W0254199

Emerging Afghanistan in the Third Millennium

Emerging Afghanistan in the Third Millennium

Edited by

MONDIRA DUTTA

Foreword by

H.E. Dr. Sayed Makhdoom Raheen
Ambassador of Afghanistan to India

Emerging Afghanistan in the Third Millennium

Published in 2009 by

PENTAGON PRESS
206, Peacock Lane, Shahpur Jat, New Delhi-110049
Phones: 011-64706243, 26491568
Telefax: 011-26490600
email: rajan@pentagon-press.com
website: www.pentagon-press.com

ISBN 978-81-8274-388-5

Printed at New Elegant Printers, New Delhi.

Dedicated to my mother
Maya Dutta

Contents

Part II
Strategic and Security Concerns

Foreword

Afghanistan today is yet at another critical juncture in its history. Having left a dark and violent past behind us over seven years ago, today we continue to struggle for a stable, democratic and prosperous future. The forces that are challenging our future are menacing and have a global reach. Therefore the turning or direction we take from this crossroad and our success and failure in this struggle will have important consequences for our region and for the world at large.

Regrettably, the picture which you get of Afghanistan these days, mainly focussing on terrorism and insecurity, is rather a little narrow and pessimistic. It is not very often these days that you hear about the remarkable progress that we in Afghanistan have achieved over the past seven years with the help of the international community. Seven years ago Afghanistan was a country without a state's institution, a country destroyed by invasions, wars, foreign interferences, terrorism and oppression; one-third of our population were either refugees outside our borders or displaced internally; our people were denied even the most basic human rights including education and health.

Seven years on, the picture is very different. Today our people are participating in a genuine political process to shape their own destiny as a nation. A new constitution has been adopted, new democratic institutions created and a new and democratic government has been elected. Despite all the odds, the freedom enjoyed by our media and civil society organizations is totally unprecedented and unparalleled.

Our national economy is also growing and over the past four and a half years we have enjoyed a total real GDP growth of 85 percent, while the rate of inflation has been kept at around 10 percent. We have created an enabling environment for business to grow and for our farmers to produce and market their products. We have encouraged Foreign Direct Investment and private sector investors to seize opportunities available in Afghanistan.

Health services covered 15 percent of the people in 2003. In 2007, the percentage was raised to 80. Three years ago, the annual per annum income was only US$ 85. Now it is US$ 350.

Another important factor in the successful transition to democracy is education. In comparison to 1985's student enrolment in Afghanistan, which was around 6, 50,000 students, today we have approximately 7 million students enrolled in formal education and nearly half of them are girls.

While our achievements are enormous indeed, the challenges that remain are equally daunting. Our initial victory over the Taliban and Al-Qaeda, our continued military efforts and the fight against terrorism and our investment in rebuilding Afghanistan's national army and national police have not yet produced the assured security that we desire.

Despite our economic growth in recent years, Afghanistan is still among the poorest countries of the world. The continuing production and trafficking of narcotics represents an existential threat to Afghanistan. It is absolutely important that with the active and sustained support of the international community, we pursue a multi-faceted strategy against narcotics. Providing adequate alternative livelihood to afghan farmers should be the central essence of our struggle against narcotics.

On the political and governance side too, Afghanistan has a very long way to go before our institutions take root, before our progress towards democratization becomes irreversible and before our people can finally enjoy their full rights and freedom. Terrorism remains our number one concern. As a multi – faceted phenomenon, it is conditioned by its environment. The terrorist mindset is an extreme corruption and degradation of human existence: it denies the sanctity of life and allows killing and dying as not just acceptable but, in a way, desirable. Terrorism is a much more sinister enemy that we share in common.

Despite the remaining challenges, Afghanistan has chosen its destiny. Afghanistan wants to be prosperous, free, democratic and a responsible and active member of the international community. I am confident that with the sustained and active support of the international community we can realize our deserved dreams. We have come a significant distance in this journey and India has given constant support throughout.

The relation between our two nations have been characterized by continuing friendship, co-operation, mutual respect and mutual contribution in almost every field from literature, poetry, architecture, religion, politics to art and music. In fact, one cannot narrate the history of Afghanistan without recalling its numerous interactions with India and vice-versa. Also from the beginning of a new chapter in Afghanistan's history following the toppling of the Taliban regime in Afghanistan, in 2001, India has been among the most generous and sincere friends of Afghanistan. I would like to take this opportunity to thank the people and the government of India for their consistent, generous and sincere support for Afghanistan during the last seven years!

H.E. Dr. Sayed Makhdoom Raheen
Ambassador of Afghanistan to India

Preface

Afghanistan traditionally has been most close to the civilization of the South Asian region. The former domain of ancient Hindu kingdom of Gandhara lies in and around the present day Kabul. Despite the closeness, relations deteriorated between India and Afghanistan after the Taliban came into power. It was only after the fall of Taliban that India started resuming its previous ties. Ever since India has entered into partnership with the Afghan government in a wide range of sectors such as hydro electricity, road construction, agriculture, industry, telecommunications, information and broadcasting, education and health, it has become a topic of speculation for most. Several security analysts opine that India's presence in Afghanistan could contribute greatly in preventing the creation of an 'Islamic belt' allied to Pakistan. Secondly it could preclude encirclement by world powers like China or the USA and protect India from the narco-terrorism that now plagues its northern borders.

Afghanistan has been trying hard to recover from the torment and sufferings after more than two decades of conflict. The Interim Afghanistan National Development Strategy (IANDS) was presented by the Afghan government, displaying the priorities for accelerating development, increasing security, tackling the drug menace and strengthening the governance at the international conference in London in January 2006. Following which, the sudden splurge of initiatives towards the reconstruction process of Afghanistan has made the country alive among the international community. Nevertheless in spite of the overwhelming response from the International Community, Afghanistan is still under a severe resource crunch for implementing its development policies and the Karzai government has requested the world community to come forward in a big way. The international community had vowed to build up a contribution to the tune of US$ 25 billion over the next five years for helping with the reconstruction process.

The government of India has been forthright in assisting the Afghan government towards reconstruction with a sum total of US$950 million. Recently this has been enhanced by the government of India to the tune of 1.2 billion US$. Other donor agencies include the USAID, European Union, the World Bank, ADB and many others. Nevertheless it is also believed that a substantial proportion of the funds from the donor agencies reverse to the donors through huge costs incurred for the maintenance and upkeep of their own staff.

It is also true that millions of children have returned back to school in Afghanistan, and the economy is growing since 2002. Nevertheless a majority of Afghans continue to live in utter poverty without access to safe drinking water, electricity or opportunities to improve their lives. The Life expectancy is short in Afghanistan. On an average it is about 47 years as compared to 59 years of the low-income countries of the world. Maternal mortality rates are one in 50 births and one of every five children dies before the age of 5 according to the World Health organization.

The Taliban still control parts of Afghanistan and has been displaying their tentacles from time to time. It is no longer a secret that they are mostly concentrated in the south and continues to launch guerrilla attacks against forces of the US and its allies, India and the current government of President Hamid Karzai.

It is estimated that the expenditure on the war in Iraq and Afghanistan is approaching the $450 billion for USA. Nevertheless security concerns continue to be a haunting problem and pose a grave scenario. Buying back peace and stability in the region does not seem a sustainable preposition in the light of the fact that there exists a large presence of more than 6,500 UN and 20,000

American and coalition forces in addition to the NATO peace keeping forces.

This abrupt clambering of getting a foothold into Afghanistan does attest its geo-strategic significance and the importance of its centric proximity from the regions of South, West and Central Asia. Several national surveys depict that places considered insecure and where a concentration of US soldiers or United Nation workers are engaged in, need not necessarily be insecure for the ordinary Afghan natives living there.

With major developmental projects being undertaken in Afghanistan such as roads, schools, hospitals, bridges, construction of high-voltage power lines and so on it is of importance that the country must restore peace and law and order in Afghanistan.

In addition the opium terror estimates that the total export value of Afghanistan's opium was $3.1 billion in 2006, representing approximately 32 percent of the country's total (licit and illicit) gross domestic product. The majority of poppy cultivation takes place in two provinces Helmand and Kandahar and the most important fact which needs to be attested is that many farmers grow the crops not for financial gain but because of death threats from warlords and the Taliban.

The not so long ago was the joint Afghanistan-Pakistan Jirga, a convocation headed by the Afghan president and his Pakistani counterpart, dedicated to formulating new strategies to confront Taliban and Al-Qaeda elements. However a lack of understanding and dialogue on the role of culture and religion in the region can hardly usher in the desired trickling-down effects. A political, economic, and social transformation is yet to be apparently visible.

More than half a decade has passed since the Bonn agreement was signed. What are the ground realities today? How far have the objectives been met with? How secure is Afghanistan today? What are the major security concerns and how to address these? The present book is a collection of articles presented at the International Conference held on 23-24 April 2008, sponsored by the Ministry of External Affairs, and Jawaharlal Nehru University, New Delhi. The major recommendations of the Conference include:

- Given the strong ethnic, historical and cultural ties between India and Afghanistan, India needs to extend its current initiatives focusing on micro level issues involving people from all walks of life. It needs to strengthen the ties for stronger bonding.
- India is fourth in rank as far as contribution towards the reconstruction process is concerned. The Ministry of External Affairs, Government of India has been forthright in assisting with the reconstruction process and needs to initiate a study to assess the Indian initiatives impact on the reconstruction process of Afghanistan
- Enhancing the Capacity Building and skill development through programmes and training of resource persons especially in the field of Education, Health and the Social sector. These trained personnel could carry forward the projects and programmes initiated to their logical end
- Development of micro level projects at the grass root to enhance the absorptive capacity of local resources. External support needs to be restricted to capacity building measures but the actual implementation of the programmes and major decisions taken, should involve the local people through participatory approach.
- Promoticn of Good Governance, Judiciary and Enforcement of the law and Order needs to be activated through vigorous security sector reforms of the Afghan National Army, Police Forces and the Justice system
- Better livelihood and Enhancement of Employment Opportunities for the local community. This would usher in a rippling effect and also bring about a reduction in the opium cultivation.
- Replacing the drug-lord's lending system with legal credit institutions and micro credit financing
- Stronger and active Regional Cooperation and bilateral agreement for security and economic cooperation
- Coordination and Monitoring of NGOs for complementing the developmental activities.

- Framing of proper labor policies for providing gender equity based job opportunities, equal wages and incentives for appropriate working conditions

The present book focuses on some of these issues. The book highlights what needs to be done further and how far away we are before peace can return to this unfortunate nation trapped amidst the peace makers. Given the background, the present book has been divided into three sections namely 'Economy and Society', 'Aid Effectiveness and International Initiatives' and 'Strategic and Security Concerns'. In all there are around 25 papers revealing the ground realities and have been meticulously presented in the backdrop of the current scenario. The book will come in useful to researchers, academicians and policy-makers.

Mondira Dutta

List of Contributors

Abdul Ghafoor Liwal: Director, Regional Studies Center of Afghanistan (RSCA).

Afsir Karim (Retd. Major General): Editor of 'Aakrosh', Asian Journal on Terrorism and Internal Conflicts.

Ambrish Dhaka: Assistant Professor, School of International Studies, Jawaharlal Nehru University, New Delhi.

Anil Bhat (Retd. Lt. Col.): Chief Managing Editor of WordSword Features and Media.

A.P.S. Chouhan: Head, School of Studies in Political Science and Public Administration, Jiwaji University, Gwalior (MP).

Arpita Basu Roy: Fellow, Maulana Abul Kalam Azad Institute of Asian Studies (MAKAIAS), Kolkata.

Chintamani Mahapatra: Professor, American Studies, School of International Studies, Jawaharlal Nehru University.

Farkhod Tolipov: Associate Professor, National University of Uzbekistan, Tashkent.

Haroun Mir: Co-founder and Deputy Director, Afghanistan's Center for Research and Policy Studies (ACRPS), Kabul.

Jagmohan Meher: National Defence Academy, Khadakwasla, Pune, India.

Kalim Bahadur (Retd.): Professor, Centre for South, Central, Southeast Asian and Southwest Pacific Studies, School of International Studies, Jawaharlal Nehru University, New Delhi.

Manash Ranjan Mishra: Research Scholar, Centre for South, Central, South East Asian and South West Pacific Studies, School of International Studies, Jawaharlal Nehru University, New Delhi.

Mariam Rawi: Member, Revolutionary Association of the Women of Afghanistan (RAWA), Pakistan.

Mohammed Bashaar: Good Governance Officer, United Nations Development Programme (UNDP) in Afghanistan, Kabul.

Nasrine Gross: President, Kabultec, Kabul

Nalin Kant Jha: Rajiv Gandhi Chair Professor in Contemporary Studies, Allahabad Central University, Allahabad.

Nilofar Sakhi: Director/Chairperson of Women Activities and Social Services Association (WASSA), Kabul.

P.L. Dash: Professor of Eurasian Studies, Centre for Central Eurasian Studies, University of Mumbai, Mumbai.

Pramod Kumar Sharma: Research Scholar, Centre for South, Central, Southeast Asian and Southwest Pacific Studies, School of International Studies, Jawaharlal Nehru University, New Delhi.

Prashant Agarwal: Reader, Department of Defence and Strategic Studies, University of Allahabad, Allahabad.

Saleem Kidwai: Faculty Member, CCUS&LAS, School of International Studies, at the Jawaharlal Nehru University, New Delhi.

Sanjeev Bhadauria: Associate Professor, Dept. of Defence and Strategic Studies, Allahabad Central University, Allahabad.

Saurabh Sharma: Research Scholar, Centre for South, Central Southeast Asian and Southwest Pacific Studies, School of International Studies, Jawaharlal Nehru University, New Delhi.

Savita Pande: Associate Professor, South Asian Studies, Centre for South, Central, Southeast Asian and Southwest Pacific Studies, School of International Studies, Jawaharlal Nehru University, New Delhi.

Sudhir Singh: Faculty, Department of Political Science, Dayal Singh College, Delhi University, Delhi.

Sayed Makhdoom Raheen: Afghanistan's Ambassador to India, New Delhi.

Wadir Safi: Professor, Faculty of Law and Political Sciences, Kabul University, Afghanistan.

Yeshi Choedon: Associate Professor, Centre for International Politics, Organization and Disarmament (CIPOD), School of International Studies, Jawaharlal Nehru University, New Delhi.

PART I

RECONSTRUCTION AND PEACE BUILDING

CHAPTER 1

Political Transformation in Afghanistan

Abdul Ghafoor Liwal

Afghanistan is one of the world's most conflict-ridden countries, displaying a complex interaction of internal and external conflict lines that have devastated the country in the past three decades.

Internal ethnic, religious, geographic and political cleavages have accentuated with modernization processes in the twentieth century. A spiral of violence has dominated Afghanistan since the mid-1970s and was not reversed until the aftermath of Operation Enduring Freedom in late 2001, which for the first time in over two decades refocused the international community's constructive attention on Afghanistan and brought an end to major military confrontations.

POLITICAL REFORM POST BONN

The events of September 11 in the United States reminded the world of the fact that since 1990, Afghanistan had become a nest for foreign terrorism and that it supported a fundamentalist regime of Taliban. Notably, the Bonn negotiations were held by the United Nations in December 2001, in which the international community, particularly, the United States, pledged to help the Afghan nation secure democracy in its country.

During the past years, the new Afghan government has taken important steps towards democracy. For example, it adopted a new constitution for the country through a public consultation process that was approved by a Loya Jirga (the grand assembly of Afghanistan). In addition, the government took steps to grant more freedom to the women of Afghanistan, and to the media. Notably, for the first time in the history of Afghanistan, people participated in a presidential election on October 9, 2004. More than forty percent (40%) of the voters in the election were women.

Some three million internally and externally displaced Afghans have returned to their country/home. More than four million children, a third of them girls, are in school, and immunization campaigns have achieved considerable success. The Government has supported good economic performance by following prudent macroeconomic policies; it has begun to build capacity and has developed the nationally-led budget process and made the budget into its central instrument of reform; and it has made extraordinary efforts to develop key national programs (for example public-works employment programs and community development programs) and to revive social services like education and health.

OBSTACLES IN THE PATH OF DEMOCRACY

Current State of Society in Afghanistan

Along the positive developments there are still challenges, which pose threat to the stability of the country. Afghanistan's current social condition is a result of years of fighting between warring factions throughout the country. Hostility and bitterness dominate everyday life. Political-military groups continuously challenge the stability of the central government and foreign interference helps some of these groups in their challenges. Thus, even pro-democratic forces within Afghanistan are unsure of the success of this new venture—democracy. There is a need for stability for democracy to succeed at this time. Due to the social structure of Afghanistan, a system of "presidential democracy," where the president has the last word, and a congress, is agreed up in the Loya Jirga to be the best. A presidential democracy alone could lead to a dictatorship, and a sole parliamentary democracy would lead to anarchism, due to certain influential factors. Only a presidential democracy, combined with a congress, fits today's Afghanistan. It is essential for this combined system to guarantee, freedom of speech, freedom of thought, freedom of political movements, marches, meetings and every kind of protest.

"The main obstacles are almost everything," said Professor Barnett R. Rubin, Director of Studies and Senior Fellow in the Center on International Cooperation at New York University, who has had several trips to Afghanistan working as a special adviser to the UN and Afghan government. He added, "The state is so weak that the government officials cannot control it or just use it for their own benefit. There is very weak rule of law compared to the rule of armed people. Courts are very weak. Political parties are non-existent. The drug economy is the largest sector, so illegal activity is predominant. And so on. Things have improved a lot and they may continue to improve, but it will take a long time."

People's Attitude Towards Democracy

As in most Islamic countries, Afghanistan authoritarian regimes have used religion as a safeguard of their power for centuries. There is a famous saying among Afghans, which says, "The king is the shadow of the God." A lot of people still believe in this proverb.

Afghan society has spent much of its history under authoritarianism. It is clear that dictatorial governments have followed their own interests, and the society had to suffer under all kinds of economic, political and cultural hardships. Dictatorships have made Afghan people face all these problems. The people have been kept hungry, illiterate and far away from politics. This has significantly contributed to the fact that this country is still among the least developed countries of the world.

Major Hurdles for Democracy

Democracy as the only alternative system to dictatorship is something new and untested in Afghanistan. Sociological studies and experiments show that every action has some specified reaction to it. But today, the current obstacles to democracy in Afghanistan are:

- *Illiteracy*: The majority of Afghans are illiterate; their awareness about democracy and its advantages is very low. During the war educational institutions were destroyed and more than three generations of Afghans have grown up seeing just guns, tanks and bombs around them. They had little opportunity to see conflicts resolved by means other than arms. Democracy has never been explained to them in their language. Even Afghans who favour democracy usually talk to Western organizations or each other more than they do to the public.
- *Deep Roots of Dictatorship in the Awareness of the Society:* The prevailing perception among people is that governments are installed by God. A nation is blessed by a just and fair government only after all the people have become pious. Dictating governments are there because of their unfair deeds, like bribery, murders and other sins.
- *Propaganda against Democracy:* In the conservative and traditional society of Afghans, there has been strong propaganda that only their values are noble. Others especially those which come with democracy are in the way around and will push the society towards converting from Islam. West is thought to be focusing too much on materiality (opposite of spirituality). Belief of life after death is weak or sometimes non-existent among West. Centuries of preachers have deep roots in the public minds.

Such outbursts of thoughts have been preached to the public continuously for centuries. Since the beginning of the war, radical religious parties have taken great advantage of this conviction. Their plan was to obtain the government through force and to stay there with the help of religious dictatorship instead of a royal dictatorship. So they used all the opportunities, particularly their meetings in the mosques, to propagate against democracy. They presented democracy as a western non-Islamic system. These parties have always declared that in Islam a government cannot be established on the basis of democratic rules.

Interference of Armed Groups

Several groups have received enormous amounts of weapons through out the conflict. They accumulated a lot of wealth with these weapons and are ruling areas under their control. They can do whatever they want. They have murdered thousands and can still kill their opponents in public in or away from public eye. These groups and their commanders know that people are not happy with them and that in a democratic system they will, for sure, lose their power. All those groups who cannot get power in a democratic way are obstacles to democracy. They use all kind of sabotage and terrorism to prevent democracy. Foreign hands support these Islamic parties because of their own agendas. They finance them to ensure these groups can survive so that they can still bear some influence in Afghanistan.

Weaknesses of the Movement

Pro-democratic movements are weak. They either don't have the much-needed personnel who can stand for democracy or don't have the means to carry out their mission. First of all, there is no security for them to operate effectively. For economic reason they are busy in jobs other than their political role, so they cannot spend their time on politics. The silence and weakness of these peoples is one of the main causes why the democratic process is so slow.

Poppy as an Anti-Democratic Force

Afghanistan grows the largest number of opium poppies in the world. There is a black market network that is involved in trafficking of this deadly plant. These networks have political, economical and military power. Some of the strongest warlords are involved in this business. Several of these individuals hold important positions in current government, are strongly against democracy and can easily sabotage the process of democratisation.

INTERNATIONAL COMMUNITIES

Often this question has been deliberated upon as to whether the U.S, and other European countries involved in Afghanistan really want democracy? The answer is a definite 'Yes' for they think, without a democratic system this country is again going to be a nest for foreign terrorists. Despite this there is no doubt that some of their activities are damaging the process of democratization.

According to Prof. Barnett Rubin's views the U.S.policies on Afghanistan both assisted and hampered Afghanistan in its transition to a democratic society. The U.S. overthrew the Taliban, has kept the warlords from fighting each other, and has supported the U.N. led program of making the government more legitimate. It also strengthened some warlords at times and committed some abuses in its military actions. If it forces the Afghan government to engage in opium poppy eradication without adequate economic development, it will undermine democracy further. Therefore Afghans wonder if the U.S. and European countries really want democracy, if so, why they support some warlords who never want democracy.

AFGHAN ECONOMY

Afghanistan is in a serious mess as far as its physical infrastructure and social make up is concerned. This is manifested by the appalling levels of poverty and dismal health care standards that most Afghans experience. Poverty in turn forms a background for the more direct threats to peace and security that challenge the country. Some of these threats include warlords, radicalism and narcotics. Poverty forces large numbers of Afghan to serve warlords and rely on them and not on themselves or the state for survival and protection. Poverty, the lack of ability to affect one's life and insecurity for the future forces numerous Afghans to cultivate opium. Poverty and underemployment also fuels resentment that helps Islamic radicalism to conquer new ground. The struggle against poverty is hence the crucial element in Afghanistan's future and a monumental task. Indeed, the salient question is how Afghanistan can be rebuilt, since the aid money, though large, is unlikely to accomplish this task. Further this question points to a need to resurrect Afghanistan's role as a trading nation. A nation on the crossroads of great civilizations, something that development cooperation can best contribute to through investments in infrastructure.

Afghanistan remains one of the poorest countries in the world in terms of both per capita incomes and social indicators, with large gender gaps. The difficult challenge of poverty reduction is made even more difficult by continuing insecurity, weak rule of law, and narcotics. Worsening security in many parts of the country threatens to derail reconstruction, undermine state building efforts and adversely affect other aspects of political normalization, reduce private sector activity, and keep it in the informal/illicit economy. The burgeoning revival and spread of opium production during the last two years (opium accounted for about a third of the Afghan economy) has fueled insecurity and funded antigovernment interests. Drugs, insecurity, "capture" of large parts of the country by regional powerbrokers, and the weak capacity of the state (including difficulties in centralizing revenue) all contribute to a self-reinforcing "vicious circle" that would keep Afghanistan insecure, politically fragmented, weakly governed, poor, dominated by the informal/illicit economy, and a hostage to the drug industry.

Afghanistan, with strong support from the international community, will break out of these vicious circle—and move toward a "virtuous circle." This would improve security, the state capacity building measures, revenue mobilization, formal private sector development and sensible, coordinated actions against drugs eventually reinforcing one and another to put Afghanistan on a path of sustained economic growth and poverty reduction mission. This will require simultaneous progress on several key fronts. Action in any one area alone will not be effective given the strong interests working to maintain the current status quo. On the other hand limited resources and capacity dictate that the Government prioritizes core reforms that will enhance governance, focusing on the implementation of ongoing tasks rather than going for a large number of new initiatives. This is a daunting agenda, which will require strong commitment, actions, and persistence on the part of the Government. In each area listed above sustained, coordinated assistance from the international community will be required.

The support extended by the international community can become more meaningful towards Afghanistan's state building and reconstruction agenda through the following measures:

- Maximizing assistance that goes through government budget channels and moving toward programmatic support;
- Maximizing use of coordinated government led technical assistance mechanisms and coordinating pay policy with the government
- Stopping payments and other support to non-legitimate regional authorities
- Being alert to macro-economic shocks (such as drought) by accelerating and adjusting assistance as and when required.

AGRICULTURAL DEVELOPMENT

In terms of agriculture, half the Afghan economy is critical for its future growth, poverty reduction, and export development. Maintaining robust agricultural growth requires adequate investments and a sound enabling environment. Some of the key priority areas include the following:

Irrigation: The Government and the international community both have been emphasizing on rehabilitation of surface irrigation facilities and subsequently on major new investments. Such a vision seems appropriate.

Agricultural Research and Extension: Dissemination of improved agricultural techniques and management practices will be essential to realize the full benefits of irrigation and other investments. Afghanistan needs to focus on adaptive research which must be demand-driven. Public and private sector roles in extension need to be clearly defined, extension services contracted out wherever possible, participatory and community-based approaches adopted, and extension focused on marketing not just production.

Marketing: Investments in both "hardware" (market facilities, cold storages—requiring electric power, roads, etc.) and "software" (grades and quality standards, market research, standards for wholesale markets, market management by market players) will be very important.

Rural Credit: Micro-finance supports are an important initiative underway. However, over the medium term additional forms of private, deposit-taking, and commercially-oriented rural credit will need to develop (e.g. through contract farming and similar arrangements).

Land Tenure: Issues are widely considered to be a source of insecurity and problems for agriculture. Such issues are part of the larger governance agenda and can be complex and controversial to resolve, so it would be prudent for the Government to proceed through pilot survey and involving the local communities before scaling up.

PUBLIC INFRASTRUCTURE

The destruction of Afghanistan's physical infrastructure is a tremendous obstacle to the development of the country and therefore also to its peace and stability. In the course of warfare, the near entirety of infrastructure such as roads, hospitals, schools, irrigation, government buildings etc. was destroyed. Lack of infrastructure for communication and transportation increases parochialism, prevents travel and exchange of ideas and goods between the provinces of Afghanistan. This contributes to suspicion and hostility among the diverse ethno cultural groups of the country. But in addition to this, as alluded to the above, the trauma imposed on Afghanistan by two decades of war has led to a less tangible but equally daunting consequence. Severe harm has been inflicted on collective as well as individual mental health as well as to the destruction on structures and norms upholding society and generating a sense of stability for the individual. The immense suffering brought on to Afghanistan's population led to strong damage to individual mental health, given the hardships in form of death, injury, migration, fear, misery, and hopelessness that the population was forced to endure.

The societal disruptions of the war, especially the shifting patterns of authority in society, are yet another element in the destruction of Afghanistan's societal makeup which carries important consequences. Groups one after another, aided by foreign powers, have destroyed the irrigation systems, mined the pastures, leveled the cities, cratered the roads, blasted the schools, and arrested, tortured, killed and expelled the educated.

HEALTH SYSTEM

Even before the most recent war, Afghanistan's health care system was on life support. In June 2000, the World Health Organization ranked the country 173rd out of 191 countries worldwide. Since then, the situation has gone from bad to worse. Take, for example, the maternal and infant care. As many as 16,000 women die yearly as a result of childbirth and Infant mortality rates are at 16.5 percent.

Afghanistan's devastated health infrastructure needs to be rebuilt. Few public health facilities are left in the country, generally operating without running water or proper sanitation. In addition, most existing health care facilities are in urban areas, leaving 60 to 70 percent of the population with little access to care. Doctors and other medical professionals are also urgently needed as many fled the country during the past two decades.

The recent studies estimated that more women died last year as a result of childbirth than those that were killed by war. Infant mortality rates are at 16.5%, compared with 9% in Pakistan and 2.6% in Iran. Malnutrition is a significant problem, and measles and other preventable diseases remain major killers. Afghanistan's devastated health infrastructure needs to be rebuilt. Few public health facilities are left in the country, generally operating without running water or proper sanitation. In addition, most existing health care facilities are in urban areas, leaving 60–70% of the population with little access to care. Doctors and other medical professionals are also urgently needed as many fled the country during the past two decades. In the light of these problems, the international community should prioritize for rebuilding Afghanistan's public health system which must include:

- Restoring basic health care services.
- Upgrading medical facilities.
- Creating a public health framework.
- Deploying of local human resources after being identified by the government.
- Improve security which would lead to increased mobility, enabling health team to reach previously inaccessible parts of the country.
- Food security to be improved, through distribution of seeds and food aid.
- Crash program needs to be implemented in the housing, water and sanitation sectors to address humanitarian and recovery needs in coordination with the health sectors on the basis of health evidence.
- Adequate, flexible and sustained international aid will have to be forthcoming to foster peace and stability.

CHALLENGES BEFORE THE AFGHAN GOVERNMENT

One of the most pressing challenges ahead for the Government is to strengthen the links between Kabul and the provinces and to strengthen the capacity of the provincial and local governments themselves. Effective governance at the local level, with reliable fiscal, administrative and policy links to the central government would enable the population across Afghanistan to gain confidence that the Government could affect their lives positively. This is possible only if security outside Kabul is significantly improved. It is important to see security sector reforms not as an end in itself but as a mechanism to enable the central government to extend its control over the country. In turn this would allow the interrelated political and economic development processes to occur within the space created by the functioning security sector.

The United Nations Assistance Mission in Afghanistan (UNAMA) should focus and continue to assist the Afghan Government to consolidate its authority throughout the country and implement national policies that reached the entire nation.

REGIONAL COOPERATION

Despite the problems, regional cooperation involving governments, the private sector, and other non-state actors is essential to the sustainable reconstruction of Afghanistan because however prolonged the involvement of the international community may be, the country will eventually be on its own. The changed political circumstances in the region in the aftermath of the U.S. led invasion provide an opportunity to improve regional relations by expanding legitimate trade and initiating other forms of positive cooperation. Such regional cooperation could be based on participation in the reconstruction of Afghanistan. The surrounding states would in turn profit from a more stable and just Afghanistan. The regional cooperation is a major focus of Afghanistan's foreign policy.

The reconstruction of Afghanistan will require not only the repair and expansion of infrastructure and the revitalization of the economy, but also the reconstruction of national institutions, beginning with the state itself. The political tasks of reconstruction means that the Afghan authorities are leery of forms of cooperation that may serve to reinforce direct ties between regions of Afghanistan (which are controlled by competing warlords) and their immediate neighbors as between Kandahar and Pakistan or between Herat and Iran. While Afghans are still debating how centralized their future government should be, the vast majority oppose a pattern of reconstruction that would reinforce local control based on armed forces and alliances with neighboring countries.

And while the Central Asian states would like to benefit from both relief operations and reconstruction, they are still wary of opening their borders to the south, which they fear may leave them even more vulnerable to drug and arms trafficking, and to the spread of ideologies they cannot control.

The prospects for regional cooperation will thus be strongly influenced by the actions of the international community. If it were to make the reconstruction of Afghanistan the keystone of regional cooperation, international community would provide a sustainable basis for maintaining peace when the international community moves on. Until then, a strong international community commitment for preventing regional interference in Afghanistan will reassure the Afghan authorities, lessen their fears of being overwhelmed by outside interference, and give them the confidence to cooperate more closely with their neighbors.

Regional cooperation is more likely in some areas than in others. Cooperation on security issues, except for specific anti-terrorist operations, is likely to be the last area to be broached. Precisely because of their history with respect to Afghanistan, neighboring states have been excluded from participation in both the International Security Assistance Force and from U.S. and European efforts to build Afghan national security forces. Broad international security guarantees will be required for regional cooperation in other areas. Some have even advocated formal neutrality for Afghanistan, as for Austria. If all its neighbors agreed to respect Afghan neutrality none would have to intervene to preempt actions by rivals. If the region, with international assistance, does manage to attain a level of stability and security, governments and the private sector can begin to cooperate in a number of areas. Governments can cooperate bilaterally with Afghanistan and with each other, if necessary through Kabul in reconstruction efforts and to redress their common development deficits. Indeed the two are linked, as a more cooperative region could provide larger markets for Afghanistan's trade and production, which could fund improvements in infrastructure.

Cooperation among the law enforcement agencies will be necessary to control drug trafficking although it is possible that such collaboration would mostly provide greater opportunities for corruption, as the police forces and militaries of several regional states are already involved with drug mafias. In order to control opium production, crop substitution will be necessary and here shared regional agricultural expertise can come into play. Farmers will probably want to plant alternative cash crops for export, rather than revert to subsistence farming, and nearby countries could provide important markets for fruits, vegetables and cut flowers. Promoting trade within the region and beyond is the sector where cooperation is most necessary and will be most beneficial. An increase in regional trade will create a powerful lobby for peaceful relations within the region.

REHABILITATION OF ROADS

The Afghan administration has named road construction and repair as a top priority.

Re-establishing its position as a land bridge, out of the total 13,586 kilometers of roads that are needed for regional trade 3,657 is built in Afghanistan. Their benefit to the country will be significant. The hope and potential for these new roads is that they will allow Central Asia once more to interact with South Asia, China and the Far East and to re-engage with Europe and beyond. The highway system is currently under going a total reconstruction process. Most of the regional roads are also being repaired or improved.

The roads built in Afghanistan, which connect the regional countries, are:

- Kabul—Kandahar highway
- Kabul—Jalalabad-Torkham highway
- Kabul-Mazar highway
- Kandahar—Boldak highway
- Kandahar—Herat highway
- Herat—Islam Qala highway
- Herat—Mazar highway

These developments would offer a large number of options for private transport through Afghanistan.

In addition to the trans-Afghan corridor, a route through Afghanistan appears to be the best option. For the Central Asian region it is the shortest route to the sea and has relatively favorable terrain for a pipeline. The route through Afghanistan is the one that would bring Central Asian oil closest to Asian markets and thus would be the cheapest in terms of transporting the oil.

The construction and repair of bridges and tunnels, repairing facilities for trucks and insurance that is recognized across borders are vital to the economic health of this mountainous region. Kabul has signed trilateral trade agreements with Iran and India, which, among other things, commits them to upgrading the rail lines connecting the three countries. Iran and Afghanistan recently reopened a customs post in Milak in southwest Afghanistan and Iran is planning to upgrade the road system connecting that transit point to the port of Bandar Abbas, which would decrease the cost and time of transit for goods. This new crossing point would also make it easier for the Afghan government to collect customs because the post is in a relatively deserted area, away from the control of the local warlord.

INTERNATIONAL AID

International aid agencies still organize or operate the majority of reconstruction in Afghanistan, and the country relies heavily on them. But as war continues in the south, insurgents target aid workers as a military strategy against the U.S. led coalition forces and the government of President Hamid Karzai. The effect is felt not only in the south, where millions have no access to health care, but across the whole country.

COMMITMENT OF DONORS, THEIR EFFECTIVENESS AND EFFICIENCY

Afghanistan is being deprived of $10bn (£5bn) of promised aid, and 40 percent of the money that has been delivered was spent on corporate profits and consultancy fees. The failure of western donors to keep their promises, compounded by corruption and inefficiency is undermining the prospects for peace in Afghanistan. Civil aid programs are a fraction of what is spent by America, Britain and other countries on military operations there. Much of the money earmarked for aid is diverted to political or military purposes.

The report by ACBAR, an alliance of international aid agencies working in the country, including Oxfam, Christian Aid, Islamic Relief and Save the Children, says the international community has pledged $25bn to Afghanistan since 2001 but only $15bn has been delivered.

Over the same period the European Commission and Germany distributed less than two-thirds of their respective $1.7bn and $1.2bn commitments while the World Bank distributed just over half of the $1.6bn it committed. Britain pledged $1.45bn and distributed almost all, $1.3bn. The report estimated that 40% of the aid money spent in Afghanistan has found its way back to rich donor countries.

Most full-time expatriate consultants working for private companies in Afghanistan incur a cost around $250,000 and $500,000 per annum, including salary, allowances and associated costs.

Around 90 percent of all public spending in Afghanistan comes from international aid. The huge shortfall hinders efforts to rebuild infrastructure damaged by over two decades of war, and the delivery of essential services such as education and health. The reconstruction of Afghanistan requires a sustained and substantial commitment of aid—but donors have failed to meet their aid pledges to Afghanistan. Too much aid from rich countries is wasted, ineffective or uncoordinated. The American media reported that the PRT (Provincial Reconstruction Team) don't have any sustainable plan for the reconstruction projects, because they spent their money on small projects, which can not fulfill the basic needs of Afghan people.

"Given the slow pace of progress in Afghanistan, and the links between poverty and conflict, the international community must urgently get its act together."

Some degree of donor under-spending could be expected because of the lack of government capacity, large-scale corruption and difficult security conditions. But the size of the shortfall highlights the need for donors making better efforts to face up to the problem. The disproportionate amount of aid follows the conflict and is being used for political and military objectives rather than reducing poverty.

"This is a short-sighted policy, there must be strong support for development in the south but if other provinces are neglected then insecurity could spread."

The volume of aid, particularly to rural areas, should be increased, aid donors should be more open about what they want to provide and cooperate better with the Afghan government. There should be better ways to measure the impact, efficiency, and relevance of aid money, and an independent commission to monitor the appropriateness and effectiveness of donors' programmes be set up.

RECOMMENDATIONS

International Community

- Cut off foreign support for armed or private militia groups by applying political pressure and blocking their financial sources.
- Apply political and military pressure on these groups to make them give up their weapons to the international forces. Abolish military groups.
- Build governmental institutions on a professional basis instead of following political interests.
- Promote the economy of the Afghan people. Some production-economy must be established in order to fulfil the basic needs of the people; attention must be paid to agriculture; land should be distributed to farmers; other countries should be invited to invest in the mines of Afghanistan; water and electricity-dams should be built.
- Building of cultural bridges and increase of cultural exchanges. Make it easier for Afghans to visit other developed industrialized countries. Afghan students should be given scholarships to universities abroad.
- Women should be helped to gain an independent personality. They should be encouraged to work and be independent.
- Develop the values associated with democracy in Afghanistan. Assistance should be provided in researching and translating political and philosophical literature
- All democratic forces have to be united to build a strong democratic movement. At the same time it is important to develop a loyal opposition.
- Lessons regarding democracy and human rights should be incorporated in school books.
- Promotion of accelerated international support and cooperation.

Government of Afghanistan

- **Enhancing security and rule of law** through vigorous security sector reforms and capacity building (especially the Afghan National Army, police forces, and justice system), combined with external security assistance including outside Kabul.
- **State building** through increasing capacity and intensifying public administration reforms, with a focus on enhancing center-periphery relations (with provincial and District administrations), revenue mobilization, and service delivery (national programs, social services, basic infrastructure).
- **Political normalization**, focused on making key institutions (cabinet, legislative bodies, judiciary) work effectively, with neutralization of warlords and other illegitimate powerbrokers.
- **Maintaining economic growth** with macroeconomic stability, and pro-actively pursuing private sector development through a good enabling environment, support services, and capacity building within the private sector.
- **Meaningful, coordinated actions against drugs**, consistent with the overall state building, security, and development strategy.
- **Enhancing the effectiveness and efficiency of international assistance**, focusing on the attainment of core reforms and enhancing donor alignment with the nation.

CHAPTER 2

Issues of Ethnicity in Afghanistan

Nasrine Gross

INTRODUCTION

This paper explores some ideas on the issue of ethnicity in the current situation of Afghanistan. It first identifies the ethnic groups and their structures. It then discusses the importance of ethnicity as a major element of the national identity and gives a historical perspective on its development. The paper then studies the political structure and relationships. In the fourth and final section it presents some observations about the situation and makes some recommendations. The author hopes that the paper encourages a more scholarly discussion among Afghans, informs the international friends and solicits ideas from the Indian audience.

DEFINING ETHNICITY IN AFGHANISTAN

Afghanistan is a multi-ethnic country. Although a complete count of all the ethnic groups has not been done and although there has never been a credible modern census, the major ethnic groups are the Pashtuns, the Tajiks, the Hazaras, the Uzbeks, the Turkomans, the Baloch, the Nuristanis, with smaller other groups. Afghanistan also divides itself into religious denominations: Sunni Muslims, Shi'a Muslims, Ismailis, some Hindus and Sikhs and some Jewish people. We also divide ourselves into different languages, the main ones being Pashto, Dari/Persian and Uzbeki along with others. This is why one normally talks about social groups rather than just ethnic groups and avoid the words majority and minority, which although correct for the numbers of each group, denote a pejorative sense.

The internal structure of the ethnic groups is worth noting. The tribal group called the Pashtuns is segmentary. Membership in the tribe is blood based. Loyalty is given to the tribe. The mode of thinking in a tribal society is circular thinking. The concept of good and bad is related to the conditions and requirements of time and place. The modus operandi is tactical. The most important aspect of life is to promote, protect and enlarge the tribe. Consensus of the tribe is paramount. The tribal council's decisions are binding and dissent is not promoted. Because the Pashtuns have been the rulers of Afghanistan for the last three hundred years, this way of thinking and the values and traditions it bears permeate most of the other communities. As well, as there is more education and urbanization, this way of thinking mixes with the other modes as well and loses some of its supremacy on individuals.

The non-tribal ethnic groups are more locally based, and are more village and urban dwellers. Division of labour is based on the needs of the community and not on ancestry. Membership is not blood based. The mode of thinking is linear. The concepts of good and bad are mutually exclusive. The modus operandi is strategic. Dissent and multiple points of view are more easily accepted. However, most non-Pashtun groups understand the circular and tribal way and the more rural and traditional they are the closer they are to a circular way of thinking. All ethnic groups in Afghanistan with the exception of the Jews are patriarchal and patrilineal. They are most often patrilocal although living with the mother's family or the bride's family is not a taboo. Intermarriage has been very common among the Muslim groups.

Another point regarding the ethnic groups is worthy of note here: the social groups of Afghanistan whether tribal or non-tribal, also have internal divisions. For example, the two largest social groups, the Pashtuns and the Tajiks, each have vertical and horizontal differences in themselves. The Tajiks because they are dispersed and local, have horizontal differences among themselves. Perhaps their being of localities gives them differences that create more steps in the formation of the national identity. In other words, what is the difference between a Panjshiri Tajik identity and a Takhari Tajik identity? Should a Tajik be first both of these two and then an Afghan? In relation to the national identity, how has their being of a locality affected their identity, thought processes and hence their actions? What is in a Kabuli Tajik which separates him/her from a Herati Tajik? What brings them together? And which one should they be first? Among the Pashtuns there exist both horizontal and vertical differences. For example, the Pashtuns have several structures below the tribe level and several structures parallel to each other that would give the goal of reaching a national identity several other steps. What is the difference between a Barekzai identity and a Popalzai identity from the horizontal and among an Ahmadzai identity, a Zurmat identity and a Durrani identity from the vertical? In other words, what characteristics differentiate an Ahmadzai from a Durrani? And does a Pashtun have to be all of these identities and then an Afghan? Which one should he be first? If we count these difficulties in all the social groups, we might reach the Forty Steps of Kandahar or the Seventy-Two nations of Hafiz! What a task!

These internal divisions have resulted in long-term rivalries especially among the Pashtun tribes and subtribes. Unfortunately, the ethnic groups of Afghanistan have not been studied or researched in any great detail. Good sociological and anthropological data is not readily available. Some experts do make some points (that need to be researched). For example, the Swiss couple, the cantilevers who have studied Afghanistan for over half a century thinks that the Aymaqs have the most equitable gender relationships. Others believe that the culture of the Turkomans is the most peaceful. Still others think that the Hazaras and the Panjshiri Tajiks have the most unity among themselves. Many believe that the Tajiks of Afghanistan have had the easiest relationship with all ethnic groups.

ETHNICITY—A COMPONENT OF NATIONAL IDENTITY

National identity is that identity which a separate, independent and sovereign country has for defining its people. This identity gives a single dimension to all the inhabitants of a country as one nation. It shows the relationship of social groups to the country and vice-versa. This identity which is higher than social group identities creates the highest loyalty in the people and becomes part of the social thought process of each individual. National identity, which has its own unique characteristics, cannot be created in a vacuum; rather it has to originate from the fundamental beliefs, values, and mores of the society.

Building of a national identity is a comparatively easy task in countries that have simpler social structures, such as Japan. But in countries such as Afghanistan, which are situated at a geographic crossroads and are composed of many diverse social groups, nation building becomes a difficult and sensitive task. The process has several components and several stages of development.

The Afghan national identity may comprise of four separate identities. These are individual identity, religious identity, ethnic identity, and national identity, forming consecutive steps. In the first step, there is the individual identity. In Afghanistan, the individual is raised by his/her family and the primary values of the individual emanate from the family. Among Afghans, the individual identity is very robust and important, especially among men and older women.

The second step is the religious identity. In Afghanistan, there are several religions and sects and in this respect all of them have been successful. For example, Islam which is the religion of the majority of the people, has taught each Afghan the five pillars of Islam, prepared the individual for the community of Islam, i.e., the society; and trained him/her in the importance of the everlasting world and the unimportance of the temporal world. In this way, Afghans, be they Sunni or Shi'a, have been pious believers and the Islamic aspect of their identity has been fully developed.

The third step is the ethnic identity. This identity is the guardian of the history of the social group and teaches the values and relations of the social group to its members. As mentioned above, Afghanistan includes many ethnicities (qawms) and in this regard, Pashtun-wali, i.e., the oral code of traditions and characteristics of the Pashtun social group is the most famous, most identifiable and most described. But for sure, Tajik-wali, Hazara-wali, Uzbek-wali, etc. also exist. And all these 'walis' give rise to the identities that have existed in historical Afghanistan. At the local and social group level, Afghans know well their own particular identity.

The fourth step is the Afghan national identity, which is over all and is the guardian of the country and nation of Afghanistan. In other words, with this identity, an Afghan must stand with full equilibrium and balance at the cross-section of family, religion and ethnicity; count him/herself a part of the Afghan nation; and consider the country above everyone and above him/herself.

During the peaceful periods, Afghanistan in the twentieth century, especially after independence, was much occupied with building and nurturing this national identity, i.e., the Afghan identity. In a way, the twentieth century Afghanistan can be viewed as a struggle and evolution towards this equilibrium and balance among the four component identities. In my opinion, the major phases of this evolution are: From independence until the Communist take-over (1919-78), the Jihad period (1978-92), the Mujahedeen state (1992-96), the period of the Taliban militias (1996-2001), and the era of the new Afghanistan or Post-Taliban (2001-present).

From independence until the Communist take-over, in relation to building the Afghan national identity, Afghanistan utilized three important tracks: First, Afghan identity building was being pursued by the central government and was one of its major goals. Second, mass public education created the Afghan identity in the same mold and made it easier to uniformly transport it across the land. Third, the foundation of national identity was built more on the principles of one single social group, i.e., on Pashtun-wali. This Afghan identity building was to a large extent successful, especially in the cities where most education took place and also among many Pashtun tribes who saw more clearly their relationship to the national identity.

At the same time this Afghan identity building also gave rise to a major problem. The other social groups could not sufficiently identify with this national identity because it did not originate from their own social bases. On the contrary, not only did they mentally reject it because they took it as representing the Pashtun identity and therefore as being lorded over, but also they were compelled to deny their own ethnicity and keep it inside themselves. In other words, the relationship and relevance of each ethnicity to the country of Afghanistan and its national identity were not apparent in this Pashtun-wali centered definition of national identity.

As a result of this flawed development, in a way, the powers that told each of the other social groups 'do not expect much from the Afghan identity, it is not for your group; it is for something new.' But in addition, all were left in the dark about each other's ethnic identities on a national level and did not know who they all were. Because the national identity itself did not have the same level of familiarity for all and one could not comprehend it deeply, what it expected from each of them also became confusing. Finally, paying so much attention to the traditions of one social group in creating the national identity gave others resentment towards the chosen social group (the Pashtuns). For a long time, perhaps until the end of the Taliban, this resentment had kept the chosen group in a defensive posture and preoccupied others to spend an inordinate amount of time in acrimonious behavior instead of worrying about development of their own identity.

However one must add that with the maturation of the educational system and increase in the ranks of the educated group, the national identity in both the monarchy of King Zaher and Prince Daoud's republic would have got stronger and the ethnic problems weaker if the Communist take-over had not taken place. But the Communist coup began the period of Jihad when the evolution of the Afghan national identity witnessed other developments. In this period, every ethnic/social group of Afghanistan performed its national duty on its own volition and choice. Every martyr, every success and every undertaking added new dimensions to their own ethnic identities and clarified them further. Also, because the central government itself was the belligerent and guilty party, road to reaching national identity lost its good name and instead other avenues opened up to directly reach the national identity. This phenomenon bestowed on all social groups honors that in the past, until the Communist coup belonged to the central government and its national identity. In other words, for the social groups of Afghanistan three things happened: Their own ethnic identity developed more, their claim to the national identity became direct, and their relation to the central government, the old builder and defender of the national identity, diminished.

During the Mujahedeen state, social groups of Afghanistan came into national power for the first time since independence and experienced the taste of central power directly. In this period, social group identities, emboldened by their victory in the Jihad, rough and somewhat arrogant, emerged individually. However, quickly and clearly it became apparent that separate social groups each with direct claims to the country, alone could not respond to national needs. In other words, it was not enough that we would be Tajik, or Pashtun or Hazara or Uzbek of Afghanistan; we had to first be Afghan and then Tajik, Pashtun or Hazara, etc. To put it another way, the national identity had to be larger than the sum of the ethnic identities. In my view, this polarity of national and central needs on the one hand and multiple strongly-developed ethnic identities on the other was one of the reasons that the Mujahedeen government did not last.

The Taliban militias pursued the opposite. The Taliban identity was a single identity, very well defined, totally central and non-ethnic who's most important and perhaps the only component was religion, i.e., doctrine and dogma. The Taliban militias seemed to want to change the historic substance of Afghanistan and its national identity. The Taliban identity, for all social groups of Afghanistan including the Pashtuns, seemed artificial and transplanted because it was not completely like Pashtun-wali; it was not quite the central government; it did not look like other social groups; and because it was more like Sunni

Hanbali than Sunni Hannafi or Shi'a Ithna Ashari, people could not distinguish their religion in it either.

Let me not be misunderstood, the sacred and compassionate Islām that the pious and God-fearing people of Afghanistan have followed in the last 1300 years is one thing and the Taliban militias' decrees altogether something else. Also, the courageous Afghanistan-building and Afghanistan-loving Pashtuns are one ethnic group and this group is altogether something else. Therefore, the social groups of Afghanistan once more did not see their relationship to this national identity and this central authority. Nor did they comprehend it. So, in the evolution of Afghanistan as an independent and sovereign state, this identity like others caused problems earlier also. The foreignness of the Taliban identity also gave an opportunity to all other social identities of Afghanistan to develop further.

The ethnic groups became more interested in their own ethnic identities. For example, if we discard the fanatics, during the Taliban, the Pashtuns felt more (especially in their private conversations) that not only a Pashtun tribe by the name of Taliban did not exist; they also questioned whether the actions the Taliban militias took in the name of traditions of the Pashtun village, were truly a part of the Pashtun-wali or a caricature of it or, in fact, just part of any traditional society. In other words, the Pashtuns who in the past had a well-developed sense of national identity, during the Taliban started to pay more attention to their internal ethnic identities (local and tribal). The non-Pashtun groups, who in the past did not feel as much included in the national identity, felt a much stronger sense of "Afghanness." Every sacrifice, every loss and every battle further polished the ethnic identity of each and deepened their relationship with the country and with the national identity, such as those of Badakhshan or Sheberghan. And thus the correct—or incorrect—evolution of the Afghan national identity continued and did not find its effective structure.

With the Bonn Agreement that put together the framework for the new Afghanistan began the latest evolutionary phase. This phase included a very important point: the all inclusive spirit and tenet of the Bonn Agreement included all major social groups.

This at first gave hope to all the ethnic groups. In fact, in my view, the first six months after the transfer of power (also called the interim period), was one of the best times ever for the ethnic groups of Afghanistan. However, beginning somewhat with the emergence of Loya Jirga and fully apparent in the Constitutional Loya Jirga, the situation changed. But to understand this change, we must first understand the political structure and relationships of the ethnic groups.

POLITICS AND ETHNICITY

The social groups who have a central role in the national identity, in relation to each other have historically had a classic vertical structure with many levels, like a ladder.[3] In other words, the social groups are situated in the upper, lower or middle level steps and their position in the ladder represents their importance. Some ethnic groups like the Pashtuns are situated in the uppermost echelons and some others in the lower social, political and economic echelons. This structure when the economy and type of power and society were traditional and based on a specific group may have run rather effectively. Even in one way, this structure in Afghanistan, compared to other places like Croatia, did not result in hatred, and all the social groups lived in comparative peaceful coexistence. Every social group owned up to a certain dignity for itself and the put downs of others did not affect them too much. In addition, our religion, Islam, also unified every one and saved us from extreme discrimination. But over the long period of war and up to today, inter-Afghan conflict is very much because of this ladder structure of the social groups. This inequality of the dignity of social groups has also become the most-used tool and secret of success for outsiders' interference in the internal affairs of Afghanistan.

Today's world also expects 'one man, one vote' and has other demands from social structures which are very important for Afghanistan and we must adapt ourselves to them and restart on this desired road. But the highway of reaching the Afghan individual, as explained above is his/her social group. Therefore, Afghanistan must first acknowledge its multi-ethnic nature and recognize the Afghan individual and impress upon him/her that 'I respect you with the identity that you have'.[4]

Transforming the vertical structure of the social groups to a horizontal structure is one of the most important steps in this undertaking. In other words, the social groups must be imagined around the circumference of a circle, situated in one level, next to each other such that destruction of one link results in the destruction of the whole circle. Although accomplishing this in practice is very difficult and success very slow, on the political level today we have a good opportunity to start the process and we must seize it.

But today the spirit of the Bonn Agreement that required inclusion of all Afghans in Afghanistan is totally shattered. It is replaced by promoting governance by one ethnic group, i.e. the Pashtun ethnic group. Some say this was from the get go at the behest of Pakistan. Several books written about post 9/11 Afghanistan talk about this. It started in the guise of bashing and marginalizing and excluding the Mujahedeen, and has now reached into a painful and divisive ethnic situation. However, this has actually made the Afghan Pashtuns more vulnerable and put them under tremendous pressure; many of them feel very defensive; and many of them do not feel it is a right strategy to make Afghanistan the land of the Pashtuns alone. This situation has resulted in the creation of so many groups, even among the Pashtuns, that reaching consensus on any issue is becoming extremely difficult. It has made politics of exclusion rampant among all groups.

Today, the new Afghanistan is no longer the country that existed 40 years ago. Today each ethnic group is fully politicized, fully experienced in struggle and fully alive. Each feels entitled to the equality that democracy requires. On a daily basis, these ethnic groups talk, write and voice their unhappiness about the situation. Let me emphasize that nobody in Afghanistan thinks that the Pashtuns are not entitled; on the contrary, everyone thinks that the Afghan Pashtuns are legitimate citizens. But most think that the other ethnic and social groups are also entitled, can also offer benefits, and that Afghanistan is the homeland of all of them. This unfortunate strategy has led many Afghans to think that the new international friendships are a modern rerun of nineteenth century colonialism and at the very least another way of implementing in Afghanistan what Pakistan failed to do with the Taliban. They feel cornered by their international friends. It is this unspoken, divisive situation that is fueling corruption, discontent and distrust, and it is creating unwillingness in Afghans to cooperate with the state.

On this point the recent Afghanistan Study Group, prepared by Ambassador Pickering and General John Jones, which has many good recommendations, remains silent perhaps because it still continues as an underlying strategy. One needs to rethink this strategy and really insist that the Afghan state and the international friends actually walk the talk of democracy; however it does mean we renegotiate with Pakistan.

So, before investing too much on this which will eventually put us in a corner, we must realize that in the current realities of Afghanistan no one ethnic group can perform all that is necessary. All groups have suffered as a result of the length of conflict. Their own social structures have been weakened. New power structures have emerged. None has the strength to build Afghanistan by itself and overlord the rest.

During the years of war, all social groups have also had great developments in education, and awareness of its own group, and they all demand inclusion. Especially Hazaras and Pashtuns have developed wonderfully. The Hazaras use their martyrdom to great advantage. The Hazara leadership and intellectuals are very close to the masses. The Pashtuns are victimized and are quagmire in being used by groups such as Al-Qaeda. The Pashtun leadership and intellectuals are more removed from the Pashtun masses in the Pashtun belt. The Uzbeks are still weak in terms of the number of leaders and the number of educated people. But they are quite aware of themselves and are in one block.

The Tajiks have the largest group of leaders and the largest group of intellectuals. But both the large numbers and the fact that traditionally the Tajiks view themselves as the king makers of Afghanistan plays a negative role among them. Also, the Tajiks for the first time are facing the fact that they are of localities, Heratis, Takharis, Badakhshanis, Ghoris, etc. and need to gel into a more cohesive group. In the last presidential elections they were the deciding factor in President Karzai's favor and thus they failed to define their weight in Afghanistan. By contrast, the Hazaras and Uzbeks voted for their own ethnic candidate and thus fully established their weight.

RECOMMENDATIONS

To have success in Afghanistan, we must proceed to develop new ways of truly including all Afghans and dealing with all ethnic and social groups equally. On the strength of the basic need theory of ethnic groups for recognition, we must acknowledge and entitle each ethnic group. As part of this, the government and civil society must conduct diversity training for various segments of society, civil servants, service providers, civil society advocates, and others.

- We must go with open arms and garlands of good will to receive our multi-ethnic society and celebrate every ethnicity, religion and locality. We must be neither ashamed nor afraid of our diversity. We must wear it like a unique jewel and show it off. We must not deny our diversity. We must rejoice in our own identity. Our diversity makes Afghanistan unique and one of a kind and is extremely important in its continuation. We must take our diversity as strength and use it for Afghanistan's stability and for an effective definition of the Afghan national identity.
- We must demand a balanced budget for all the 34 provinces of the country. According to a newspaper article published last November, full fifty percent of all donor money goes to only four Pashtun provinces. The debates in the Parliament in the last two years over the national budget have also centered on the inequality of expenditures among the provinces. The author's personal visits to Bamyan, Ghor and Jowzjan, some of the most peaceful and secure provinces, where one can clearly see that not much has been done.
- We must define the Afghan nation in such a way that

all ethnic groups can see themselves in it clearly. The new constitution making the national anthem only in one language of Pashto sends an unmistakable message of exclusion to the rest of us! or, the national TV delivering the evening news one item in Pashto, another item in Dari, obviously wants Afghans to know only half of the news, never the full news! All Afghans have the right to learn the entire news in their own mother tongue. This is the least we can do for a population that suffers so miserably from imposed isolation by various ideological groups in the last 25 years.

- Friends of Afghanistan can now define their own strategies based on their own first-hand knowledge of the ground realities instead of taking Pakistan's wishes as written in stone. To ignore the ethnic structure in the building of the new Afghanistan is an error.

This time we must not be afraid and do the right thing for Afghanistan—for our beloved Afghanistan and for the cherished modern world at large. The Afghans are ready. World, are you ready for the Afghans?

REFERENCES

1. In fact, the Taliban militias may have been the greatest threat to the Pashtun-wali and Pashtun identity of Afghanistan. The two phrases 'I am first a Muslim' and 'I don't have a qawm' which slogan-like used to come out of the mouth of many Taliban militias are very much against the traditional and historical Pashtun-wali as practiced in Afghanistan. The Pashtuns have always been Muslims; we have not heard of Jewish, Hindu or Christian Afghan Pashtuns. So, to state this obvious fact betrays the outsider. By the same token, Pashtuns always belong to a tribe or to one of its structures (qawm) and by way of introducing themselves properly they usually mention their qawm affiliation, often in the introductory sentences of a salutation. So, to deny one's qawm is also a non-Pashtun behavior that belies the outsider. I do not have much information on the Pashtun-wali of the non-Afghan Pashtuns or their support for the Taliban militias' brand of Pashtun-wali.

2. Regardless of what we now know to be the truth, the Taliban militias since early had aspects so reminiscent of other foreign occupiers with bankrupt ideologies, that the already-tested Afghans unquestioningly recognized them as an outside element. These are: Fascism in most areas of governance, a global tendency that transcended borders, creating society around doctrine, denial of diversity, and open reliance on one foreign country, in this case, Pakistan.
3. Horowitz, Donald L., Ethnic Groups in Conflict. Los Angeles, CA: University of California Press, 1985.
4. Burton, John W., Conflict Resolution: Its Language and Processes. Lanham, MD and London: The Scarecrow Press, Inc., 1996.

CHAPTER 3

Afghan Women, Violence and Abuse of Human Rights

Marium Rawi

Afghanistan, officially the Islamic Republic of Afghanistan is a landlocked, dry and mountainous country that is located approximately in the center of Asia. It is bordered by Pakistan in the South and East, Iran in the west, Turkmenistan, Uzbekistan and Tajikistan in the North, and China in the far Northeast. The 31 million populated Afghanistan consists of many ethnic groups, mainly Pashtun, Tajik, Uzbek, Hazara and a few more. The history of Afghanistan is marked by brutal civil wars and foreign influences and invasions. Most of the early 18th century rulers were under the influence of the English and Indians until in 1919 King Amanullah Khan took over and Afghanistan was completely independent. This day (18th August) is celebrated as Afghanistan's Independence Day.

The 1970s of Afghanistan was a political turmoil consisting of the Khalq, Parcham and the unpopular Ikhwanis (Islamic fundamentalists). Zahir Shah was the last king of Afghanistan who ruled from 1933-1973. In 1973 Zahir Shah's brother-in-law, Mohammed Daoud Khan, launched a coup and became the first President of Afghanistan. When the PDPA (People's Democratic Party of Afghanistan—another criminal band in Afghan history) came to power in 1978 it introduced laws which gave so-called women's rights and freedom of religion. In March 1979 Hafizullah Amin took over as prime minister and removed Taraki, who was killed. On December 27th, 1979 over 100,000 Soviet troops entered Afghanistan. They were supported largely by the Parcham faction. During this time Amin was killed and replaced by Babrak Karmal.

The Soviets and its puppet regime killed at least 600,000 to 2 million Afghan civilians,[1] mainly progressive intellectuals and young university students who opposed the Russians and the government. Many who were arrested were executed, killed under brutal torture or buried alive. Over five million Afghans fled their country to take refuge in Pakistan, Iran and other parts of the world. Thousand of people still remain "disappeared."

The U.S. saw the situation as a major opportunity to weaken the Soviet Union. In 1979 it began to fund and train the Mujahedeen forces who were Islamic fundamentalists divided into different factions according to their ethnic backgrounds, through the Pakistani secret service known as Inter Services Intelligence (ISI). With all the pressure mounting on the USSR, they finally withdrew from Afghanistan in 1989 though did support the puppet government of Najib till 1992.

From 1992-1996 fighting continued among the victorious Mujahideen factions for power. These four years under the Islamic fundamentalists are remembered as the most bloody and dark years in the history of Afghanistan. The seven infamous factions belonging to warlords trained and equipped by the USA namely Hezb-e-Islami of Gulbuddin Hekmatyar, Ittihad-e-Islami Afghanistan of Sayyaf, Jammiat-e-Islami Afghanistan of Rabbani, Hezb-e-Wahdat of Khalili, Shoray Nezar of Ahmad Shah Massoud and Junbish-e-Islami Afghanistan of Dostum; fell into a cruel war for power, crushing the innocent people of Kabul in between. In these four merciless years, more than 65,000 people were killed in Kabul only and 90% of the city was turned into ground zero.

Like anywhere else fundamentalists target women's rights as a first priority, citing medieval *Sharia* (Islamic law) as their authority. Islamic fundamentalism of any kind in essence looks upon women as sub-humans, fit only for household slavery and as a means of procreation. This regime of fundamentalists practically proved that women are indeed the first and most easy victims. Women were raped, kidnapped and killed by armed men of different factions. In certain cases, young girls committed suicide to escape forced marriages or rape by commanders or armed men. From 4-year old girls to 70-year old grand-mothers were raped and kidnapped; hundreds of young boys were also raped and forced to fight or work for some commander, people were abducted for money and in most cases were killed; public properties and houses were openly looted; Rockets were exchanged between factions from different areas of Kabul and more often the houses of innocent people were targeted; many people were killed and injured in the cross firing as well. Nails were driven into skulls and a famous "camel dance" was invented. (A helpless victim's throat would be slashed and boiling oil would be poured on it.) And much more bone chilling tortures and crimes were committed. The men of a certain faction committed these abuses against people of other ethnic. For example the Pashtun faction of Sayyaf's, roasted innocent Hazara men in containers which had a fire blazing below it. Similarly, Mazari's Hazara faction pulled out eyes of Pashtun men. The preys were mostly innocent civilians who didn't belong to any faction or political current but suffered simply because they had different physical feature.

In connection to custodial violence against women, documentation of sexual violence against women during times of conflict and violence against refugee and internally displaced women the first and foremost report that can be referred to is Amnesty International's reports such as "Women In Afghanistan: A Human Rights Catastrophe" (March 1995) or "Afghanistan: International Responsibility for Human Rights Disaster" (November 1995), as an eloquent testimony to the situation of women under the fundamentalists. Many other such documents can be found on the web site of Amnesty International and Human Rights Watch. Apart from the above, a number of eye witnessed accounts of atrocities by the Taliban and their Jihadi brothers can be found on RAWA web site.

After four years of the Jehadis' rule came the next creation of the US. The Taliban were ignorant, medieval-minded men who had been trained in religious schools (Madrasa) in Pakistan. They were mainly of Pashtun ethnic group. At the very beginning the

Taliban killed Najib and his brother. During their seven-year rule, the Taliban created impositions on women that proved their real nature. Women were banned from jobs and girls forbidden to attend schools or universities. They had to wear burqas (a long cloth that covered them from head to toe and had a mesh for the eyes). Make-up, jewellery and heels were forbidden and those who violated these laws were severely punished. Women also suffered public floggings in the streets. Thieves were punished by amputating one of their hands or feet. Sports stadiums were used for public executions, like the famous execution of Zarmeena.

At the start of the Taliban regime, the Northern Alliance was formed. Ahmed Shah Massoud, Karim Khalili, Atta Mohammad, Piram Qul, Sayyaf, Mahqiq and many others were the prominent leaders of this alliance. They aimed to defeat the Taliban and unified for that cause. After the 11 September, 2001 attacks on the U.S., America invaded Afghanistan and in late 2001 the United Nations Security Council authorized the creation of an International Security Assistance Force (ISAF) for helping the war-battered Afghanistan in recovering. Multi-billion US dollars have also been provided by the international community for the reconstruction of the country. The US and her allies tried to legitimize their military occupation of Afghanistan under the banner of "bringing freedom and democracy to our people and particularly the women," but after the fall of the Taliban regime in 2001, with great disappointment and surprise, Afghan people witnessed how the US government replaced one terrorist fundamentalist of Taliban with the other of the Northern Alliance.

The re-installment of the Northern Alliance to power crushed the hopes of the Afghan people for freedom and democracy. The US created a government from among those people who were responsible for the massacres, rape of women, destruction of the country, killing, looting and many more crimes. They were not honest in their claim of "war on terror" as relying on one enemy or terrorist to defeat another is a wrong policy and these blood suckers, who unfortunately happen to be part of Karzai's team, continue to be the main obstacle towards the establishment of peace and democracy.

Following an election in October 2004, Hamid Karzai won and became the President of the Islamic Republic of Afghanistan. In the presidential elections the majority of the people gave their votes to Karzai in the hope that he will prosecute and punish all the criminals and fundamentalists for their crimes and atrocities and will establish democracy and freedom, as he had repeatedly promised during his campaign. But he betrayed the vote and trust of the sorrowful people by compromising with the already tried fundamentalists and drug-lords and appointing infamous warlords to high governmental posts.

In 2005, a strategic partnership agreement committing United States and Afghanistan to a long-term relationship was signed. The National Assembly was made which was the first elected legislature in Afghanistan since 1973. Unfortunately the government consists of criminals who had to be tried and punished in courts; the parliament today consists of corrupt, powerful criminals who had got votes by threats and corrupt methods.[2]

With the exception of the glorious and suffocated voice of Malalai Joya, which they could not stand and finally expelled her from the parliament and a few others, Afghanistan has a parliament full of warlords and killers mainly belonging to Northern Alliance, Khalqis, Parchamis and Taliban.

It is a quite painful fact that those who ought to be prosecuted for their crimes against the Afghan nation, particularly women and children, are ruling over them and continuing with their crimes. The hanging of Saddam frightened the Northern Alliance killers and they used all their power to block the way to their trial. The parliament of Afghanistan passed the infamous bill of "National Reconciliation" whose aim was forgiving and providing immunity to all traitors and war criminals of three decades. With this act once again, the parliament proved its anti-nation and treacherous nature and that it is a tool practically only in the service of fundamentalists. The criminals present in the Afghan parliament think that by playing the game of "National Reconciliation," they can forgive themselves of the responsibility of looting, raping, destructing, shedding the blood of more than 60,000 civilians only in Kabul in the early 90's, but they have forgotten that our people and freedom-loving people and democratic organizations like RAWA will never forget and forgive and will not allow them to play with the sufferings of our people forever.

Not only by passing the "National Reconciliation" bill, but also by the formation of the National Front, the fundamentalist leaders joined hands with the Parchamis, Khalqis and Taliban to protect themselves from being brought to justice and to extend their black sovereignty. And besides the National Front, with the help of their so-called intellectuals they have formed a cultural united front against the people. Through their strong propaganda machine in the media these intellectuals are trying hard to whitewash these criminals and portray them as democratic, progressive-minded and freedom-loving people. They run these activities mostly with the help of their Iranian bosses. RAWA believes that Taliban and the Northern Alliance are like brothers. Ideologically they have the same thinking and this was proved once more when the National Front said that it has been in secret talks with the Taliban in the last six months. RAWA announced several times that when the legislature, administrative and judicial bodies are ruled by drug-lords and warlords of Northern Alliance, Taliban, Gulbidinis, Parcham and Khalq accomplices, nothing positive in Afghanistan can be expected. As we see human rights violations, crimes and corruption have reached their peaks. The existence of illegal private armies, private security companies run by these mafia bands are enough to realize their sinister intentions and the danger they pose. The human rights violations, crimes and corruption have reached their peaks. The lack of security is the main issue Afghans—men and women, face everywhere: thousands of people who became victim of the US and NATO bombing and air strikes, thousands of those who lost their lives and many more who became injured as a result of suicide attacks of Taliban, and an unknown number of those men and women who were killed, abducted, arrested, tortured, raped, looted by gunmen of fundamentalist Jehadis.

Afghanistan emerged as the world's third most volatile country, topping even Iraq.[3] The Post writes: "The HRW in its comprehensive report of 2005 revealed that several war criminals and warlords are still active and engaging in widespread human rights abuses. Many highly placed members of the present government and legislature were implicated in war crimes during brutal fighting that killed or displaced hundreds of thousands of Afghans in the early 1990s and precipitated the rise of the Taliban, the report added."[4]

It would not be wrong to state that the corruption, fraud and unsecured situation are the main reasons of the resurgence of Taliban. Despite billions of dollars donated to Afghanistan, corruption flourishes like never before and rots right into the heart of the government, with many high government officials involved in it. "The international aid effort in Afghanistan is in large part 'wasteful and ineffective' with as much as 40 per cent of funds spent going back to donor countries in corporate profits and consultant salaries, Kabul-based charities will say today. At the same time, the administration of Hamid Karzai has failed to tackle high-level corruption in a government that relies on international handouts for 90 per cent of public spending."[5]

The opium production is sky-rocketing; Afghanistan is estimated to supply more than 90 per cent of the world's illicit opium.[6] The United Nations Office on Drugs and Crime said that opium is now equivalent to more than half (53%) of the country's licit GDP.[7] Afghanistan's opium crop has risen every year since US and Afghan forces toppled the Taliban government in 2001 and another record crop was recorded in 2007. Nearly one million addicts exist in this nation of about 30 million people, including 60,000 children under age 15. Among the country's addicts, about 13% are women and 7% are children.[8] And the list of those involved in the drug trade reaches the former warlords who are in the Karzai's government. Freedom of speech and media is one of the main pillars of democracy in a nation but unfortunately it is extremely weak in Afghanistan. Famous TV channels and newspapers and publications are highly biased and if a single word is said against any of the fundamentalists of Northern Alliance they are threatened. The warlords misuse it for their own advantage but when it comes to exposing their real faces to the world they suppress and stop it in every way possible.

Women in Afghanistan in the 21st century still don't have the rights and equality considered even as basic human rights in today's world. The so called freedom gifted to Afghan women can be enjoyed only by a few women living mostly in the capital city of Kabul and not all provinces. In the fundamentalism-blighted Afghanistan the misogynist, barbaric and ignorant fundamentalists hold the Quran and the anti-women culture and traditions in one hand and the weapons in the other and suppress the rights of women in every way possible. Women today are suppressed under two layers of oppression. From one side it is the oppression from the Northern Alliance forces that are currently in power along with the Taliban who has control of some parts of the country and from the other side it is the male chauvinism existing in our society.

The current administration of President Hamid Karzai has control over only 30% of Afghanistan.[9] The other 70% is mainly controlled by the Islamic fundamentalists of the Northern Alliance. Security does not exist in such places. There are hardly any schools and even if there are some, girls can't attend them as they can be raped, kidnapped and attacked by gunmen. Schools have also been burnt down.[10] So families can't take such great risks of sending their girls for education and paying a heavy price in return.

The life of a woman in today's Afghanistan may be summarized as follows:

- **Health:** In terms of health about 24,000 Afghan women die every year while giving birth. 1,600 out of every 100,000 women that give birth die in the process. In Afghanistan the lifetime risk of maternal death is 1 in 8. (By contrast: The rate in neighboring Pakistan is 1 in 74).[11]. Preventable diseases such as diarrhea, cholera, dysentery and pneumonia kill about 600 under-five Afghan children every day, according to the UNICEF.[12]
- **Education:** In the education sector, everyday violence in all parts of the country prevents families to send their children, especially girls to school. Since the last 7 years several schools were attacked[13] and burnt.[14] The Taliban

shut down nearly 400 schools in Afghanistan[15] and 200,000 children are unable to attend school.[16] According to a survey by Oxfam almost half of all Afghan children are not in school. Girls in particular are losing out, with just one in five girls in primary education and one in 20 going to secondary school.[17]

- **Self-Immolation**: Under the so-called democratically elected government the violence against women almost doubled, the rate of suicide and self-immolation also has increased alarmingly. A growing number of Afghan women are attempting to escape a life of abuse by setting themselves on fire. Some women do manage to end their lives, but many survive with huge burns on their faces and bodies.[18] Womankind Worldwide says there has been a dramatic rise in cases of self-immolation by Afghan women since 2003. It believes many are as a result of forced marriages. It is believed 80% of Afghan women suffer domestic violence, 60% of marriages are coerced, and half of women are married before the age of 16.[19]
- **Domestic Violence**: "Violent attacks against females, usually domestic, are at epidemic proportions with 87 per cent of females complaining of such abuse – half of it sexual."[20] Women are victims of honor-killings and torture by husbands and in-laws. Herat's 22-year old Fatima's husband cut her toes, pulled her hair out, poured hot water on her and shot her.[21] Other young women like Nafisa suffered an equally horrendous fate.[22] Sixteen-year old Nazia's husband cut off her nose, ears, shaved her head, broke her teeth within three months of marriage and due to these she suffers psychiatric distress as well.[23] A man killed his two wives in February 2008, with an axe in Mazar-e-Sharif.[24] The list is endless. Women can be exchanged like property in Afghanistan's society. In disputes women (especially young girls) are usually sold into a life of slavery, rape and other tortures to solve the problem. A painful part of the women of our society is termed

as "opium brides." Poor farmers who grow poppy and are unable to pay back their loans to drug-traffickers give their daughters to them to settle the debt. A 10-year old girl was given to a 46-year old drug-trafficker in this manner.[25] On daily basis, girls commit suicide due to domestic violence like the 18-year old Farzana of Jowzjan who hung herself due to poverty and family problems.[26] Everyday one notices news like "Afghanistan: Violence against Women Almost Doubles," "I was sold four times," "Violence Has Increased: Girls and Women's Escape their Homes," "Man slaughtered his 14-year-old wife," "Women forced to quit work because of insecurity" and so on.

- **Sexual Abuse**: On March 30, 2008 an 8-year old girl was raped in Takhar province.[27] In the month of February, four cases of rape were reported alone in the North. Seventeen—year old Najibullah, son of an MP and powerful commander in the North, gang-raped a 12-year old girl named Bashira with his friends on 18 February, 2007; but he was easily released from prison and is roaming around with impunity. With her innocent and painful face and cry she said on TV that no one hears her voice and no one has paid attention to her case.[28] Similar were the cases of Ayesha, a four-year old girl in Balkh province; eleven-year old girl in Jowzjan and another girl in the district of Gosphandi.[29] A small 7-year old girl was gang-raped by two men but the men were easily released after arrest.[30] The 16-year old Guldana was kidnapped by five unknown, armed men in Baghlan.[31] Many cases of suicide due to rape and forced marriages have been reported to hospitals as well.[32]
- **Widows**: Kabul is referred to as the city of widows. According to some statistics there are more than 1.5 million widows living without any support.[33] IRIN News says in a report published on January 30th, 2008 "The average age of an Afghan widow is just 35 years, and 94 percent of them are unable to read and write,"

Deborah Zalesne, a board member of the Beyond 9/11 and a law professor at the City University of New York, told IRIN, "About 90 percent of Afghan widows have children, and the average widow has more than four," she added. To survive many Afghan widows weave carpets, do tailoring, beg or even engage in prostitution.[34]

- **Social Condition**: Afghanistan is a country where women are exchanged for dogs, a country where two women are thought as one man, and families are forced to sell their daughter for only US$10.[35] Like property they can be exchanged or sold and used to settle community disputes. A painful part of the life of Afghan women today is called "Opium Brides." Poor farmers who grow poppy and have not been able to pay their debts usually sell their daughters to a life of rape and slavery. Lately a 10-year old girl was given to a 45-year old drug-trafficker.[36] Over 3000 prisoners including 346 women are currently being held in the Pul-i-Charkhi jail.[37] Women and young girls in all the 31 provinces of Afghanistan are the most unprotected vulnerable creatures. There are hundreds of cases of women's right violations by powerful warlords or their gunmen but only a few of them are reported by the media. Out of thousands of such terrible cases there are a few reported by the people who have dared to come forward and tell the media about their sufferings. Most people hide these painful sufferings for their protection and out of fear that they may be disgraced in the conservative society. In most cases of violence against women the convicts are not prosecuted or punished. One of the well-known examples was the case of Daulat Bibi—a 40-year old woman who was raped by 13 men belonging to Piram Qul. She went everywhere looking for justice. People told her that there is no law and just forget about it and she finally gave up.[38]
- The real problem is that there is no law and judiciary practically in women's favor or the police and all the

> governmental authorities are either deeply involved in such crimes or are simply powerless. Our government today is made up of misogynists, drug kingpins,[39] thieves who have stolen billions of dollars of aid and is composed of all the criminals who have committed brutal crimes against our people from 1992-96. All the judiciary and law-making bodies are occupied by these criminals and obviously none of the laws written on paper would be implemented against such atrocities. The warlords have their tribal governments in rural area and people of their gangs are highly involved in such crimes, so of course no action would be taken against them.

It is unfortunate that the world believes that the US and its allies have freed the Afghan women. It is better to say that they have used "liberation of women" as a justification to bomb Afghanistan. RAWA claims that democracy, freedom, peace and liberation of women would be impossible without the abolition of this government filled with Islamic fundamentalists. And this has been amply evident seeing the condition of Afghanistan in general. After the fall of the Taliban, Afghanistan's new government pledged swift action to improve the lives of women. But a recent report by different international sources proves that millions of Afghan women and girls continue to face discrimination and violence in their day-to-day lives. The BBC's Afghan service has been talking to Afghan women about their lives. "Afghan women's rights groups acknowledge that women now have a variety of rights which they didn't have under Taliban rule. But in practice, they say, many of those rights are ignored and activists face intimidation, or worse." Our women have questions which remain unanswered?

For ten years our women suffered under the most terrible and dangerous terrorisms of Northern Alliance and Taliban, but why did the whole International Community sit silent and refused to listen to the helpless cries of our oppressed women at that time?

Why did they ignore the warnings of democratic organizations like RAWA who said that these creatures are not only harmful for our people but for the whole world, which was also finally proved by the 9/11 attacks? After all that time, the US and its allies finally invade Afghanistan in the name of freeing its people especially the women.

We have been stating that America has been dishonest in its war against terror and we have reasons for it. If they would have been honest in stabilizing Afghanistan's volatile situation why did they replace the barbaric Taliban with the much criminal, anti-women and atrocious Northern Alliance?

Northern Alliance has been the criminal group that has committed heinous crimes. Amnesty International and Human Rights Watch are forced to acknowledge it. If they were true friends of Afghanistan, they would have tried these criminals and traitors in international courts and punished them severely for their unforgivable crimes.

If they were honest, why don't they struggle and try solving the main problems faced by Afghanistan such as the opium production, women's worsening situation, alarming rise in insecurity, suicide bombings; whose roots lies in the virus called fundamentalism. Instead of attacking fundamentalism and uprooting every brand and kind of it there is a Tom and Jerry game going on between US and Taliban.

If they would've been honest in their claim of war against terror they could have disarmed the Taliban completely but instead they are supporting them behind the scenes. It is quite ridiculous to believe that a super power like America can't defeat a band of ignorant and backward criminals. RAWA has been stating this from the very first year of US invasion in Afghanistan that the West is playing a very dangerous and dirty game in Afghanistan and caught among them are our people—the main victims. With around 46,000 troops in Afghanistan, this war on terror has been failing. The true nature of the US's "war on terror" drama has been exposed today and we witness that they are killing thousands of our innocent people under the name of "fighting terrorists." The killing of around 6000 innocent civilians by 'mistake' is a disaster as Professor Marc Herold put it as 'twin tragedy' to 9/11.

These treacherous acts of demagogy have proved to our people and to the world that the US government and its allies are just pursuing their strategic, economic and political gains in Afghanistan and pushing our people to increasing destitution and disasters. If the West had been a true friend of Afghanistan, they would have supported the democratic movements against these fundamentalists but instead they are supporting the powerful Northern Alliance drug lords and warlords and these democratic forces have received no moral, financial or political help from the US government to bring peace, freedom and democracy into Afghanistan.

Afghanistan is a good example which shows that fundamentalists are big obstacles for restoration of women's rights and democracy. For this reason RAWA always emphasizes that only a society based on secular democracy can assure the rights of women and pave the way for freedom and social justice.

RAWA's mission is a flame in the dark life of Afghan women. Struggling for freedom, democracy, social justice and human rights, the Revolutionary Association of the Women of Afghanistan (RAWA) is the oldest anti-fundamentalist political and social feminist organization founded by its martyred leader Meena[40] in 1977 in Kabul. RAWA represents the most deprived and oppressed women of Afghanistan whose voices are not often heard and they continue to be the first and silent victims of terrorist and fundamentalists' tyranny.

RAWA members have risked their lives documenting human rights abuses, running schools and literacy courses (which were a great risk during the Taliban regime as they didn't allow education for girls and called schools "Gateway to Hell"), orphanages, income-generating projects, hospitals and health care centers which all provide free service for women and children. Today our most pressing concern is RAWA's financial problems, which put our projects at risk. Despite the serious security and financial problems, we are active inside Afghanistan and in refugee camps in Pakistan.

RAWA has concentrated on raising awareness and organizing masses of women in legal and social sectors, and increasing education and literacy among them. We strongly believe that education is power and Afghan women cannot fight for their rights as long as they are not equipped with this sharpest weapon against ignorance and fundamentalism. With the weapons of education, Afghan women's rights could not be ignored by any government in the country. Revolutionary Association of the Women of Afghanistan (RAWA) once again proclaims that all miseries of our country and specially its women have roots in the existence of fundamentalist forces be it the Jehadi or Taliban style and as long as this filthy virus is not removed from the body of our country, our nation and country will never see even a ray of happiness and development. Although Mr. Karzai has declared that he is not in the position of bringing the criminals around him to justice, we state repeatedly that we are determined, despite many limitations and the fact that we are besieged by warlords and their foreign masters, to drag the warlords and criminals of the last three decades to law courts and punish them regardless of their religion and ethnic backgrounds, with the help and support of our people.

REFERENCES

1. Wikipedia Encyclopedia (http://en.wikipedia.org/wiki/Afghanistan).
2. Ruder Eric, 2004: "Massive Fraud in Afghanistan Vote," S.W. Online (October 15, 2004).
3. *New York Times*, 2008: "Afghanistan named third most Volatile Country, Topping even Iraq" (March 26, 2008).
4. The Post, 2007: "Afghan Criminals and Warlords" by Musa Khan Jalalzai (November 3, 2007).
5. The Financial Times, 2008: "Afghan Aid 'Wasteful and Ineffective'" by Jon Boone.
6. Council on Foreign Relations, 2007: "Afghanistan Opium Survey, 2007," September 19, 2007.
7. United Nations Office on Drugs and Crime (UNODC), 2007: "Opium amounts to half of Afghanistan's GDP in 2007, November 16.
8. Associated Press, 2007: "Drug Addiction Rising in Afghan Children," January 3, 2007.

9. CBC News, 2008: "70% of Afghanistan Still Lawless" by Michael McConnell, National Intelligence Director, February 28, 2008.
10. Pajhwok, Afghan News, 2007: "Threatened and Snubbed: 50,000 Students Banned from School in Ghazni" by Sher Ahmad Haidar, January 2, 2007.
11. UN News Centre, 2008: "Maternal Health Biggest Challenge Facing Afghan Women—UN agency," March 3, 2008.
12. IRIN News, 2008: UNICEF Report, January 22, 2008.
13. The New York Times, 2007: "As War Enters Classrooms, Fear Grips Afghans" by Barry Bearak, July 10, 2007.
14. Pajhwok Afghan News, 2007: "School set on fire in Balkh in Northern Afghanistan" by Zabeehullah Ihsas, September 9, 2007.
15. Turkish Press, 2007: "Taliban unrest shuts nearly 400 schools in Afghanistan," September 8, 2007.
16. Reuters, 2007: "Gunmen kill two schoolgirls in Afghanistan," June 12, 2007.
17. IRIN and BBC News, 2006: "Almost Half of all Afghan Children Not in School by Oxfam," November 27, 2006.
18. Spero News, 2008: "Afghanistan: Violence Against Women Almost Doubles," March 9, 2008.
19. *Ibid.*
20. The Independent, 2008: "Afghanistan: Women's Lives Worse Than Ever" by Terri Judd, February 25, 2008.
21. RAWA News, 2008: "Husband cuts toes of his wife, pours hot water on her," February 26, 2008.
22. RAWA News, 2008: "Nose and Ear of Nafisa was Cut Off by her Husband," February 15, 2008.
23. IRIN News, 2007: "Nazia: "My husband Cut Off my Ears and Nose and Broke my Teeth"," December 26, 2007.
24. RAWA News, 2008: "Man Kills his Two Wives with Axe," February 18, 2008.
25. NDTV, 2008: "Afghanistan: 'Opium Brides' Pay the Price," March 31, 2008.
26. PAN, 2008: "A Young Afghan Girl Commits Suicide Due to Domestic Violence," March 10, 2008.
27. Ariana Television Network, 2008: "8-year Old Girl Raped in Takhar Province" by Qasim Nasrullahi, March 30, 2008.
28. RAWA News, 2008: "Bashira, Gang-Raped in Sar-e-Pul Province, Calls for Justice," February 25, 2008.
29. RAWA News, 2008: "Gang-Rape of Young Girls in Northern Afghanistan," February 21, 2008.
30. The Guardian, 2007: "7-Year-Old Afghan Girl Raped by Two Men" by Alisa Tang, August 23, 2007.

31. PAN, 2008: "A Young Girl Kidnapped in Baghlan Province" by Shir Mohammad Jahsh, March 22, 2008.
32. Spero News, 2008: *Op cit.*
33. IRIN News, 2008: "Bleak Prospects for Estimated 1.5 million Widows in Afghanistan," January 30, 2008.
34. *Ibid.*
35. Pajhwok Afghan News, 2008: "Afghan Woman Sells Daughter for $10" by Abdul Matin Sarfaraz, January 27, 2008.
36. NDTV, 2008: *Op cit.*
37. Pajhwok Afghan News, 2007: "UN Concerned at Plight of Women in Afghan Jails" by Habib Rahman Ibrahimi, September 2, 2007.
38. IWPR, 2007: September 13, 2007.
39. Pajhwok Afghan News, 2007: "Senior Officials Linked to Drug Smuggling: Afghan VP" by Zubair Babakarkhel, September 27, 2007.
40. Meena (1957-87) is the founding leader of Revolutionary Association of the Women of Afghanistan who was assassinated on February 4, 1987 in Quetta by Gulbuddin Hekmatyar's men with the help of ISI.

CHAPTER 4

Displaced Population from Afghanistan: A Case Study of Delhi

Mondira Dutta and Pramod Kumar Sharma

Decades of civil war and serious human rights abuse have forced millions of Afghan men, women and children to flee from their homes and seek refuge in other parts of Afghanistan or outside the country. Several hundreds have been killed or injured in indiscriminate bombing and shelling of residential areas. Thousands have been arbitrarily arrested, tortured and raped, disappeared and even murdered for their political affiliation, ethnic identity, gender, or in reprisal attacks by the various armed groups fighting for control of territory. Schools, hospitals, homes, and farms have been burned and destroyed leaving millions of Afghans displaced and dispossessed, their towns and villages being destroyed.

Afghanistan happens to rank the highest not only in terms of opium production but also in terms of human displacement. Afghan refugees make up the greatest population of the same origin ever transplanted outside their own borders – an exodus from the south to the south, or the poor towards other poor. The Afghan refugees constitute more than 60% of the refugees in the world. The UNHCR estimates more than 5 million Afghans as either a refugee in the neighborhood or are internally displaced population. About 2 million of these are located in Pakistan, one and a half million are in Iran while the rest are scattered in India and elsewhere.

It has been attested by several studies that the massive outflow of this human population can largely be attributed to the involvement of superpowers in this strategically important region. The total number of asylum applications made by Afghans in European countries between 1989 and 1998 was, 99,350 according to UNHCR. Of these, the total number recognized as refugees (as per the 1951 Convention) or granted humanitarian status was 39,436 (approximately 26%). Germany and the Netherlands had received the most number of applications. However the countries of Europe and other northern states have no doubt taken concerted steps to make it nearly impossible for refugees to enter their territories and have denied protection to many even with a valid claim to asylum. Hundreds of Afghan asylum-seekers in Europe who have had their claims to asylum rejected are living in fear of being deported. Their status is unclear and subject to change. In Germany many asylum applications of Afghans have been rejected on the grounds that since there is no effective state in Afghanistan to commit human rights violations, there is therefore no obligation for the asylum country to grant refugee status.

The refugee problem became a significant issue for Afghanistan and its neighbors ever since the 1978 coup by the 'Peoples Democratic Party of Afghanistan' (PDPA). The refugee flow began as a trickle in April 1978, reaching to a peak during the first half of 1981 when an estimated 4,700 (http://en.wikipedia.org) crossed the Pakistan border daily. By the fall of 1989, the flow gathered momentum due to Soviet offenses, pushing up the number of Afghan refugees to an estimated 3.2 million in Pakistan, 2.2 million in Iran, and several hundred thousands resettled in scattered communities throughout the world including India.

Afghans represented the single largest concentration of refugees in the world on whom an estimated $1 million a day (http://countrystudies.us/afghanistan) was spent in 1988. A new wave of refugees entered Pakistan following the fall of the PDPA regime in 1992. Taliban's takeover of Kabul in 1996 had narrowed the out flow of refugees but this quickly surged back after the Taliban took over Jalalabad and Kabul in September 1996. In fact the flow of returnees, which had started to gather momentum dramatically reversed raising the number of families crossing into Pakistan, inspite of the fact that the refugees were now no longer welcomed and were allowed only minimum emergency assistance. These two neighbors of Afghanistan—already overwhelmed by 3.5 million Afghan refugees crossing the borders over the past two decades—sealed their borders fearing more exoduses (UNHCR, 2006). However, according to UNHCR, "Between 10,000 to 20,000 new refugees has managed to slip across the border by roads and other remote paths" (The Muslim, 1983).

After the UNHCR cut down its subsidies to the host countries providing shelter to the Afghan refugees, the initial euphoria among the host countries started dying in Pakistan and Iran. The host countries weary of hosting this huge refugee population were in favor of repatriation. Both Pakistan and Iran are now giving persistent calls for their repatriation on the grounds that the burden of hosting such vast numbers of refugees for such a long period has taken a toll on their economies. Within local communities there have been signs of growing resentment to the prolonged presence of the refugees in Pakistan.

Simultaneously the internally displaced persons estimated at about one million have been equally disruptive both for the rural areas as well as the cities bringing about changes in the demographic balances with countless consequences. Some families have moved several times as violence flared up in different areas for control of territory.

Studies in relation to the magnitude of Afghan refugees' show wide scale variation among the researchers. A study (Hiram Ruiz, 2001) estimates 15,000 Afghan refugees have fled to Pakistan and hundreds of thousands are reportedly on the move within Afghanistan. It also states that about 2 million Afghan refugees are living in Pakistan and more than 1.4 million in Iran, with an estimated 30,000 in India, Tajikistan, Uzbekistan and other countries. According to the British and U.S. government estimates (Human Rights Watch Backgrounder, 2001) the September 11 fears of U.S. retaliatory military action, forced conscription and politically motivated attacks by the Taliban against particular ethnic groups in Afghanistan resulted in 20,000 to 30,000 refugees' crossing over Pakistan. The United Nations High Commissioner for Refugees puts the figure as more than 3.5 million refugees residing in Pakistan and Iran alone (CNN.com, 2001). Nevertheless it is amply evident that a substantial number of refugees have fled from Afghanistan especially during the aftermath of 9/11.

Table 1: Magnitude of Displaced Afghans in India

UNHCR	22000
Government of India	11750
Human Rights Watch	60000
Sample Survey (Conducted by the Authors)	30000-40000

However it is difficult to estimate and arrive at a meaningful number as far as their magnitude and spread is concerned. India has had to face the spill over of such population. It is believed that approximately 60,000 Afghans live in India, of which a mere 16,000 possess certificates issued by the UNHCR. The Indian Government does not recognize them as refugees. The UNHCR often plays a complementary role to the efforts of the Government, particularly in regard to verification about the individual's background and the general circumstances prevailing in the country of origin (Ananthachari, 2001). Relations between Afghan refugees and the New Delhi based office of UNHCR is particularly not a cordial one. A report (South Asia Human Rights Documentation Centre [SAHRDC], 1999) highlights the predicament of the Afghan refugee population in New Delhi. It examines the services offered by United Nations High Commission on Refugees (UNHCR) to Afghan refugees in Delhi, the relevance, accessibility, and overall effectiveness of services available. The policies of the Indian Government that pertain to Afghan refugees and the problems faced by Afghan refugees in Delhi have also been discussed. In 1999, a group of more than 100 Afghan refugees staged a sit-in protest outside the UNHCR mission in New Delhi. The UNHCR (UNHCR, 1997) has also slashed its subsistence allowance rolls, from 12,000 families at the end of 1994 to 1,500 families in 1998 in an arbitrary and insensitive fashion, and impoverished thousands of Afghan refugee families, adversely affecting their standard of living and driving many of them into debt (Human Rights Documentation Centre, 1999).

According to the Indian constitution through articles 14 and 21, any resident on the soil of India have all the basic rights at par to Indian citizen. Refugees under UNHCR's mandate in India (approximately 12,000 in number) constitute 90% Afghan beneficiaries. Out of this almost 85% belong to the Hindu and Sikh faith. A sizeable number of the displaced Afghans living in India as against those living in Pakistan and Iran are reluctant to return back to their homeland despite improvements back home.

The present paper attempts to study the magnitude and identify issues of concern among the displaced population of Afghanistan in Delhi. The study is based on primary sources of information collected through a random sample survey conducted with the help of a structured questionnaire. A sample of 953 displaced people from Afghanistan was selected for the study. A random sample was conducted during the months of March-May 2007.

The sample was selected on the basis of areas of concentration and discussions with the Afghan group leaders and their religious leaders. The paper will attempt to assess the magnitude of the displaced population from Afghanistan in Delhi and present a situational analysis. It will also attempt to assess the status of their identity and political implications involved.

SAMPLE DETAILS

To begin with a sum of 1169 samples was interviewed. After careful scrutiny a total of 953 questionnaires were selected for the study. The sample was selected on the basis of areas of concentration and discussions with the Afghan group leaders and their religious leaders. A major chunk of these refugees were however contacted during the occasion of 'Baisakhi' (New Year's Day of Sikhs) in the various Gurudwaras where a large section of the Afghan refugees were present. The respondents in the age group of 40 to 50 years in age were more receptive. They were Afghan born and had spent more time in Afghanistan.

Besides the survey on Afghan refugees, the study also undertook several visits to other offices for data collection. Some of them include:

- The UNHCR, Jorbagh, New Delhi.
- The Afghan Desk, Ministry of External Affairs, South Block.
- YMCA, Lajpat Nagar, New Delhi.
- Don Bosco, Lajpat Nagar, New Delhi.
- The Khalsa Diwan Bhawan, Old Mahavir Nagar.
- Interview with Ms Nasrine Gross, Kabultech, during her lecture in Jawaharlal Nehru University, New Delhi, November 2006.
- Foreigners Regional Registration Office (FRRO), R.K. Puram, New Delhi.
- Human Rights Law Network (HRNL), Jungpura, New Delhi.

However some of the secondary sources of information such as the FRRO were reluctant to impart with any information on the pretext that the RTI Act does not apply on them. The Afghan embassy on the other hand directed the surveyors to contact the UNHCR for any information related to refugees.

The details of the sample survey and their distribution pattern area-wise have been displayed in Table 3.

Table 2: Afghan Refugees in India

State/UT	*No. of Refugees*
Andhra Pradesh	02
Bihar	01
Chandigarh	01
Delhi	10521
Haryana	1215
Maharashtra	10
Orissa	01
West Bengal	02
Total	11753

Source: Lok Sabha Unstarred Question No.4544, 22.4.2003.

From the table (Table 2), it is evident that whatever may be the magnitude of Afghan refugees in India; these are mostly concentrated in Delhi or near Delhi (Haryana).

The sample survey was thus conducted in the areas of maximum concentration.

Table 3: Sample Distribution

S. No.	*Areas Covered*	*Sample Size*	*% of Sample*
1.	Tilak Nagar, Delhi; Gurdwara-Mahavir Nagar, Guru Nanak Darbar, Manohar Nagar; Guru Harrai Saheb Kakrola, Palam Mor; Karala, Mongolpuri; Guru Har Govind Saheb, Karala; Angad Devji, Karala; Angad Devji, Chandra Vihar	641	67.3
2.	Karol Bagh, Delhi: Gaffar Market, Tank Road	4	0.4
3.	Greater Kailash: Gurdwara	6	0.6
4.	Munirka, Delhi	4	0.4
5.	Sangam Vihar	7	0.7
6.	Malviya Nagar—Khirki Extension	23	2.4
7.	Ballimaran—Delhi	65	7.0
8.	Defence Colony	5	0.5
9.	Laxmi Nagar	57	6.0
10.	Mehrauli	12	1.3
11.	Lajpat Nagar	116	12.0
12.	Jangpura	13	1.4
	Total	953	100%

According to the secondary sources of information the Afghan refugee population by country of asylum (UNHCR, 2006) is given in Fig. 1.

As is evident, from Fig. 1, the countries of Pakistan and Iran have received huge magnitudes of refugees from Afghanistan during the last twenty-five years. Pakistan has received the maximum number of refugees in quick succession and registers a quick decline in numbers as well. This suggests that the repatriation process has been an ongoing one. As far as India is concerned, it's a steady graph, which has remained more or less constant. Although it does not depict an instant rise but the figure does not register a decline either. If such were the trend, India would continue to receive the displaced Afghans and ultimately

Fig. 1: Afghan Refugee by Country

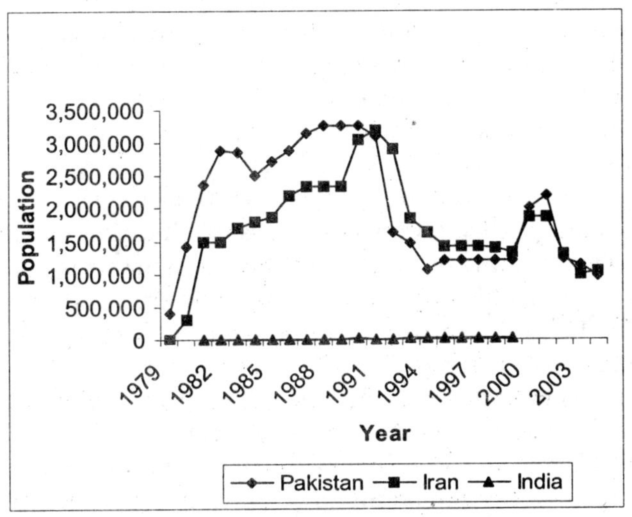

may land up in a similar situation like that in Assam and West Bengal with the Bangladesh refugees!

From 1984, UNHCR and the World Bank set up a joint project in cooperation with the Pakistan government, known as the Income Generation Project for Refugee Areas. This programme, in which US$ 85 million was invested over the next 12 years, involved some 300 projects in three refugee-affected provinces. It included reforestation, watershed management, irrigation, road repair and construction etc. The programme was generally considered to have had a significant and positive impact. As with other projects in Iran, however, donors were less willing to provide funds for the project. Of the US$18 million initially requested by UNHCR and IFAD for this project, only a third was forthcoming during the project's first five years (*The Times of India*, 2000).

Another major difference between services provided to refugees in Pakistan and to those in Iran was in the field of education. In Pakistan, many boys received an education in UNHCR-funded schools in refugee villages, although fewer girls did so owing to discriminatory cultural practices, which made it difficult for many of them to attend these schools. A significant number of boys also received an education in private Madrasas (religious schools) with which UNHCR was not associated. In the mid-1990s, some of the boys who grew up as refugees in Pakistan, and who attended these madrasas, became leading members of the Taliban Islamic movement that seized power in Afghanistan (Rashid Ahmed, 2000).

In Iran, by contrast, refugee children were enrolled in Iranian schools and girls had far greater access to education. During the 1990s, when repatriation to Afghanistan began in earnest, refugees frequently cited this access to education for girls as a reason for not wanting to return to Afghanistan, where the Taliban prohibited such accesses.

The Taliban, drawn from one ethnic group, the Pashtuns, consisted of a curious mixture of extremist Sunni Muslim clerics, students from madrassas (Islamic colleges) who had been denied anything like a normal family life as a result of two decades of war, and Pushtuns who identified with the movement out of ethnic solidarity rather than ideological affinity (Maley, 1998). This led to an increased ethnic crisis of the Afghan conflict (Saikal, 1998). The remarkable and bizarre restrictions on women, which the Taliban sought to impose, blocked the movement's attempts to secure international respectability.

The main losers were the Hazara ethnic group. For much of the twentieth century, Hazaras witnessed significant discrimination. In February 1995, the Taliban killed Abdul Ali Mazari, leader of the Hazara-backed Hezb-e Wahdat ('Party of Unity'). In August 1998, some 2000 Hazaras were slaughtered when the Taliban took the northern city of Mazar-e Sharif; the killings were fuelled by incidents of broadcasts by the Taliban 'Governor' of Mazar, Mullah Muhammad Niazi (Human Rights Watch, 1998). The nomadic Pushtun tribes allied with the Taliban in order to obtain control over the land in the region or recover old debts. This has complicated the position of Hazaras in the Hazarajat region (Rubin, 2000). For the Hazaras, the future in Afghanistan appears anything but bright. Such, victims of the Taliban are no longer welcomed in neighboring countries. Pakistan, which is not a party to the 1951 Convention, closed its borders to Afghan refugees in late 2000, in a move widely viewed as an attempt to support the Taliban's military objectives by increasing the vulnerability of civilian populations in areas outside Taliban control, and has been forcibly deporting Afghan refugees to Afghanistan.

SOCIAL CHARACTERISTICS

The sample survey shows that majority of the respondents were Sikhs constituting 64% of the sample size. Hindu and Muslim displaced population constitute only less than 20 percent each. Historical past reveals that Ghazni conquered India and had taken Indian slaves back with him. Even during the rule of Maharaja Ranjit Singh, some Indians (mainly Sikhs) settled down in Afghanistan to practice trade. At the time of partition in 1947, some Hindu families migrated to Afghanistan as well in search of a safe haven. Thus the refugees that have come to India during their time of crisis necessarily belong to the same ethnic group.

The age groups have been classified from 20 years onwards. Care was taken to avoid too young people. The sample comprises of 32% in the age group 31-40, which is the highest, followed by 28% and 24% in the age group of 20-30 (youngest) and 51-60 (Oldest) respectively. Most of the youngest group have been born in India and can hardly associate themselves with the Afghan culture and tradition. The older generation of the sample respondents spoke with nostalgia in their voices about their golden days in Afghanistan. (Fig. 2)

Fig. 2: Religion of the Respondents

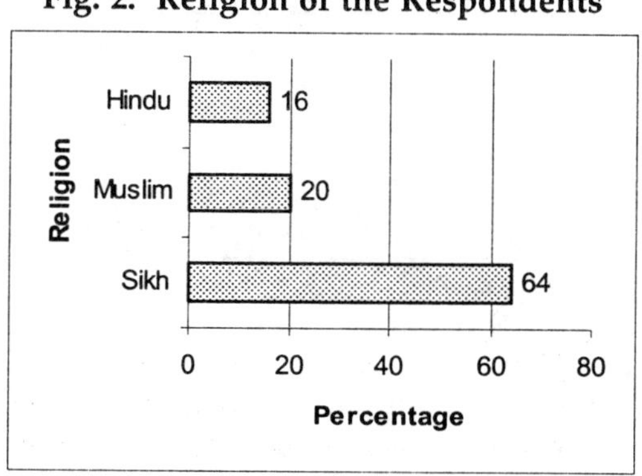

The sample reveals a total of 28 percent the respondents as illiterate. This is a substantial proportion of the displaced and will affect the quality of the refugee community population in fighting for their rights. The displacement has forced many of them to abandon their basic education practices. Out of the literate people, only 4 percent were found to be graduates. However Education is now being realized as a major skill development and the parents are taking an interest in enrolling their children in schools. Sometimes Language can be a big barrier in intermingling with the local people. Due to the ethnic ties, the respondents already were familiar with the local language and had no difficulty in expressing themselves freely with the fellow counterpart in Delhi. Almost all respondents knew Dari and Pushto irrespective of their religion. Similarly almost all knew Hindi at least they could understand and speak the language very well.

On an average the number of dependents per respondent varied from one to 5 dependents. More than 72% of the respondents had to take care of more than 2 dependents enhancing the responsibilities of the refugee even during his present crisis. Majority of the respondents migrated in the year 1992 although the process or displacement started way back in 1982. However among the respondents majority got displaced during the period 1992 to 1996 that is when the Talibans were in power.

Table 4: Migration Period

Year	*Percent (%)*
1982-1985	12
1986-1991	24
1992-1996	55
1997-2001	05
After 2001	04
Total	(953) 100

Based on Sample Survey, 2007.

The majority (90%) of the displaced respondents were with family. Ten percent of them still had families back home in Afghanistan as they were unsure where they might have to settle.

Majority of the displaced respondents were from Kabul (84%), followed by Jalalabad (12%) and Kunar (8%).

Table 5: Place of Origin

Origin	*Jalalabad*	*Kabul*	*Kunar*	*Total*
Percent (%)	12	80	08	100 (953)

Most of the respondents availed the train to reach their destination. They reached Pakistan and from there they entered India through the Wagah border. Few traveled by road as well. Another 20 percent came by air.

It was important to ascertain the reasons for displacement. Time and again studies have revealed that many of the refugees were arriving on account of economic constraints. The sample survey, showed otherwise. The entire sample respondents stated 'hostile environment' as the major reason for their displacement. Security, threat to life, law and order were the other major reasons stated for their displacement status. Another 22 percent also stated the fear or Taliban's resurgence as one of the reasons for fleeing from Afghanistan. (Fig. 3)

Fig. 3: Reasons for Displacement

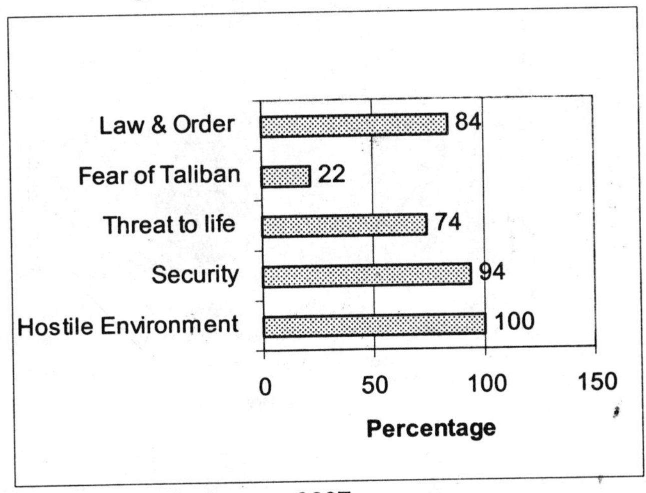

Based on Sample Survey 2007.

The ethnic affiliation and ancestral roots normally plays a dominant role in attracting the distressed. Among the respondents, all Sikh and Hindu respondents accepted that ancestral roots did convince them to shift to India. Almost all stated that the secular image of India was indeed a reason for attracting them. Majority of the respondents did accept that India portrayed a better image in terms of economic prospects, supportive relations and cultural ties as compared to Iran and Pakistan. (Fig. 4)

The survey not only revealed some of the traumas of displacement but also displayed the horrendous experiences of the respondents so much so that they simply shudder at the thought of returning back to their homes in Afghanistan. A respondent Shri Uttam Singh from Sevadar Gurudwara Nanak Devji, Manohar Nagar narrated his agony when he stated how the Mujahideen thoroughly checked and searched him with suspicion when he visited the Kabul market. He died a hundred deaths during the entire process.

Majority (nearly two-thirds) of the displaced people stated they can never dream of going back permanently to Afghanistan. Only 28% are willing to give it another try provided they are

Fig. 4: Selecting India as a Destination

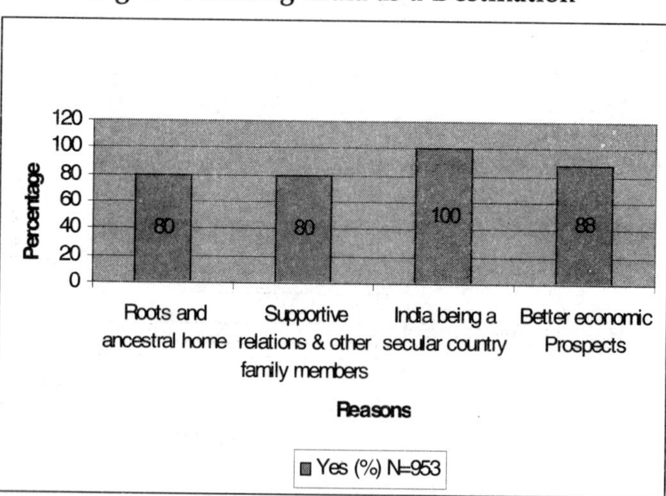

Based on Sample Survey 2007.

assured of their lives and security. Most of these would like to go back on an Indian passport so that in case of any adverse situation back home they can always return back. The respondents feel that they are neither accepted in Afghanistan nor are they accepted in India. According to Shri Narendra Singh of Khalsa Dewan office located in Malviya Nagar of South Delhi says,

> "Whenever we go to Afghanistan, they tell us 'Oh have you returned from your country?' and when we come here to India, we are asked 'when are you returning back to your country?' We are not recognized either as Afghani or as Indians. What can be more pathetic than this?"

OCCUPATION AND INCOME

Occupation for an alien community under distressing situation, possessing little technology and skills has hardly any option but to be self-employed. Accordingly majority (52%) of the respondents was found to be self-employed, 24% were unemployed and another 24% were working under some private owners of factory and shops. (Fig. 5)

Fig. 5: Occupation of the Respondents

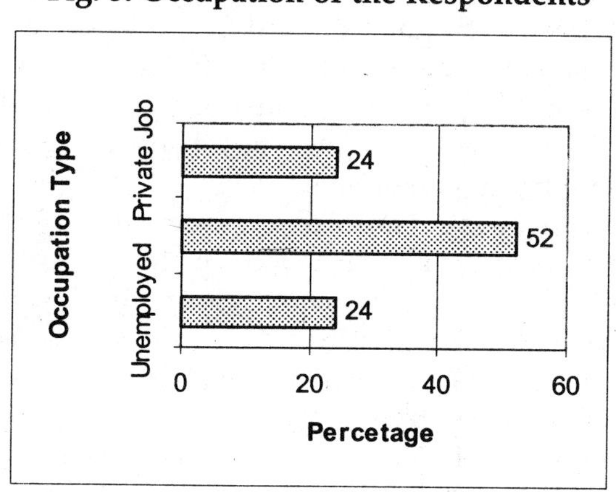

Based on Sample Survey 2007.

Fig. 6: Occupation Status by Age Group

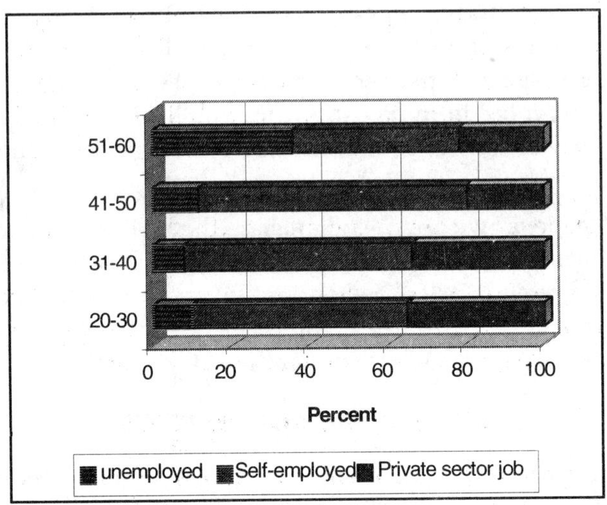

The occupation as per the various age-groups (Fig. 6) shows a large section of the displaced population in the age group (51-60), are unemployed. A major chunk of the respondents in all age group are self-employed. The availability of jobs in the private sector seemed to be limited and also low paid.

Fifty five percent of the respondents in the age group of 20-30 are self-employed while 35% of the respondents are employed in Private Sector Jobs and 10% are unemployed. Most of the employed belong to the age group 31 to 50 years. In the age group of 31-40, 58% of the respondents are self-employed followed by 34% in the Private jobs and 8% are unemployed. In the age group 51-60, 36 percent are unemployed. (Fig. 7)

Age factor does seem to play a dominant role in the job market. Figure No 7 shows that most of the self-employed are illiterates (45%). On the other hand it is amply clear that higher education does not imply better jobs in the private sector. The private sector prefers educated youths but not with very high education status. Secondary level education can get a job to the respondents in the private sector. Thus it gives an edge to the employers in the private and unorganized sector to employ the displaced without having to follow the labour laws.

Fig. 7: Occupation Status by Education Level

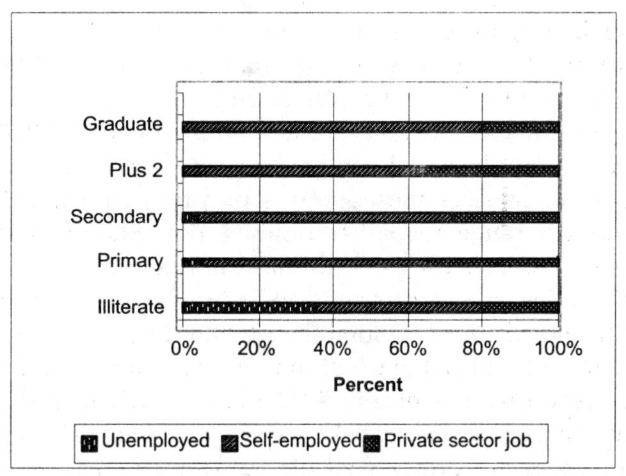

ECONOMIC EARNINGS

With the kind of occupational structure, income is hardly expected to be sustainable especially so as each respondent has a minimum of two to four dependents. Majority of the displaced person (84%) stated that their income was hardly enough to survive. Only 16% felt that the income is just enough. This is quite expected, as majority of them are self-employed.

Table 6: Economic Earnings of Respondents

Sustainable Income	*Percent (%)*
Yes	84
No	16
Total	100

Based on Sample Survey 2007.

Almost all the respondents irrespective of their religion did accept that they were much better off and comfortable in Afghanistan. They realized the hardships of displacement and craved for the situation to become normal so that they could return to their respective places of work and lead a peaceful life.

An 18-year old Suni Pathan girl from Kabul called Razia came with her father 15 years back. She stays with her family in Mehrauli. During the course of the survey, she was found arguing hard with the YMCA Refugee Aid Programme (RAP) Officer in Lajpat Nagar. She was being paid three thousand rupees as monthly assistance. With an exorbitant house rent of 3,000 rupees for a small room, she wondered how on earth she would buy her ration and other necessities. She was pleading with the Officer in Charge to arrange a small accommodation. She insisted that the Officer give in writing that this was not possible.

Amarjit Singh a youth from Kunar province of Afghanistan felt that the government divided the Afghans into two categories. First one includes the Afghans of Indian origin like the Sikhs and Hindus. Secondly the ethnic Afghans – which includes the Pashtuns, Tajiks, Hazaras, Uzbeks, etc. He was skeptical that some of the refugees are pretty well off but don't reveal their real income while some are really poor and suffer.

PROBLEMS FACED

The respondents did not complain much about problems in general such as buying of property, receiving health facilities, providing education to their children or in buying of assets like car, etc. It was heartening to find that many of them possessed the PAN number, which allows them to buy assets and house. Only a marginal section complained about the availability of health facilities. (Fig. 8)

As such the respondents did not come out with much political hurdles in their day-to-day functioning. Majority of the Sikh and Hindu respondents were keen on attaining the status of Refugees but Muslim respondents were keen to return back. Most of the respondents however were of the opinion that currently the fee for citizenship is very high i.e. Rs. 15000 and is hardly affordable.

Shri Raghubir Singh, Secretary of Guru Arjun Devji Gurudwara, Mahavir Nagar suggested that the President of India should announce the citizenship to all Afghan Sikhs and Hindus without any fees. He emphasized that ultimately they were Indians no matter wherever they lived. India is their motherland

Fig. 8: Problems Not Faced

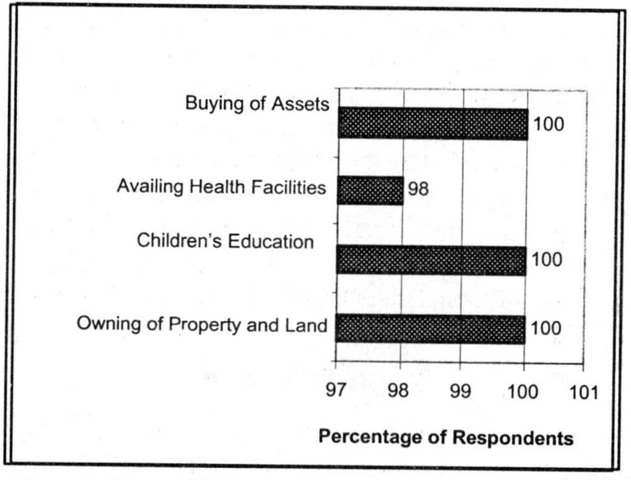

Based on Sample Survey 2007.

and they would sacrifice everything for India.

Respondents felt that the Government of India approving the 'stay visa' for one year is too short. They felt that the visa period should be extended up to three years. The respondents also stated that the same should be applied for the return visa and be extended up to 3 times a year so that one could look after their properties in Afghanistan and not close the option of returning back completely.

Applauding the role of Shri Trilochan Singh, the then Chairman of Minority Commission of India a respondent stated that about 20,000 Afghan Sikhs are in Delhi itself. They are spread in Greater Kailash, Faridabad, Tilak Nagar, Govindpuri, Kalkaji, Vikaspuri, Fatehpuri, etc. He further said that they should be issued visas to go to Europe, US, and Canada. Citizenship to all community members is a genuine demand that should be fulfilled as early as possible.

However the legal status of refugees in India may be categorized under two heads:

(a) Refugees who are provided relief and rehabilitation by

the Government of India, like Tibetan, who fled from Tibet after Chinese annexation of Tibet and Sri-Lankans, who fled from Sri-Lanka after the ethnic civil war. Government of India has made ample provision to safeguard their basic rights till their departure.

(b) Refugees recognized by UNHCR like Afghans and Myanmars. For such refugees India is only a transit country till they are permanently settled in a third country. They live on the subsistence allowance given to them by UNHCR. They are provided legal stay in India during their transitory stay and rights available to any other foreigner.

REFUGEE STATUS

The Government of India has allowed all displaced people from Afghanistan to avail the stay visa. They are free to practice trade, business and even work. However, the current status does not allow them to enjoy political rights. This implies that they are not allowed to cast their votes nor can they avail ration cards. Although they can work and practice trade after seeking certain permissions.

Table 7: Status Wanted by Respondents

Status	*Percent (%)*
Citizenship	76
Refugee	24
Total	100 (953)

A majority of the respondents wanted citizenship status:

- A respondent named Kulwant Singh running a small hosiery business in Tank road, Karol Bagh says,
  "In America if a child is born he becomes an American citizen and in India our children born here are not treated as Indian citizens."
- Jathedar Charan Singh Nagpal of Gurudwara Arjun Devji, Mahavir Nagar spoke about how Pakistan offered them to stay in Pakistan but they denied. They

came to India and didn't show any interest in staying on in Pakistan because the Sikh community has apprehensions that after settling down in Pakistan they can forcibly send us to Amritsar for creating insurgency in the Indian part of Punjab.

- Kulwant Singh who runs a chemist shop in the Udipi complex in Munirka says,
  "My father came to India in 1987 due to apprehensions about conflict escalation. We remained here on 'stay visa', since then. It was two years back that we applied for citizenship and finally my family became Indian after a long wait of 18 years."
  Not everyone is as lucky as Mr Kulwant Singh. He further stated that he knew nothing about Afghanistan, as he was only 6 years old when his family came to India. He has grown up in complete Indian atmosphere and knows Hindi very well. He has almost completely forgotten Dari and Pashtu. Further he said that they have already become Indian so they don't want to get dragged into controversy nor be treated as an Afghani.
- Kishore Kumar, a Hindu Khatri from Kabul while appreciating India and Indian government for extending a helping hand hoped that they would get the citizenship status soon.

However it seems to be a distant dream for the Afghans in India! Mr. Acquino Vimal, IFS, Ministry of External Affairs (MEA) states that the Ministry of Home Affairs (MHA) deals with Afghan Refugees. The Government of India has given the refugees a 'Stay Visa' and feels they should return back to Afghanistan. The Afghan Desk, Ministry of External Affairs (MEA) states that India has already spent a huge sum to the tune of US$ 750 million assistance package for Afghanistan's reconstruction process. This is an on going project. The Afghan refugees should return back to their country at the earliest.

However there are people like Din Mohammed, a 45-year old Suni Pathan from Kabul came in 1985 via Iran. He remained in Iran for 2 years, married an Indian girl in 1993. However he does not want a citizenship because refugee facilities will get withdrawn. He works with Don Bosco and earns a sum of Rs 2500 per month in Lajpat Nagar. The UNHCR has given him a Refugee status and he is able to receive a Refugee Allowance of Rs.1400 per person plus some other charges such as education and so on.

CONCLUSION

Though the magnitude of Afghan refugees in India differs from study to study but all of them do agree that the figure is well above 10,000 and also that in India they mostly concentrate in Delhi. The refugees in India are treated at par with other foreigners as per domestic legal requirements as regards their stay, entry and exit, which are included in the following Acts such as the (Ministry of External Affairs, 2007):

- Foreigners Act, 1946
- Registration of Foreigners Act, 1939
- Passport (Entry Into India) Act, 1920
- Passport Act, 1967

Given the Government of India's Legal stand on Refugees, their stay visa extends most of the freedom to the refugees barring a few such as exercising their political rights to cast votes or obtain a government document such as the ration card.

The sample survey reveals that generally they lead a subsistence lifestyle in India, mostly engaged in the unorganized sector. Though the Afghan refugees do not face many problems in their day-to-day life but most of them live under the constant fear of being deported back to Afghanistan as their Stay Visa is too short. Before they get a year's extension it is time again for them to renew their 'Stay Visa'. So they are constantly on tenterhooks!

The constant reporting by the media projecting the Afghans as criminals, terrorist, thieves and captions such as 'Talibanization of South Asia' have contributed to a popular stereotype image of the Afghans as fanatics and criminals. This has encouraged the victimization of the Afghan population in India both by the private individuals and the states. People are scared to let their houses out on rents to Afghans. Time and again there has been a huge influx of returnees to Afghanistan, but they too face great difficulty in gaining access to land, shelter and basic services.

This is a global problem which needs handling at the international level involving all concerned. The role of states such as Pakistan, Iran, India, Afghanistan, Central Asian Republics and others is crucial. The reconstruction process in Afghanistan will remain incomplete until the people concerned are able to return to their homes where safety and peace would await them!

REFERENCES

Ananthachari, T. (2001): Refugees in India: Legal Framework, Law Enforcement and Security, World Legal Information Institute

CNN.com, (2001): Online

Hiram Ruiz & Margaret Emery (2001): Afghanistan's Refugee Crisis, Middle East Report, Online, pp. 1-5.

http://countrystudies.us/afghanistan/index.htm

http://en.wikipedia.org/wiki/People's_Democratic_Party_of_ Afghanistan

Human Rights Documentation Centre, (1999): Afghan Refugees Face Insecure Refuge, a Joint Initiative of SAHRDC and HRDC, www.hrf.org.in.1999.html

Human Rights Watch Backgrounder (2001) : No Safe Refuge. The Impact of September 11 Attacks on Refugees, Asylum Seekers and Migrants in the Afghanistan Region and Worldwide, www.hrw.org

Human Rights Watch, 1998: New York, p.199.

Maley, William (ed.), 1998: Fundamentalism Reborn? Afghanistan and the Taliban, London; C. Hurst & Co., p. 47.

Ministry of External Affairs, 2007: A Report. Government of India

Rashid Ahmed, 2000: Taliban, I.B. Tauris, London, p. 119.

Rubin, Barnett, R., 2000: The Fragmentation of Afghanistan, Yale University Press, p. 179.

Saikal, Amin, 1998: Afghanistan Ethnic Conflict in Survival, Vol. 40, No.2 Summer, 114-26.

South Asia Human Rights Documentation Centre [SAHRDC], (1999): www.hrd.org.in

The Muslim, Islamabad, 1983: 19 December.

The Times of India, 2000: 17 April, New Delhi.

UNHCR (1997): The State of the World's Refugees: A Humanitarian Agenda, www.unhrc.org.in

UNHCR, 2006: *op cit*, p.145.

UNHCR, 2006: The State of the World's Refugees, Oxford University Press, New York, p. 144.

CHAPTER 5

The Triangular Paradigm: Child Labour, Education and Poverty in Afghanistan

Saurabh Sharma

Three decades of armed conflict have devastated the lives of millions of Afghan children. A generation of Afghan children have grown into adults either being the direct target of human rights abuses or have been a witness to acts of violence and destruction which have destroyed the social fabric of the society. The old, women and the children are amongst the most vulnerable groups which are the worst hit in times of conflict. Children are the country's future. However the collapsed infrastructure, healthcare and educational systems in Afghanistan all have a tremendous impact on the children. More than 50 percent of the estimated population of 32 million people in Afghanistan is under the age of 18 years (CIA 2008). UNICEF estimates that nearly 30 percent of the primary school going age children are working and are often the sole source of income for their families. With a per capita GDP of 200 US$, child labour is bound to increase significantly.

Afghanistan signed the convention on the Rights of the Child in 1994, but it is merely on paper while the real situation of child labour has been constantly on the increase. The present paper attempts to study the inter linkages between poverty and child labour which ultimately leads to low levels of education. It highlights the international instruments to curb child labour, followed by the Afghanistan's constitutional obligations in ensuring the welfare of children. The present paper will focus on the situation of child labourers in Afghanistan, the factors leading to child labour and the means to control this and provide them with qualitative education.

CHILD LABOUR IN INTERNATIONAL INSTRUMENTS

Child labour specifically refers to children who are engaged in work that is in violation of the established standards. It also implies that children in the school going age who do not go to school are engaged in child labour. Therefore any children engaged in economic activities under the age of 12, children in the age group of 12 to 14 employed in hazardous work and children under the age of 18 involved in worst forms of labour are included as child labourers. The worst forms of child labour includes exploitation of children, child trafficking, forced employment, coercing into performing illegal acts and exposure of children to hazardous work. The effective instruments governing child labour are C138 Minimum Age Convention and C182 Worst Forms of Child Labour Convention adopted by the International Labour Organization (ILO).

The Minimum Age Convention, (C138) states that *the minimum age, at which children may be admitted to employment in certain types of work, must be specified*. The Convention emphasizes that the minimum age must not be less than the age of completion of compulsory schooling and in no circumstances must be less than 15 years. However, the Minimum Age Convention has taken into consideration the situation in countries that are not able to implement such standards and has provided the space for the specification of 14 years of age for admission of children to work in such countries. It permits the employment of persons over 12 years of age on light work, the employment of persons of 15 and over for non-hazardous work, but absolutely prohibits work that exposes children to physical and mental torture and that which interferes with their education.

According to ILO "light work is a work that is not likely to be harmful to child's health or development and that does not hinder their attendance at school or at professional training centre.

The Convention also defined hazardous work based on the number of hours and the conditions in which the work is undertaken. But, it has not set as standards on hours of work, conditions of work and has entrusted the states to determine such standards.

The Worst Forms of Child Labour Convention, C182 was adopted in 1999. It has set limitations on the types of child employment. The convention has prohibited the following:

- All forms of slavery or practices to slavery, such as sale and trafficking of children, debt bondage and serfdom and forced or compulsory labour, including forced or compulsory recruitment of children for use in armed conflict;
- The use procuring or offering of a child for prostitution, for the production of pornography or for pornographic performances;
- The use, procuring or offering of a child for illicit activities, in particular for the production and trafficking of drugs as defined in the relevant international treaties; and
- Work which, by its nature or the circumstances in which it is carried out, is likely to harm the health, safety or morals of children.

It must be noticed that the Convention has vested the States with broader powers to define child labour and minimum age of child admission to employment. This has prevented the adoption of a unified approach to universally define child labour and specify the minimum age of employment for children.

Under the internationally recognized instruments such as Universal Declaration of Human Rights (UDHR), Convention on the Rights of the Child (CRC) and International Covenant on Civil and Political Rights (ICCPR), Afghanistan is required to protect children and prohibit certain types of work and this responsibility also includes:

UDHR—Article 16	State obligation for the protection of the family
CRC—Article 27	State obligation to protect children and assist parents of needy children for their sound development
CRC—Article 32	Prohibition of economic exploitation of children
ICCPR—Article 24	Protection of children by the State, society and family without discrimination in all its kinds

CONSTITUTIONAL SAFEGUARDS FOR THE AFGHAN CHILDREN

The Afghanistan Constitution stresses the need to protect children and fulfillment of state obligations ensuring the welfare of the child, which is stated in Article 54. Yet, the Afghan children are subjected to worst forms of labour. They encounter severe bodily and mental harms and are stripped of access to qualitative education. This happens even though Afghanistan's Constitution has specific provisions relating to the issue of child labour and child rights for having access to education and explicitly reads:

"Forced labour is forbidden. Active participation, in times of war, calamity, and other situations threatening public life and welfare is one of the primary duties of every Afghan. Children shall not be subjected to forced labour." Afghanistan Constitution, Article 49 (Afghanistan Constitution 2004).

Further, the Constitution (Afghanistan Constitution 2004) in its Article 43 states: "Education is the right of all citizens of Afghanistan, which shall be provided up to the level of Bachelor of Arts free of charge by the State. The State is obliged to devise and implement effective programmes for a balanced expansion of education all over Afghanistan, and to provide compulsory intermediate-level education. The State is also required to provide the opportunity to teach native languages in the areas where they are spoken."

But the child labourers are not being provided with any kind of education and this is alarming as it indicates the emergence of an illiterate and non professional generation. Such child labourers are the soft targets of criminal gangs engaged in drug trafficking and smuggling. These children have also been recruited by the local militias engaged in inter factional fighting (Chrobok 2004).

The tense and unpredictable security environment, particularly in the South and South East and also in some of the North and Central highlands, contributes to putting Afghan youth at the risk of being mobilized by armed groups.

TYPES OF CHILD EMPLOYMENT

Large numbers of Afghan children are involved in a variety of child labour activities of which majority include working on the streets, carpet weaving, working in farms, selling, blacksmiths, labouring and begging (AIHRC 2006). A large number of children are being exploited in activities related to narcotics, heavy vehicle repair workshops and metal works representing the harsh realities of the twenty three years of continuous turmoil. These children are devoid of even the primary education and grow up illiterates. This lot of illiterate mass can be easily excited by the religious fanatics and used by them for spreading insurgency and terrorism all over the region. Therefore, it is of utmost importance to provide them with primary education as well as some kind of vocational education.

Afghanistan being an agricultural country, farming is an indispensable source of income for families which involve children in farming activities in the rural areas. As poppy is being grown at a large scale in Afghanistan, children also become part of the poppy production and unknowingly become victims of the same. A considerable number of children are made to work in carpet weaving workshops. They are made to work for long hours in dim places. These children suffer from weak eye sight and also get afflicted with respiratory diseases due to breathing dusts of wool.

Children living in urban centres are predominantly involved in selling in markets, bus stations or beside restaurants. They also work as helpers in restaurants and in car repair shops. Begging is also a common practice by children living in cities. This has increased with the rise of foreigners visiting Afghanistan in the post 9/11 period. These children are widely seen on roads and streets, asking for money from people especially from the foreigners. The city children have also taken up the task of shining shoes as well as selling scrap metal, paper and firewood.

The working hours for the children vary from 6 to 15 hours and a considerable number of them work even more. Due to the long working hours children get deprived of their education. But, how can parents think of educating their children when they are struggling for bare survival? Priority of the family is to arrange the daily meals not that of educating their children. Due to the prolonged conflict a large number of women have been widowed or their husbands are unable to work due to physical disabilities or illness. A large responsibility then falls on the shoulder of the young children who have to work and become the bread winners for the family. So, due to the economic pressure approximately 7 million (Oxfam 2006) children are being denied of any kind of education.

CAUSES OF CHILD LABOUR

Generally children have to work due to poverty and bad economic conditions. Sometimes families believe that the children have to work when they grow so it would be better if they could learn the working skills at an early age. But, mostly, it is the weak economic condition which leads to child labour. According to a study report on economic and social rights, conducted by the Afghan Independence Human Rights Commission in 2006, 29% of the families have no regular and stable income and only 13.4% of the interviewees had regular self-employed incomes. 2% of the interviewees are dependent on charity and begging. According to the above study the major reasons for the child labour are:

- To enhance the family earning. Children can easily enter the labour market, as they can be employed with a low payment and can be easily abused.
- Illness or death of parents especially father. Due to the sickness or after the death of the father the children are forced to work and at times they are the bread earners of the family.

Reasons for child labour can vary from one family to the other but poverty does form the basic cause. In addition lack of access to education worsens the scenario. If social security is promoted and equal access to education is increased, the scope of child labour will gradually decline.

Effects of Child Labour

In the long-term child labour has an adverse effect on the nation's growth. Working children miss the opportunity of access to education that empowers them with knowledge, skills, self confidence and prepares them to participate effectively in the social and economic life. The direct and clearly visible impact of child labour in the society is the increase in child confrontation with laws. If children are forced to work under unsafe conditions and not in compliance with the accepted norms and standards, they could be led to the verge of delinquency and confrontation with the laws. Child labour under unsafe condition can cause addiction of children to narcotics. Many of the children engaged with cultivation, production and trafficking of narcotics are gradually addicted to narcotics and other drugs.

Children are in vulnerable situation and as a labourer they are exposed to both economic and sexual abuses. They cannot defend themselves and further more they lack necessary awareness, therefore they become an easy target. Street children and the young beggars are at high risk of being abused. Children employed in carpet weaving, small industries and factories work in small dump and dingy rooms where the ground for abuse and crimes is paved.

The long-term impact of child labour is even more harmful. It will lead to the higher levels of illiteracy. The illiterate unskilled youth will then be incompetent for professional jobs requiring education and technical competence. They get merely employed as pity labourers at low wages. In the long-term, this will have a negative impact on social and economic condition of Afghan society. Such illiterate and poverty stricken youth becomes an easy target of the religious fanatics as well. They can be easily motivated to perform illegal acts in the name of religion and '*jihad*'. Therefore, child labour ultimately creates hurdles for the social and economic development. So, the steps must be taken to eradicate child labour and to provide education to the children.

Education of Afghan Children

Education is essential for human development and is considered a right throughout the world. Article 28 of the Convention on the Rights of the Child indicates that states "recognize the right of the child to education, and with a view to achieving this right progressively and on the basis of equal opportunity, they, in particular:

(a) Make primary education compulsory and freely available to all;
(b) Encourage the development of different forms of secondary education, including general and vocational education, make them available and accessible to every child, and take appropriate measures such as the introduction of free education and offering financial assistance in case of need;
(c) Make higher education accessible to all on the basis of capacity by every appropriate means;
(d) Take measures to encourage regular attendance at schools and the reduction of drop-out rates."

Afghanistan signed this Convention in 1994 but nothing was done regarding the education of children. The education infrastructure was completely damaged by the time Taliban were ousted in 2001. This sector needed utmost attention and the demand for education was required to be bolstered. The new Afghan government and its international partners have initiated programs to widen the educational opportunities of all children. They have been successful to a certain extent but have fallen short of the promise they held in 2001-02.

There has been a significant leap in enrolment since the collapse of the Taliban. More than 4.3 million children were enrolled in primary and secondary school in 2003, of which one-third (The World Bank 2005) were girls. In the age group 7-12 years, 67% were boys and 40.5% were girls. Presently, approximately 5 million children attend school but still an estimated 7 million children remain out of school. The majority of this group of children constitutes the working force of child labourers in Afghanistan.

The Constitution of Afghanistan reiterates the commitment to education from a rights perspective and declares that it should be available free of charge from grades 1 to 9 up to secondary level. However, in reality, more than half of Afghan children are out of school. Furthermore, there are huge regional disparities as well as rural-urban divide. Besides poverty, factors that adversely affect children and especially girls' access to school are the lack of school facilities in particular girls' schools and girls' secondary schools, lack of female teachers as well as severe insecurity in school premises.

Girls are the most disadvantaged in the present scenario of Afghanistan. Of the total children in school in 2006-7 only one-third i.e. 1.7 million was girls. Even at the primary level they lag behind. While at the secondary level enrolment is low for both boys and girls, but it is worse for girls despite considerable improvement since the end of 2001 with 5 percent for girls compared to 20 percent for boys. Access to secondary schools is limited particularly due to the low number of secondary schools and their location. The girls suffer, as they are not permitted to go to the distant schools. They are not permitted to walk beyond their village and these results in enormous difference between girls and boys accessibility to secondary schools in their districts.

Traditionally, the majority of Afghan parents are largely indifferent towards and sometimes even hostile to formal education for girls. They believe that formal education will corrupt girls and this will poison the whole community as women and girls are the repository of the family 'honor'. There is a common perception that formal schooling is irrelevant as it cannot prepare girls for their future gender role—as wives. According to parents, after marriage the girls have to look after their home so the use of formal education is seen as a waste. Instead they must learn the household chores early in life. So girls are made to assist in the household domestic chores adding to the magnitude of child labour. Parents believe that boys may not get suitable jobs once they are educated, so the families with weak economic condition prefer that the male children of the family also start working and start earning at an early stage. Therefore, apart from providing basic schooling, attention must be given to convince parents the importance of education.

POLICY IMPLICATIONS

Poverty and insecurity have long prevented generations of Afghans from becoming educated. If education is the key to breaking down the cycle of poverty, then child labour threatens Afghanistan's economic growth and human development. Major investment in education, security, and social services is required in order to ensure an inclusive education system and effectively control child labour in Afghanistan. Free, compulsory and quality education till the child attains a minimum age of employment is considered a key solution to control child labour.

Certain policy actions which can be implemented to control child labour and alleviate education amongst the children are:

- Infrastructure development: There is an immediate need to have more schools in the rural areas and large number of primary teachers must be appointed.
- Additional gender sensitive initiatives need to be adopted to ensure that at least 50 percent of those recruited and trained are women.
- Funding agencies must support nutrition programmes in school. Providing a simple nutrition midday snack of milk and fortified biscuits with universal coverage of all school going children will attract them to attend schools.
- The State should compulsorily provide basic education for those child labourers who have not completed elementary education, by organizing special programmes.
- The State should pay serious attention to the situation of child labourers and moreover provide opportunities for their enrolment.
- The State should provide, on the basis of standards established by ILO, protection to children through adopting regulations, making amendments in the Law on Labour and embodying clear and specific provisions

regarding employment age and definition of child labour.

- The State and civil society organizations, should make people aware of the consequences of child labour, and also encourage the employers to provide children with opportunities for light and educative work.

Peace will come in the region when we replace poverty with an active energy in which childhood leads to jobs, not Jihad!

REFERENCES

Afghanistan Constitution, (2004), "The Constitution of Afghanistan," [Online: web] Accessed 5 April 2008, http://www.afghan-web.com/politics/current_constitution.html.

AIHRC (2006), Afghanistan Independent Human Rights Commission (Kabul), "An Overview on Situation of Child Labour in Afghanistan," [Online: web] Accessed 10 December 2007, URL: http://www.aihrc.org.af/rep_child_labour_2006.pdf.

Chrobok, Veera (2004), "The *demobilization and reintegration process targeting Afghanistan's armed youth*" [Online: web] Accessed 25 February 2008, URL: http://afghanistan.developmentgateway.org/uploads/media/afghanistan/Article%20on% 20youth -DDR%20in %20Afghanistan%20(2).doc.

CIA, (2008), "CIA-The World Factbook ", [Online: web] Accessed 5 April 2008, URL: https://www.cia.gov/library/publications/the-world-factbook/geos/af.html#top.

Oxfam (2006), "Free, Quality Education for Every Afghan Child," Oxfam Briefing Paper, Oxfam International, November 2006.

The World Bank, (March 2005), "Afghanistan: National Reconstruction and Poverty Reduction – The Role of Women in Afghanistan's Future," p. 33, [Online: web] Accessed 20 March 2008, URL:http://siteresources.worldbank.org/AFGHANISTANEXTN/Resources/AfghanistanGenderReport.pdf.

CHAPTER 6

Challenges to Peace Building in Contemporary Afghanistan

Arpita Basu Roy

Peace building in a society where conflict seems to have been controlled to a large extent is an enormous challenge and often entails a wide range of sequential activities, proceeding from cease-fire and refugee-resettlement to the establishment of a new government and economic reconstruction (Ho-Won, 2006). Most reconstruction programs rely heavily on "democratic" institution building and economic recovery through free-market oriented policies. The end of violent conflict has to be accompanied by the rebuilding of physical infrastructure and the restoration of essential government functions that provides basic social services. It is generally assumed, often as a fallacy, that peace building process ends with the establishment of a new government along with an economic recovery package. This paper attempts an analysis of the key issues in contemporary Afghanistan within the theoretical paradigm of "peace-building'. It analyses the people's perception based on first hand interactions and studies the recent comprehensive surveys conducted in Afghanistan to understand the complex nuances of the peace-building process in progress. By combining analysis of Afghan opinions with broader contextual interpretations, this presentation attempts an appraisal of change in the underlying socio-political realities and the history of Afghanistan.

This paper argues that it is imperative to address the local contexts, the people perceptions and underlying causes of problems for a long-term viability of the UN peace-building project. One can argue that failing to provide solutions to the root causes of the problems that generate the war allows new conflict dynamics to undermine peace. Therefore, addressing the local political and socio-economic context is crucial and a symptomatic peace building process, unrelated to the nuances of the Afghan society will fail to provide a lasting solution to the causes of the conflict.

ACHIEVEMENTS AND CHALLENGES OF PEACE BUILDING PROCESS

Six years after Bonn Agreement, opinions differ as to whether the model of Afghanistan state–building that is being pursued is approaching unheralded success or tragic failures. Emerging from more than two decades of violent and extensive conflict, Afghanistan faces tremendous political, administrative, social and economic challenges. Amidst these daunting challenges, it is important to underscore the developments in recent years. The political and democratic infrastructure mandated by the Bonn Agreement is now in place with a new constitution, a Presidential election (Oct. 9, 2004) and the parliamentary elections brought into place the representatives of the Lower House and the Provincial Councils (in September 2005, 249 representatives of the *Wolesi Jirga* were chosen and 34 Provincial Councils). So far, the struggle to assert power and define roles within the new political system has been energetic. Apart from relative stability and completion of the Bonn process, there are certain other significant positive developments like substantial refugee repatriation (1.9 million returnees), infrastructure building (schools, roads, hospitals have been rebuilt), child immunization programme and improved women's conditions have gained momentum. There has also been significant technological advancement for instance with the internet and telecommunications and improved banking quality and accessibility which is at least benefiting the urban population. Private media, despite criticism about its content is dynamic and popular culture (music, drama, sports) is being revived (Perceptions of Field Trip, 2000).

Despite the developments in recent years like, Afghanistan faces tremendous political, administrative, social and economic challenges. Moreover, these achievements may prove short-lived if donor, government and public support falter during the next several critical years of transition. Comprehensive and accurate demographic information to guide policy making does not exist: the Afghan government often uses information developed from the 1979 census. Donors usually stitch together results of each-others issue and need-based assessments to craft their programmes of assistance. The Afghan media which is now a main avenue of expression and information does not have the capacity to utilize rigorous research method in covering policy-relevant issues. Neither is policy arguments crafted on the basis of larger nation-wide samples of public opinion or analysis of demographics or economic statistics. Since the viability of a new Afghan state depends upon the capacity of Afghan civil society to participate in the political process, hence public perception of national conditions are important and should be of great interest to a wide range of individual and institutions.

Normally, local elected officials provide a modicum of feedback from grassroots' constituencies which can in conjunction with good social science research become credible, policy-relevant information. The dearth of Afghan organizations capable of rigorous survey research-requires substantial investments in capacity-building to support research-based policy reforms the viability of a new Afghan state depends upon the capacity of Afghan civil society to participate in the political process. In many ways the environment of 2007 is different from that of 2001-02 when there was reportedly much optimism and large expectations from the new interim government of Karzai. Much of this optimism now seems to have been dissipated to a large extent and the cause of frustration seems to be the alleged slow pace of economic and social development, poor government performance and widespread unemployment (Observation Based, 2007). Lack of faith in the government is extensive. Fairly or not, the government is seen to have not delivered the expectations. It is still too early to know whether the Parliament and Provincial assemblies will be perceived as providing a voice to the people or simply as ineffective and 'self-serving institutions'. While there has been improved ministerial and administrative capacity and performance in some cases, continuing weak capacity, particularly of the judiciary, reduces the legitimacy of the state (Observations Based, 2007). This has also been a factor in weakening the states' ability to set and implement policies.

This increasing frustration over unfulfilled expectations is also reflected in a rising level of disillusionment with the international community. Apart from a lack of delivery and results from the assistance money that was allocated to reconstruction, imported ideas, a perceived lack of respect for Afghan culture and traditions and ostensible lavish lifestyles of reconstruction workers have become sore points. There is a perception that much of the aid money has been wasted and fed by opportunistic politicians and officials. With out positive acuity of the Afghans at large, the peace building process may waver, hence it is important to study the perception of the people in depth.

Activities involved in rebuilding war-torn societies are designed to enhance public security, generate economic recovery, facilitate social healing and promote a political "institution." The discussion here would therefore revolve around certain important aspects of peace-building like security and demilitarization, political transition, the concept of democracy, public perception of state institutions, economic recovery, social rehabilitation and empowerment.

SECURITY AND DE-MILITARIZATION

Maintaining a cessation of all violent conflict is the foundation for a peaceful transition to the creation of a new government, economic development and social reconstruction. By making the disbandment of illegal armed groups (DIAG) a major policy priority for the post-Bonn era, Afghanistan aims to continue its transition towards the rule of law and stronger civil administration. The Afghanistan Compact stresses that this process must be government-led, and backed by strong international support (Strategy of DIAG, 2006). This will require strong leadership and political resolve at all levels, reinforced by stronger governance and necessary law enforcement. In Afghanistan, attempts to reduce tensions and mutual suspicions are however low. Attempts at demilitarization which composes of force-reduction, demobilization and reintegration of ex-combatants into the society have also achieved limited success. "Freedom from fear" is a concern in several provinces and the fiercely intensified insurgency causes harm to the lives, livelihoods and daily affairs of the average Afghans. Fear is widespread in many areas of the country and personal security has been a 'core concern' for those living in insurgency affected zones. The Taliban's ability to function in southern Afghanistan depends in part on the labyrinthine complexities of tribal politics, and on their ability to paint themselves as defenders of poor opium farmers (and their dependents, notably wage-labourers) who fear the eradication of crops in an economy where decades of destruction have limited the range of viable livelihoods.

PERCEPTIONS OF SECURITY BY REGION

Region	*Excellent (%)*	*Good (%)*	*Fair (%)*	*Poor (%)*
Central	31	54	12	3
East	24	37	29	9
South	7	39	39	15
South West	7	40	29	24
West	8	50	33	9
North	20	56	21	3
Central	15	52	28	5

Source: The Asia Foundation Survey.

The Taliban are not in a position to march into Kabul, but that has never been their immediate intention. Their principal strategic aim, and that of their backers, is rather to sustain that level of violence required to sap the will of NATO and other states currently supporting the Karzai government. The mere spectacle of such a weakening discourages ordinary Afghans from actively supporting the government and encourages them to sit on the fence. From the Taliban's viewpoint, it opens the door for them at some point in the future to press their demands on Kabul from a position of strength (Daoud Yaqub, 2008). Since the beginning of 2006, insurgency has claimed more lives of Afghan civilians than soldiers and police. Insurgents continue targeting individuals' voice about human rights and are effective in spreading the message of peace and developments. Given that the judiciary and the law enforcement agencies are 'the standardized and replicable pillars of the rule of law," a weak justice system handicaps the transition to a new democratic state, and in Afghanistan this is exactly the case.

There are several indicators to declining personal security, the first indicator being the strategic location as feelings of insecurity is more in the southern and eastern provinces (the provinces which are Pashtun-dominated) compared to north and northeast provinces (which have a Tajik or Uzbek dominance). The reason logically is that most severe fighting has been in the Pashtun belt. Most security experts confirm that insurgent attacks are planned and prepared over the Pakistan border. In 2006, within a few months, the insurgency spread westwards as far as Farah and Nimroz). A second indicator is unemployment. In Farah, high insecurity coincides with high unemployment. The third indicator is the presence of substitute authority in peripheral provinces and in pockets of society that recognize such groups or individuals as legitimate rulers. The Taliban have won sympathy in certain districts, enough to actually have some local residents join their ranks. Warlords who have become stronger since they were co-opted into the government have also exercised their influence to gain more personal resources.

Groups and individuals are prepared to tolerate different levels and manifestations of insecurity. A survey of community perceptions of security in Afghanistan showed that Afghans have a very sophisticated understanding of security, which encompasses not just physical safety, but also livelihood security, human rights and equality. The study found that "negative peace – the absence of armed conflict – is an important consideration, but the absence of positive peace – stable and secure livelihoods – is the key determinant in the security perceptions of local communities." For example, an effort to provide skills training and small business start-up programs might help in securing livelihoods (www.theirc.org/news). Hence the novel approach to peacemaking, that "human security" and "human development," rather than military force and diplomacy alone, are key to resolving Afghanistan's complex problems is largely true in the case of Afghanistan (UNDP, 2004). The majority of Afghans surveyed agreed that the presence of Coalition Forces and ISAF has improved security. However, they continue to feel threatened by commanders, despite the formal disarmament process, and cited conflicts over land and property, bribery and corruption and police brutality amongst their key concerns. According to NGOs, 'the security spiral is downward, and the people of Afghanistan are now speaking of the "days of better security under the Taliban" (International Rescue Committee Report, 2003).

POLITICAL TRANSITION

A peaceful transition requires the establishment of a functioning government acceptable to the different parties, along with the formation of mutually agreeable expectations and rules for inter-group dynamics (Ho-Won, 2006). A minimal consensus regarding the rules of political competition is essential to institution building. There are varied processes within a transition towards a functioning government. In the absence of a local capacity for self-governance, an interim administration is set up before administrative control is transferred to newly elected officials. Afghanistan has already completed the mandate established by the Bonn Agreement. The political and democratic infrastructure mandated by the Bonn Agreement is now in place with a new constitution, a Presidential election (Oct.9, 2004) which secured Hamid Karzai's position as the elected president and the parliamentary elections brought in place the representatives of the Lower House and the Provincial Councils.

Trust and confidence in a national government can be gained through the establishment of democratic principles reflecting an inclusive representation. In contemporary Afghanistan this lack of trust towards the government is widespread and extensive. The reported optimism of 2001 and large expectations from the new Interim government of Karzai now seems to have been dissipated to a large extent and the cause of frustration seems to be the alleged slow pace of economic and social development, poor government performance and widespread unemployment. Lack of faith in the government is extensive. Fairly or not, the government is seen to have not delivered on expectations. It is still too early to know whether the Parliament and Provincial assemblies will be perceived as providing a voice to the people or simply as ineffective and 'self-serving institutions'. It is regrettable that the Parliament is backed by the drug lords, war lords and criminal elements. Besides, the government is plagued by organized crimes, the challenges posed by the Taliban, the Al-Qaeda and the organized criminals (UNAMA, 2007). While there has been improved ministerial and administrative capacity and performance in some cases, continuing weak capacity, particularly of the judiciary, reduces the legitimacy of the state. This has also been a factor in weakening the states' ability to set and implement policies. In the course of our interactions with ordinary Afghans we could get a clear picture about the lack of trust in the government. For example people expressed their dissatisfaction in clear terms. For example, our driver Ghulam Rasol expressed his dissatisfaction over the current system and I quote him, "Yeh hukumat accchi nehin hain, Taliban ki hukumat acchi thi." When we further questioned him on the reasons of his observation, he however cited the failure of the system to provide employment opportunities as the primary cause for disillusionment with the government and democracy as a whole.

PERCEPTION OF DEMOCRACY

Any international peace-building effort presupposes that the state-building efforts will be based on democratic principles of nation-wide elections resulting in the appointment of the head of the state and other representatives. Afghanistan's tumultuous and non-democratic history raises initial questions about the democratic attitudes of the Afghan public and the potential growth of these attitudes. There are many positive elements of the contemporary political culture, but also areas where challenges remain. For example the single largest comprehensive public opinion poll conducted in Afghanistan by the Asia Foundation finds that while the vast majority of Afghans express support for democracy as the best form of government, there are also tensions between support for democratic values in the abstract and a willingness to apply these values in specific instances. Moreover these sentiments are relatively equal across major ethnic or religious groupings, and regions within the country. Afghans also express general support for key democratic values, such as equality of women and minority rights.

The question on democracy as a form of government (Democracy may have its problems but it is better than any form of government) has been asked in public opinion surveys in a range of other nations in the region. Afghans tend to be supportive of democracy more than Iranians, Iraqis and Indonesians and Pakistanis, at a level comparable to Jordanians, but less than Egyptians or Moroccans. The survey reflects that the Afghans are willing to accept democracy as a form of governance although they realize that it is being imposed by outsiders. (Fig. 1)

Similarly, while democratic aspirations seem widely dispersed, democracy tends to co-exist with social and political norms derived from Afghanistan's traditional and Islamic heritage. A substantial minority sees potential challenges between democratic and Islamic values, and these sentiments have increased over time. It is found that while there is a significant support (82%) for the separation of religion and politics, people

Fig. 1: Democracy vs Other Forms of Government

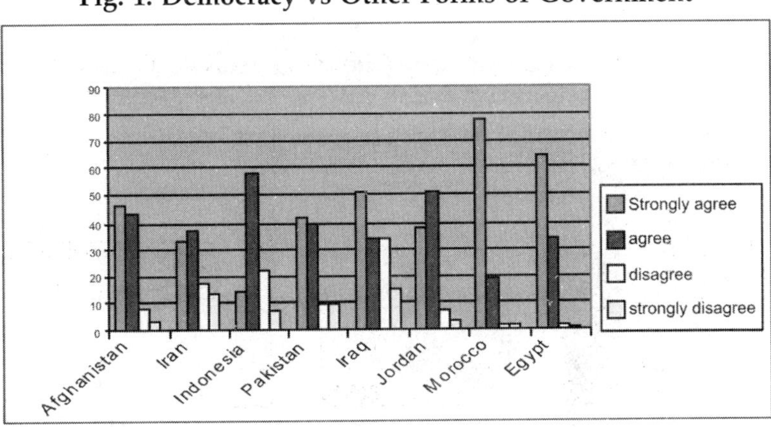

Source: Asia Foundation Survey 2007.

nevertheless believe that local religious leaders should be consulted on matters that affect the community. Support for these local religious leaders is greater among the more traditional sectors of the society (rural residents, older Afghans, the less educated, residents of Eastern Afghanistan and central Hazarazat). This is reflective of the respect and acceptance of the traditional role of the mullahs and their values in the politics of the community. There also remains potential tensions between democracy and Islam, reflective in the contradictory approaches of the people where a sizeable number of respondents could say that a country can become democratic without sacrificing Islamic values while on the other side, they believed that democracy could bring too much westernization and challenge Islamic values. For example, in 2004, a young Uzbek woman in Kunduz said: "We want democracy in an Islamic frame that respects national and religious traditions. We don't want western democracy."

In Afghanistan today, while a bare majority of (52%) viewed democracy and Islam as compatible, a sizeable section (37%) saw democracy as a challenge to Islam. (Fig. 2)

TRUST IN POLITICAL PARTIES

Some also remain hesitant to accept opposition parties that are a key element of electoral democracy. Although parties are central to democracy, people are seldom positive about political

Fig. 2: Does Democracy Challenge Islamic Values

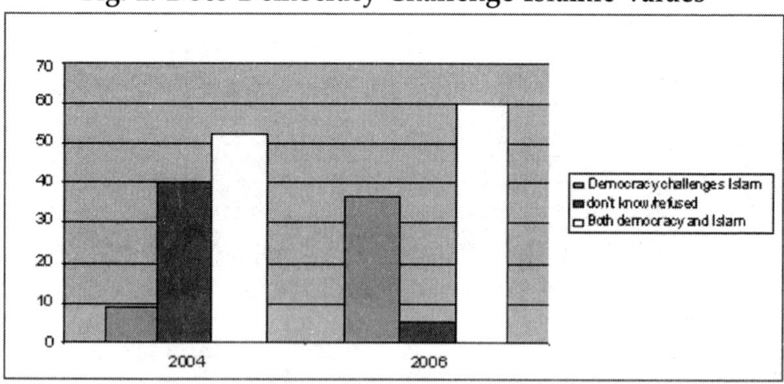

Fig. 3: Trust in Political Parties: Afghanistan in 2006

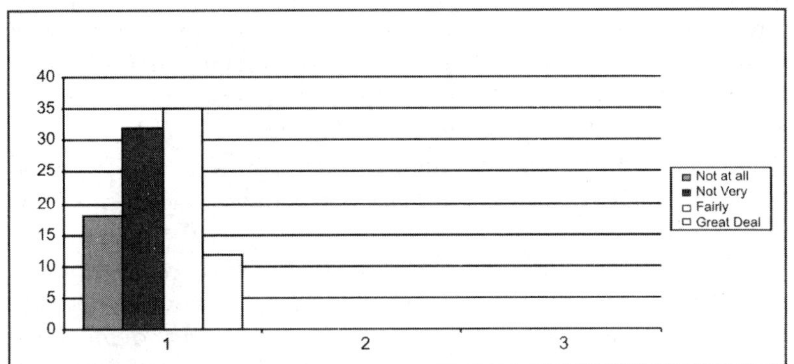

parties even in established democracies. The Afghan people share these doubts. Less than half of the Afghan public (47%) expresses great or fair trust in the parties, most Afghans say that they do not trust parties at all or not very much (Afghanistan in 2007). (Fig. 3)

While the public broadly endorses democratic attitudes, political conflicts within Afghanistan can limit the willingness to express and act on these opinions. Successful democratic reform has to be built upon public support for the democratic ideal that will sustain new political institutions. To assess public support for democracy the 2006 survey asked Afghans whether they agreed with the Churchillian statement: "Democracy may have its problems, but it is better that any other form of government'. A full 84% of Afghans agree with the statement, which is a positive sign of democratic aspirations. Moreover, Afghan experiences of the alternatives to democracy (from the Zahir Shah regime to the Taliban) have not been satisfying. In the words of a rural Pashtun, "I have heard that democracy gives freedom, it is very different in our own country, where all depends on guns."

At the same time 11% of the public do not favour democracy. Some doubts are inevitable which is illustrated by the comments of a man in Mazar-e-Sharif: "We saw democracy at the time of Khalq and the Parcham (parties). The name 'democracy' has bad implications in the minds of the people. People have suffered a lot. The 'democratic' people have punished us a lot. If it's like the Khalq and Parcham 'democracy', we won't like it." Similarly, our driver Ghulam Rasol expressed his dissatisfaction over the current system and I quote him, "Yeh hukumat acchi nehin hain, Taliban ki hukumat acchi thi." When we further questioned him on the reasons of his observation, he however cited the failure of the system to provide employment opportunities as the primary cause for disillusionment with the government and democracy as a whole.

In the lead upto the 2004 election, there was frequent evidence that many Afghans were still uncertain about democracy and the electoral process, but latest surveys show that democratic awareness has grown substantially as experience with elections and public education programmes have increased. 84% of the public defines democracy in terms of liberal political rights—freedom, rights and law, elections and government by the people. Although the identification of democracy with peace and stability (38%) and economic prosperity (17%) has increased over time, these remain secondary meanings of democracy.

Another interesting finding is that the belief that democracy would benefit the individual has grown over time. In 2004, 37% did not cite any personal benefit from democracy. The statistic drops to only 4% in 2006. It is interesting that most Afghans have started identifying political rights as personal benefit, especially freedom, rule of law and civil liberties. In addition, an increased percentage in 2006 cites peace, stability and prosperity as important benefits of democracy.

The understanding of democracy as political rights varies only modestly within the population, and tends to be slightly higher among minority groups. For instance, 80% of Pashtuns (the majority) define democracy in terms of political rights, but 86% of the Tajiks and 91% of the Hazaras think of democracy in these terms. Similarly 83% of Sunnis define democracy in reference to political rights, but 90% of Shias share these opinions. The clearest example of this pattern involves the rights of women. Citing women's rights in the definition of democracy is more common among women (27%) than men (12%), and women's rights are similarly cited as benefit of democracy more often by women

(30%) than among men (15%). The pattern suggested that minorities see democracy as providing political rights that protect or benefit them.

Social Science research repeatedly demonstrates that abstract expression of democratic values does not always predict actual behavior. This means, people can be 'questionnaire friendly' wherein the democratic reality can typically fall short of the democratic ideal. Nevertheless a high degree of expressed support for equality and peaceful opposition are positive features of contemporary Afghan political culture.

Afghanistan's recent tumultuous and non-democratic history raises initial questions about the democratic attitudes of the Afghan public. However, experience and public education programmes are apparently improving support for democracy in Afghanistan. The general uniformity of opinion is again a positive indicator for further democratization. One of the major questions for democratization in Afghanistan is whether these contrasting norms of Islam and democracy can be reconciled, because belief in the political role of Islam erodes support for a democratic form of government. The benefits of democratic aspiration by the public will be limited in the absence of a democratic context. Satisfaction with the democratic process is linked to the economic performance of the system. However, economic reversals can erode these sentiments. The public still looks to the government to provide basic needs, and will be judged by its success.

PERCEPTIONS OF STATE INSTITUTIONS

Assessment of state-building project to date has disproportionately involved elite actors, perceptions and concerns. Apart from insightful journalistic accounts and partial surveys, there has been little systematic analysis of how ordinary citizens perceive the state. To what extent ordinary citizens trust formal state institutions such as the Afghan National Army (ANA), Afghan National Police (ANP), Parliament, Provincial Councils (PCs) and the judicial system? Which of these bodies do they approach to address, judge, and resolve their concerns, needs and conflicts? Or do ordinary Afghans continue to seek assistance from traditional social authorities or de facto centres of power, such as local militia leaders, elders of the local shura or tribal chiefs? To what extent do ordinary citizens believe that formal state institutions function in an impartial and effective manner and represent their interests? In short, what is the 'view from below' of the state building project? To analyze the local perception of state in Afghanistan one has to examine the levels of trust in various formal institutions of the state vis-à-vis traditional social authorities.

Three major findings emerge from the analysis. First is the levels of trust in the army and police are relatively high, despite their widely reported failings.

Table 2: Levels of Trust in Various Public Institutions

Institutions		*Fair*	*Not Fair*	*No Trust*
ANA	50	38	10	2
ANP		42	10	3
Electronic Media	38	48	9	5
Print M	34	48	12	6
NGOs	16	42	25	
Political Parties	11		33	22
Justice		28	23	29
Local Militias	10	21	26	42

Source: Asia Foundation Survey, 2007.

Public confidence in ANA bodes well for the state building process. In contrast, the expressed support for the ANP, seen by most commentators as the refuge of demobilized, corrupt and ill-disciplined private militias, is very puzzling; the level of trust towards NGOs is more evenly divided. Regionally, NGOs receive their highest endorsement in the south of the country, 72%, compared to Hazarazat and the East). Public support for the members of Parliament, provincial councils and community development councils is also strong, in contrast to political parties, government courts and local militias. Yet perception of levels of corruption is high.

Concern over corruption is high. Around 43% of respondents perceive corruption to be a major problem in their daily life, a comparable number (40%) sees it in similar terms in their neighborhood. The underlying understanding being, Afghans believe corruption is a major problem in general and particularly acute in provincial and national affairs. People also feel that corruption is rising everywhere.

Table 3: Perceptions of Corruption in Afghanistan

Sphere	(%)	*Minor* (%)	*Not a Problem* (%)
Daily Life	43	32	25
Neighborhood	40	45	15
Provincial Govt	67	28	5
Nationally	80	17	3

Source: Asia Foundation Survey, 2007.

Most Afghan citizens express great confidence in traditional local institutions to address their grievances, disputes and conflicts. There is a high-level self-confidence in local community structures to resolve outstanding disputes. The local shura elders being the most important ones. Interestingly, those who sought help predominantly turned to elders of the local shura (12%) or ANP (11%). Some elicited the support of a religious leader (4%); a tiny number contact MP or a government agent. Consequently, buttressing the capacity, authority and legitimacy of the state depends on its relations with these traditional social authorities and implementing the rule of law. We can, therefore necessarily say that formal state institutions can strengthen legitimacy only by respecting local community structures. The need to establish better relations with traditional social authorities like the local shura elders is clear.

DEVELOPMENT

Development policies should be considered to be an integral part of a broader peace process, given that poverty and inequality, sustained after internal conflict, remain to undermine peace by breeding discontent and anger. Peace agreements create high expectations for economic improvement and continuing gaps between expectation and existing realities become a major source of social unrest. In January-February 2006 international donors pledged an estimated $10,500 million of aid for the country within the framework of a new 5-yr development plan, The Afghanistan Compact. In conjunction with this, the Afghan government introduced the Interim Afghan National Development Strategy (I-ANDS) which encompassed plans and goals for economic, political and social development. Afghanistan now is taking time to rebuild systems of transport and communications, banking, health care and education. It is a very slow process of economic progress. Initiating economic recovery precluded by violent conflict, major attention is generally paid to a production increase in agriculture, manufacturing and construction.

Agriculture, in the case of Afghanistan has largely been damaged or destroyed by fighting. Many agricultural lands remain land-mine affected. In addition, inadequate distribution of land and resources weakens a community's ability to recover from war wounds. It is difficult to provide an accurate information and economic profile of Afghanistan. However more reliable statistics have become available as government and financial institutions have been re-established. Social indicators in Afghanistan have been the worst in the world. In 2002 problems such as severe food and fuel shortages, the lack of infrastructure and the difficulties posed by the return of millions of refugees began to be addressed. A National Development Framework for the reconstruction programme focused on these challenges. It placed emphasis on allowing the private sector to lead Afghanistan's recovery and on streamlining the public administration. However a bulk of assistance to Afghanistan was invested in humanitarian assistance in the country rather than towards reconstruction. From 2003 the economy showed signs of progress. A new currency was launched in late 2002, the exchange rate has been largely stable and domestic and international confidence in the new currency has been increased. Efforts to develop a modern banking sector commenced in 2003; the central bank was granted autonomy and the government approved a law allowing foreign banks in Afghanistan. Reconstruction of the education system was also underway; women were given equal employment rights as well as access to education.

However, with the formal economy recovering, the criminal economy is also flourishing. Despite an introduction of a ban in

January 2002 on poppy cultivation and processing, trafficking and abuse of opiates during the collapse of law and order in late 2001 had allowed Afghanistan to resume its place as the world's largest supplier of opium. Even in September 2006, the UN Office on Drugs and Crime (UNODC) warned of record levels of opium production, along with an estimated increase of 59% in the area under poppy cultivation, compared with 2005. The opium trade and associated violence and corruption, therefore posed a serious threat to the Afghan economy.

The repatriation of refugee populations is an integral part of economic recovery and rehabilitation especially in the support of the impoverished communities that absorb the bulk of the burden. Their challenge of resettlement derives from the sheer number of refugees and displaced people to be supported. The repatriation of refugees needs to be connected to reintegration and longer-term development activities.

The logic of market economy provides opportunities to pursue self-interest but does not create conditions for social harmony. Moreover the low domestic capacity for raising revenue as in the case of Afghanistan and high demands for expenditure, foreign donors with financial resources play a dominating role in economic recovery where the establishment of liberal economic policies is often a condition attached to international assistance. Development policies therefore, can be organically linked to the priorities of reconstruction rather than a series of disconnected technical projects. Drawing on the capacity of indigenous organizations to mobilize resources in their local settings is a key-strategy to long-term peace-building and Afghanistan has a long way to go in mobilizing indigenous resources.

SOCIAL REHABILITATION AND EMPOWERMENT

Future sources of conflict can be removed by enhancing civil society's abilities to resolve conflicts. Despite differences among elites at the national level, communal groups have served as vehicles for non-violent expression of different interests and values. By serving as a space for communication, civil society creates opportunities for broad public involvement ranging from community councils to neighborhood associations, consequently contributing to more sustainable post-conflict reconciliation. The media can be used for reconciliation by exposing diverse views instead of diving groups. Private media in Afghanistan were found to be dynamic but the essential question remains whether the media will act as a constructive force for social change or merely be a provider of entertainment undermining social values and authority. Popular culture (music, drama, sports) have being revived in the post-Taliban period as a measure to achieve some degree of social cohesion.

The activities of the women groups also occupy high moral value, given their status of being frequent victims of ethnic conflict and civil war. Empowering people derives from restoring cultural norms and achieving the well-being of those who were victimized by violence. In contrast to development and democratization, reconciliation programmes tend to be very small and attract less funding in official peace building projects. Reconciliation cannot be expected to be a project yielding immediate results because years or decades may be needed to be required to rebuild broken relationships originating in genocides, mass killings and repression.

There has been a positive change in the status of women in the last few years as women have gained tangentially and benefited in crucial areas like education and political participation. Although Afghan women enjoy more liberties and freedom of movement, they seek greater rights and opportunities (Afghan Women, 2007). However, the new government in Afghanistan has not been keen and pro-active at the ground level in women's advancement and upliftment perhaps because they do not want to alter the social patriarchal norms and inherent gender biases, in fear of a social rebuff. Though rights to equality and freedom have been guaranteed to women under the new constitution, these remain largely on paper. From the interviews conducted we found out that although the patriarchal male mindset is yet to change, some Afghan men encourage women's education, political participation and liberty to move freely with a hijab, not the all-enveloping blue burqa which was mandatory during the Taliban period (Interaction with afghan men, 2007).

The stătus of women in Afghanistan has been ranked in recent years in various gender and developmental discourses as one of the lowest compared to their counterparts in others countries. The maternal mortality rate is the second highest in the world with 1600 deaths per 100,000 live births, mainly due to poor access and non-availability of pre-natal health care services. The life expectancy of women is 43, one of the lowest in the world. The literacy rates among women are reported to be very low and an assessment of the literacy levels of women in 2003 showed that only14% of girls and women over the age of fifteen were literate (UNICEF). The highest women's literacy levels among Islamic countries in the region were in Iran (82%) followed by Iraq, Pakistan (25%) and Bangladesh (20%). Illiteracy, lack of rights, forced marriages and dowry, restrictions on freedom of movement and security were some of the major problems faced by women in contemporary Afghanistan.

The political status of women in any society can be judged by the degree of equality and freedom enjoyed by women in sharing political power. Some findings here are significant. In the National Assembly election held in 2005, out of the 2,835 people who filed their nominations as candidates for the Wolesi Jirga (Lower House), 344 were women. Despite threats to stay away from the ballot box women did come out to vote in large numbers (40% of the 41% registered women voters). But an interesting aspect was that women won more seats than those reserved for them in the Lower House (27.31%) being ahead of their counterpart in other Islamic countries of the region. Such representation although amazing has no value in real terms. Reports indicate that although they have entered parliament in large numbers, they are not allowed to freely participate in discussion or raise questions concerning the people of their region and national interest. Their voices in Parliament are gagged in parliament by threats and abuses from former military commanders and their conservative male counterpart. There are reported threats to women parliamentarians from different sources and sporadic acts of violence against them.

Hence, there has not been a major shift in the position of women and the strict patriarchal norms of society. Empowerment of women in the form of representation in the Lower house also seems to be a token without real impact in terms of decision-making and political participation. Women's movement in Afghanistan is tentative and yet to take firm roots. Empowering people victimized by long periods of conflict is essential to peace building and women's empowerment is just a part of this larger social issue. And Afghanistan women have a very long way to go before achieving real empowerment.

Regarding the empowerment of women, while provisions for the empowerment of women was negligible during the Taliban era, now more opportunities are being created, yet it will probably take a considerable period of time for them to be truly emancipated and this could come true, through access to health, education, creation of jobs and a secure environment. And in the process of empowerment of women, quantity should be matched by quality.

He questioned the implementability and affordability of a model of governance which in order to become successful has to be adaptive to the local situations. He in fact regretted the tendency to place all blame upon the Al-Qaeda and the Taliban.

CONCLUSION

The effort at peace-building in Afghanistan is a daunting and challenging task, remaining partial and lopsided. Projects of establishing new governments as well as social reconstruction have been driven by the demand to create a local political order that is compatible with the global strategies. Not much analysis has been conducted as to how institution-building and political transitions are undermined by the lack of social and economic foundations. The government and the peace building process are now being criticized by several Afghans as a puppet government being extremely dependent upon donor nations. An important element of mis-governance stressed by them was that incompetent people were placed in highly responsible positions and that the Parliament was backed by the drug lords, war lords and criminal elements. He also stressed upon the absence of a good media policy and a poorly designed civil service commission imposed upon by external experts who failed to understand the ground realities. Many even refer to the process being based on faulty assumptions. While establishing a stable government at the center is important, enough attention should be paid to the local political and social context (UNDP – Governance Officer, 2007).

The end of violent conflict has to be accompanied by the rebuilding of physical infrastructure and the restoration of essential government functions that provides basic social services. In the long–run, peace building and stability also cannot be achieved without the participation of former adversaries in a suitable political process and socio-economic reform.

Peace building efforts devoted to democratization and development have been geared towards supporting military and diplomatic activities. And reconciliation and social rehabilitation remains a distant goal until ongoing hostilities and armed resistances come to an end. Therefore, peace-building in Afghanistan can largely be explained in the context of a new war on terrorism rather than the transformation of local conflict dynamics through negotiation.

REFERENCES

1. Afghan women working at beauty parlours in Kabul in interaction with the author, October 2007.
2. Afghanistan in 2007, A Survey of the Afghan People, The Asia Foundation, Kabul, 2007.
3. Daoud Yaqub and William Maley, "NATO and Afghanistan: Saving the State-Building Enterprise," The Bucharest Conference Paper, 2008. <www.bucharestconference.org> The Bucharest Conference is organized by the German Marshall Fund of the United States in cooperation with the Romanian Ministry of Foreign Affairs and Chatham House. The event brings together leaders from both sides of the Atlantic to discuss the most pressing challenges facing NATO and its member states. Published ahead of the Bucharest Conference, the Bucharest Papers are written by independent authors on the topics of NATO's mission in Afghanistan; NATO enlargement; NATO's relationship with Russia; and global cyber defense and NATO.
4. Ho-Won Jeong, 2006: Peace Building in Post Conflict Societies: Strategy and Process, Viva Books Private Limited, New Delhi (first

Indian reprint, Copyright Lynne Rienner publishers), 2006, p. 1.

5. Interaction with Afghan men (working as drivers, hotel mangers, shop owners) in Kabul, October 2007.
6. International Rescue Committee Report, 2003
7. Observation based on interactions with locals in Kabul, October 2007.
8. Observations based on interaction with officials of ANDS, UNDP and UNAMA, Kabul, October, 2007.
9. Perceptions gathered by the author during the field trip to Kabul, October 2007.
10. Strategy for Disbandment of Illegal Armed Groups in Afghanistan (DIAG), DIAG Strategy FINAL 2006-01-26.<www.diag.gov.af/DIAG>
11. UNAMA, 2007: An Afghan officer with the UNAMA who did not want his identity to be disclosed, elaborated on the current corruption and composition of the government—interaction with the author in Kabul on 24th October, 2007.
12. UNDP – Governance Officer, 2007: The author in conversation with Zubair Popalzai, an Afghan Officer, the then Governance Officer at UNDP, Kabul, October, 2007.
13. UNDP, 2004: "Security with a Human Face," Afghanistan—National Human Development Report.
14. www.theirc.org/news 'Helping the vulnerable make a living in Afghanistan', Nangarhar, February 03, 2006, News from the field—Afghanistan, International Rescue Committee.

CHAPTER 7

Status of Health in Afghanistan—Post 9/11

Mohammad Bashaar

BACKGROUND

Decades of conflict and human displacement, compounded by three years of drought, have had a severe impact on Afghanistan's health sector. The health infrastructure was damaged throughout the country; health workers disappeared without being replaced, and demand for care increased at an exponential rate. high vulnerability to natural disasters, food deficit, limited safe water supply, poor standards of hygiene and sanitation, and restricted access to health care for women and girls have become important features of the situation in Afghanistan, exacerbated by difficulties of geographic access and by the limited delivery capacity of the existing health facilities.

As might be expected, information is scarce but sufficient evidence exists to point to priorities in terms of burden of disease and local resources and capacity.[1] The general health outlook of the Afghan people was bleak. Life expectancy at birth was 47 years for men and 45 years for women. The country was suffering from very high levels of child and maternal mortality—the under-five year old mortality rate was 257/1,000 live births/year, and the maternal mortality ratio was estimated at 1,600/100,000 live births/year, among one of the highest in the world. All these are adding to the complexity of health sector development.

Back in 2002 the challenges facing the Ministry of Public Health (MOPH) included an infrastructure that had been almost entirely destroyed, lack of professionals and a paucity of health services to the population. The role it adopted, then, was to be a steward of the health sector. Six years ago, in 2002, if a child in a village in Afghanistan was very ill and needed to see a doctor, there was rarely a nearby facility or health worker to which the mother could take the child. There was a great chance that the child would die.

The health sector is gradually being re-established by the Afghan Government with the help of the international community. The health services inherited at the end of 2001 were limited in capacity and coverage, and while the Ministry of Health has shown leadership and stewardship, the health status of the Afghan people is still among the worst in the world. The majority of the population lacks access to safe drinking water and sanitary facilities. Disease, malnutrition and poverty are prevalent and an estimated 6.5 million people remain dependant on food aid.

The World Bank, the United States Agency for International Development, UNDP, Global Fund and the European Community are helping the Afghan Ministry of Health, through NGOs, to provide a basic healthcare service to the entire population devoid of any discrimination. The Basic Package for Health Services (BPHS) consists of services for maternal and newborn health; child health and immunisation; nutrition; communicable disease; mental health; disability; and the supply of essential drugs. The Ministry of Health has established a Child and Adolescent Health Department and a Department of Women and Reproductive Health to tackle high infant and maternal mortality rates.

OBJECTIVES

The present paper has the following objectives:

- To reflect upon the post 9/11 achievements of Afghan Health Sector
- To study the formidable challenges towards health sector development
- To suggest recommendations in order to increase access

to quality basic health services for the women and children

- To create a safe space for rational use of medicine

ACHIEVEMENTS IN HEALTH SECTORS

Since the collapse of Taliban in 2001, MoPH has achieved several milestones in the area of institutionalization, capacity building, service delivery, monitoring and evaluation. A number of health sector policies, strategies, laws and standards have been developed or revised, such as National Health Policy & Strategy, PPC national standards, NBC National Standards, National Medicine Policy, Malaria Treatment Protocol, Introduction to IMCI, Guidelines on Reproductive Health, EPI Policy, Contraceptive Logistic Guidelines, Child health Policies, Blood Transfusion Policy, ANC National Standards, National Essential Drug List, BPHS, EPHS, and human resources policy. The under five child mortality rates in Afghanistan has declined from an estimated 257 per 1000 live births in 2001 to about 191 per 1,000 in 2006, according to preliminary findings of Johns Hopkins University (JHU) household survey. It shows 25% reduction in the child mortality in Afghanistan that means 89000 deaths among < 5 years children are averted each year compared to the years prior to 2006. The coverage of Basic Package of Health Services (BPHS) has increased from 9% in 2002 to above 85% of Population to Date[2] and the number of health facilities providing the BPHS has increased to 897 (from 746).[3] Essential Package of Hospital Services (EPHS) has moved forward. So far EPHS has been implemented in 13 Hospitals. In these hospitals occupancy rate has been doubled from 41% in 2005 to 81% in the third quarter of 2007. To monitor and evaluate the BPHS delivery an innovative strategy called the Balanced Score Card was designed to carry out these evaluations. The use of such a "scorecard" to evaluate a health system has not been implemented in any other developing country, and is a credit to the MOPH and its partners. Immunization coverage has reached more than 83% of infants (<one year). Vaccination for measles has increased from 50% to 70%, DPT3 from 54% to 83% and TT2 from 40% to 60% in 2007.[4] Polio eradication initiative is nearing their final goal and has

made a significant progress over the past few years, only 17 polio positive cases have been confirmed, which shows 50% decrease, in contrast to 2006 where we had 32 cases.[5] Antenatal Care for pregnant women has increased from 18% in 2001 to 35% in 2007. (Also the institutional delivery and skilled birth attendance during labour and delivery have increased dramatically over the last 6 years).

126 Sentinel sites are functioning in 34 provinces of the country under the Disease Early Warming System (DEWS) Surveillance System. All Sentinel Sites have to send their reports on weekly basis to Afghan Public Health Institute, Ministry of Public Health. The incidence of tuberculosis has dropped sharply. Just a year ago, about 23,000 Afghans died because of the tuberculosis. However, because of the implementation of the BPHS and DOTS strategy for controlling tuberculosis, this year 12,000 Afghans lost their lives due to tuberculosis (50%). A total of 28769 TB cases were diagnosed in 2007.

Establishment of AIDS Control Department, Government of Afghanistan has responded proactively by establishing a National AIDS Control Program and a multi-sectoral HIV/AIDS Co-ordination Committee of Afghanistan (HACCA). The World Bank has committed 10 million US dollars to support implementation of Afghanistan HIV/AIDS National Strategy. A Provincial Public Health Coordination Committee was established at a provincial level with the membership of Provincial Health Director, 4 Provincial Health Officer, UNICEF, WHO, private sector representative, NGOs and other health stakeholders. This forum is coordinating health activities at a provincial level. About 80 NGOs, both international and local, are working in the health sector, most of them operating a few clinics or providing specialized support.[6]

The five cross-cutting Afghanistan National Development Strategy (ANDS) addresses the themes of gender, counter-narcotics, regional cooperation, transparency and accountability, and environmental protection.[7] The number of health facilities providing Comprehensive Emergency Obstetric Care has increased to 89 (from 79), and the number of health facilities within the 'Integrated Management of Childhood Illnesses' reached the figure of 309 (located in eight provinces and 39 districts). 30 mobile health facilities in 26 provinces were established to provide BPHS to the Kuchi (Nomad) population.[8] Similarly a drastic reduction was noticed to the tune of 93% and 76% in the Plasmodium Falciparum and Plasmodium Vivax malaria cases, respectively, in Afghanistan between 2002 and 2007. 1.2 million insecticide treated bed nets is distributed in 2008 through 900 public and private outlets in 10 provinces by the National Malaria Control Programmed while 326000 was distributed during 2007. "Prevention and control of Malaria is an important priority programme of the Ministry of Public Health of the Islamic Republic of Afghanistan. Malaria prevention and control programme is integrated with all other health care interventions in all 1429 health facilities in the country. In Afghanistan transmission is seasonal, unstable and dependent upon altitude, temperature and rainfall. Transmission occurs below 2000m, in areas around Jalalabad and Khost to the east, Kandarhar to the south, Farah and Herat to the west and Mazar-i-Sharif, Kunduz, Baghlan and Pul-i-Kumri to the north. The central highlands of Afghanistan are malaria free. The programme has achieved remarkable progress in the development of national strategic plan, establishment of training and research institute, implementation of different research projects, establishment of national surveillance system and conducting of comprehensive training Programmes at different levels.

Provincial teams in eight provinces were established to track the prevalence of avian flu. In total, 233 health facilities have been renovated or constructed.[9] The anti Narcotic activities are in 16 centers and are working in 14 provinces to treat addicts. 4547 addicts have been treated in 2007 and 55333 have received awareness on the disadvantages of narcotics and its addiction.

CHALLENGES

Despite all the successes, many significant challenges remain, and we have long way to go. The health challenges are terrifying. Afghanistan needs to rebuild the infrastructure of its health services. Some of the major challenges are:

- Fifteen percent of the population doesn't have access to basic health services.[10] These are five million Afghans—who live in remote and marginalized areas of the country. Increasing the coverage of basic services to the people of Afghanistan means reduction of maternal mortality, reduction of infant and child mortality.
- Every day, 60 mothers die due to pregnancy-related problems[11] or to problems which are preventable. The province of Badakhshan is the worst among all with a Maternal Mortality Ratio of 6,500/100,000 life births—the highest in the world and ever recorded in history.[12]
- More than 400 infants die every day in Afghanistan[13] due to vaccine-preventable diseases or other treatable interventions, which are very simple, and very cost effective.
- Control of communicable diseases, such as TB, HIV/AIDS, sexually transmitted diseases (STDs), malaria, schistosomiasis, amoebiasis, leprosy, trachoma, lymphatic filariasis, intestinal helminthiasis, leishmaniasis, and preventing outbreaks like cholera and acute watery diarrhoea (in the outbreak in 2002 there were 70000 cases), as well as other diseases of concern like pertussis, and diphtheria. Afghanistan is still one of the 22 TB high-burden countries in the world and women are particularly vulnerable. Despite marked progress, (Afghan women make up about 67 percent of all TB patients in the country and are considered particularly vulnerable to TB infection due to their acute food insecurity, multiple pregnancies, they are indoors far more than men and therefore suffer greater degrees of exposure and a general lack of awareness about TB)
- HIV/AIDS currently, Afghanistan is facing a looming threat of HIV/AIDS epidemic. Afghanistan is considered to be a country of low HIV prevalence but at high-risk for spread of HIV infection. The reasons behind this are several: over two decades of protracted

armed conflicts, the extremely low socio-political and economic status of women, huge numbers of people displaced internally and externally, the extremely poor social and public health infrastructure, drug trafficking, use of injecting drugs and lack of blood safety practices. These risk factors lead officials to warn of the urgent need for early interventions to prevent a potentially rapid spread of HIV in Afghanistan.

- Lack of clean drinking water and sanitation, children will become sick and we will have continued high infant and child mortality. 23% of people have access to clean drinking water, which comes down to 18% in rural areas.[14]
- To improve the quality of drinking water, the relevant government ministries start testing water for E. coli, total coliforms, and chlorine residue (where chlorination is used), stop the uncontrolled drilling of deep wells, and establish a sanitary zone of at least 30 meters (and preferably 300 meters) around all sources of water supply.
- Environmental health, following decades of conflict and drought, Afghanistan had lost nearly all of its wetlands and much of its forests, and its citizens were increasingly at risk for infections and epidemics caused by poor waste management and unequal access to fresh water.15
- In Afghanistan, more than 80% of the population relies directly on natural resources such as rangelands and water bodies for their livelihood and daily needs, and only 12% of the land is arable. Thus, widespread environmental degradation poses a threat to livelihoods and places the poorest Afghans at particular risk.[16]

Over two decades have decimated Afghanistan's environment and public health. Common post conflict scenes show industrial pollution, environmental contamination by human and medical wastes, agriculture devastated by drought, and the maladies that arise from malnutrition and poverty. Deforestation is perhaps the most serious environmental problem facing Afghanistan. Timber mafia cutting the forest illegally in order to earn illicit revenue which adversely affecting environment and economy of the country. With many power plants and electrical lines destroyed, impoverished Afghans have few energy options. Millions of daily cooking fires are devouring the last vestige of the forests that once covered millions of acres of their country.

Diseases with the largest total annual health burden from environmental factors, in terms of death, illness and disability are:

- Diarrhoea largely from unsafe water, sanitation and hygiene, which is common in Afghanistan.
- Lower respiratory infections largely from air pollution, indoor and outdoor especially in urban or populated cities like Kabul, Hirat, Jalalabad, etc.
- Malaria largely as a result of poor water resource, housing and land use management which fails to curb vector populations effectively.
- Road traffic injuries largely as a result of poor urban design or poor environmental design of transport systems and increment of traffic.
- Chronic Obstructive Pulmonary disease (COPD) largely as a result of exposures to workplace dusts and fumes and other forms of indoor and outdoor air pollution.

Other major illness includes:

(1) Due to more than two decades of war and internal conflicts, most of the Afghan lost their beloved ones and property, which caused metal disorders such as the major psychoses, anxiety and depressive disorders, substance abuse disorders, and psychological disturbances such as posttraumatic symptoms, depression, anxiety, anger, violent behavior, and suicide. Women have the highest levels of depression, traumatic grief and anxiety. By comparison, most men report moderate levels17. Widowed women are at greatest risk for emotional problems and impaired psychosocial functioning.

(2) Shortage of competent, well-trained, motivated healthcare and public health providers in the country, brain drain, especially, lack of female health personnel is particularly problematic. In our conservative society, it is difficult for the head of the family to agree that his wife or daughter or sister be treated by a male health worker. Everybody in Afghanistan wants their wife, mother, or sister diagnosed, examined and treated by female staff.

(3) Health facilities are not equipped with the appropriate technology such as biomedical equipment. The technology which were present prior to war, have been destroyed by decades of turmoil.

(4) Low Wages and Incentives, the government employees earn 3000 AFS (60$), which is not enough to feed and support their families, which in turn forces competent staff to supplement their income through private practice or seek employment in the private, NGO or UN sectors where income is higher and many urban women's health practitioners are unwilling to relocate to rural areas because of the lower wages and security concerns

(5) Ongoing insecurity and political instability[18] in some areas, particularly in the southern and southeast part of the country, also affects health services. For Instance, (Medicines Sans Frontiers (MSF) pulled out of the country after 24 years after the killing of five of its workers. Since then, another non-governmental organization, Malteser, from Germany, suspended its operations in Afghanistan's restive south east after two of its healthcare workers were ambushed and killed).

(6) Funding challenges (it is also a major challenge for the impoverished and lower-resources country like Afghanistan).

(7) Counterfeit and Poor Quality Medicines are an additional barrier to equitable access to medicines. Antibiotics and other essential medicines are often counterfeited and their use leads to treatment failure

and sometimes death. In extreme cases, counterfeit medicines may cause serious harm to health or exacerbate the conditions being treated because of the harmful ingredients they contain. Substandard drugs could result from poor manufacturing practices, unsuitable packaging, storage and distribution, or when generic drugs are produced by unregistered manufacturers.[19]

(8) As Afghanistan mostly depends on donated medicine and mostly these medicines can fail to meet quality standards. For a variety of reasons (poverty, lack of relevant information or inadequate control) medicines which are less safe and effective may be used. The pharmaceuticals market is much more chaotic than the other markets studied in Afghanistan Research and Evaluation Unit's (AREU) political economy research stream. Pharmaceuticals are brought into Afghanistan from many different sources, and there is a confusing array of products on sale. The number of players is larger at every point in the supply chain than in other markets studied. There are more importers, more wholesalers, many more pharmacies, many grocery stores that sell pharmaceuticals and street vendors of medicines, as well as purveyors of traditional medicine. The figure below provides a guide to the main players in the private sector pharmaceuticals supply chain. However, there may also be middlemen, or "agents," facilitating transactions such as distribution of pharmaceuticals from a producer, importer or wholesaler to provincial pharmacies. Researchers were frequently told that such agents were used, but did not encounter any agents directly.[20] (Fig. 1)

(9) Existence of unregulated markets: The existence of unregulated markets where substandard and sometimes even lethal medication is sold to unsuspecting customers. Unregulated markets are often supplied with stolen and diverted drugs, illicitly manufactured pharmaceuticals. Inspection, sampling

Fig. 1

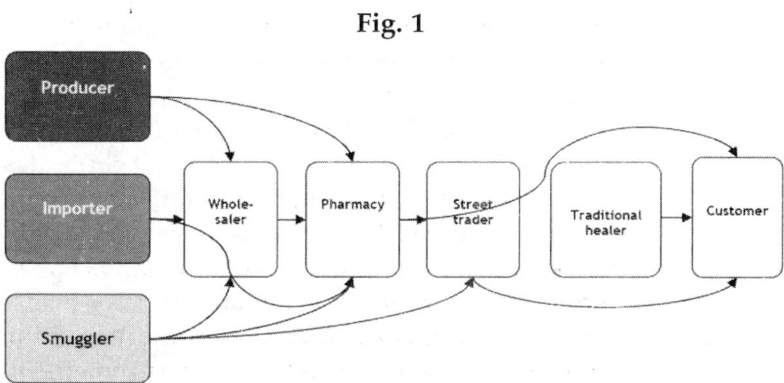

and testing facilities are inadequate to secure basic standards of medicines on the market. It makes sense to concentrate efforts on inspection and testing at the point of wholesale and retail, given the scale of smuggling. However, the lack of testing facilities at border points, and resultant long delays in clearing imports, pending sample results from Kabul, is a serious disincentive for importers to bring their imports through official channels. The feasibility of installing testing facilities at borders or of a mobile laboratory could be considered.[21]

(10) Lack of Access/Irrational us of Essential Medicines: There are serious concerns over the rational use of drugs in Afghanistan, and anecdotal evidence from various sources suggests a tendency among doctors to over-prescribe medicines generally and antibiotics in particular, and that combinations of medicines are prescribed without due consideration of possible side effects. Patients often ask pharmacists to prescribe medicines even though a large proportion of private pharmacies do not have a qualified pharmacist on staff. Exacerbating all these factors is the presence on the market of low quality and counterfeit medicines containing insufficient or no active ingredients.

(11) **Lack of Good Governance of Health Systems**

(12) **Complicated/complex administrative procedures and bureaucratic process** within the health ministry and outside.[22] There are no laboratories for testing medicines or raw materials for pharmaceuticals production at border ports or in provincial customs offices, medicines and raw materials are held in these offices while samples are sent to the MoPH laboratories in Kabul to be tested. This process can be very lengthy, as the laboratory in Kabul is itself lacking in staff and equipment. As a result pharmaceuticals can be held for up to three months, according to importers, before being released from customs. As many medicines require refrigeration and some are damaged by extremes of heat or cold, many pharmaceuticals are damaged or destroyed while they are being held by customs. This represents a serious disincentive to involvement in official customs/administrative procedures for importers of pharmaceuticals.[23]

(13) **Land Mines and unexploded ordnance (UXO) which causes disabilities**: There are an estimated 10 million land mines in Afghanistan—one for every child. Land mines are distributed in agricultural land; water canals mined, grazing land mined, residential areas mined, access to drinking water and firewood mined, roads and access to public places mined.

Land mines seriously undermine the economy, food security and health services. The expense of medical care and rehabilitation add economic disability to the physical burden. 1.5 million Men, Women and children were physically disabled by war injuries, including amputation, blindness and paralysis. Children by nature of their small size, are more likely to suffer a fatal mine injury. In addition, the most common mines found in Afghanistan are designed to cause immediate fatality. It is felt that many children and adults die before reaching hospital due to the remote location of the accident, a lack of appropriate first aid at the time of injury and inadequate or unavailable transport for definitive treatment. Of the 59% of landmine victims estimated to die from their injuries, most are likely to die before arriving at hospital (Medecins Sans Frontieres, 1997).

If the child survives the blast, they can be expected to suffer one of the three patterns of injury from antipersonnel mines that have been described (Coupland and Korver 1991; Coupland 2000). Eye injuries and blast injuries to the ear are common in all mine victims. The pattern 3 injury is most common in children and relates to accidental detonation whilst handling a mine. It involves severe wounds to the hands and face. Wounds from landmines do not correspond to any of the modern surgical specialties and surgery even in experienced hands is difficult and time consuming. Organic matter, dirt and debris are driven up into tissues necessitating extensive excision and delayed primary closure. The wounds are often associated with fractures requiring splinting and skin loss requiring grafts. Surgical amputation of entire limbs that are beyond repair is not unusual.

(14) **Narcotics/Poppy Cultivation and Corruption,** Corruption in the health sector is a concern in all countries, but it is an especially critical problem in developing and transitional economies where public resources are already scarce like Afghanistan. Therefore; corruption reduces the resources effectively available for health, lowers the quality, equity and effectiveness of health care services, decreases the volume and increases the cost of provided services. It discourages people to use and pay for health services and ultimately has a corrosive impact on the population's level of health.

(15) Preventing and controlling corruption therefore is important to increase resources available for health, to make more efficient use of existing resources and, ultimately, to improve the general health status of the population. The only way to control the corruption is to increase the salaries of the health workers, doctors,

nurses etc (3000 AFS (60$) is not enough and establishment of competent financial mechanisms and systems.

(16) **Dispersed population & geographical constrains** make access to rural areas difficult.[24] &[25]. Most of the Afghan villages, communities are living scattered, since Afghanistan is mountainous country. It is really difficult for the people to reach on time for their treatment.

(17) **Lack of Roads and Public Transportation** adds to all the other challenges in health sector. Most of the families are living in valleys and in mountainous areas, where there is no asphalted roads, which could pose most of population with hard times during the delivery of their patients. Although health sector made progress in providing basic health services in the great majority of districts, hospital care requiring advanced curative procedures are not yet in place even in our provincial hospitals.

(18) **Lack of effective financial mechanism** for poorer households. The policy should be developed in pro poor and pro rural area manner.

(19) **Lack of Coordination,** Health services are supported by a multitude of partners, creating occasional difficulties for coordinated approaches.

(20) **Lack of mechanism for regulation of the private sector clinic and pharmacies.** Establishment of regulatory bodies which could efficiently control all activities of private health clinics and pharmacies nationwide in order to provide quality health services.

FUTURE POLICIES AND BENCHMARKS

National Health Policy 2005-09[26]

The 18 priorities listed in the National Health Policy 2005-09 have been turned into strategies. As with the priorities in the national policy the strategies are grouped into the 3 areas of: Implementing health services, Reducing morbidity and mortality, and Institutional development. The 18 strategies each state what is going to be done and the main mechanism for implementation to ensure successful achievement. The strategies are:

A. Implementing Health Services

- Extend coverage of the basic package of health services through mobilising additional human and financial resources and strengthening the delivery of quality, effective, efficient health services.
- Strengthen the coverage and implementation of the essential package of hospital services through mobilising additional financial resources and improving hospital management.
- Develop and implement at least three prevention and promotion programmes through inter-ministerial collaboration.
- Lay the foundations for greater community participation through developing links with local shura.
- Further strengthen the coordination of health services through ensuring better communication between the different levels of the health system and the effective and efficient functioning of provincial health coordination meetings.
- Increase the coverage of quality support services through mobilising resources and strengthening health plans, systems and implementation.

B. Reducing Morbidity and Mortality

- Improve the quality of maternal and reproductive health care through strengthening the delivery of care, especially emergency obstetric and gynaecological care and of routine reproductive health services.
- Improve the quality of child health interventions through introducing Integrated Management of Childhood Illnesses (IMCI) and enhancing the control of vaccine preventable diseases.
- Strengthen the management of cost effective integrated communicable disease control programmes through

capacity building and effective guidelines and supervision.

- Ensure effective delivery of nutritional interventions through the basic package of health services and social marketing.

C. Institutional Development

- Further strengthening institutional and management development through clarifying roles and responsibilities, encouraging team work, and increasing delegation at all levels of the health system.
- Further strengthen human resources development, especially of female staff through quality basic training and continuing education in parallel with further development of human resource planning and retention strategies.
- Further develop health planning, monitoring and evaluation through: enhancing evidence-based, bottom-up and participatory strategic planning at all levels of the health care system; the availability of accurate, user-friendly baseline and other information; and regular planning, monitoring and evaluation cycles.
- Further develop health financing through increasing the flow of funds to the health sector, especially for health and hospital services, ensuring spending is in line with priorities, monitoring different mechanisms to finance the delivery of health services and developing an integrated budgeting and planning system.
- Further strengthen provincial level work by developing the leadership skills and knowledge of Provincial Health Directors (PHDs), increase delegation and decentralisation, and undertake monitoring and evaluation to see whether the provision of health care is responsive and efficient.
- Ensure effective implementation of Priority, Reform and Restructuring (PRR) through efficient performance appraisal and human resource support systems.

- Introduce and develop a culture of quality assurance through setting good examples in day-to-work and the development and use of a ministry quality processes covering service delivery, clinical care and health management.
- Develop health reform related regulations and laws for the public and private sectors by mobilizing and using technical and other resources and developing processes for effective enforcement.

Critical Success Factors

In achieving the strategy objectives there are a number of critical factors that can influence how well they are implemented, including the need for:

- Strong political will and commitment.
- Visible and effective leadership and stewardship.
- Ownership of the strategy among managers at all levels of the health system.
- A corporate culture that includes team work.
- Additional human and financial resources.
- Strong human and financial resource planning and management.

Necessary Conditions

In addition to the above critical factors, there are a number of conditions necessary for successful implementation of this strategy. The key ones are:

- All stakeholders to be committed to the values and working principles of the Ministry of Public Health.
- Development partners to work within the framework of the strategies and their desired outputs.
- Continued emphasis on building capacity in human and financial resources.
- Development of a learning environment and a strong institutional memory.

- Involvement of many health workers at community and districts levels in deciding ways to implement strategy priorities and necessary programme activities.
- Good links between strategic planning and activities and budgeting through the formulation of annual business plans.
- Increased delegation of managerial authority to provincial and district levels in order manage more effectively and efficiently at local levels.
- Better integration between vertically organised interventions and programmes.
- Availability of improved baseline information on health risks, diseases, and management and financial issues.
- Use of best practice tools and guidelines in all aspects of services during implementation.

Risks and Assumptions to Strategy Implementation

A number of risks to successful implementation have been identified during the development of this strategy. To the extent possible they need to be monitored, minimised and managed during implementation. This is because a number of factors can seriously hinder the successful achievement of the best written strategies. The risks outlined in Box 2 below are some of the most important ones. The Ministry of Public Health has also identified various assumptions which are also shown in Box 2. These assumptions will be an important part of the monitoring and evaluation process when assessing the rate of progress towards achievement of the outputs.

Risks to Strategy Implementation

- Poor macroeconomic growth resulting in no increase in the government allocation to health sector.
- Stopping of support by international organizations due to security problems.
- Insufficient numbers of women trained as female health workers.
- Lack of sustainability of PRR and its salary supplementation component Health salaries not

included in PRR do not rise leading to salary between workers.

- Attitudes of health personnel towards clients fail to improve.
- Health staff fail to take actions to improve quality of available health services.

Assumptions Underlying Strategy Implementation

- Economic growth and continuity of national and international financial resources.
- Stability of the political situation spreads out from Kabul to much of the country.
- Continued willingness by Ministry of Public Health to undertake reforms.
- Effective decision making mechanisms continue.
- Useful coordination forum continue.
- Continued transparency about all financial incomes and expenditures.
- Continued management performance and needs-based human resource management.

FIVE-YEAR STRATEGIC BENCHMARKS TO BE ACHIEVED BY THE END OF 2010[27]

Programme 1: Extending the Basic Package of Health Services

By end-2010, in line with Afghanistan's MDGs, the Basic Package of Health Services will be extended to cover at least 90% of the population, maternal mortality will be reduced by 15%, and full immunization coverage for infants under-5 for vaccine preventable diseases will be achieved and their mortality rates reduced by 20%.

BPHS has two objectives: to provide a standardized package of basic services which form the core of service delivery in all primary health care facilities; and to promote a redistribution of health services by providing equitable access, especially in underserved areas. The defined package is being offered as four standard types, ranging from outreach by community health workers, to outpatient care at basic health centers, to inpatient services at comprehensive health centers and district hospitals. The package has a strong focus on conditions that affect women and children. It entails basic services at low cost, addressing the main causes of morbidity and mortality and aiming to provide health services to all Afghans, especially those who are poor and live in remote and rural areas.

Programme 2: Extending the Essential Package of Hospital Services

1. By end-2010, the EPHS will be implemented in 50% of provincial and regional hospitals.
2. By end-2010, community boards will be established in 50% of all provincial and regional hospitals.
3. By end-2010, the proportion of district and provincial hospitals providing good quality emergency obstetric care will be increased to 80%.

Hospitals in Afghanistan play an important role in the health sector since they are part of the referral system that aims to reduce the high maternal and early childhood mortality rates. The overall goal of the 'Essential Package of Hospital Services' (EPHS) is to improve the quality of care at secondary and tertiary health care level. Main strategies to implement the EPHS are developing standards for hospital management, clinical care, and supportive services; building the hospital and clinical case management capacities of hospital staff; completing the Priority Restructuring and Reform process at secondary and tertiary health care level; providing hospitals with required medical supplies and equipment in a timely and regular fashion.

Programme 3: National Communicable and Non-Communicable Disease Control Program

1. By end-2010, a low prevalence of HIV positive cases (<0.5%) in the population will be maintained in order to reduce mortality and morbidity associated with HIV/AIDS.
2. By end-2010, malaria morbidity will be reduced by 50% and malaria mortality will be reduced by 80%.

3. By end-2010, the risk of infection, morbidity, and mortality due to tuberculosis will be reduced by increasing Direct Observed Treatment-Short Course (DOTS) population coverage to 100% by end-2006.
4. By end-2010, at least 70% of infectious TB cases will be detected and at least 85% of those cases will be cured.

This program entails those that are not part of the 'package' programs, but follow a vertical approach for disease control up to a certain level (e.g. the provincial). At the lowest level of delivery these programs are integrated, though due to special logistical and input requirements they have to be managed outside the BPHS and EPHS structure. They are designed to have significant impact on the health of the population and include, beside the principal programs, control of tuberculosis, malaria and HIV/AIDS, eye care, the control of leprosy, and leishmaniasis.

Programme 4: Health Sector Human Resource Management

By end-2010, suitably qualified, appropriately skilled, balanced, and motivated staff for the health sector will be equitably deployed throughout Afghanistan to deliver the BPHS and EPHS.

The attainment of the overall goal of the health sector is dependent upon the appropriate selection, appointment, and management of appropriately trained health professionals. The current evidence on the status of health workers indicates that there are major challenges to ensuring the availability of suitably qualified, appropriately skilled, balanced, and motivated health workers throughout Afghanistan. In order to achieve the main strategies of the program, MoPH has partnered with the Civil Service Commission to implement the transparent, competitive recruitment process to affect PRR. Work will be undertaken with donors and technical partners to upgrade capacity of the recruited workforce and to encourage more female school leavers to enter the health profession, particularly nursing and midwifery in upgraded health training institutions. Continuing education and retesting will increasingly be required for health workers.

Also fundamental to improved health care will be food security programs aimed at reducing the extremely high rate of infant and maternal malnutrition. This strategy recognizes the multiplicity of factors that contribute to good nutrition in rural communities and gives priority to increasing food diversity and opportunities for the improvement of real incomes. Nutritional education proposes ways to improve access to markets, measures to reduce pre- and post-harvest crop losses, measures to improve food safety, and the development of an early-warning capacity

RECOMMENDATIONS

- **Support of the international community to train specialists, equip hospitals and to build the capacity of provincial health directorates, managerial and administrative staff.** This will further strengthen health sector and will save thousands of Afghans from becoming bankrupt due to catastrophic out of pocket spending on surgeries and treatments in neighboring countries.[28]
- **Prioritizing the needs of the population,** to reach first who are in critical situation and have more chances to survive.
- **Strengthening Good Governance of Health Systems:**
  - (a) Strengthens good management in health systems;
  - (b) Supports the decentralization of health systems with a focus at the district level;
  - (c) Strengthens civil society to become a stronger stakeholder in the health system;
  - (d) Computerization of health system and services.[29]
- **Improving Reproductive Health:**
  - (e) To promote the concept of Reproductive Rights;
  - (f) To promote gender sensitive approaches to Reproductive Health;
  - (g) To promote integrated Reproductive Health services (inc. HIV/AIDS and sexually transmitted diseases);
  - (h) To promote maternal and infant health;

(i) To support efforts to reduce gender based violence.

- **Improving public health condition by allocating sufficient budget:** The importance of health for socio-economic growth and reduction of poverty is reflected in the Millennium Development Goals (MDGs). Three out of the eight goals refer directly to health. One additional goal refers to access to affordable drugs in developing countries. To ensure universal and equitable access to quality health services, governments must earmark a sufficient share of public revenues for health. While most rich countries spend at least 5% of GDP on health, many developing countries spend less than half of this figure.
- **Establishment of Radiotherapy centers for Cancer treatment**
- **Regulation on pharmaceutical markets and Establishment of Medical (Quality Control) Labs at borders:**

(j) Given the gargantuan nature of the task of bringing Afghanistan's borders under control and the sheer number of smuggled imports of pharmaceuticals, it makes sense to concentrate in the first instance on regulating pharmaceutical products at the point of wholesale and retail. Simple measures such as publishing more widely the list of permitted medicines and obliging retailers to display this in a prominent place on their premises might be a useful tool. Lists of common counterfeits and banned medicines could also be displayed;

(k) Continued support for the training of pharmacists in the Faculty of Pharmaceutical Sciences in Kabul University would help to secure the supply of qualified staff both for pharmacies and for regulatory authorities;

(l) Licensing procedures should be fair and transparent, and licensing authorities should be independent and demonstrably free from any influence by the private sector. Streamlining of the process for licensing importers could provide an incentive for importers to enter the official economy and would eliminate room for corruption, favoritism and bribe taking;

(m) The feasibility of installing testing facilities at main border entry ports, or even a mobile laboratory for testing of pharmaceuticals, should be assessed. Such facilities would improve the testing of pharmaceuticals and avoid delays and damage caused to pharmaceuticals imports while they are stored in customs offices.[30]

- **Establishment of Pharmacovigilance Centers:** It will benefit everybody. The patients are protected from risky and counterfeit drugs; doctors and pharmaceutical industries maintain their status integrated and the drug regulatory authorities will receive relevant data that helps them to take regulatory judgments.

  Pharmacovigilance aims at making the best use of medicines for the treatment or prevention of disease. Good Pharmacovigilance will identify the risks and the risk factors in the shorts possible time so that harm can be avoided or minimized. This will ultimately help each patient to receive optimum therapy, and on a population basis, will help to ensure the acceptance and effectiveness of public health Programmes.[31]

- Updating Curriculum of Medical Universities & Colleges, since the medical education has been halted with few publications or books later than 1986 available.
- Creating Coordination and Synergy between Health NGOs (National/International) and relevant ministries.
- Launch health education and awareness campaigns.

CONCLUSION

Healthy Afghanistan is dependent on long lasting peace and security. Persistent insecurity and political instability will hamper health sector activities, international aid efforts and avert the health sector from provision of its services across the country.

Afghanistan is at critical cross-roads today. We achieved more, but the way forward is long and hard and need more struggles. From where we stand, the direction we take, and the extent to which we succeed in achieving our long and short term objectives, all these will have important implications for Afghanistan and for the world in general.

The key elements for a successful public health services in this post-conflict era include; rock-solid commitment, security, coordination, establishment of realistic goals and objectives, the careful prioritization of services and activities and the development of efficient and effective management and information systems that allow senior health management to closely monitor the progress and make decision.

I do agree with this fact that, since 9/11, we together, with International Community including India reached significant results in Afghanistan. This is imperative to continue along the course we have taken so far. Loosing momentum would be to take the wrong step at this critical cross-road.

REFERENCES

1. Reconstruction of Afghanistan health sector, a preliminary assessment of needs and opportunities, Dec 2001 Jan 2002, WHO.
2. Accountability of government to nation 1386 by Dr Fatemi as of 12 April 2008 (Anis Newspaper as of 25 Hamal 1387).
3. http://www.ands.gov.af/ands/progress/ANDS%20Progress%20Report%20IMF&WB%20%20English.pdf
4. Accountability of government to nation 1386 by Dr Fatemi as of 12 April 2008 (Anis Newspaper as of 25 Hamal 1387).
5. Accountability of government to nation 1386 by Dr.Fatemi as of 12 April 2008 (Anis Newspaper as of 25 Hamal 1387, page 03, column 03).
6. http://www.adb.org/Documents/News/2002/nr2002268.asp
7. Health sector presentation by Minister of Health to Afghanistan Development Forum.
8. http://www.ands.gov.af/ands/progress/ANDS%20Progress%20Report%20IMF&WB%20-%20English.pdf
9. http://www.ands.gov.af/ands/progress/ANDS%20Progress%20Report%20IMF&WB%20-%20English.pdf

10. Accountability of government to nation 1386 by Dr Fatemi as of 12 April 2008 (Anis Newspaper as of 25 Hamal 1387)
11. http://www.moph.gov.af/, An Interview with Dr. Sayed Mohammad Amin Fatimi
12. UNFPA, Afghanistan.
13. http://www.moph.gov.af/, An Interview with Dr. Sayed Mohammad Amin Fatimi.
14. Ajmal Paiman, Spokesperson of MRRD, interview with Lemar TV, as of 16 March 2008.
15. Environmental Triage in Afghanistan," EHP 111:A470–A473 (2003)
16. Zaidi and Belinda Bowling, UNEP's environmental law expert in Afghanistan, fall 2005 issue of Sustainable Development Law & Policy.
17. http://www.apa.org/monitor/dec04/afghanistan.html
18. Accountability of government to nation 1386 by Dr Fatemi as of 12 April 2008 (Anis Newspaper as of 25 Hamal 1387, page 4, column 4).
19. The safety of medicines in public health programme, WHO, Chapter 2, pp. 14, 15.
20. Case Study Series, UNDERSTANDING MARKETS IN AFGHANISTAN: A Study of the Market for Pharmaceuticals, Anna Paterson and Asif Karimi, Dec. 2005.
21. Case Study Series, UNDERSTANDING MARKETS IN AFGHANISTAN: A Study of the Market for Pharmaceuticals, Anna Paterson and Asif Karimi, Dec. 2005.
22. Accountability of government to nation 1386 by Dr Fatemi as of 12 April 2008 (Anis Newspaper as of 25 Hamal 1387)
23. Case Study Series, UNDERSTANDING MARKETS IN AFGHANISTAN: A Study of the Market for Pharmaceuticals, Anna Paterson and Asif Karimi, Dec. 2005.
24. CG Briefing Report, CG5: health, JUNE 2007-JANUARY 2008.
25. Accountability of government to nation 1386 by Dr Fatemi as of 12 April 2008 (Anis Newspaper as of 25 Hamal 1387, page 4, column 4).
26. www.moph.gov.af (downloads) Draft Afghanistan National Health Policy 2005-09 and National Health Strategy 2005-06.
27. http://www.president.gov.af/english/np/health.mspx
28. http://www.moph.gov.af/ (Progress and Challenges of Ministry of Public Health of Afghanistan 2008-02-04).

29. Accountability of government to nation 1386 by Dr Fatemi as of 12 April 2008 (Anis Newspaper as of 25 Hamal 1387).
30. Case Study Series, UNDERSTANDING MARKETS IN AFGHANISTAN: A Study of the Market for Pharmaceuticals, Anna Paterson and Asif Karimi, Dec. 2005.
31. The safety of medicines in public health programme, WHO, Chapter 2, p. 7.

PART II

STRATEGIC AND SECURITY CONCERNS

CHAPTER 8

Pakistan-Afghanistan Relations—Post 9/11 and its Implications

A P S Chauhan and Sudhir Singh

Pakistan—Afghanistan relations have been one of the most interesting bilateral relationships in post second world war world. It is interesting because Pakistan has perceived an Islamic Afghanistan in their backyard as the common friend and allies but whosoever has ruled over Afghanistan has always opposed Pakistan. The first confrontation was taken place in early 1950's, when Pakistan applied for the membership of the UN. Afghanistan opposed their membership on the plea that Pakistan is not willing to implement basic tenets of UN values and it has violated it through negating the right of plebiscite of the Pathan of the frontier. Afghanistan never accepted Durand Line as the legitimate boundary between both countries. We are aware about the fact that this line was demarcated by the British Empire. It is also pertinent to mention here that throughout the history due to its excellent geo-strategic status, Afghanistan has had been an obsession for major powers. That factor propelled both Czarist Russia and British Empire in the 20th century to establish their sphere of influence over Afghanistan. The demarcation of the Durand Line was the result of that competition between both contemporary dominant colonial powers.

The British left India in 1947 and India was divided into two entities namely India and Pakistan. Pakistan became successor state of the British Empire in South-west Asia and came close to

Afghanistan by geographical proximity. The Pakthun ethnic tribes have been known for their bravado. They are settled between present Pakistan and Afghanistan. The Pakhtun believed that the demarcation of the Durand Line was a deliberate attempt of the British Empire to establish peace and normalcy in its western borders and deter Russian impacts and they never accepted this division because they perceived it as an act of divide the Pakhtun community.

Located at the crossroad of Asia and the route of the invasions of the Indian sub-continent, Afghanistan has had great strategic significance since centuries. It is thus surprising that while most countries of Asia succumbed to European imperialism, Afghanistan managed to preserve its autonomy in international affairs. With enormous courage it was almost successful to deter the influence of czarist Russia from the North and the British Empire from the South. However a multi ethnic and multi lingual country but it is known for its internal plurality and till the emergence of the Taliban, Afghanistan was known for its liberal version of Islam. After the independence of India and Pakistan and the withdrawal of the British from Indian Sub-continent, a New Great Game was started in this region. However this new Great Game was different from the 19th century, a Great Game between Czarist Russia and the British Empire. In 19th century, Britain was hell bent to prevent the expansion of the Czarist Russia from beyond the Amu Draya River with anticipated fear that its further expansion would jeopardize the inherent interests of the British Empire. In pursuance of the containment of Czarist Russia the British once in 1839 and on another occasion in 1878 occupied Kabul and Khandhar and part of eastern Afghanistan.[1] On the other side, Russia frequently invaded the autonomous regions of Central Asia and almost captured it before Bolshevik Revolution of 1917. Finally the two powers were agreed upon the maintenance of an independent and neutral country in a region between Hindukush Mountains and Khaiber Valley. Later in 1893, the British signed an agreement with Afghanistan defining the boundary between Afghanistan and the British India. This boundary is known as Durand Line because Sir M. Durand the geographer, drawn this line. Neutral status of

Afghanistan continued till 1979 when the Soviet Union invaded Afghanistan to preserve the communist credentials of the regime.

This is the point from where the saga of Afghanistan starts which still continues. It is pertinent to mention here that since that 1979 Soviet intervention, Afghanistan never stood as an independent country and after the elimination of the Taliban and Al-Qaeda in the leadership of the Hamid Karzai, an iota of stability has been revived in Afghanistan. However this article will focus on various dynamics of Pakistan—Afghanistan relationship since the emergence of Pakistan and it is also intended to analyze that why Pakistan is not really willing to allow the consolidation and the stability of Afghanistan and finally it will debate that what kinds of consequences it is putting on the reconstruction process of Afghanistan. We are aware about the fact that almost three decades of war has devastated the entire country and infrastructure therefore it needs massive reconstruction.

Since the formation of Pakistan as an independent country the issue of Pakhtunistan issue had been an apple of discord between Pakistan and Afghanistan. Even during British rule, the Afghan rulers never accepted Durand Line as a legitimate boundary between British India and Afghanistan. When the Britishers declared their intention to leave India and it was widely debated within the government circle in Afghanistan where NWFP would go and probable options for Afghanistan to deal with newly emerged situation. Because it is an open secret that NWFP was ruled by the Congress Party even after independence. It was one of the great challenges to the authority of the Muslim League being the custodian of Muslim community given the fact that NWFP had brutal Muslim majority. It is also very pertinent to note here that NWFP was among seven states, which were under Congress rule before independence. Needless to say that NWFP was Muslim majority state and Congress rule in any Muslim dominated state was a severe embarrassment for the League. It was conceded by Mohammad Ali Jinnah himself on 15 January 1942 through a statement regarding NWFP. Mr. Jinnah remarked that " In the NWFP, he would openly admit that he had failed, before the 1937 elections, to get them to form a Muslim

League. Congress had got in ahead of him, and local candidates there had defeated him at that time, but since then, the Muslim League had won every by-elections, and he was quite confident that, if general elections were held in that province, the Muslim League would win."[2]

We are aware about the fact that even after plebiscite organized in the Frontier province, Afghanistan never accepted NWFP as an integral part of Pakistan. The Afghan claim over Pakhtunistan could be seen as their desire to get an outlet to the Arabian Sea due to its landlocked status. Prime Minister of Afghanistan, Mohhammad Hasim, during an interview, expressed his opinion about the subject "if an independent Pakhtunistan cannot be set up, the Frontier province should join Afghanistan. Our neighbor Pakistan will realize that our country with its population and trade needs an outlet to the sea, which is very essential ...if the nation of the world desire peace and justice. It will be easy for us to get an outlet to the Sea."[3]

It is an open secret that Afghanistan inked an agreement with the British Empire and acceded Durand Line as a boundary between British India and Afghanistan. But at the same time it is also the reality that Afghanistan always opposed the demarcation of Durand Line. This acceptance from Afghanistan was given under duress due to lack of any alternatives. After the withdrawal of the British and the emergence of Pakistan, Afghanistan has taken a new course of action in this dispute. Afghanistan asserted that this agreement was inked under duress and under international law any deal done under duress has no legal value. Second point, Afghanistan has taken the stand that since Pakistan is not the successor state of the British India therefore this agreement has no legal value for Afghanistan.

Although Pakhtunistan is an important irritant between Pakistan and Afghanistan but there are other issues also where there are divergences of interests between both countries. Since the basic goal of this article is to focus post 11th September scenario therefore there is hardly any space of accommodation of those issues in detail in this paper.

In December 1979, Soviet red army annexed Afghanistan. It was the zenith of the cold war politics. The United States declared that they are forging an alliance for fighting against the invading Soviet red army. All members of the western blocks contributed in this project but one of the strange contributors was China. It was cold war era and both China and USSR were harbingers of the Communist block but they were in different blocks in this conflict. The Chinese stand with the US in Afghan conflict in 1979 was unique example for the realist school of foreign policy and according to that school bilateral relation has been shaped by the national interest not by the principles of idealism and commonality of ideology. Right from Kautilaya's Arthsastra to Morgnethau's Politics among Nations, this basic notion has been perpetuated and the strange Chinese stand during Afghan crisis (1979) was not an unique incident but replication of the universal truth in the realm of international politics.

PAKISTAN'S DOCTRINE OF STRATEGIC DEPTH IN AFGHANISTAN

Why Pakistan had contributed enormously in Afghan resistance war. This is not an easy question for reply but if one can forsee the entire configuration of Pakistan-Afghanistan relationship than it will be very easy to understand that dynamics and here lies the basics of Pakistan-Afghanistan relationship. As we have mentioned earlier that Afghanistan never accepted Pakistan as a conducive neighbor. Afghanistan always sustained the saga of Pakhtunistan and kept Pakistan busy in countering those effects. This was the state of affairs before 1979 Soviet invasion in Afghanistan. This prolongs thorny relationship also deny the theory of clash of civilizations propounded by Samuel P. Huntington, in which he propounded that future clash will be clash among civilizations. It is an open secret that both Pakistan and Afghanistan are Islamic state. But due to clash of interests they are fighting. Even after the restoration of democratically elected Karzai government in Kabul and being an important US ally in international war against terror, Pakistan is paying only lip services to its duties for the reconstruction process. Since late 2003, the Taliban and Al-Qaeda forces are on rise and they have posed a severe threat for the reconstruction process and needless to say that it is a big hindrance to the reconstruction process, which including Pakistan international community has pledged to Afghanistan. We are aware about the fact that since the withdrawal of the Soviet red army, the internal peace has remained a remote reality in Afghanistan due to gamut of factors. Among variety of factors one of the important factors is the unprecedented interests of Pakistan to keep Afghanistan fragile to serve its vested interests. One of the major reasons which have prevented Pakistan not to allow a stabilized Afghanistan has been Doctrine of Strategic Depth. This Strategic Depth has been extremely positive for the sustainability of the dominance of the army within Pakistan. We know that out of 61 years of independence, Pakistan has been ruled by the army for 33 years and only 28 years by the democratic regimes. During Afghan resistance war, the US and its allies including China had contributed enormously for all kinds of empowerment of the Mujahedden forces. They poured almost $10 billion to this project.[4] Interestingly one of the important amounts of that money had been contributed through sophisticated weapons. That war attracted Young Muslim recruits from Morocco to Mindanao (Philippines) to fight against infidel Soviet red army. We are aware about the fact that later on they emerged as the breeding ground for the international terrorism. These forces had been given military training and weapon by the Pakistani ISI in a tacit understanding of the American CIA. We must remember the fact that this was the time when military dictator General Zia Ul Haq was badly struggling for legitimacy due to the fact that he had hanged one of the most popular leader of Pakistan, Zulfikhar Ali Bhutto on flimsy grounds. The Soviet intervention was extremely positive for Pakistan. At one hand it provided legitimacy to the illegimate military regime of General Zia and on other hand it served the purpose of the principle of the Doctrine of Strategic Depth for Pakistan. It was the reason which kept either military or democratic regime tied with the notion of Unique Afghan Policy. In 1988 after the sudden demise of military dictator General Zia, elections took place and Benazir Bhutto of Pakistan People's Party emerged victorious and formed democratic government. But before military allow her to take over she gave three assurances to the military and all three were related overtly or covertly with India.[5] The first assurances was that Benazir will not change Unique Afghan Policy, second was she will not change Kashmir policy and third was that she will not change Nuclear Policy.[6] Even she could not change unique Afghan policy and Zia's foreign policy was allowed to continue under military pressure. The candid proof of this argument was the continuation of Sahabzada Yakoob Khan as the Foreign Minster. He was Foreign Minister under Zia regime also and he fought election from opposition group against Benazir, s PPP in 1988 elections. Benazir agreed to allow Khan to continue after she inked an unofficial deal with the military before military gave her green signal to take over. Again during second term of Benazir Government (1993-96) Taliban was originated. This idea was the brainchild of Interior Minister Babar of second Benazir Bhutto regime. Benazir Bhutto was willing to bifurcate Afghan affairs from the ISI. Initially it was aimed that the Taliban would ease the hurdles into the potential trade between Pakistan and Central Asia. But in due process of time it has become a tool of Pakistani design of Strategic Depth in Afghanistan against India. During Taliban regime (1994-2001) Afghanistan become extended Pakistan and terror groups from across the globe took their training there including the terror groups active in Kashmir, Chechnya and Xingjiang. That had provided Pakistan a new leverage to its larger project to destabilize India. One can reconnect their memory and find that resurgence in terror movement had been coincided with the withdrawal of the Soviet army from Afghanistan and during Taliban era in Afghanistan it touched new height. With a Hobson state of nature in Afghanistan, Pakistan has used terror as an instrument of its foreign policy. Now Taliban and Al-Qaeda is no more the ruler of Afghanistan. In this scenario when the entire international community has pledged their determination for the reconstruction of Afghanistan to eliminate the tentacles of terror from its root, it will be extremely significant to examine that Pakistan despite as an ally of the US in international war against terror, cooperating in the reconstruction process or not. It will be interesting to examine that what are those factors which propelled Pakistan to not to allow the cementing process of the reconstruction process. Now we will examine those issues.

INDIA AS A FACTOR BETWEEN PAKISTAN—AFGHANISTAN RELATIONSHIPS

India has remained an important factor in Afghan tango. We have seen that Pakistan has successfully used its leverage in Afghanistan in keeping India busy to counter terrorism and low intensity conflicts. This factor has kept India compelled to formulate effective strategy to deal with the emerging situation. During Taliban rule in Afghanistan, India with Iran and Russia contributed enormously into the sustainability of the Northern Alliance which was based in Tajikistan just on another side of the Amu Darya River. It is pertinent to mention here that the Northern Alliance not only resisted the Taliban but also played an important role in its elimination in the aftermath of 11th September 2001 terror attacks on the US soil.

PAK-AFGHAN RELATIONSHIP & INDIA AS A FACTOR

In the second week of September 2001, coincidently the then ISI chief Lt. General Mahmood Ahmed was on US tour as a CIA guest. On 12 September he was called by the US officials and told that Taliban and Al-Qaeda is the mastermind of the terror strikes on US soil.[7] The officials also lamented that they are going to teach a lesson to the Taliban and Al-Qaeda. They sought following 7 points cooperation from Pakistan.[8] The following seven points are important to understand entire episode :

1. Stop Al-Qaeda operating coming from Afghanistan to Pakistan, intercept arms shipments through Pakistan, and end ALL logistical support for Osama bin Laden
2. Give blanket over flight and landing rights to US aircrafts.
3. Give the US access to Pakistani Naval and air bases and to the border areas between Pakistan and Afghanistan.
4. Turn over all intelligence and immigration information.
5. Condemn the 11th September attacks and curbs all domestic expressions of support for terrorism. Pakistani

volunteer's from going into Afghanistan to join the Taliban.

6. Cut of all shipments of fuel to the Taliban, and stop Pakistani volunteer's from going into Afghanistan to join the Taliban.
7. Note that, should the evidence strongly implicate Osama bin Laden and the Al-Qaeda network in Afghanistan, and should the Taliban continue to harbor him and his accomplices, Pakistan will break diplomatic relations with Taliban regime, end support for the Taliban, and assist the US in the aforementioned ways to destroy Osama and his network.

The US Deputy secretary of State, Richard Amritage in a hard-hitting conversation tol'd the ISI chief that Pakistan has to make a choice; "you are either 100 percent with us or 100 percent against us and there is no grey area."[9] With the passage of bit over a week, Pakistan succumbed under US pressure and accepted all 7 points asked by the US. We have already mentioned that Pakistan sown the seed of the Taliban and it was an open secret that Pakistan with Saudi Arabia and United Arab Emirate were only three countries who gave recognition to the Taliban government under the provisions of the international law. In the later phase of attack, Pakistan started showing distance from Taliban but it is a fact that Pakistan created Taliban and even paid monthly salary to that government in Kabul.[10] Even after 11 September 2001 attack on US soil, Pakistan tried its level best to convinced the Taliban to hand over Osama Bin Laden and evade the onslaught of the US attack. For this purpose, Pakistan dispatched three member delegation to Khandhar to convince the Taliban leadership to hand over Osama bin Laden on 16th September 2001.[11] The member's of this delegation were ISI Chief, Madrasa Chief and Mufti Nizamuddin Shamzai, head of the famous Deobandi Madrasa in Karcahi. It is the same Madrasa where Osama bin Laden met Mullah Omar, leader of the Taliban first time, few years ago. This mission failed because Taliban decline to succumb under pressure and vowed to fight against probable US attack. It was expected reaction of the Taliban but interesting development was that Mufti Shamzai, instead of conveying the official message, encouraged Mullah Omar to wage Jihad against the US if it attacked Afghanistan.[12] However the Taliban declined this offer and vowed its determination to fight against the US might. The Taliban took their training in Pakistan based Madras's. The ISI provided maximum support to the Taliban and it has had intense relationship with the Islamic parties in Pakistan and even according to eminent expert of Afghanistan -Central Asia affairs, Ahmed Rashid, the Taliban established more effective contacts within Pakistan which was not available even for the groups operating within Pakistan.[13] Although Pakistan declared its open support to the US attack on Afghanistan and provided military logistic for the smooth progress of the US attack and on 7th October 2001, the US launched its attack. Despite this official policy of Pakistan government it is estimated that around ten thousand Pakistani Jihadis crossed the border into Afghanistan to fight along with the Taliban.[14]

Why Pakistan allowed the US to eliminate the remnants of the Taliban and Al-Qaeda from Afghanistan despite an open reality that since a long time Pakistan had nurtured the Taliban. There are gamuts of opinions about this sudden change. While talking a select gathering of retired generals, seasoned diplomats, and politicians, on September 18, Musharraf argued that the decision to extend "unstinting support" to the US was taken under tremendous pressure and in the face of fears, that in case of refusal, a direct military action by a coalition of the United States, India and Israel against Pakistan was a real possibility.[15] It was a sudden U-turn by Pakistan despite the fact that it had shaped its Unique Afghan Policy to pursue its objectives of strategic depth against India. Pakistan based Jihadi groups were taking training in Afghanistan and operating in Kashmir, one could connect the withdrawal of red army with the starting point of insurgency in Kashmir in 1990. Pakistan Afghan policy right from the inception of Pakistan in general and since 1979 have been India centric and developments in Afghanistan till the elimination of the Taliban regime had provided strategic leverage to the Pakistani ISI to push extra pressure in Kashmir through the mechanism of the Jihad. It is vindicated with the assessment of eminent French scholar Olivier Roy's. As Roy has noted:

> "Pakistan's Afghan policy was absolutely in line with its policy on Kashmir ; first and foremost the use of international militias composed of Islamic volunteer's ; direct support for the Mujahedden; the same religious network to train volunteer's, the same implacable denial that they are interfering. These are often the very organizations that are found in Kashmir helping the Taliban, such as Harkat-Ul-Ansar. So it was indeed a policy of aggression on all sides that Pakistan pursued."[16]

We are aware about the reality that the army had taken three assurances from Benazir Bhutto, when she became Prime-Minister first time in December 1988. Not only that Pakistan provided their own military personnel both for training and for fighting at the fronts along with the Taliban. There are concrete proofs that the ISI bribed the local commandeers to surrender before the Taliban.[17] On direct instructions of the ISI, the Taliban targeted Shias within Pakistan and Afghanistan that make Iran bitter enemy of the Taliban and in 1998 after severe massacre of the Shia Hazaras in Mazar-e-Sharif by the Taliban the Iranian attack on Taliban was almost a reality.[18] Riaz Besra, a Sunni terrorist (SSP) killed Iranian consulate Sadiq Ganji in Lahore in 1990. This high profile elimination in a broad day light gave much popularity to Besra within the cadres of the SSP. Needless to say that the SSP is determined to eliminate the Shias from the political landscape of Pakistan. This incident provoked Iran and embarrassed the political leadership in Pakistan. Finally Basra was arrested on 5th June 1992 but he escaped from the custody in April 1994. A former intelligence officer revealed that Besra was operating in league with some junior ISI officials.[19] Lashkar-e-Jangvi (Army of Jangvi), which was splinter part of the SSP and Besra gave new twist to the sectarian violence in Pakistan. Besra started to kill elite Shias and even common Shia mosque became his targets led to the killing of innocent people. The Lashkar started its operation in Kashmir but keeping its philosophy, it embarked on this journey by starting to murder Kashmiri Shia leaders before targeting the Indian forces.[20] The relationship between Besra and the Taliban was excellent and it is vindicated with the fact that whenever he executed heinous crime, he was escaping to Afghanistan for safe heaven and he had played his important role into the elimination of the Shias within Afghanistan. He was so powerful within the Pakistani intelligence system that Pakistani police never caught him for a long time. He killed a senior police officer Asraf Marth in front of his official residence, who did much work in the crackdown of sectarian groups including various off-shots of the SSP. The attack was so planned that half a dozen armed guards of Marth could not move and the attackers vanished from the scene. According to noted Pakistani columnist, Samina Ahmed, the army used the instability caused by sectarian violence to pressure the democratic governments.[21] The zenith of the courage of the SSP and its off-shots was an attack on Prime Minister Nawaz Sharif in Lahore in January 1999 in which he escaped.[22] It was the manifestation of the might of the terror groups and they had sent a signal to the PM that if he would be tough against them then he could be eliminated.[23] Besra was killed finally while fighting with the Taliban and Al-Qaeda against the US attack in early 2002. He may be one example there are many examples of this significance. India is one of the most important factors behind this line of thinking and Afghanistan was used as the heaven for training and safety for terrorists operating against India, which is vindicated with the fact that after high jacking of the Indiana Air-Lines plane it was taken to Khandhar in December 1999. This is the basic reason under which Pakistani military and the ISI has extended their tacit support to the resurgence of the Taliban especially in the Southern part adjoins to the Pakistan border even after its commitment to war against terror. The Pakistani military and the ISI are still sustaining their business to support the terror groups to use them as an instrument of its foreign policy. Pakistan participated in war against terror as an ally and drawn huge largesse for this support but they never abandoned the terror groups and almost pretended that they are eliminating them from Pakistani soil. It is candidly clear from the views of eminent Pakistani scholar, Hussain Haqqani, who has become one of the advisers of the newly elected Prime Minster Jillani in March 2008. According to Haqqani:

> "During the decade following the American threat to declare Pakistan a state sponsor of terrorism, Pakistan repeatedly promised to crackdown on Islamist militant groups operating from its territory. Each time, some measures were taken to create the impression that the task of uprooting the Jihadias was a difficult one and that the Pakistani government was struggling with the problem...the official explanation was featured with the difficulty of the mountainous terrain along Pakistan's border with Afghanistan..(and that US pressure) would throw Pakistan into the hands of the mullahs. That argument was first made in 1993 and continues to be made today."[24] After the Mazar-A-Sharif victory of the Taliban, Pakistan openly appealed to the international community to provide recognition to the Taliban as the legitimate ruler of Afghanistan.[25]

Why Pakistan was doing all this exercise despite changes in the nature of governance. It was due to two immediate projections. First was that chaotic situation within Afghanistan will keep Pakistan out of fear of the revival of Pakhtunistan in foreseeable future. Second plan was the use of terror as an instrument of foreign policy especially against India with especial reference to Kashmir.[26] We are aware about the fact that Afghanistan was extended Pakistan during the Taliban regime (1994-2001). The ISI used this leverage to train the terror groups and then they exported it into Kashmir. However with the due process of time they covertly exported if into Russian Chechnya and the Chinese Xingxiang also. When in 1998 the US attacked the terrorists training ground in Khost (Afghanistan) the number of casualties vindicated the fact that it was the breeding grounds for international terrorism.[27]

Another additional ambitious idea which ISI had in its mind that after the Taliban total consolidation over Afghanistan they would have expand its influence and minus Shia Iran almost all Islamic countries of South-West and Central Asia would be dominated by Pakistan. There projections were that even Russia and the US would have been compelled to deal with the Taliban in route to Islamabad.[28] The ISI also dreamt that Pakistan would be number one powerful country within Islamic block and then it would have been very easy to snatch Kashmir from India by the use of brutal force.

One of the obsessions of Pakistan has been its desire to provide access to land locked Central Asian Republics (CAS). Since their inception, the Central Asian Republics have been eagerly pursuing their reach towards the sea. There are only two nearest routes and both are traverses through Afghanistan either it is going finally to Iran or Pakistan. We are aware about the sensitivities of Iran for the Taliban and Central Asia. It is pertinent to mention here that Iran never supported Taliban or any other forces close to Pakistan and always supported either Northern Alliance led by late Ahmed Shah Masud or after that Karzai led government. In the meanwhile, Iran has persuaded its desire to provide sea route to Central Asia. With the Chinese support, Pakistan has developed the Gwador natural port at the mouth of the Persian Sea to provides a sea route to Central Asia. Close to Baluchistan's Makran area where Gwador is situated, Iranian port Chabar is also located. India and Iran has inked an agreement under which they are connecting this port to Central Asia by road through Afghanistan. The 217 KM highway from Iranian city of Zaranj to Delaram near Central Asia-Afghanistan border is part of this garland highway. This highway also interlinks Afghanistan's major cities—Kabul, Khandhar, Heart, Mazar-e-Sharif and Kunduz. It is expected to be completed by July 2008. Built by the Border Road Organization (BRO, India) it will link Afghanistan major cities to Iran as well as Central Asia. Additionally it will provide much needed sea route to Central Asia. Afghan-Pakistan relations have plummeted in the recent past and this road link, which gives Iran and India a greater role and Afghanistan a choice to avoid Pakistan made Pakistan very upset. Its diplomats have been alleging that India has used its involvement in reconstruction projects including this highway one into convert Afghanistan its intelligence outpost. Since the beginning of the work on this highway India has lost five workers and Afghanistan also lost 56 of its security person in guarding

Indian workers and crew for the same road project.[29] However India has asserted that it will not pullout from the reconstruction process despite those precious human losses. India perceives those projects extremely necessary for the rehabilitation and reconstruction of Afghanistan. Why instead of cooperation in the reconstruction process, Pakistan is working as a hurdle. It is primarily because Pakistan did not appetite that Central Asia is connected with Iranian Sea route through Afghanistan at the nearest point in partnership with India. The objectives and strategic orientations of the Taliban are closely tied with the Pakistani state. They share hostility with India, which is a significant challenge to Pakistan's strategic sway in South West Asia. This incidence is an ample proof which vindicates that why Pakistan is not cooperating into the reconstruction process.

PRESENT PAK-AFGHAN RELATION AND RECONSTRUCTION PROCESS

Why Taliban came into being although it is not the purview of this paper but a cursory glance for the emergence of the Taliban will be fruitful to pursue to understanding the diverse dynamics of Pakistan-Afghanistan relationship in present circumstances and its impact on the reconstruction process. Firstly the Taliban came into being to facilitate the Pakistani trade with the newly emerged Central Asia in a tacit understanding with Pakistan. Of course the US has also contributed and both could be classified as the illegitimate father of the Taliban. Later on Taliban inclined to strengthen its base as the ruler of Afghanistan. Needless to say that contemporary prevailing scenario had also helped a lot to the Taliban to prosper in a very short time. But the way Pakistan has handled the Taliban has vindicated the allegation that they are not going to allow to prosper to any established regime in Afghanistan. After the US attack on Taliban in 2001, the Karzai government is ruling over Afghanistan and significantly Pakistan is a partner of US led coalition against terror network. All reports either Pakistani or western origins agrees that the Taliban is in upswing and needless to say that it has posed a severe threat to the reconstruction process. There are several occasions when president Karzai has alleged Pakistan for non cooperation and some time interference in Afghan's internal affairs. The fact of the matter is that insurgency is going on in Afghanistan and the Taliban is emerging as a bigger threat to the reconstruction process.

In counter insurgency efforts more than 340 American soldiers have been killed in action in the later part of the 2006. In comparison with first five months of 2005 in 2006, there was a 200 percent increase in terror attacks. Last couples of years have witnessed an acceleration of deadly attacks thorough Guerilla warfare.[30] One of the significant features of this growing insurgency has been witnessed in eastern and southern parts of the country, which has a common border with Pakistan. Taliban and Al-Qaeda allies are gaining ground. There have been numerous attacks in 2006 in areas other than in south and east and now it is approaching in the north. President Karazi and Foreign minister, Rangin Dadfar Spanta blamed that Pakistani security forces chase Al-Qaeda within Pakistan but make little efforts to arrest Taliban fighter's or stop them to crossing the border into Afghanistan.[31]

We are aware about the fact that including both towering leaders of the Taliban and Al-Qaeda (Mullah Omar and Osama bin Laden) all prominent leaders of these outfits are hiding somewhere within Pakistan. They have sustained their propaganda that they are vowed to eliminate the dominance of the west and Afghanistan and Iraq invasion they have termed as an attack on Muslims by the Christians and needless to say that this line worked with the notion of clash of Civilization of Huntington. Although through declaring open support to the US led coalition in war against terror Pakistan has taken a U-turn but there are evidences which prove that they have sustained tacit support to the Taliban. In due course of elimination, the Taliban has converted Quetta as their undeclared capital of the government in exile. Without Pakistani support how it is feasible. Since inception of Pakistan Mullah and Military have been working with tacit understanding to promote and protect the Pakistani state. However General Zia-ul-Haq has been termed as the dictator who Islamized Pakistan but the crude fact of matter proves that it is partially true. Political Islam has been prominent within Pakistani system since its inception and right from Jinnah to present ruler's, every successive ruler have ruled the state with this broad understanding that Islam is the moral guardian of Pakistani state. This line of thesis prevents Pakistani state to curb the Islamic forces.[32] The Afghan Jihad has of course has provided new leverage to the teeth of political Islam and its Jihadi outfits, which has been openly used by the Pakistani state as an instrument of foreign policy to garner leverage especially against India. Although since US attack on Afghanistan the Jehadi's are almost out of order to the Pakistani state but not absolutely. It is the fact that in the year 2007, Pakistan has surpassed the number of terror victims from India but it is the survival tactics and the moment state will provide them new theater of action they will come under the state direction. This dilemma has encouraged the Pakistani rulers to provide tacit support to the resurgence of the Taliban. It is extremely urgent for the survival of the Pakistani state because without collaboration with the Jehadis how they will use their Kashmir card and maintain peace and order within Pakistan. It is vindicated with this statement of Henry A. Crumpton, the US Department of State coordinator for counter terrorism :[33]

> "The Americans are finding the Pakistani's much more reluctant to face down the Taliban—who are brethren from the Pashtun ethnic group that dominates in Afghanistan—then they have to confront Al-Qaeda, who are largely outsiders. Has Pakistan done enough? I think the answer is no... not only Al-Qaeda, but Taliban leadership are primarily in Pakistan, and the Pakistanis know that."

President Karzai and his many sub-ordinates have alleged number of occasions that Pakistan is not cooperating properly in war against terror despite the fact that the US has poured the largesse of almost $ 10 billion since 9/11 to Pakistan and additionally they have given the prestigious status to Pakistan as major Non-NATO Ally.[34] It is significant to mention here that cooperation from Pakistan is extremely necessary for the elimination of perpetuators of terror but the reality is that Pakistan could not affords to crack down on these elements for a longer period of time. It is simply due to the fact that Pakistan could not afford to allow for the emergence of an independent and strong Afghanistan. Since last two and half decades virtually they had high jacked the sovereignty of Afghanistan and used it for the pursuance of their broader strategic interests. Pakistani claim on Kashmir has been the basis of the sustainability of mullah–military alliance in Pakistan and despite all tall claims by present Pakistani Prime Minster Jillani it is going to be sustainable in foreseeable future. The concept of Strategic Depth is so much obsessed with Kashmir it is vindicated with this statement:

> "In Pakistan, 'they' are Indians. And between 'us' and 'them' the great wall is Kashmir. It is Pakistan irredenta. It represents the continuation of the 'Pakistan' Movement; a movement of Muslim unity. It embodies the unfinished work of Islam on the sub-continent. It is a daily reminder of the perfidy and untrustworthiness of Hindu India. Kashmir rightly belongs to 'us', but it has been stolen by 'them'."[35]

The restoration of the Karazi regime has prevented Pakistan with this significant leverage and that propels Pakistan to assist the Taliban in a covert manner to destabilize Karazi regime. The Pakistani attachment with the Taliban could be understood with the following statement of President Musharraf, which he gave on May 25, 2000:

> "He gave the clearest articulation to date of the reasons for Pakistan's continued backing of the Taliban. He explained that in view of the demographic and geographic pattern. Afghanistan's minority ethnic Pathuns have to be on our side. This is our national interest. Pastuns are represented by the Taliban at the moment, and Taliban cannot be alienated by Pakistan. He insisted that we have a national security interest there."

The prevailing scenario has proved Musharraf assertion that Pakistan could not afford to oppose the Taliban for a longer period of time despite the fact that Pakistan has received a huge largesse for their support to the US led attack against the Taliban. The Taliban and its off-shots have been able to raise their ugly face again in southern and eastern Afghanistan only because of the tacit Pakistani support to reestablish their much desired doctrine of strategic depth against India in particular and against Iran in general. However for the larger success of the reconstruction process, the need of the hour is to pour more lucrative resources to provide basic amenities to the common Afghan masses that are fed up with ongoing three decade conflicts resulted into the loss of almost 2 million people. In a country of 23 million people, 2 million people matters and decade long war has devastated the infrastructure in a massive way and needs to be restored at the war level. The ongoing reconstruction process has remained confined into the Northern parts of the country and restive south and eastern parts have almost away from the creation of basic amenities largely due to security irritants. There is a need for the advancement of socio-economic development in restive Southern and Eastern parts of Afghanistan also. With these renewed efforts for the reconstruction there must be sustainable efforts to engage Pakistan within the process.

In the reconstruction process the basic focus has been given on military build-up and socio-economic dynamics of reconstruction has been given lip-services, which needs to be taken into account. It is vindicated with the facts that since 2001 to 2006 the USA poured 88.2 billion $ as military aid and during that period only 11.4 billion $ has been poured for the reconstruction process. Even military need to understand local people, their diverse cultural identity, put some mark of their respect and than only an alien force could do a challenging job of providing military cover to the reconstruction process. The Dutch forces have done this in Uruzgan province. They started first to mix with the local people and then construct a bridge, road and local bazzar. This way they have won the hearts and minds of common Afghan, which is the task of the coalition forces in Afghanistan. In the meanwhile they did not leave the core job to eliminate the Taliban, but first they mixed with the local people, did some charity with their due representation and then fought against Taliban. This policy of the Dutch forces is well known as "Oil Spot" approach.[36] History is evidence and also a lesson for the future also. The focal lesson of Afghan history reminds us that it is extremely sensitive society and in this type of society you need to be extra cautions. There is a strong necessity to replicate this Dutch model by all segments of the coalition forces.

CONCLUDING REMARKS

Reconstruction of Afghanistan in not only necessary for the Afghan society but it is in the larger interest for the well being of all the adjoining societies in particular and for the rest part of the globe in general. Once before the Soviet intervention of 1979, Afghanistan was well known for its connecting role not only into various parts of Asia but with Europe also. Even despite its strange geographical and climatic status it was almost self-reliant in terms of its agricultural and all significant horticultural productions. Its horticultural products were extremely popular in the surroundings areas. But almost three decade long war and devastation has changed the face of the Afghan society in a horrendous manner. Eminent Pakistani expert of the Taliban, Ahmed Rashid has noted that after the Soviet withdrawal, 90,000 Afghan families were headed by the widows, 66,000 by the disables and around 45,000 were wounded in the conflicts. We are coming on the point that why Taliban came into being and again citing Ahmed Rashid it was due to prevailing anarchy after the withdrawal of the Soviet army and Hobbesian state of nature. The Taliban came into being in 1994. In 1993 this prevailing anarchy spread across Afghanistan, as vividly described by journalist Steven Coll:

> "Trucking mafias that reaped huge profits from Herion trade and other smuggling rackests propped by local warlords. Any groups of young Pakhtun fighters with a few Kalashnikov (Russian Rifles) and rocket propelled grenade launchers could set up a checkpoint and extort payments on the highways. By 1994 the main road from Quetta in Pakistan through Kahndhar and on towards Herat and Iran was choked by hundreds of extralegal roadblocks. So was the road from Khandhar to Kabul. Shopkeepers in the ramshacles markets ... battled ruthless extortion and robbery gangs. Reports of unchecked rapes and abduction, including child

rape, fueled a local atmosphere of fear and smoldering danger."

It was the state of affairs of entire Afghanistan which propelled an environment for the emergence of the Taliban. Pakistan played an important role in the emergence of the Taliban by all practical purposes. According to Ahmed Rashid,

> "In the 1980s, the ISI handled the billions of US dollors which had poured in from the West and Arab States to help the Mujaheeden, with technological support and encouragement of the CIA, that money had been used to carry out an enormous expansion of the ISI. The ISI inducted hundreds of army officer's to monitor not just Afghanistan, but India and all of Pakistan's foreign intelligence as well as domestic politics, the economy, the media and every aspect of social and cultural life in the country"[37]

This debate of the emergence of Afghanistan may prolong therefore we are shifting on the other dynamics of this paper with the note that Taliban came into being due to certain loopholes left by the important players particularly Pakistan and the US but less similar negative role was also played by Iran, Central Asian Republics, Russia and Turkey.

Today after seven years of post Taliban experience one must say that the pledges which international community had promised through the Boon and Tokoyo conferences. We put the circumstances of the emergence of the Taliban to remind us that any Hobessian state if prolong again that will bring the Taliban back into power and this time they will sustain their writ of power for a longer spell of time. First of all what kinds of reconstruction promises were made through Boon and Tokayo conferences and how far it has been met till now. We know the fact that Hamid Karzai has been ruling over the country since the elimination of the Taliban. Since 7th October till June 2007, 5,235 civilians and 610 coalition soldier's have already lost their precious life.[38] But the fact of the matter is that with the tacit understanding of the Pakistani ISI all Taliban and Al-Qaeda including Mullah Omar and Osama bin Laden is hiding in the safe havens within Pakistan and Taliban is resurfacing its nefarious designs and gaining grounds into southern Afghanistan adjoins to the western Pakistan border (Durand Line).

The ongoing conflict in Afghanistan has devastated the social fabric of Pakistan. The culture of Heroin and Kalashnikov is now prevailing, which resulted into severe losses. A compilation of terrorism related casualties indicates that 1,471 people were killed in Pakistan during 2006, up from 648 in the previous year and during the year 2007 it has crossed India in this direction.[39] We are also aware about the fact that Pakistan is not cooperating adequately into war against terror as well as in the reconstruction process because both efforts are dependent on each other due to gamut of vested interests. In this scenario it is important to examine that how the reconstruction process could be ensured in its true manifestation. One thing is absolutely clear that without full scale reconstruction process, conflict is not going to over because of the simple fact that unmet promises of reconstruction has provided new leverage to the Taliban among the common masses particularly into southern Afghanistan. The policy of inclusion must be incorporated as the focal strategy of reconstruction through socio-economic rights and respects of every ethnic group.

We are also aware about the fact that Afghanistan is a multi-lingual, multi-ethnic country and within this scenario one can ensure peace only through accommodation of peripheral interests into the mainstreaming process. President Karzai has been successful at some extent in this direction but an unmet promise of reconstruction has weakened his position.

The Pakistani establishments despite their all Himalayan claims will not going to cooperate into the reconstruction process in a cordial manner. Although Pakistani support is important due to its geographical proximity with Afghanistan and all efforts should be continue to obtain Pakistani support but at the same vein coherent efforts of reconstruction must be sustainable. Iran has been one of the original opponents of the Taliban in particular and Pakistan's, Afghan policy in general. Even when Taliban was its peak, Iran supported Northern Alliance against Taliban with Russia, India and Central Asian Republics. The US must ensure

Iranian cooperation into the reconstruction process despite their differences on gamut of other issues.

The reconstruction process and war against terror is interdependent and needless to say that one success would be helpful for another. Not only that the prevailing menace of Kalashnikov and Heroin culture could not be eliminated without ensuring reconstruction process. In Iran the numbers of drug users were three millions and so in Pakistan and it is growing into Central Asian Republics and even in Russia, China and India too. It is high time to allocate adequate attention for the success of the reconstruction process. It would not only bring peace and prosperity in Afghanistan but establish peace in Iran, Pakistan and Central Asian Republics in particular but within Russia, China, India and rest part of the globe in general. It will also facilitate energy flow from Central Asia to South Asia in a natural manner and will be extremely helpful to restore law and order in all of its surroundings in particular and in the rest part of the globe in general.

REFERENCES

1. Ameri, Nasser Sachafi, "Afghanistan Crisis; Geopolitical Aspects" in V.D. Chopra edited *Afghanistan and Asian Stability*, Gyan Publishing House, New Delhi, 1988, pp. 184-85.
2. Sir Roger Lumley to Linlithgow, 15 January, 1942, TP 1; 28.
3. *The Statesman*, New Delhi, 22 June 1947.
4. Haqqani, Current History, April 2007, p. 151.
5. Rizvi, Hasan Askari, *Military, State and Society in Pakistan*, St. Martin Press,London, 2000, p. 113.
6. *Ibid*.
7. Text of President Bush Speech published in *New York Times*, New York, 12 September 2001.
8. Abbas, Hasan, *Pakistan's Drift into Extremism, Allah, the Army, and America's war on Terror*, M.E. Sharpe, New York, 2005, p. 218.
9. Owen, Bennett Jones, *Pakistan; Eye of the Storm*, Yale University Press, New Haven, 2002, p. 2.
10. Rashid, Ahmed, *Taliban, Islam, Oil and the New Great Game in Central Asia*, I.B. Tauris, New York. 2000, p. 183.
11. *Op. cit*, No. 8, p. 221.
12. *Friday Times*, Lahore, October 7, 2001.

13. *Op. cit*, No. 8, p. 203.
14. *The Frontier Post*, Peshawar, October 11, 2001.
15. *Op. cit*, No. 8, p. 221.
16. Roy, Olivier, "Islam and Foreign Policy" in Christopher Jaffrelot, *A History of Pakistan and Its Origins*, Anthem Press, 2004, p. 142.
17. *Op. cit*, No. 8, p. 205.
18. *Op. cit*, No. 8, p. 207.
19. *Ibid*, p. 207.
20. *Ibid*, p. 208
21. Ahmed, Samina, "Centralization, Authoritarianism, and the Mismanagement of Ethnic Relations in Pakistan," in *Government policies and Ethnic Relations in Asia and the Pacific*, ed, Micheal. E. Brown and Sumit Gangulay, Cambridge Press, 1997, pp. 107-27.
22. *The Frontier Post*, Peshawar, February 7, 1999.
23. *The News*, Islamabad, November 27, 2000.
24. Hussian Haqqani, "Pakistan: Between Mosque and Military," Carnegie Endowment for International Peace, Washington, 2005, p. 297.
25. *Op. cit*, No. 10, p. 194.
26. Dawn, Karachi, March 19, 2001.
27. *Op. cit*, No. 8, p. 202.
28. *Ibid*.
29. *The Times of India*, New Delhi, 13 April 2008.
30. Witte, Griff, "Afghans Confront Surge in Violence; Foreign Support seen Behind Attacks That Mimic"; Those in Iraq, *Christens Science Monitor*, November 28, 2005.
31. Ron, Synovitz, "Afghanistan; Upsurge of Violence Reflects New Taliban Tactics," *Eurasia Insight*, May, 26,2006.
32. Akhtar, Sajjad, Asha Amirali and Muhammad Ali Raza, Reading between the lines; the Mullah-Military Alliance in Pakistan, *Contemporary South Asia*, 15(4), December 2006, p. 387.
33. *The New York Times*, New York, May 28, 2006.
34. *Op. cit*, No. 4, p. 147.
35. Stern, Robert W., *Democracy and Dictorship in South Asia; Dominate classes and Political Outcomes in India, Pakistan and Bangladesh*, Westport; Praeger, 2001, p. 141.
36. *The New York Times*, New York, April 6, 2007.
37. *Op. cit*, No. 10, p. 184.
38. http;//www.icasualties.org/oef/
39. *Op. cit*, No. 4, p. 148, *The Times of India*, New Delhi, January 13, 2008.

CHAPTER 9

Afghanistan Political Transition and its Impact on Reconstruction

Nilofar Sakhi

POLITICAL TRANSITION AFFECTED FROM DEC. 2001

On Dec 5, 2001, various Afghan groups came together under U.N. guidance to sign the Bonn Agreement, laying the groundwork for democratic development in Afghanistan. In accordance with the agreement, an emergency loya jirga took place in June 2002, electing a transitional government under President Hamid Karzai.

The Bonn agreement of 2001, which has been implemented along with the Parliamentarian election of 2005, was focused on the principles of state building and democracy implementation. The decision has been taken in Bonn agreement shows a new political transition form religious extremism/dictatorship to democracy. The political transformation started after 2001 brought with it a new turn to politics in Afghanistan. It is for the first time that the international community including United States started strategizing seriously about the reconstruction processes in the country.

The process started from economic development – such as building infrastructure, businesses and bank system to political development with a main focus on state building. The 2002 political transition in Afghanistan created a new turn to

Afghanistan's history. The international community started working on different strategies for Afghanistan as a model implemented in other post conflict countries. The political transition happened with duplication of models from other post conflict countries without having complete knowledge of the situation in Afghanistan. It started with involvement of many actors, capital and resources, that is why it was difficult to identify the strategies at the beginning. At the political level preparation started for the state building and most prominently government institutions and police. It was an energetic and excited movement by the international community with United States leadership to make their best for the promotion of democracy in the country.

At the beginning of transition there were two prominent observations , the first was the positive level of coordination and cooperation among the supported states and the second one was the weak position of the freedom fighters/warlords in power—made the nation optimist about the future of Afghanistan. Most Afghans believed that the Bonn Agreement represented the best chance possible for establishing peace, security, and protection of human rights in Afghanistan. The situation changed over a passage of time; the previous fight-fighters or warlords became the guardian of top political positions and gained power in government institutions. The parliamentarian election was positive by its essence as it kept a foundation for the future of democracy but on the other hand the result was not satisfactory since the individuals from unexpected political groups from the past were elected in the parliament.

Soon after the parliamentarian election the insurgency raised in different part of the country with more focus in the South, Taliban consists of Pakistani and Afghani nationalities started making the security worse. It was at that stage when the role of Pakistan in contributing in insecurity in Afghanistan became obvious. This situation was unexpected for all the actors working for positive change in Afghanistan. It seemed that the international community and Afghan government did not expect imported terrorism from neighboring countries in Afghanistan that is why there was no strategy available at that time for the prevention. As a result it took time for Afghanistan to launch certain activities for the prevention of insurgency from neighbouring state as well as to negotiate with their perspective country. This process slowed down everything else going on around the country and created fair and frustration among the nation.

As Burnett Rubin, the expert on Afghanistan says in his Saving Afghanistan article, "With the Taliban resurgent, reconstruction faltering, and opium poppy cultivation at an all-time high, Afghanistan is at risk of collapsing into chaos. If Washington wants to save the international effort there, it must increase its commitment to the area and rethink its strategy—especially its approach to Pakistan, which continues to give sanctuary to insurgents on its tribal frontier."

The strategy for Afghanistan's future should not be unilateral in approach. It should be a multi-approaches strategy since the experience showed that Afghanistan stable politics and reconstruction is not possible without regional coordination and cooperation. It is obvious that the political transition started after 2001 has been a transition from a dictator and fundamentalist regime to a democracy. Here the question arises that weather this transition has helped Afghanistan so far or no? Yes, But if we compare it with the dark and a fundamentalist regime of Taliban only, no doubt that the transition has helped the country to move from a closed state where there was not any legitimate political system, no international links, no commitment to international convention, and no particular strategy for running the state and now Afghanistan is committed to international treaties, has a parliament, opening ways to strengthening civil society and laid the foundation for the promotion of democracy but still the promotion of democracy and its sustainability in future is questionable under today's situation in Afghanistan.

Democracy is not only confined to election—that happened in Afghanistan. It is about people's participation and representation in building the government institutions in order to govern the state. Under such definition if the level of education is low then how can one expect the nation to take active part in the election, and elect their representatives who deserve and have potential to run the state. Unfortunately the new political transition has made the local warlords again in legitimate power.

Although DDR (Disarmament, demobilization and reintegration) process happened all over the country but unfortunately it didn't have much success, and most of the areas are still under the control of previous fight fighters/warlords. Their strong representation in parliament shows that the election at this stage couldn't help fair participation of individuals. It shows that those who do not believe in democracy are guardians of democratization.

It is important to note that a post conflict model applied in Afghanistan did not work well in maintaining security as well as speeding up the reconstruction process. The political transition in Afghanistan is not completed yet. It is in early stages of developing a framework for building the state although nation building process has not started yet.

The political transition in Afghanistan had some major drawbacks which has become obvious with the passage of time. They are as follow:

- The implementation of strategy from other post conflict countries without the complete and accurate knowledge about Afghanistan.
- Bringing in power the freedom fighters/warlords.
- Lack of strategies to deal with the regional terrorism most prominently terrorism emerge from neighboring states.
- Lack of long-term strategy to deal with the country's hard reality i.e. poverty.
- Lack of activities for the nation building in Afghanistan.

The three above factors created security issues all over the country and made it worse day by day. People started losing trust from the government. On the other hand there is a class struggle started among the nation.

IMPACT OF POLITICAL TRANSITION ON RECONSTRUCTION OF AFGHANISTAN

Reconstruction has a very direct link with the political transition in Afghanistan. Afghanistan reconstruction was mentioned in Bonn agreement. It was also followed by the

Afghanistan Compact in London that the international community and Afghanistan government should work together for the promotion of sustainable economic growth and development; strengthening state institutions and civil society, rebuilding capacity and infrastructure, reducing poverty, meeting the challenges of counter-narcotics and meeting basic human needs. International community committed to be a part of this process. At the beginning of transformation when there was a coordination and consistent follow up mechanism, the reconstruction efforts was initiated and speeded up with full support of international community. In fact, many positive changes related to reconstruction occurred during two years of transition period. For instance, tremendous changes in education sector, improvement in central provincial hospitals, building highways and providing a plate-form for the economic investor to launch their program but this process did not continue for long time.

One of the most important factors that made the reconstruction efforts possible at the beginning of the transition was security. Indeed a secure situation opened a plate form for enhancement of different reconstruction related programs including, infrastructure, democracy promotion such as, human rights, freedom of speech, election preparation, free media and economic investment started to build up people's trust on the changes that that the transition brought with it. In general the nation became hopeful for their future and considered election as the way for the stability of Afghanistan as they have experienced the level of reconstruction started in different parts of the country.

Everything changed into different direction after parliamentary election. On the other hand security got worse day by day. Different provinces had different security concerns. For instance, north became the center of suicide attacks, west became the center for kidnapping and murder, and the south became the target of insurgency and east the main door of violence. Schools were burnt in the south, innocent people were kidnapped and murdered in the west and people's property and life was no safer. The situation was out of control suddenly at the end of 2006 and the entire 2007. The insecurity in Afghanistan became the main challenge for the reconstruction processes. Donors stopped their projects in remote areas due to security reasons.

Besides security the second factor that slowed down the reconstruction process has been the specific interest of different international actors in Afghanistan. Different donors have specific agenda and they lead their programs according to their states' interest. Some one has interest in short-term programs and others plan for the long-term activities. There has not been consistency and coordination among donors which has created a duplication of work and in some areas spend of money on projects that do not have any sustainability in future. The third factor that did not make the use of funds so effective has been the return of high percentage of funds to the donor agencies ad their staff. A recent study of Agency Coordinating Body for Afghan Relief ACBAR says that since the ouster of the Taliban regime in late 2001, the international community has pledges some $25 billion in aid to Afghanistan. But it says only $15 billion of that total has been delivered—in a country where some 90 percent of public spending is international aid. The study "Falling Short" by the same organization also finds that a "staggering" 40 percent of the Western funds that are spent on aid projects are returned to the donor countries through fees to contractors and salaries to employees from those countries. The fourth challenge of reconstruction has been corruption among national organizations. Due to a lack of system and capacity, the Afghan NGOs failed to make effective use of grants provided for the implementation of various projects.

The process of reconstruction including the pressure on building infrastructure slowed down and projects has remained limited to small short term projects through NGOs. Due to lack of a system there has not been monitoring mechanism for the international aid coming for the reconstruction of Afghanistan. In the current situation of Afghanistan if there is no strong system that can monitor the aid coming into the country, corruption and waste of money can easily take place. I think if the state is weak there is no question of effective implementation of reconstruction programs especially in post-conflict situation. Weak states can promote corruption and block the reconstruction processes.

Based on the situation it is clear—for building Afghanistan the activities were started from economic development but not with substantive and long-term project rather with shorter project focus on few elements of democratization. Unluckily democracy was confined to elections only. Education and economy—the main factor that makes democracies sustainable and also can speed up reconstruction efforts has given less attention. Democracy promotion remained only confined to the big cities and urban population with knowing the reality that the majority of the population inhabits in urban areas. Education was not taken to the remote areas due to lack of security and existence of extremist forces.

Despite many efforts and many actors, and with the most intense phase of military campaign in Afghanistan, the country faced many difficulties. Political and economic transition at this stage, with security was the main concern, pushed the country into a state of instability. "The political transition in strife-torn Afghanistan continues to face a number of serious challenges, including terrorism and a booming drug industry," according to a new United Nations report, which urges an integrated approach among all international partners to stabilize the fledgling democracy.

This political transition can move into a better position if there will be a proper assessment from last seven years. No doubt there have been positive changes as I mentioned in my paper, and it is not logical to expect substantive and stable Afghanistan overnight. Considering political transformation is a journey, it needs dedication, commitment of international community and Afghanistan government and the most important the people of Afghanistan to work effectively for making Afghanistan stable. Indeed it is the people who can bring change. Knowing this reality Afghans should take the lead and coordinate with the international community to build Afghanistan.

CONCLUSION

- As seven years have passed since the Bonn Agreement, there may be a need for an assessment to examine what went wrong at the national and international efforts that the country is facing a deteriorating security and a fragile political situation.

- The things must get afghanize at the national level. Afghan must be given the opportunity to be a part of policy making.
- Afghanistan needs partnership with international community. This partnership should not be dominated by any side.
- Afghanistan Government should make ways for making democracy work through the nation. Democracies are not possible if nation will not understand the value and importance of it. The current political transition in Afghanistan is a transition to democracy where it should have different strategies for making democracy work and prevent its collapse. It should have consistence programs for the promotion of education and economic development to make democracy people's choice and movement. There should be a focus on nation-building at this stage of the political transition.
- Instead of top-down approach, there should be bottom-up approach in reconstruction processes.
- To resolve security issues, serious steps are necessary to be taken since insecurity can block the reconstruction processes.

United States and its international partners for the reconstruction of Afghanistan should continue their support but meanwhile should rethink their strategy for effectiveness of their resources they devote to Afghanistan.

RECOMMENDATIONS

The following recommendation are suggested:

- State building should be given priority in Afghanistan. A strong leader with vision has to be promoted in order to get legitimacy from the nation.
- Economic investment through long term sustainable indigenous mechanism should be created.

- A new strategy should be made to promote education throughout the country more specifically remote areas of Afghanistan.

REFERENCES

1. The Afghanistan Compact, 31st January-1st February, p. 1. http://www.ands.gov.af/admin/ands/ands_docs/upload/UploadFolder/The%20Afghnistan%20Compact%20-%20Final%20English.pdf
2. Foreign Relations, Saving Afghanistan, January/ February 2007 http://www.foreignaffairs.org/20070101faessay86105/barnett-r-rubin/saving-afghanistan.html
3. REF/RL's Radio Free Afghaistan: Report on Afghanistan, Tuesday, March 25, 2008 www.rferl.org/featuresarticleprint/2008/03/
4. The Afghanistan Compact Report, "Building in Success," London 31 January-1 February 2006.

CHAPTER 10

The Turmoil in Afghanistan and Regional Security

Afsir Karim

Afghanistan received aid both from the United States and the Soviet Union till 1971. The soviet invasion in 1979 changed the situation radically, in 1989 an assorted force, named mujahidin, assembled and trained with the American and Pakistan collaboration forced the Soviet army out of Afghanistan.

In 1998 when Kabul was under the control of the Taliban, the U.S. missiles attacked the al-Qaeda training complex near Kabul as Osama bin Laden's was suspected to be the man behind the bombings of the American embassies in Kenya and Tanzania in 1998.

In March 1999, an UN-brokered peace agreement was signed between the Taliban and the Northern Alliance, under Ahmed Shah Massoud, a Tajik mujahidin leader. But the truce broke down soon and fighting among various guerrillas groups started once again. In 2000 when the Taliban controlled almost ninety percent of the country, continuous turmoil and infighting caused over a million deaths, and this forced about 3 million Afghans to take refuge in Pakistan and Iran. The turmoil and instability in Afghanistan was directly connected to training of fundamentalist groups by America and Pakistan with financial aid from Saudi Arabia after the Soviet invasion. In 2001, after 9/11 the US attacked and destroyed all Al-Qaeda bases in Afghanistan, but its top leadership and large numbers of its trained cadres escaped to Pakistan where they found shelter.

The main cause of alienation of people from the present regime is its alliance with America, presence of foreign troops on Afghan soil and harsh military action of the US-NATO forces against the common people.

The present resurgence of the Taliban also essentially points towards lack of acceptance of a weak democratic regime propped up by the US-NATO forces. In these conditions insurgency, terrorism, illicit drug trade has created conditions of total anarchy; re-construction and development have taken a back seat in most parts of the country.

In this situation the resurgence of the Taliban, establishment of al-Qaeda bases and revival of fundamentalism in Pakistan has created serious security problems for the entire South and Central Asian region. India with its on going tussle with fundamentalist elements within the country that are supported by the radical groups in Pakistan faces a greater security challenge now.

COUNTRY AND THE PEOPLE

The geographic location, difficult terrain, lack of means of communication and poor development of human resources in Afghanistan facilitate insurgency and terrorism, some of these factors have been highlighted here with this point of view.

Afghanistan is a land locked country bordered by Iran in the west, by Pakistan on the east, and by Central Asia in the north; a mass of rugged mountains cover the country, various ranges fanning out from the Hindu Kush (reaching a height of more than 24,000 ft) run across many parts of the country. The geo-political importance of Afghanistan is obvious from its pivotal location serving as land bridge between West Asia and South Asia and as an outlet to the sea for the Central Asian region The population comprises Tajiks; Uzbeks and nomadic Turkmen, Hazaras and Pashtuns—who are the country's largest ethnic group. The unifying factor is religion; the majority is Sunni, minority groups is Shiite. Baluchis live in the extreme south. Dari (Afghan Persian), Pashto (Afghan), and various Turkic tongues (mainly Uzbek and Turkmen) are the country's principal spoken languages.

The central mountain chains such as the Selseleh-ye Kuh-e Baba, the Paropamisus and the Amu Darya (Oxus), define the northern boundary; the highlands of Badakhshan, Afghan Turkistan, the Amu Darya plain, and the rich valley of Herat on the Hari Rud (Arius) River are in the northwest corner of the country.

Waters of the Hari Rud and of the Amu Darya and Helmand—which flows in a southwesterly direction from the Hindu Kush to the Iranian border and is the longest have been used since ancient times for irrigation. The Kabul River, flows past Kabul and from where it flows towards the Khyber Pass and thus to Pakistan. Most rivers are, however, not navigable.

Kabul, Kandahar and Herat are important cities but these and all the major trade route of the country have been ravaged by recent wars. Industry has largely disappeared; there is up to 70% employment, road communications are poor all over the country despite ongoing reconstruction since the end of Taliban regime. The tunnel under the Salang pass, built in 1964 by the Russians still provides an all-weather route between Northern and Southern regions.[1]

Mineral resources are undeveloped, besides natural gas there are deposits of coal, copper in the country. Billions of dollars in aid have entered Afghanistan but the reconstruction effort has been hampered by the ongoing insurgency and poor governance. Afghanistan is the world's largest producer of opium which is its most important cash crop.

There are still significant obstacles in the way of female education in Afghanistan stemming from lack of proper perspective of Islamic values and cultural inhibitions. Some parents will not allow their daughters to be taught by men, this hinders female education.

Literacy of the entire population is estimated (as of 1999) at 36%, the male literacy rate is 51% and female literacy is 21%. Up to now there are only 9,500 schools in the country and generally there is lack of infrastructure and funding required increasing the level of educational facilities.[2]

POLITICAL RELATIONS AND SECURITY

Before the Soviet invasion, Afghanistan pursued a policy of neutrality and non-alignment; it was one of a few countries that remained neutral during both World Wars. During the Cold War Afghanistan was able to exploit the Russian and American quest for allies and managed to receive economic assistance from both countries. However, since Russia offered extensive military aid also, the government of the day developed closer ties with the USSR, while remaining officially non-aligned. After the December 1979 Soviet invasion, Afghan policymakers tried to improve their standing in the noncommunist world, by signing of the Geneva accords, soughting to end Afghan isolation from the Islamic nations and in the Non-Aligned Movement.[3]

Many countries initially welcomed the Taliban, whom they saw as a stabilizing factor, and as an alternative to the war lords who had ruled the country since the fall of Najibullah's government in 1992. The Taliban soon became unacceptable to most countries because of the imposition of harsh Sharia laws in Taliban-controlled territories The harsh attitude towards women who attempted to work or wanted to go to schools, inhibited outside assistance to the country.

Pakistan, Saudi Arabia, and the United Arab Emirates recognized the Taliban as the legitimate government of Afghanistan, but all three countries withdrew recognition to the Taliban following the September 11, 2001 terrorist attack on the United States. Pakistan had recognised the Taliban regime in 1997 and developed close ties with it with the aim of gaining strategic depth in any future conflict with India. Following the 2001 invasion and overthrow of the Taliban, Pakistan, however, recognized the transitional administration led by Hamid Karzai.[4]

The relationship between Pakistan and Karzai regime are currently precariously balanced. Two areas that have complicated Afghanistan's relations with Pakistan are: Pakistan's clandestine support to the Taliban and establishment of al-Qaeda and anti-Karzai elements in frontier areas of Pakistan. Instability has prevailed since the establishment of the Durand Line in 1893 that divided Pashtun and Baluch tribes living in Afghanistan and frontier areas that form part of Pakistan now. As of now, Afghan-Pakistani relations continue to fluctuate due to continued controversy over the Durand Line and Afghanistan's close relationship with India. Afghanistan has long relied on Pakistan for trade and travel to the outside world, and Afghanistan is Pakistan', primary route for trade with Central Asia, these routes remain closed due to insecure conditions.[5]

Most Afghans believe that Pakistan is an agent of Western countries, assisting the diplomatic subjugation of their country. Some in Pakistan seek to form a confederation with Afghanistan. Such a confederation would virtually re-establish the original Afghanistan that existed under Ahmed Shah Abdali. Prominent European and North American scholars believe that such a union would bring peace and stability to both countries and will be in the interest of both these countries and the region as a whole. This logic, however ignores the fact that such a confederation will become an Islamic stronghold where orthodox elements and Al-Qaeda will rule the roost, their aggressive policies towards moderate states of South and Central Asia will make it a permanent war zone.[6]

India has traditionally sought to maintain good relations with the Afghan government, primarily to check Pakistani influence in the region beside age old ties. It supports the elected government and has donated buses, aircraft and has imparted training to its fledgling police force to assist the warn-torn nation.[7]

During President Hamid Karzai's visit to New Delhi, India pledged aid totaling to about $650 million—of which $200 million has already been provided. India is reconstructing a road in the remote southwestern Afghan province of Nimroz The project is being carried out by s Border Roads Organization (BRO), the mission statement of which states that the BRO is India's "most reputed, multifaceted, transnational, modern construction organization committed to meeting the strategic needs of the armed forces." The killing of BRO employees by the Taliban and suicide attacks on them lately shows that the Taliban and some other elements are working against Indian interests; have has prompted the Indian authorities to provide armed guards for the security of Indian personnel working on various construction projects in Afghanistan.[8]

THE SECURITY ENVIRONMENTS

Since the late 1970s Afghanistan has faced continuous internal conflict violence as a result of the 1979 Soviet invasion and the 2001 US-led invasion that ousted the Taliban regime. In late 2001 the United Nations Security Council authorized the creation of an International Security Assistance Force (ISAF). This force composed of NATO troops is involved in assisting the government of President Hamid Karzai in establishing law and order as well as rebuilding key infrastructures in the country. In 2005, the United States and Afghanistan signed a strategic partnership agreement committing both nations to a long-term relationship. In the meantime, multi-billion US aid has also been provided by the international community for the reconstruction of the country. However, the security situation remains highly disturbed despite stepped up American-led NATO operations.[9]

Gradually the Taliban have reemerged as powerful guerrilla force that is successfully challenging the US-NATO forces and the Karzai regime. During US-led operations indiscriminate bombings of civilian areas have invariably resulted in large number of civilian casualties and further alienation of the majority of the population in Afghanistan besides creating great resentment in the Pushtun belt shared by Afghanistan and Pakistan. In 2006 The U.S.-led coalition launched its biggest campaign against the Taliban since 2001; some 11,000 troops took part in a summer offensive in four southern provinces, where the Taliban had become firmly entrenched. In July 2006, NATO assumed operational responsibility of South Afghanistan, where the found themselves engaged by well armed Taliban forces particularly in Kandahar province. In the second half of 2006, NATO operations floundered and casualties mounted and this prompted NATO commanders joining Afghan leaders in blaming Pakistan for allowing use of their border areas as safe haven for the Taliban.[10]

In March 2007, NATO forces launched a new offensive in Helmand province against the Taliban and Al-Qaeda. Pakistan's construction of a fence along the border with Afghanistan in this period led to protests from Afghanistan, and several border clashes between the forces of the two countries were reported.

Afghan civilian casualties during military operations in 2007 became a great source of anger among Afghans and further increased resentment against the foreign forces. As of March 1, 2007, according to Department of Defense (DOD), the United States had 24,845 military personnel deployed in Afghanistan. Of these more than 21000 formed the active component and the rest were National Guard and reserves.

There were 77 suicide attacks just in the first six months in 2007, about twice the number for the same period last year. Towards the end of this year that figure had risen to around 140, in Baghlan province a suicide bomber blew himself up in as school children welcomed visiting parliamentarians. The nearly 80 died including 59 school children and six parliamentarians.[11]

Baghlan attack that targeted Afghanistan's first democratically elected parliament showed the increasing influence and support of the Taliban in the North. The war continues and the Taliban are growing stronger by the day. Foreign troops have been accused of killing hundreds of innocent civilians in their operations and this has greatly undermined people's confidence in the Karzai regime.

President Hamid Karzai blames "terrorist hideouts outside Afghanistan" and support in some countries for "terrorist elements and Al-Qaeda" in a pointed reference to Pakistan. However, influential tribal chiefs in Kandahar province, where the Taliban have been strong say that the problem is the government has failed to reach the people who are living under the fear of the Taliban.

A study titled "Counterinsurgency in Afghanistan," says that Pakistan's Inter-Services Intelligence Directorate and paramilitary Frontier Corps "have failed to root out Afghan insurgent groups based in Pakistan and, in some cases; individuals from these Pakistani organizations have provided direct assistance to such groups as the Taliban and Haqqani network.

It is reported that a number of Pakistani army personnel continue to support the Taliban and al-Qaeda; this is one of the reasons why many tribal agencies have become safe hideouts of the al-Qaeda and the Taliban.

Intelligence reports indicate that some of the Jihadi terrorist groups may have shifted to new bases in PoK that provide a springboard for terror attacks in J&K. One of the key concerns of India has been the deteriorating security situation in this region and the threat posed by violent Islamic activism emerging in Afghanistan and Pakistan the Taliban resurgence in Afghanistan and their support bases in Pakistan can involve the entire South and Central Asian region and Iran in religious instigated strife and violence. The short sighted American policies that generally translate into unbridled military action and blind support of Pakistan army are mainly responsible for the growing fundamentalism and resurgence of fundamentalist forces in this region.[12]

The Taliban leader Mullah Mohammad Omar has vowed to continue war as long as the foreign troops remain in the country On the other hand, in an attempt to allay fears of the international community the Taliban leader, Mullah Omar also said that the "Taliban represent no threat to anyone as they want to have good relations with all nations in line with the Islamic law."[13]

NATO's chief during his recent visit to Afghanistan described the alliance' mission in Afghanistan as a "necessity and not a choice" and warned if Taliban and terrorists are not contained their activities would expand to Europe. The US focus still remains on Iraq as a result that the Taliban and Al-Qaeda are gaining in strength. According to all major US intelligence agencies Pakistan border is Al-Qaeda's primary safe haven and represents the greatest direct threat to the US.[14]

The US policy makers view a military victory in Afghanistan as central to the war on terrorism. "What is happening in Afghanistan and beyond its borders can have even greater strategic long-term consequences than the struggle in Iraq," observed the Atlantic Council of the United States. The United States is already going beyond Afghan borders and launching attacks into Pakistan through 'Unmanned Predator' aircraft to kill Taliban leaders, but alas they kill scores of innocent civilians.[15]

Frederick Kagan recently put together a planning group at the conservative American Enterprise Institute to urge the Bush administration to surge troops into Afghanistan and threaten Pakistan with air strikes. However, rather than suppressing the Taliban, this kind of stepped up military action is likely to unite the Pushtuns on both sides of the border and escalate violence.[16]

Ronan Thomas, a British correspondent notes, "Strategic success in Afghanistan has often been envisaged by outside powers—British, Soviet and now Coalition forces—but rarely if ever achieved." Like its predecessors, the United States is losing the "great game" in Central Asia. It seems this is no way for US-NATO to win a war against terrorism.[17]

Afghanistan currently has more than 70,000 national police personnel and there are plans to recruit more so that the total number reaches 80,000, who will be trained by the Afghanistan Police Program. Although the police officially are responsible for maintaining law and order, many regional military commanders continue to exercise control in the hinterland. Although in 2003 the mandate of the International Security Assistance Force, now under command of the NATO, was extended and expanded beyond the Kabul area in some areas, unoccupied by those forces, local militias rule the roost In most areas, crimes have gone uninvestigated because of insufficient police force and lack of communications. Units of the Afghan National Army have been sent to maintain order in some areas lacking police personnel.[18]

SECURITY CONCERNS

The Taliban are still not capable of fighting a set piece battle against US-NATO forces, but in their own way they are capable of launching local offensives. The newest US military acronym for the insurgent in Afghanistan is now AAF, or anti-Afghan fighter, replacing the last, ACM, or anti-coalition militant. These terms show the US planners understand now that they are confronting a loose affiliation of disparate groups with different tactics and goals.

Fighting season in Afghanistan depends on the weather conditions; warm weather before the harsh winter sets in is more suited for conventional operations, it would be correct to assume that violence rises to higher levels with the spring. Taliban are now also waging "information operations." By making noises about an "spring offensive" in the past, the Taliban have hit headlines and gained publicity. They are now well versed in asymmetric warfare, (also known as fourth-generation warfare or 4GW), where the main objective is to wear down the enemy and erode his will and ability to continue fighting. In such operations perceptions count and information to the media, regarding an upsurge in violence in the spring raises the spectre of a big spring offensive that may never actually materialise.[19]

In an interview Karzai said foreign troops had failed to go after "the sanctuaries of the terrorists" which Afghan officials say exist over the border in Pakistan. Though Karzai did not directly mention this but the Afghan government has said that the West should have done more to crack down on Taliban and Al-Qaeda bases in Pakistan.[20]

Karzai lamented "some of the Taliban who have laid down their arms, who are living in the Afghan villages peacefully, who have accepted Afghanistan's new order, they were chased, they were hunted for no reason, and they were forced to flee the country." He also stated, "The international community came to Afghanistan in the name of fighting terrorism and that fight has to be real and effective. There is no way we can win this war against terrorism unless and until Afghanistan is ... detached from the other interests or views that some of our partners have in this region."[21]

A UN report on suicide attacks says that an increase in "Talibanization" in the Federally Administered Tribal Areas of Pakistan threatens the stability of Afghanistan. Pakistan's efforts to eliminate al-Qaeda bases and military operations against local Taliban have met with little success. The report brings out the emerging danger and the requirement of a more meaningful international response as the Pakistani efforts are half hearted. The newly elected government in Pakistan wants to broker peace with the local Taliban but not much headway has been made so far and terrorist activities and their resistance against Pakistan army has not ceased.[22]

In the regional context India is a major player in Afghanistan, and has ongoing economic aid and assistance programmes for infrastructure development. The emerging strategic equation between India and the US may help in faster development of infrastructure by Indian agencies. Killing of Indian engineers and workers by the Taliban are meant to slow down development work and discourage Indian constructive efforts. Stability of

Afghanistan is of major concern to India because of the tie up between terrorist groups of this region and the terrorist outfits of Kashmiri origin. Fundamentalist forces, however, pose threats to all the countries of the region and a cooperative effort by various countries is essential to curb their activities.

The desire for a quick, low cost victory and a cheap constructive effort is what has brought Afghanistan to the present state and an increasingly dangerous situation. A report published last November said that despite international efforts Afghanistan was still fifth from bottom on a global index of human development, this is a factor that require greater international effort, it is necessary to change the living conditions of the common man to wean him away from terrorism. As the armed conflict is likely to last many years the population needs to be reassured that there is a clear goal of improving their lot despite the prevailing conditions. Fight against insurgency must be based on enforcing the rule of law with priority given to police reforms and good governance. Short-term ad hoc anti-terrorism measures, reliance on poorly disciplined militias and discredited politicians will only undermine the long-term goal of achieving sustainable economic development. Political strategy based on making a deal with the Taliban is not likely to yield any tangible results. The key to restoring peace and stability in Afghanistan is meeting the legitimate grievances of the population who so for have supported the process of democratization.[23]

As the Afghan government lacks the capability to wear down Mujahidins and assorted militias insurgency will continue to threaten security of the country, particularly in the southern and eastern areas. NATO forces have struggled to bring these elements under control without much success, 2007 saw the worst violence since the fall of the Taliban with over 6,200 deaths including about 900 Afghan policemen; many experts see a bleak future for peace in 2008 even with the speculation that new strategies might succeed in attempts to reconcile some insurgent elements.

One of the troubling problems is the large number of unmarked landmines and scattered unexploded ordnance (UXO). Afghanistan is considered one of the most heavily mined countries in the world and there was a marked increase in the number of persons killed or wounded by landmines in 2007. The government has added de-mining as a 9th MDG priority.[24]

Peace is still far away in the wake of continued attacks and repeated cross-borders skirmishes between Afghan and Pakistan troops. Afghan President Hamid Karzai recently threatened to send Afghan troops across the border to fight militants in Pakistan, a forceful warning to the Pakistani government that his country is no longer ready to tolerate cross-border attacks. Hamid Karzai threatened to attack Taliban insurgents on the soil of his supposed ally in the "war on terror," saying his war-torn country had a right to do so in self-defence. On the other hand Pakistan's foreign office spokesman Mohammad Sadiq was quoted as saying by the government-run Associated Press of Pakistan news agency "Pakistan shall defend its territorial sovereignty."[25]

These are dangerous developments that could escalate into a military confrontation between Afghanistan and Pakistan leading to greater violence and chaos in the region.

References

1. Afghanistan—Wikipedia, the free encyclopedia, <http://en.wikipedia.org/wiki/Afghanistan>.
2. War in Afghanistan (2001–present) —Wikipedia, the free encyclopedia, <http://en.wikipedia.org/wiki/War_in_Afghanistan_(2001%E2%80%93present>.
3. Foreign relations of Afghanistan—Wikipedia, the free encyclopedia, <http://en.wikipedia.org/wiki/Foreign_ relations_of_ Afghanistan>.
4. The Troubled Afghan-Pakistani Border—Council on Foreign Relations, <http://www.cfr.org/publication/14905/troubled_afghanpakistani_border.html?breadcrumb=%2F>, *Op cit*, n. 3.
5. *Op cit*, n. 3.
6. *Op cit*, n. 3.
7. *Op cit*, n. 3.
8. *Op cit*, n. 3.
9. *Op cit*, n. 2.
10. *Op cit*, n. 1.
11. Al Jazeera English—News—Afghan Strategy Review Sought, <http://english.aljazeera.net/NR/exeres/9770A3CB-B6DB-412C-B538-D87EE1B69AD4.htm>.

12. Afghanistan: who is behind Baghlan suicide blast? | World War 4 Report, <http://ww4report.com/node/4645>.
13. Conn Hallinan: Afghanistan, A River Running Backward, <http://joun.leb.net/hallinan03182008.html>.
14. Foreign Policy In Focus | A River Runs, <Backwardhttp://www.fpif.org/fpiftxt/5059>.
15. *Ibid.*
16. *Op cit*, n. 14.
17. *Op cit*, n. 1.
18. *Op cit*, n. 1.
19. A spring offensive by any name | World news | guardian.co.uk, <http://www.guardian.co.uk/world/2008/may/21/spring.offensive>.
20. Karzai says Western forces bungled war on Taliban | Reuters, <http://in.reuters.com/article/southAsiaNews/idINIndia-33863420080602>.
21. Ibid.& Karzai says Pakistan supporting Taliban—South and Central Asia—msnbc.com http://www.msnbc.msn.com/id/16166102/
22. *Op cit*, n. 1.
23. OneWorld UK / In depth/Country Guides /Afghanistan, <http://uk.oneworld.net/guides/afghanistan/development?gclid=CNvNgYGR55MCFQMLewodXFsAWw>.
24. *Ibid.*
25. Pakistan, Afghan Leaders Swap Threats, <http://www.military.com/news/article/pakistan-afghan-leaders-swap-threats.html?ESRC=eb.nl>.

CHAPTER 11

War on Terrorism in Afghanistan: US Policy and Responses

Sanjeev Bhadauria

> *There is nothing more difficult to take into hand, more perilous to conduct or more uncertain in its success than to take the lead in the introduction of a new order of things...*
>
> —Niccolo Machiavelli, The Prince (1532)

The 9/11 attack on the World Trade Centre and the Pentagon changed the calculus by demonstrating how terrorists can use sanctuaries in the most remote and hitherto ignored regions of the world to mount devastating attacks against the United States and its friends and allies. In the post-9/11 world, national security experts are coming to the consensus that threats to U.S. security may arise from areas within states or at the boundaries between state that, for various reasons, are not controlled by a central authority. And so the US took the lead in undertaking the War on Terrorism in Afghanistan. But some critics have pointed out that it would not be appropriate to call the 'Afghan Insurgency' as 'war on terrorism' as the conduct of the United States and its allies indicates so far that they have probably deviated from their earlier objectives. As a result of the so called 'war on terrorism' or 'local insurgency', a serious disruption of the functioning of the community or society in Afghanistan is evident causing widespread human, material, economic and perhaps environmental losses which exceed the ability of the affected community or society to cope using its own present resources and hence the role of the stake holders especially that of the United States becomes extremely important.

The sudden changes brought on by the conflict has exacerbated problems that people face daily, and could challenge Afghanistan's national security by heightening conditions for conflict such as inequality, resource scarcity, social grievances, political tension, and distortions. The developmental failures have added to the vulnerabilities of the population and the political, economic, and social systems. Hence, these are serious concerns for Security which may be seen as lack of conflict, territorial claims, inequalities, defence of ideologies, racism and vulnerable human conditions. Thus, besides reducing Resource scarcity, Poverty/inequality, Political instability, Lack of development and Lack of human security the task of the US has to deal with the Militant Conflict and ensure the physical security of individuals in Afghanistan and reduce their vulnerable conditions

INSIDE AFGHANISTAN

The situation has improved in Afghan's capital-Kabul. But most rural parts of the country, where majority of Afghans live, remains beyond Mr. Karzai's control. The current "security-lite" strategy being followed by the United States and its NATO partners does not inspire confidence that Afghanistan will soon do better. President Hamid Karzai or his Successor will require more help from the international community to have a decent chance of avoiding future instability in his country and gradually improving the lives of Afghans. To add to it, Pakistan is in the grip of one of its worst political crisis in recent years.

As one senior NATO official mentions, the Taliban and other forces now operate in a large swath of territory that includes Afghanistan's western, southern, eastern, and parts of central Afghanistan. NATO and Afghan forces control at most 20 percent of southern Afghanistan. The rest is controlled by Taliban or a range of sub-state groups.[1] Another recent National Intelligence Estimate from the United States argued: "Al-Qaeda is and will remain the most serious terrorist threat to the Homeland.... We assess the group has protected or regenerated key elements of its Homeland attack capability, including: a safe haven in the Pakistan Federally Administered Tribal Areas (FATA), operational lieutenants, and its top leadership."[2] One senior Afghan government official stated in October 2007 about the insurgency in Afghanistan that now engulfs roughly half the country "Thc answer is simple. The people are losing faith in the government. Our security forces cannot protect local villages, and our institutions struggle to deliver basic services."[3]

The resurgence of civil war in Afghanistan can be attributed to two fundamental causes. **One** is the failure of the United States, the Karzai government, and the international community as a whole to take advantage of the lull in that conflict that followed the collapse of the Taliban regime in late 2001 to strengthen the capacity of the new Afghan government to project its authority and provide public services, including security, to the population beyond Kabul. The **second** cause is the fragmentation of the international coalition that the United States put together in late 2001 to stabilize and reconstruct Afghanistan. The situation can be gauged from the fact that Karzai is secure only inside his own compound, and doesn't trust his own Defence Ministry troops to act as his bodyguards.[4]

In Afghanistan, all politics is local. The country's history is littered with empires/countries that failed to understand this reality. The Taliban and its allies certainly understand the importance of local politics. They have successfully re-emerged by co-opting or threatening local villagers, and promising better governance and security than the current Afghan government. Afghans are frustrated by the lack of development over the past five years, and unhappy with widespread government corruption. This makes the Taliban's threat real and significant. The Taliban and its allies have a strong presence in local villages throughout such provinces as Kandahar and Helmand, and are preparing sustained operations. The message of the Taliban clearly has resonated with a growing number of locals in southern and eastern parts of the country. It is telling that the Taliban's primary target (to be influenced) is not U.S. or NATO forces, but local Afghans. This reflects the understanding that the local population represents the centre of gravity, as Mao Zedong famously wrote. Greg Grant in his analyses says "the U.S.-led coalition faces an emboldened and more effective Taliban today than it did six years ago, and that U.S. and NATO emphasis on Taliban body counts is meaningless because the Taliban have demonstrated they can raise and disband a fighting force at will."[5]

Greg in his article further says that "As American and world attention focuses on Iraq, the military situation in Afghanistan over the past year has so deteriorated that the shaky American and NATO coalition risks losing the war against the Taliban."[6] In a remarkable statement by Bin Laden's associate Abu Musab al-Zarkawi's successor Abu Hamza al-Masri, thanked President Bush for sending the US Army to Iraq and thus giving Al-Qaeda the "great historic opportunity" to engage Americans in direct fight on Arab ground[7] is a reflection of the flawed strategy adopted. In Afghanistan, the U.S. commanders say they have readily defeated the Taliban in every fight. But critics say the United States is losing the strategic battle because of its pursuit of a counter terror strategy that emphasizes killing and capturing Taliban, instead of a counterinsurgency strategy that places more emphasis on reconstruction. Although, it is true that the United States intervened in Afghanistan to destroy Al-Qaeda and the Taliban, not to rebuild the country or spread democracy, and has not adjusted its strategy since, says James Dobbins, a former U.S. special envoy to Afghanistan and director of the International Security and Defense Policy Center at RAND Corporation.[8]

But serious thinking needs to be done on whether the US would be able to fulfill both these objectives primarily on its own with the help of its allies or the local counter-insurgency forces are to be strengthened and made capable of handling the situation on their own in future. Anthony H. Cordesman, a leading expert on military and security developments in Afghanistan, in an interview admits that despite some gains, the situation remains tenuous and says that "We have seen in Afghanistan more success for the Taliban in 2007 than we saw in 2006. If you look at intelligence maps of the area of Taliban influence in Afghanistan, it has increased by about four times in 2006. It increased arguably, according to UN maps, by somewhere between 50 [percent] and

70 percent in 2007." He further adds that "NATO [North Atlantic Treaty Organization] has decisively defeated the Taliban in virtually ever tactical encounter it has had in the last year. But what you can see if you map something different, which is the area under the Taliban under political and economic influence when NATO is not actively present, these arc the areas where the influence has increased."[9]

THE CHALLENGE

Apart from the building of political institutions, other major Security Council goals (read US) that remain unfulfilled are enhancing internal security; disarming militias; countering the narcotics trade; building an effective, independent judiciary system; expanding human rights; improving health and education; and building critical infrastructure such as roads.

The United States must place four interlocking objectives:

(1) Afghanistan must establish internal and external security to ensure economic reconstruction, political stability, and stem the rise in opium production;
(2) It must work to establish a stable, effective, and broadly representative central government;
(3) The economic development must bolster this new government and reduce dependence on donors; and
(4) It must help the people of Afghanistan meet their critical humanitarian needs while reconstruction proceeds.

The costs of this ambitious set of goals are substantial. Michael O'Hanlon of the Brookings Institution estimates that between $15 billion and $50 billion is needed for the rebuilding of Afghanistan over a 10-year period and suggests that the United States provide at least 15 percent of the total aid to retain influence over "how the aid effort is administered and how the country is rebuilt."[10] The truth of the matter is that America as of now has not shown the inclination to arrange for the resources either in terms of aid, or troops that are needed in Afghanistan.

The United Nations mandated the International Security Assistance Force (ISAF) in Afghanistan. A specific challenge of international coordination that merits special attention is the mechanism of Provincial Reconstruction Teams (PRTs). There are now 25 PRTs in Afghanistan operating under the NATO-led International Security Assistance Force (ISAF). PRTs are led by the U.S. and 12 other NATO and Coalition partners; another dozen countries contribute personnel, financial and material support. The purpose of PRTs in Afghanistan is to extend the authority of the central government into the provinces. PRTs concentrate in three areas: governance, reconstruction and security. They should reflect the strategic overview of U.S. and NATO efforts in Afghanistan and play an assigned role, tailored to the local circumstances Ideally, the international coordinator, when appointed, should be tasked with overseeing the process of assessing, optimizing and synergizing the PRT mechanism. Alternatively, NATO should aim to create this process under its auspices. The NATO allies unanimously accepted responsibility for its success. All 26 allies have deployed troops and other security personnel, as have 11 non-NATO countries. All must understand that a resurgent Taliban, ISAF failure, and allied retreat would impose severe penalties.

Although, it cannot be said that the country has not moved forward in any way but there appears no end for the mess in which the US finds itself. Allies with responsibilities for police training (Germany), fostering a viable judiciary (Italy), and stemming the renewed flood of opium poppy production (Britain) have fallen far short of what they agreed to do. Worse, there is no overall coordination of civilian activities undertaken by governments, international institutions and non-governmental organizations, and far too few resources. The only pertinent saving grace for the success of the peacekeepers is that Afghanistan held presidential elections in October 2004 and parliamentary elections in September 2005. President Hamid Karzai has retained relatively high levels of support. According to a December 2007 public opinion poll, for instance, 63 percent of Afghans rated the work of President Karzai positively.[11] But, much needs to be done to facilitate a noticeable change in the overall situation.

Indeed, the primary challenge in Afghanistan is one of ***governance***. Governance includes the set of institutions by which authority in a country is exercised.[12] It is thus axiomatic that good governance cannot be exercised without adequate security mechanisms in place and so it can be safely said that perhaps the most basic governance challenge in Afghanistan is **security.** A recent assessment from Afghanistan's intelligence service, the National Directorate for Security, concluded that there are too few competent Afghan forces to provide security to the population in rural areas of the country.[13] The result is that key villages have fallen into the hands of the Taliban and other insurgent groups. The paradox of using civilians in Security and Reconstruction efforts is that civilians usually move out of rather than into areas of political instability. A complete manual for identifying, obtaining, and organizing human resources into an unstable area thus simply does not exist. The villages are gradually emptied of pro-government political forces and individuals. These rural areas become sanctuaries for the Taliban, and the population is left with no choice but to become sympathizers of the insurgents.

Another major challenge is **corruption.** Afghans have become increasingly frustrated with national and local government officials who are viewed as corrupt and self-serving. This sentiment is just as palpable in rural areas of the country as it is in the cities. U.S. military officers decry rampant corruption in the Afghan army and police. This corruption is structural, not just a question of corrupt individuals, and it reflects the low level of income of officials, They say Taliban fighters are paid better wages, reportedly $150 a month, than the Afghan army and police, who make $60 a month, with some of that skimmed off by officers.[14] An officer of the U.S. Army Maj. Tim Byrne, who spent a year training the Afghan army, says some units refused to go out on patrol alone "because they're scared to go up against the insurgents without U.S. support."[15] There are government officials at the district, provincial, and national levels involved in drug-trafficking, who are more interested in making money than in serving their populations. Indeed, rising levels in the cultivation, production, and trafficking of poppy have undermined governance.

Afghanistan has also faced challenges from **outside actors**, which have undermined governance. The first is a limited NATO role. Its roots can be traced back to the "light footprint" approach adopted by the United States and other international actors—including the United Nations—in 2001which continues even today. The U.S. military views Afghanistan as an "economy of force mission," a euphemism for few boots on the ground. There are now 27,000 U.S. troops there, though the country is 50 percent larger than Iraq and its population 16 percent bigger. Even when NATO's 21,500 troops are added, the size of the Afghanistan operation pales in comparison to past operations in Kosovo, with 40,000 troops, and Bosnia, with 60,000. On top of that, U.S. Special Forces with counterinsurgency skills have been pulled out of Afghanistan and sent to Iraq, leaving fewer than 500 to deal with the Taliban. The peacekeepers numbers were particularly insufficient because a number of NATO countries refused to become involved in combat operations. This practice has been referred to as "national caveats," In addition; political leaders were reluctant to deploy their forces into violent areas because of low domestic support for combat operations. In a German Marshall Foundation poll, for example, 75 percent of Germans, 70 percent of Italians, and 72 percent of Spanish did not support the deployment of their troops for combat operations in Afghanistan[16] is an indication of the shallow public support across Europe for the Afghan mission.

Although, NATO's Supreme Allied Commander, Gen. James Jones, says the alliance has sufficient manpower to fulfill its mission in Afghanistan but faces ultimate failure unless counternarcotics and reconstruction efforts improve. "Anything we do militarily is perishable if it's not accompanied by reconstruction," Jones while speaking at the Council on Foreign Relations briefing was of the opinion that "I think there is a requirement to do more and to bring more focus, more clarity, more purpose, and more results in a shorter period of time. And fundamentally, this is the exit strategy for Afghanistan."[17] This is easier said than done as the stake holders are involved too deeply in Afghanistan to exit suddenly without fixing the mess.

Unfortunately, there are no short-term solutions to Afghanistan's challenges. Research that Rand Corporation has done indicates that "It takes an average of 14 years for governments to defeat insurgent groups. Many also end in a draw, with neither side winning. Insurgencies can also have long tails: approximately 25 percent of insurgencies won by the government and 11 percent won by insurgents lasted more than 20 years. If one starts counting from 2002, when the Taliban began conducting limited offensive operations, history suggests that it would take *on average* until 2016 to win."[18] That is a long time for many NATO countries but it is realistic. This does not mean, however, that the US or other NATO countries need to—or should—win the insurgency for Afghans. While outside actors often play an important role, victory is usually a function of the struggle between the local government and insurgents. **First**, outside forces are unlikely to remain for the duration of any counterinsurgency effort, at least as a major combatant force. Since indigenous forces eventually have to win the war on their own, they must develop the capacity to do so. If they don't develop this capacity, indigenous forces are likely to lose the war once international assistance ends. **Second**, indigenous forces usually know the population and terrain better than external actors, and are better able to gather intelligence. **Third**, a lead outside role may be interpreted by the population as an occupation, eliciting nationalist reactions that impede success. **Fourth**, a lead indigenous role can provide a focus for national aspirations and show the population that they—and not foreign forces—control their destiny.

Some of the policy prescriptions aimed at addressing problems of governance will also reduce the region's conduciveness to terrorist activities, for example, building the capacity of the local military and counterterrorism forces. It should be understood that the ultimate objective of any nation-building mission is to leave behind a society likely to remain at peace with itself and its neighbour's once external security forces are removed and full sovereignty is restored. It is said that democratization and development can contribute to the achievement of this objective but it is a distant reality in a country facing a virtual collapse of governance. This is certainly the challenge in Afghanistan.

US POLICY AND ROLE

America's prior nation-building experiences suggest that external aid has a limited effect in the reconstruction of so-called failed states. Afghanistan provides a model for a broader policy framework wherein American intervention would be confined to eliminating national security threats rather than getting entangled in counterproductive nation-building exercises around the globe. The U.S. Army "clear by fire" tactics of lobbing artillery shells into areas suspected of harbouring insurgent fighters which has become common practice is flawed. When US units' patrol uncleared valleys, they use indiscriminate artillery fire to clear ridgelines. Lacking personnel, the United States and NATO rely on airstrikes that result in large numbers of civilian casualties and thus play into Taliban hands by stoking resentment. In a society that adheres to tribal concepts of revenge and honour, such mistakes are fatal. According to a Pashtun saying, it is said "Kill one enemy, make 10." The death of a Pashtun guerrilla in battle invokes the code of revenge, so killing a Taliban fighter is "an act of insurgent multiplication, not subtraction." This has to be clearly understood by the US policymakers.

The U.S. military forces currently operating in Afghanistan should concentrate on smashing the Taliban and Al-Qaeda remnants that are regrouping along the Afghanistan-Pakistan border. Once this goal is achieved, U.S. forces need not remain in the nation. Following the end of military operations, the focus could then shift to monitoring Afghanistan and its neighbours to ensure that forces that threaten the United States are not resurrected.

The current insurgency in Afghanistan does not arise from a profound disaffection among large elements of the Afghan population with their government. This insurgency has been raised in Pakistan, but individual's resident in Pakistan, some of whom are refugees from Afghanistan, others who are native Pakistanis. For the tens of millions of Pashtun tribesmen on both sides of the current border, the distinction between Afghan and

Pakistani is, indeed, of little importance, as neither they, nor the government of Afghanistan, for that matter, recognize the current border between the two countries as legitimate.

In order to undertake the challenge, the old cold war mindset deserves a re look. There seems to be a view that a relentless attack against Islamic insurgents wherever they surface should be waged. The view is as seemingly logical as the Cold War belief in a worldwide communist conspiracy for global domination—and just as wrong. The belief is also harmful, for four major reasons. Firstly, as in the Cold War, the belief in a global insurgency can lead the United States to make local commitments on the basis of vague overarching global principles. This commits America to send more troops, sustain greater military casualties, and spend more money than it possibly could in multiple conflicts at times and place of the insurgents' choosing. Secondly, a U.S.-led global counterinsurgency makes it more difficult for the United States to defeat insurgencies. Successful counterinsurgents fight as patriots in the service of their own country—not as United States clients. Thirdly, equipping Americans with a mindset that places prominence on the global common features of insurgencies at the expense of fine-textured local features makes the U.S. military less effective in combating insurgencies. Fourthly, belief in a global counterinsurgency leads to mismanagement of counterinsurgency campaigns because it undercuts the leadership of governments allied with the United States and of American military commanders battling an insurgency.

The United States can best aid Afghanistan by accelerating the war against Islamic extremists, paving the way for Afghans to reconstruct their own political and economic systems. The alternative—a U.S.-imposed political structure—will only serve to increase anti-American sentiment. An increase in the U.S. commitment to Afghanistan's reconstruction is unlikely to speed up that nation's progress toward stability and peace. With fighting between rival warlords still raging, and neighbouring nations vying for influence in Afghanistan, American entanglement in Afghan civil affairs will only distract from the major goal of eliminating the anti-American forces that were instrumental in the 9/11 attacks.

RECOMMENDATIONS

Hence, keeping these lessons in mind, a collective effort must be made to: (i) fight the Insurgency in Afghanistan, and (ii) invigorate the global war on terror for which Afghanistan was a test case. The Afghanistan specific recommendations for fighting Insurgency could be summed up as below:

- Concentrate on the main aim of destroying Al-Qaeda and Taliban—countering Sanctuary in Pakistan.
- Increase funds for rebuilding Infrastructure—'Reconstruction light'.
- Restrained use of force in Civilian areas-not "Clear by Fire" tactics.
- Understand the Local culture—family, clan, and tribal ties with concepts such as revenge and honour with less attachment and respect for the centralized state government.
- Establish a regional approach to Afghanistan with the aid of UN: encourage Pak-Afghan Border to be settled and ask India to scale down assistance.
- Indigenous forces eventually have to win the war on their own, they must be developed with the capacity to do so.

In order to energize the global war on terror certain steps could be taken which may be enumerated as under:

- Updating the UN Charter and breaking the Definitional Impasse on Terrorism.
- Launch 'Operation Global Peace'.
- Transform the global war as a truly UN led war.
- OIC, Russia and China be taken on board.
- Declare 2009 and 2010 as Years to Combat Global Terrorism.
- Centralized Control and Coordination HQ be set up for Regional Operations.
- Disrupt financing of Terrorist Networks.
- Ostracize Fence Sitters.
- Wage a War of Ideas.

The way forward for the Global War on Terrorism rests upon the International community and the leading global power. The efforts (i) should be focused and result oriented, especially in areas relating to law enforcement and prosecution. (ii)They should be seen as cooperation and not as dictation. (iii)They should avoid overlapping and duplication. (iv)They should also address the root causes.

CONCLUSIONS

The lesson for the United States and NATO is stark. They will win or lose Afghanistan in the rural villages and districts of the country, not in the capital city of Kabul. And if they are to win, they must begin by understanding the local nature of the insurgency. These include local history, terrain, demographics, culture, religion, power-sharing arrangements, leadership personalities and a host of subtle but critical idiosyncrasies not collected by intelligence satellites.

As we are seeing today in Iraq and Afghanistan, America has been unable to defeat insurgencies with the sheer power of the U.S. military. Despite a wealth of prior and recent experience, the U.S.-led attempts to rebuild Iraq and Afghanistan after American forces toppled their governments have been marked by unforeseen challenges and hastily improvised responses. Ultimately it will be the local conditions, population, unique features and personalities of each nation that will determine the outcome of the insurgencies against the U.S.-backed governments. The larger lesson is to retain the clarity of a "local" versus "global" perspective in dealing with the future insurgency challenge. Viewing the Taliban as nothing more than a highly radicalized vision of Islam, and viewing all Taliban as terrorists, misses the shared Pashtun tribal ethnicity of the insurgency and the family and clan ties that are stronger than any ties to the central government.

As far as troop and financial commitments to US and UN led nation building operations over the past sixty years, Afghanistan was the least resourced of any major American led nation building operation since the end of WW II. When one invests low levels of military manpower and economic assistance in post-conflict reconstruction, what one gets is low levels of security and economic growth. This has been the experience in Afghanistan. Afghanistan has never been a self sufficient state, and it probably never will be. It is simply too poor to be able to raise the revenues necessary to provide security and effective governance to a large and dispersed population. So, liberal external assistance is a necessary prerequisite for this war torn country. Security, Stability, Transition, and Reconstruction operations are a difficult and potentially lengthy process that requires appropriate resources.

Among the principal conclusions that can be drawn from historical hindsight is the extreme difficulty in putting together broken societies without the support of neighbouring states, and the near impossibility of suppressing well established insurgencies that enjoy external support and neighbouring sanctuary. The validity of this lesson is evident today both in Iraq and Afghanistan. The US should take effective steps which could contribute in its peacekeeping efforts. **First** the United States should intensify quite efforts to encourage both India and Pakistan to resolve their differences over Kashmir, that dispute being the root cause of radicalization in Pakistani society and governments use of terrorism as an instrument of state policy as geopolitically, Pakistan fears an independent Afghan state aligned with India. **Second**, the assistance programs need to address the economic and social needs of the Pashtun populations on both sides of the border, not just in Afghanistan. There is only limited benefit in winning the hearts and minds of Pashtuns resident in Afghanistan if the larger numbers of Pashtuns living in Pakistan remain hostile and ungoverned. **Third**, there is a need to encourage both the Afghan and Pakistani governments to establish an agreed border regime and legitimize the current frontier. American efforts alone, no matter how intense and skilful, will not be sufficient to achieve any of these objectives. An effective strategy is badly needed to involve Afghanistan's neighbours and regional powers in a renewed effort to end the war.

It should be clearly understood that if one's only tool is the hammer, it would not serve the purpose every time. In the changing world, the US badly needs some new tools. Only then it will be able to face the challenge it has undertaken. On the other front, the Afghans want Security and Hope which they deserve after 30 years of near-constant war. We all must remain optimistic but realism says it will take time.

REFERENCES

1. Jones Seth G., 2007, "The State of the Afghan Insurgency," Testimony presented before the Canadian Senate National Security and Defence Committee on December 10, 2007, Rand Corporation, CA, , p. 2.
2. National Intelligence Council, 2007, *The Terrorist Threat to the U.S. Homeland* (Washington, DC: Central Intelligence Agency), p. 5.
3. No. 1, p. 4.
4. Kaufman Marc, 2003. "U.S. Role Shifts As Afghanistan Founders," *Washington Post*, April 14.
5. Grant Greg, 2007, "Govexec.com: Tribal War: Taliban 2.0,"Council on Foreign Relations, NY, March 1.
6. Grant Greg, 2007, ggrant@govexec.com *Government Executive* March 1, p. 1.
7. Riedel Bruce, 2008, Al-Qaeda Strikes Back, Brookings Institution, Washington DC, April 14, p. 7.
8. Grant Greg, 2007, ggrant@govexec.com *Government Executive* March 1, p. 3.
9. Gwertzman Bernard, 2008, Consulting Editor, in an Interview with Anthony H. Cordesman, Arleigh A. Burke Chair in Strategy, Center for International and Strategic Studies, "Cordesman : Despite Gains, Future in Iraq, Afghanistan Remains 'Uncertain," Council on Foreign Relations, NY, January 14, p. 3.
10. Atal Subodh, 2003, "At a Crossroads in Afghanistan Should the United States Be Engaged in Nation Building?," CATO Institute' Washington, D.C., Foreign Policy Briefings, No. 81, September 24, p. 3.
11. ABC News/BBC/ARD, 2007, *Afghanistan—Where Things Stand* (Kabul: ABC News/BBC/ARD, December 2007), p. 16.
12. World Bank, 2006, *Governance Matters 2006: Worldwide Governance Indicators* (Washington, DC: World Bank), p. 2.
13. No. 1, p. 5.
14. No. 6, p. 1.
15. *Ibid.*

16. German Marshall Fund of the United States and the Compagnia di San Paolo (Italy), 2007, *Transatlantic Trends: Key Findings 2007* (Washington, DC: German Marshall Fund of the United States and the Compagnia di San Paolo), p. 33.
17. McMohan Robert, 2006, NATO Official Says Counternarcotics Strategy Needed to Stabilize Afghanistan, Council on Foreign Relations, NY, October 4, p. 1.
18. No.1, p. 6.

CHAPTER 12

Durand Line—Rising Geopolitical stakes in US's War on Terror

Ambrish Dhaka and Manash Ranjan Mishra

INTRODUCTION

The line between Afghanistan and Pakistan demarcated by Sir Mortimer Durand in the agreement with Amir Abdur Rahman Khan has been one of the live testimony to the geopolitics of the sub-continent. The geopolitics has its own explanation in terms of south Asian communities unlike the play between the nation-states in Europe. The ethno-geopolitics is more comprehensive term to describe the geopolitical dynamics of the region. The ethnic communities have often found themselves in reference to core-periphery relations vis-a-vis south Asian state powers. The peripheral communities have shown unique adaptability to align themselves with the ascendant power and throw the garb of the declining state.

The paper aims at examining the hypothesis that the growing scope of US's Global War on Terror (GWOT) has recursive implications for south Asian stability and security. The ethno-geopolitical basis of Durand line can lead to destabilisation of state polity in Afghanistan and Pakistan, which has effects for India and beyond. If one looks at the history of the Durand line then it is clear that its phoenix like rise to geopolitical reverberations has been temporal since its agreement in November 1893.

The Durand line had three distinct phases of geopolitical significance since demarcation. The first phase consisting of Cold war immediately after the formation of India and Pakistan; the second phase of Soviet intervention and the *Jihad* follow up, and the third that of post-Taliban period to present times.

THE BRITISH GEOPOLITICAL PERSPECTIVE

The British had already reached western extents after the annexation of Sindh. This was followed by the first Anglo-Sikh war which lead to capture of Lahore. The finality of which came to rest with the annexation of Punjab by Dalhousie in second Anglo-Sikh war in 1849. The British after the Sikh war were besieged with the dilemma of exploring the territorial limits. Their expansionism new only the boundary being defined by a rival power which was little far away in 1850s, notably, the Russia. The Duke of Wellington called for natural frontier logic that would portray the banks of the Indus as the limits of the British India, and this was invariably corroborated by Lord Lawrence.[1] (Davies: 1932) But, the river was occupied with meanders that would flush down newer courses after every monsoon season; thus Indus not only made a weak line of defence, but also a bad political boundary. The forward policy camp under the leadership of Lord Lansdowne advocated the opening of the Gomal pass or the expansion of the British control over the Zhob and Bori valleys as well as retention of Kandahar on military, political and commercial grounds.[2] (Malhotra, 1982)

The lessons of the Second Anglo Afghan war had important bearing upon the British policy towards the tribal areas in the northwest. The Russians were not at that time in their immediate calculations, but only commanded influence among the Forward policy supporters who believed the need for advance positions, just as in Gilgit. The Close border policy advocated the limiting of British dominion to the settled parts of the eastern regions of the Hindukush mountain chains. The Treaty of Gandamak 26 May 1879 after the Second Anglo-Afghan war sealed the fate of the most of the territorial demarcation that were to follow as Durand line.[3] (NAIFD, 1879) The precursor to these had been the Anglo-Russian Treaty of the 1872 known as the Granville-

Gortachkov agreement of 1872-73. The treaty stated that the Badakhshan with its dependent districts of Wakhan from Sir-i-Kul on the east to the juncture of the Kokcha River with the Oxus forming the northern boundary of this Afghan province throughout its entire length. The Oxus continued to be the boundary as far as the ferry of Khwaja Salar, on the road between Balkh towards the sea of Aral, further west it was agreed that a line should be drawn from Khwaja Salar towards the Persian frontiers to include Andhkoi and Maimana in Afghanistan, but it was stipulated by the Russian government that the old city of the Merv and adjacent Turkoman districts should be excluded from the possessions.[4] (Sykes, 1981) These in fact created the residuary territorial control for the Amir Sher Ali. The northern influence was defined at one level between the two giant spheres. This infact, a precursor to the Durand line has gone into subsequent demarcation of Afghanistan boundary, both in Durand agreement and later the Pamir agreement of 1895.

Strategic Depth Argument—Tsarist Russia (in South Asia)

The British had concluded several treaties prior to Durand line agreement with the Amir of Kabul throughout 19th and 20th century. The Shah Shuja-Elphinstone Treaty (1809), Shah Shuja-Auckland Simla Manifesto (1838), Dost Mohammed-Sir John Lawrence Treaty of Peshawar (1855) and Yakub Khan-Lord Lytton Treaty of Gandamak (1879) exposed some of the serious concerns of the British regarding the possible incursions of the Russians facilitated by the Persians. The Kabul was regularly seen as counterpoised to Herat and Bukhara from where there was a possibility of the Russian-Persian advances. The internal component of this was that Kandahar was to be brought under the Kabul fold and desist Kabul's temptations over Peshawar which the British considered well under the Sikh dominion. The First Anglo-Afghan war in 1842 for the first time offered the reversal of movement from Indus Basin to Kabul valley through Khyber Pass. General Pollock for the first time took his troops from Peshawar to Jalalabad. This also made them realised of the unruly space between the Persian, Russian and the British Empire that was hard to put under singular control. Dost Muhammed in

1850s conquered most of the northern and south-eastern Afghanistan. He even briefly held Peshawar but, Herat was outside his purview until 1863, when he conquered in May but died in June. It is believed that Amir's relinquishing of Peshawar and even during Indian mutiny (1857), not exploiting the Treaty of Peshawar to this effect actually sealed the fate of Afghanistan's influence towards east of Khyber pass.

Political History of the Durand Line

The agreement between the Amir of Afghanistan, Abdur Rahman Khan and Sir Henry Mortimer Durand, Foreign Secretary, Government of India meant to draw a line for 'fixing the limit of their respective spheres of influence, so that for the future there may be no difference of opinion on the subject between the allied Government.' The key feature of the agreement were, as follows:

(a) The line had been drawn already at the time of agreement.
(b) The limit of influence is to be exercised with reference to this boundary.
(c) Asmar valley upto Chandak is retained by the Amir. The Swat, Bajaur or Chitral (including Arnawai and Bashgal valley) are retained by the British. The Birmal tract is given to Amir and rest of Waziristan and Dawar is given to the British, as well Chageh.
(d) The Joint British and Afghan Commissioners to mark the frontier line with all practical adjustments keeping in mind of the existing local rights of the villages adjoining the frontier.
(e) Amir relinquishes his claim on Chaman, with modifications as mentioned.
(f) Expression of satisfaction over the agreement.
(g) Raising embargo from Afghanistan purchasing war munitions with some British help. Subsidy to the Amir raised to twelve lakh rupees per annum.
(h) Dated: Kabul, 12th November 1893; signed by H.M. Durand and Amir A.R. Khan[5] (NAIFD, 1894).

The demarcation process was conceived into four stages by Amir Abdur Rahman Khan. First was under Mr.Udney and Gulam Hyder Khan the Amir's representatives were entrusted upon dealing the boundary line from Asmar to Safed Koh, south of Landi Kotal. The total length of the boundary defined by the agreement is something over 130 miles.[6] (NAIFD, 1894)The second under Mr. J.Donald and Sardar Sherindil Khan, demarcating the Kurram frontier from Peiwar Kotal to the Laram Peak. The third under Mr. R.I. Bruce for demarcating Waziristan boundary from Shariangarh Peak west of Waziristan to Domandi. Mr McMohan was appointed in the fourth commission, for the delimitation and demarcation from Domandi to Koh-i Malik Siah. Geographically that areas falls into two parts first from Domandi to Chaman at distance of 330 miles and second 470 miles length Chaman to Koh-i Malik Siah.[7] (NAIFD, 1895)

Geographic Divide: The Khyber Pass and the Hindukush

The Hindukush mountains are a major divide between the south Asia and the west, central Asian realms. The major Khannates of Kokand, Khiva, Bukhara and Khorasan were the neighbours of Kabul Amir. The Kabul was ideally located as geocultural entrepôt between the west, central and inner Asia leading to Sikiang and China. This historic location had renditions from the past recounting Buddhist times to medieval influence of Sufism descending towards south Asia. The mountains are one of the most convenient demarcation zones between two river valley civilisations or communities. The division of water through watershed offers the most suitable explanation to this. But, how one can divide the space between the two mountain dwelling communities, obviously the river thalweg is the best option. The Afghanistan-British India represented the unique situation. The Indo-Gangetic basin could be easily separated from the Persia or the Khiva-Kokand-Bukhara Khannates through Hindukush. But, delimitation of Kabul dominion which itself was located in the Hindukush mountains was a little intricate exercise. The Kabul's perception of the zone could be the line from where the plains start and the mountains end. The British however, perceived that they needed an advance line of defence that would allow them to keep them informed of any possible advances of the enemy. This meant identification of the first line of defence in the Hindukush mountains itself.

Afghanistan and Pakistan Boundary

The Durand line has been subject of debate not because of demarcation as an issue, but the role that has been assigned to it as an international boundary. The division of Mohmand and the Waziris was historic dispute as one of the consequences of the principle of watershed as boundary demarcation. The map shown here clearly demarcates the Mohamand agency in the north of Jalalabad. The Waziristan has also some of its tribes on the west of the Durand line, however the major part of these are still on eastern part. The major groups such as the Mahsuds, Daurs are concentrated in the Kurram, North and South Waziristan agencies. The boundary conception was not in terms of international borders, but in terms of frontier demarcation.[8] (NAIFD, 1894)

This precisely meant that the local level affairs would not be touched upon unless there is consequential upon the interests of the states concerned. This ultimately revealed that the while the delimitation of the territories would mark the area of jurisdiction for the Amir and the Government of Punjab as immediate party concerned. It also created the British strategic defence so far Persia and Russia are concerned. The Amu Darya which had been transformed into territorial demarcation feature for Afghanistan and Russia clearly was a hand out decision to Afghanistan as the northern boundaries for it were secured by the Anglo-Russian treaty of 1872. The geographic argument held for Durand line is not upheld for the Amu Darya, where it is the river thalweg that is considered for the boundary rather than northern mountain limits of Hindukush.

POST-SOVIET AFGHANISTAN AND DURAND LINE

The Soviets before leaving in February 1989 wanted to ensure that Najibullah is in some way integrated into the new government that would allow to stabilise the major political

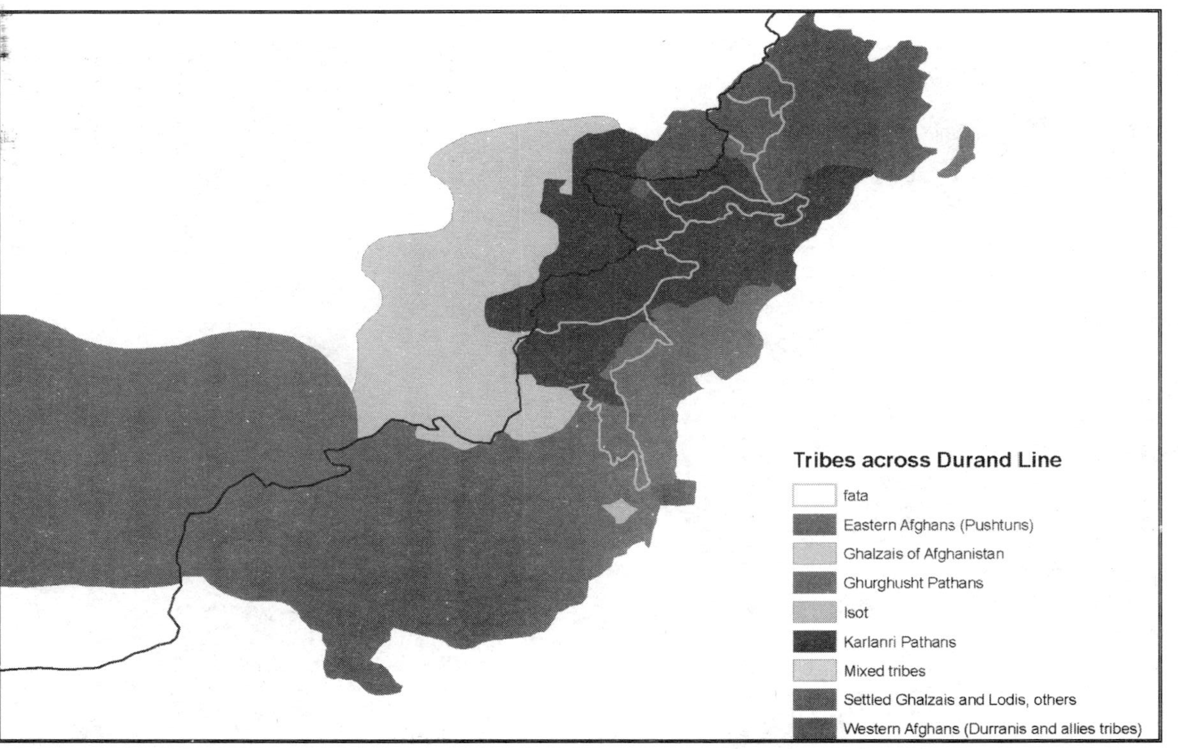
Tribes across Durand Line
fata
Eastern Afghans (Pushtuns)
Ghalzais of Afghanistan
Ghurghusht Pathans
Isot
Karlanri Pathans
Mixed tribes
Settled Ghalzais and Lodis, others
Western Afghans (Durranis and allies tribes)

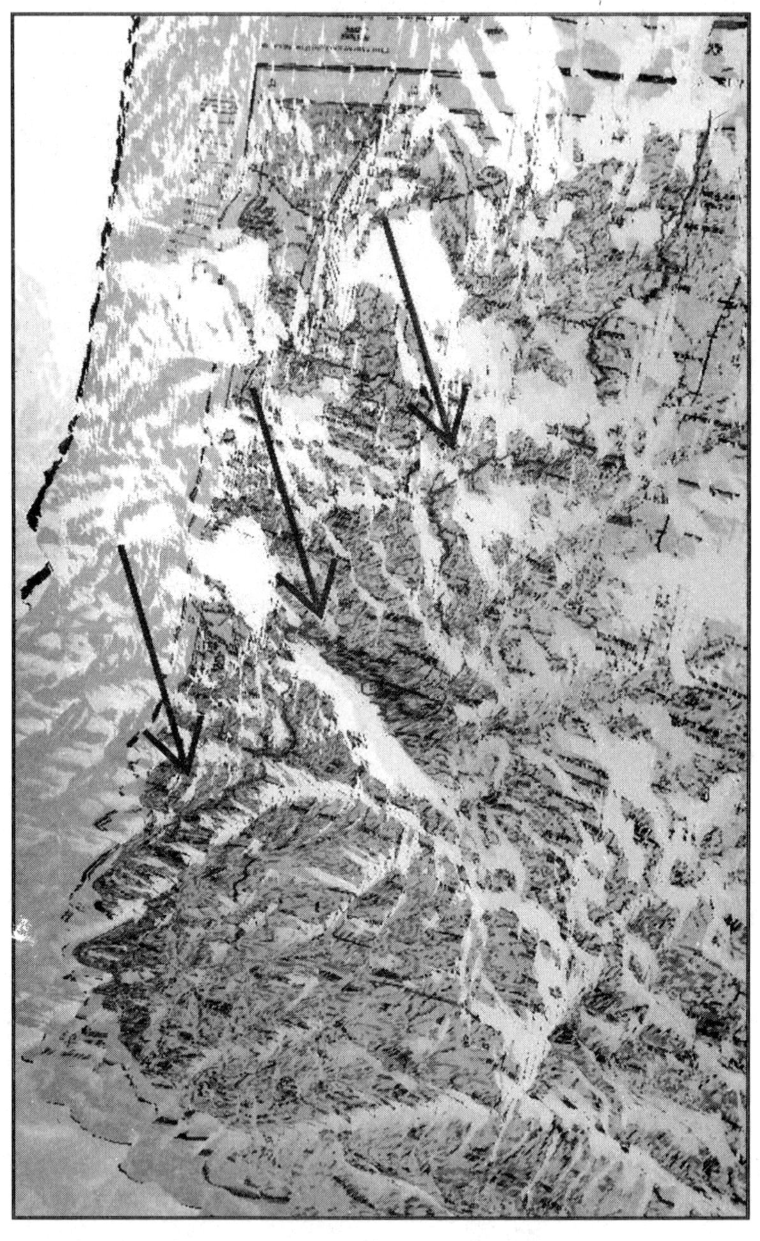

warring factions around the residuary power structure. There were five principal organised armed groups, namely, the Jombesh under the leadership of Rashid Dostum, the Jamiat groups under the leadership of B. Rabbani and A. Masud, the Jamiat faction headed by Ismail Khan, the Hizb groups under the leadership of G. Hekmatyar and Khalis, and the Wahadat under K. Khalili and Mazari.[9] (Dorronsoro, 2000)The factions were encouraged by the Soviets to mend their differences so that a stable political set up is created. The Soviet retreat created a situation where the Khalq leaders started hobnobbing with the Hekmatyar. The Hizb-i Watan party of Najibullah split days before signing of Peshawar (24 April 1992) accords and few of its members (Abdul Wakil, Nabi Azmi) defected towards Masud, helping him and Dostum occupy Kabul just at the time of the accord. The situation varied at every geographic location. The Mazar-i Sharif witnessed cooperation between the Wahadat and Jombesh. The Kabul saw cooperation between the Jombesh, Wahadat and Jamiat in the early phase of 1992. The attack by Masud on Wahadat positions led them to take sides with Hekmatyar, and even their own split. The Persians tried to influence the Shia led Wahadats to come to terms with the Hekmatyar. The Jombesh played neutral to Jamiat and Hizb conflict during 1993. The neutrality was however, compromised by one of the generals of Dostum in 1994, who decided to support Hizb against Jamiat owing to its growing insecurity from another Jamiat leadership under Ismail Khan. The territorial control of these groups fairly represented the watershed divide of Afghanistan.

Ethnicisation of Conflict

The regional pitching of the forces created the trench warfare kind of situation, where each group was holed up into their respective positions except the Jamiat and the Hizb who were relying on temporal alliances to outdo each other. The regional organisation of forces was clearly from 1992 to 1995 where the major positions considered were that of the Jamiat, Jombesh and the Wahadat areas which covered most of the Afghanistan. The south-eastern positions were especially commanded by the Mahaz, Jebhe and Ettehad groups often oscillated between the

Jamiat and Hizb alliances. But, the deep animosity between the Wahadat and Ettehad-Mahaz-Jebhe-Harkat based on Shia-Sunni differences created a deep rooted problem of leadership within the coalition.

Some of the most tricky issue is the ethno-political divide that has been weighted now under the geopolitical influences. The present situation is one where the political and administrative build up is an all ethnic affair as is evident since the inception of the Bonn process. The basic character that evolved during the conflict of personal loyalties has got itself seated into the present system as well. The appointment of the officials and the local benefits are all according to the preferences of the commanders who now are either holding their positions in elected bodies or as pressure groups in cohort with the regional set up facilitated by the NATO policy makers. One such débâcle was the Musa Kalan fiasco, where the TAQ forces finally duped the British on their previous commitments and had to be thrown out after falling into latter's disfavour.

The political outfits such as Jamiat-i Islami, Hizb-i Islami, Jombesh and Wahadat all have their leadership working in the present situation. But, their political identities have not been allowed to mobilise in the electoral process. This democracy without party system is one of the confusing situation, where the masses hardly feel themselves politically motivated. The party system though in the post-Soviet phase was reduced to ethnic formations, at least provided an opportunity to rally behind a set of interests which can be seen as national at some level, for e.g., the *jihad* against the Soviet occupation. This marked absence of national formation has limited the further maturing of the reconstruction process in Afghanistan. The reconstruction and development as promoted by ISAF is also showing the sign of regional negotiated arrangement with the groups. The post-Taliban Afghanistan had hoped that king would be of some rescue in the situation, but his old age and now his being no more is an option perhaps lost for all practical purposes. The rise of new Afghanistan as if one would envisage demands that international presence is to be there for decades to come as some of the past memories of war get wiped out and new generation takes seat.

This is the only long enduring hope that can make Afghanistan a viable society and state.

The Taliban Rule of Afghanistan from 1996 to 2001

The advent of Taliban addressed the fractured position where the law and order within the urban areas was worst where the political parties partitioned the city as their zone of influences. The most holistic position was seen in Herat under the aegis of Ismail Khan. Taliban arose under the framework of leadership consisting of the eastern Pushtuns and subsequently got an interface of the Kandhari (Durrani) Pushtuns.[10] (Dorronsoro, 2000) They were seen initially as an ally to Rabbani government due to their opposition to the Hizb-i Islami leadership of Hekmatyar. This confusion helped them to increase their proximity to Kabul, till 1995. The year 1996 saw them fully established in the capital and by 1998 they had control on most of the Taliban. The decimation of Wahadat and setback to Jombesh created a bipolar situation in Afghanistan by 1995, when only Masud and Taliban faced each other and others rallying behind them. This also created the polarisation of support with Russia, Iran and Central Asian states coming together in support behind Masud and Pakistan, Saudi Arabia and US's tacit support to Taliban.

The advent of Taliban was the weakest phase of identity of Durand line. The cross-border logistics were visible since the days of Jalalabad in 1989. The capture of Khost in 1991, Kandahar 1994, Shindand air base 1995, attack against Masud in 1995 and Mazar-i Sharif operations in 1998 were the high-points of ISI led support mechanism working in favour of Taliban. The first Gulf war alienated the Hizb-i Islami from the US policy preferences, Taliban was alienated in the second Gulf war in the similar manner.

Post September 11, 2001 US's war against Taliban and Al-Qaeda

The war against Taliban and Al-Qaeda (TAQ) forces began soon after the twin tower attack. The Taliban tried to hold ground, but were decimated in the two months of initial onslaught that stayed upto December 2001. The strategy for flushing out the

Taliban leadership essentially depended on the support provided by the Northern Alliance troops, who gave ground intelligence and front movement to the anti-TAQ coalition. These forces had resounding success in most of the northern and western Afghanistan, but their clashes were heavy all near the Durand line. The Nangerhar, Khost, Paktia and Kandhar showed localised resistance against the coalition forces. The TAQ leadership soon left the battle zone, but the southern and eastern Afghanistan showed phases of volatility in successive stages.

US Operations in FATA

The NATO clearly declared its intention of looking for the Al-Qaeda and Taliban operatives in the Federally Administered Tribal Areas (popularly known as FATA) territory. The reasons were not hard to see. The TAQ forces had erected their logistics structure and its success was visible in 2007. The cross-border support was evident as all the Afghan provinces bordering Durand line were witnessing intense retaliation by the TAQ forces. The new situation that emerged in 2007 the pattern of distinct engagement at the two fronts along the Durand line. The northern front showed activity concentrated at Khost, Kunarha and Nangerhar provinces. These operative units were attacking as far as Badakhshan and Takhar provinces where there is hardly any Taliban presence. The second TAQ unit appears to be located in Kandhar, Ghazni and Zabul area. Here, they have been attacking Nimroz, Helmand and Wardak provinces. Most noticeable is the absence of any Taliban operations in the central provinces of Afghanistan, such as, Bamiyan, Daikondi, Ghor and Samangan. These are also the Hazara dominated regions which were the worst suffers under the Taliban rule. The pattern and intensity of attacks shows that there is distinct support, both, logistic and material from outside Afghanistan. This can be confirmed by the fact that though there is general level of violence, the concerted attack to engage NATO-ISAF forces at different points reveals the strategic afterthought once the TAQ forces had suffered initial losses in 2004. This comes to explain why there is finger pointing at Pakistan and by no lesser terms on Iran too. The history is testimony to the fact that the Bajaur and Waziristan had been the twig in the eye of the British Raj,due to their habitual unpredictable behaviour. These regions have been also the suitable breeding grounds for Islamic jihadis wanted in Kashmir and elsewhere. The situation has become critical in the current year with coalition casualties already running as well as the despair among the contributing nations, who see it as an unforeseen situation of stay. The need to deliver upon the promises has prompted the US to harangue Pakistan for reigning the militants under the TAQ framework.[11] (http://www.independent.co.uk) The military operations that have been launched there have led to the further alienation of the Pushtuns in FATA region and both Pakistan and Afghanistan governments are being accused of attacking the innocent people in the operations. The small number of US experts embedded into the FATA operations conducted by the Pakistan army have been pointing finger at the hard-liners within the Pakistan army who are responsible for intelligence failure behind several operations along the Durand line.

Violation of Durand line by US forces can destabilise FATA

The US drones finding and hitting the targets has create certain scare among the TAQ logistics and their efforts to design and execute an attack has been hampered. The so far spring offensive has been much controlled as compared to the last year, although the mid-year situation shall be more credible account of any claimed success. The reports available from the various agencies have claimed major losses for the Taliban have occurred this year. These are effective in minimising the operations capability of the Talibans. The major step has been to increase troops support for ground operations. The US marines and various NATO countries have been raising their troop numbers this year. This is particularly important so far as the southern Afghanistan is concerned. The major challenge however remains of identifying the most reliable non-Taliban Pushtun leadership from Kandhar, who could significantly bolster the reconstruction process in Afghanistan. There has been no leadership from these former Taliban strongholds. The another challenge is to isolate the TAQ forces within the FATA region.[12] (http://terrorismanlysts

.com) These forces have strong traditional hold throughout Pakistan under the network of Jamiat-ul Ulema (JUI) and MMA organisational spread. The present situation is delicate where NATO forces are attacking them in south Waziristan and other areas that has incurred public criticism of Pakistan's acquiescence to these acts. The tribal elders were always trusted to bring out any negotiated settlement through jirga discussions amidst warring parties. Pakistan's President Musharraf had offered tranquillity in exchange for desisting from terror acts, but this has boomeranged in several tribal elders already paying with their lives under such a situation.

DURAND LINE ISSUES

The Afghan-Pak border has several levels of functionality owing to its geopolitical history. The immediate local functionality is defined by the territorial division it outlays for the two countries. The second important aspect is the gateway to south Asia. The oil and gas transit is much more in vogue among academic circles. There are vast array of other possibilities of trade and commerce that lies between the two regions. The most vital functionality is defined in the possible direction of the Europe-Asia system of nations and communities. This is incipient in terms of north-south trade & transit corridor, but the revival of silk route under the multinational infrastructure that can come up facilitating movement of goods and peoples would be a very significant development.

The Challenges for Afghanistan State

The level of functionality envisaged above first of all demand a stable and secure statehood in Afghanistan. This task now appears to be a protracted one. The global community is only a mute spectator to what NATO-ISAF does in Afghanistan. There needs to descend down to a UN mission that can broad base the reconstruction and development programmes that are being run in Afghanistan. The peacekeeping operations can only succeed if Afghan police and military is sufficiently capable of turning out adequate response to the sectarian forces. This apart the social base needs to be strengthened through the education and health issues that rein high in the present state. There are pressures on economic side too as the current narcotic economy heavily dependent on cross border smuggling would only keep the state a client of external forces. The land and water reforms though considered a source of discontent during the PDPA regime need a fresh initiative so that people can be provided an assured basis of livelihood where not much economic activity lies. The second important sector is the construction and mining where maximum investment can be done for expanding the employment base in the society.

Cross-border Drug Trade and Warlords

The narcotic economy of Afghanistan is one of the most worrying issue. It contributes to nearly half of the Afghanistan economy. According to the Afghanistan Human Development Report 2007, out of total value of the opium produce only a fourth share reaches the farmer whereas the rest is pocketed by the traffickers. A third of the produce goes by Pakistan making Durand line a vital link between the Afghan farmers and Pak traffickers. The narcotic earnings have been channelled into the war funding by TAQ forces, and they found it lucrative even before 2001 as a quick source of revenue. The attempt to reduce the opium production has been strongly resisted in southern Afghanistan and most of this discontent has been wisely exploited by the TAQ forces. It remains to be seen how the economy of Afghanistan can be shifted from trading into this drug economy to other agro-business products such as dry fruits, vegetables, flowers and even meat products. A better assurance to the farmers about the price of their produce could well be the starting point to look ahead.

Consequences for South Asia

Durand line is seen as limits to the US intervention in south Asia per se. This deters lest it has significant implications for political stability in Pakistan. The nuclearisation of Indian and Pakistan's arsenal and the lack of trust between the two nations could further undergo jeopardy if the US presses further. The hardliners and the army in Pakistan would not miss it an opportunity to create an insecurity scare and this has long term implications for the stability and security in south Asia. The another aspect is the political sensitisation of the tribal regions of Pakistan. Any lowering of stakes of Durand line as an international boundary might create a new regional demand, which would again have spillover effects within Pakistan, such as, the Baluchistan issue. This might not be very positive situation again for India as the Kashmir peace process would certainly find Pakistan backing out in all zeal to counter-balance the geopolitical situation. The volatile borders have always made state insecure of its territorial possessions. The Durand line being hard pressed for total border control has led to limiting of exchanges and the natural trans-border cultural, social and economic linkages being snapped by the respective state. This is more aggravating as Durand line is in a tribal region which has strong cross-border ties. Thus, a stable functionality of Durand line is needed for a cohesive development of civic life in the frontier regions of Pakistan and Afghanistan.

REFERENCES

1. Davies, C. Collin, 1932: The Problem of the North West Frontier 1980-1908, London: Cambridge University Press.
2. Malhotra, Ravi Inder. 1982: Search for Identity Frontier Settlement 1872-93, New Delhi: D.K. Publication.
3. National Archives of India, Foreign Department Files: 1879:32.
4. Sykes,Persy.1981: A history of Afghanistan, London: Macmillan.
5. National Archives of India, Foreign Department Files: 1894:196.
6. National Archives of India, Foreign Department Files: 1894:9.
7. National Archives of India, Foreign Department Files: 1895:21.
8. National Archives of India, Foreign Department Files: 1894:1.
9. Dorronsoro, Gilles, 2005: Revolution Unending: Afghanistan 1979 to the Present: Colombia University Press: New York.
10. The Independent, "Pakistan: A crucial moment in the history of a troubled nation," http://www.independent.co.uk, Saturday, 1 September 2007.
11. Perspectives on Terrorism, "Dealing with FATA: Strategic Shortfalls and Recommendations" by Faryal Leghari, http://www.terrorismanalysts.com.

CHAPTER 13

Afghanistan's Narcotics Dilemma

Haroun Mir

INTRODUCTION

Before the start of conflict in 1979, Afghanistan was not a prominent producer of opium among the "Golden Crescent"[1] countries. Iran alone was producing an estimated 600 tons per year of opium gum, Pakistan another 500 tons, and Afghanistan roughly 300 tons.[2] Opium production became widespread in Afghanistan when Iran started to curb on its production after the Islamic revolution in 1979, and when Pakistan introduced the "Hadd Ordinance" the same year.[3] Today Afghanistan has become the major producer of opium not only in the Golden Crescent region but in the entire world.

Indeed, the Soviet invasion of Afghanistan, followed by two decades of strife and internal conflict destroyed Afghanistan's economic infrastructures and political cohesion, which served as precursor for illicit economy of opium producing and drug processing in Afghanistan. Today, income from opium constitutes more than 50% of Afghanistan's GDP.

Since the collapse of the Taliban regime in 2001, there have been consistent efforts by the Afghan government, donor countries, and the United Nation to reduce opium cultivation and drug processing in the country. However, despite financial and military efforts the opium production has been increasing since 2004.

The majority of studies and analysis on Afghanistan's drug economy highlight insurgency, poverty, lack of rule of law, administrative corruption, weak government, and war lordism as major impediments for anti-drug policy implementation in Afghanistan. However, they ignore the nature and prominence of illicit and contraband business in the region which has promoted opium cultivation in the country.

The failure of counter narcotics policies in Afghanistan are not solely due to policy implementation but also with policy formulation. In fact the first major anti-drug policy in Afghanistan was formulated and funded by the British authorities, which has failed despite a large budget of more than £ 100 million. And there is serious and growing doubt about the success of the new US anti-drug strategy in Afghanistan.

One of the major obstacles for formulation and implementation of an efficient and effective anti-drug policy is lack of understanding by the Western experts of Afghanistan's peculiar and non-economic factors which have arose due to almost three decades of conflict. Until now the focal point of anti-drug policies in Afghanistan has been short-term law enforcement efforts, whereas the country needs a long-term development strategy to deal with the issues emanating from narcotics.

The objective of this paper is to highlight the causes of proliferation of drug trafficking and reasons for policy failure in Afghanistan, which have remained ignored by policy makers in the country.

ECONOMIC BACKGROUND OF AFGHANISTAN

In terms of GDP per capita, Afghanistan has remained in the trap of poverty as one of the poorest countries in the world. According to United Nations standards, the Afghan economy resides at the ranks of the world's Least Developed Countries (LDCs). The country's base of economy has always been agriculture and animal husbandry, with only few small factories. Only recently the services sector has increased due to influx of aide money, which accounts for more than 40% of the economy.

Agriculture constitutes only about 30.27 percent of GDP and industrial production represents 26.65 percent of GDP.[4]

Prior to the start of the conflicts in 1979, Afghanistan was considered self-sufficient in terms of its agricultural production, except for the years it faced severe droughts and had to import food or seek aid from the international community. In other areas of production such as industrial sector, it did as well as agricultural and livestock sectors. Statistics, from the Ministry of Planning in 1971, show that the country was well on track towards increasing domestic production and economic prosperity. However, today Afghanistan produces below its capacity of 1971. (Fig. 1)

In the 1960s and 70s, there were attempts to modernize the Afghan economy. A number of countries such as the United States, the former Soviet Union, Britain, Germany, France, Japan, and some other countries provided financial, technological and educational support to enhance and modernize the Afghan economy. In late 1970s, following the path of many other developing countries, Afghanistan took the path of a failed centralized planned economy. With the Communist coup in 1978, people lost control over valuable property rights. During the subsequent two decades of conflict, much of the country's economic infrastructure was destroyed. Most of the irrigation canals were ruined and valuable animal stocks were reduced to dangerous levels. Destruction of the schools and educational systems caused young boys and girls to grow up without any formal or traditional education. After the fall of the Communist Regime in 1992, Afghanistan fell even into deeper political chaos. Its ties with the world, particularly the international multilateral organizations were severely damaged. The majority of Afghans had to rely on assistance from Non-Governmental Organizations (NGOs) and humanitarian aid agencies for their survival.

Immediately after terrorist attacks in September 11, 2001 in the US, the world's focus turned back to Afghanistan. Despite, the influx of aid money, and presence of coalition force Afghanistan has become the largest drug producer in the world. (Fig. 2)

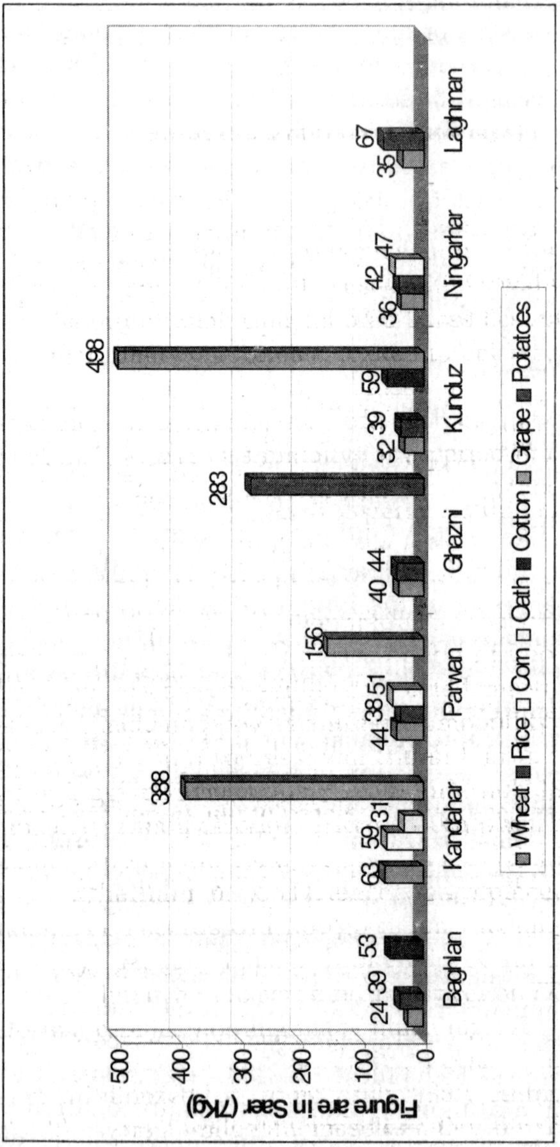

Fig. 1: Average of Main Agricultural Products (Per 2000 Square Meter of Land)

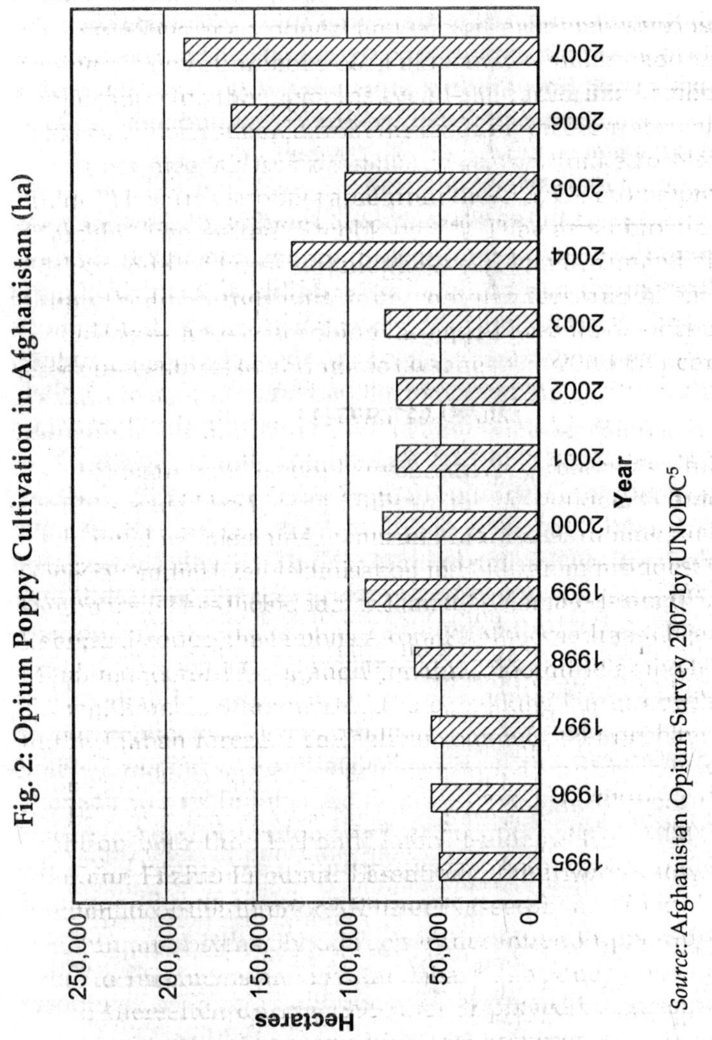

Fig. 2: Opium Poppy Cultivation in Afghanistan (ha)

Source: Afghanistan Opium Survey 2007 by UNODC[5]

The record production of opium in 2007 has alarmed the international community. Afghanistan is slowly sliding towards a failed narco-state. In addition, it compromises NATO's efforts to curb Taliban and Al-Qaeda's activities in the region. The majority of Western experts on Afghanistan have reached the conclusion that the military efforts against insurgency and narcotics are intertwined and must be coordinated jointly.

III. CAUSES FOR OPIUM POPPY CULTIVATION IN AFGHANISTAN

Indeed, there are multiple factors which have pushed farmers to abandon traditional crops for much lucrative opium poppy. But the following three elements are so far the most important determinants: First of all absence of government authority and rule of law due to almost three decades of conflict, which have created an enabling environment for the cultivation of poppy and trade of opium-Second, economic factors such as the destruction of farm lands, irrigation canals, and livestock as well as forced displacement of farmers in the neighboring countries such as Pakistan and Iran—Third, climatic change such as the continuous severe droughts which affected farm lands and livestock throughout the country.

1. Absence of Government Authority

Absence of government authority and rule of law in remote and isolated villages of Afghanistan has created a unique enabling environment for drug traffickers to provide important financial incentive for Afghan farmers to grow opium. The recent report by UNODC shows that opium cultivation has expanded in the most unsecured provinces, and it has been significantly reduced in provinces where government authority is maximally felt. (Table 1)

According to UNODC 2007 report, opium poppy cultivation has increased in the provinces where there has been significant security deterioration by the Taliban activities. (Fig. 3)

In fact Helmand has become the major producer of opium, and opium cultivation has also increased in western provinces such as Farah, where the insurgents have enhanced their subversive activities.

Table 1: Regional Distribution of Poppy Cultivation in Afghanistan, 2006-07

Region	*2006 (ha)*	*2007 (ha)*	*Change 2006-07*	*2006 as % of total*	*2007 as % of total*
Southern Region	101,900	133,546	+31%	62%	69%
Northern Region	22,574	4,882	-78%	14%	3%
Western Region	16,615	28,619	+72%	10%	15%
North-East Region	15,234	4,853	-68%	9%	3%
Eastern Region	8,312	20,581	+148%	5%	11%
Central Region	337	500	+48%	0%	0%
Round Total	165,000	193,00	+17%	100%	100%

Source: Afghanistan Survey 2007 by UNODC.[6]

Fig. 3: Main Opium Poppy Cultivation Provinces in Afghanistan

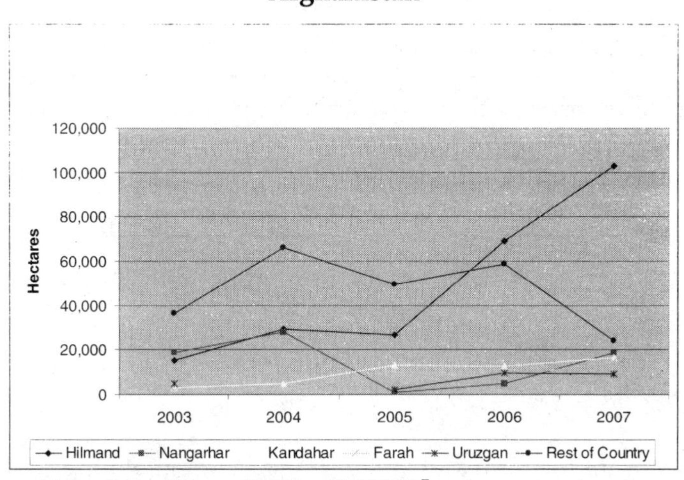

Source: Afghanistan Survey 2007 by UNODC.[7]

Similarly, the increase in poppy cultivation is Nangarhar province after 2005 is an interesting case. In fact, in the case of Nangarhar, opium cultivation was significantly reduced in 2005 because different tribes of the province had cooperated with the government authority in exchange for promised incentives. But since the Afghan authorities didn't deliver on their promises, therefore the tribes in the province have shifted back to opium cultivation.

2. Economic Factors

Destruction of Farmlands

Prior to the Soviet invasion of the country, agriculture and animal husbandry represented close to 70% of Afghanistan's GDP. There are no data available to measure the impact of conflict on Afghan economy but the number of minefield in Afghanistan due to the military conflict is indicative of damage to the farm and grazing lands in Afghanistan.

Fig. 4: Minefields in km² by year of Mining

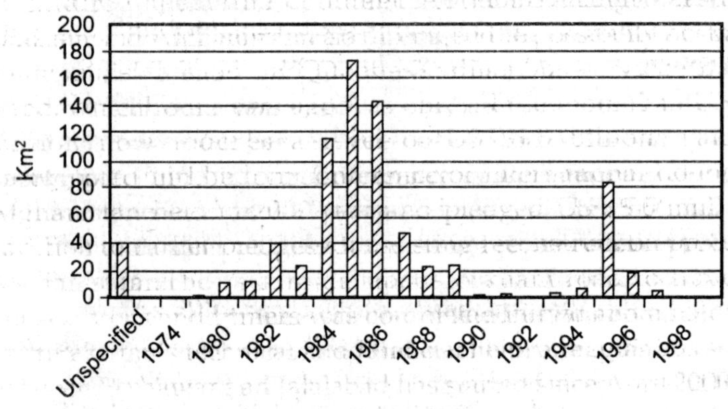

Source: SIMAA.[8]

Most of the farm and grazing lands throughout the country have remained dangerous to farmers and their livestock. As an example, in 1972 horticultural commodities supplied 40 to 60% of all export earnings for the country and Afghan's dried fruit once accounted for 60% of the world's market. Horticultural production is now estimated at less than 30% of 1978 levels because.[9]

Forced Migration of Farmers

In addition to destruction of economic infrastructure millions of farmers had abandoned their homes and farm lands for the safety of big cities inside Afghanistan and in neighboring countries such as Iran and Pakistan. In fact up to one third of Afghan population was displaced. They either fled the country or moved to safety of big cities.

Uncontrolled Growth of Population

Despite close to three decades of conflict, the population of Afghanistan has more than doubled due to improvement efforts of health care and food donation by the international community through international multilateral organizations and Non Governmental Organizations (NGOs). There has been no scientific census conducted in the country but the estimate of from the CIA World Fact Book shows that the Afghan population increased to close to 32 million. The latest Afghan census conducted by the Afghan government in 1979 estimated the Afghan population at 13.9 million. The demographic increase in Afghanistan happened when the country faced significant decrease in productivity.

3. Climatic Conditions

Climatic change has severely damaged Afghanistan's agricultural production. According to the latest study on climate change by MercyCorps, Afghanistan is among the most vulnerable countries affected by climate change. From 1998-2007 mountain snow cover has been constantly below the long-term average throughout the year.[10] While in many other parts of world climate change is still subject of a political debate, Afghanistan has already seen its direct impact through consistent and continuous droughts.

For example, Afghanistan's livestock has been dangerously reduced to record level never seen before even during the heights of military conflict. (Fig. 5)

Fig. 5: Livestock Numbers per Family from the FAO Surveys and Census

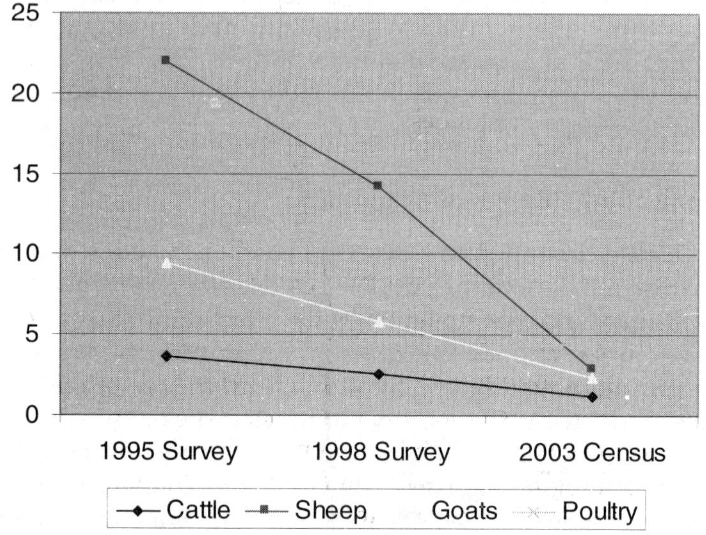

Source: FAO Census 2003.[11]

The declining livestock trend in Afghanistan after 2001 is closely related to climatic change in the country, which has pushed more farmers to migrate to cities inside Afghanistan or outside in the neighboring countries.

In fact since the Soviet invasion of the country in 1979, all of the above factors have forced Afghan farmers to rely on their own capacity to survive in an insecure and inhospitable environment.

IV. PROMINENCE OF ILLICIT ECONOMY ON DRUG PRODUCTION IN AFGHANISTAN

The Causes of Illicit Economy

After the collapse of the communist regime in 1992, Afghanistan was abandoned by the international community and left alone at its own mercy. The productivity in the country was severely reduced and successive governments in Kabul had to print money in order to pay for public and military expenses. The chart below shows the rate of inflation in Afghanistan immediately after 1992. (Fig. 6)

Fig. 6: Exchange Rate (Afghani per US$)

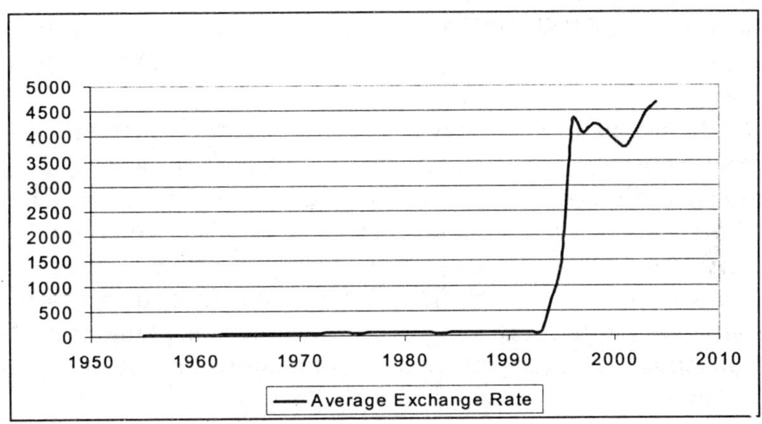

The majority of Afghans had become dependent of food distribution by the international organizations and NGOs.

In fact in the absence of a viable income, the illicit economy has become the major source of income for the country. Its origin in this region goes back to the era of "The Great Game" Between Victorian England and Tsarist Russia. British Colonial authorities had brought economic development, modern education and governance everywhere in the Indian Subcontinent except for the Pashtun tribes and Balouch because of their fierce resistance to foreign domination. In order to be able to control them, British authorities had conducted their famous policy of "divide and govern" by subsidizing a number of rival tribal chieftains and keeping the rest of population economically underdeveloped.

After the partition of India in 1947, the same ill-conceived tribal politics has been followed by Pakistan ever since. Thus, it has pushed people in the tribal area to promote illicit economy as the only means of generating income. In addition, the geography of the region the distribution of same ethnic groups across national borders has also created an enabling environment for illicit business. For instance, The Golden Crescent of drug trafficking is the name given to the geographical area shared by the three countries Afghanistan, Pakistan, and Iran, where same ethnic groups share a contiguous but artificially divided territory. After the soviet invasion the illicit business has found a prosperous ground in Afghanistan, and it could explain why Afghanistan became the major drug producer in the Golden Crescent.

Traditionally, trafficking of goods across the border has been a major business and economic activity in this part of the region. Indeed, the long-term conflict, combined with political chaos, has created an enabling environment for illicit economy in Afghanistan. During the years of conflict re-export of imported goods to Pakistan and Iran, cultivation of opium poppy, flourishing of drug processing factories, and trafficking of timer from Afghanistan have constituted a lucrative illicit economy in Afghanistan.

Re-export of Imported Goods

Afghanistan signed Afghanistan Transit and Trade agreement (ATTA) with Pakistan in 1965 which has enabled it to import goods through ports in Pakistan without paying customs duty. It was signed under a U.N. agreement to protect the interests of landlocked nations.

This agreement became a lucrative contraband business for a number of business clans and families across the border in Afghanistan and Pakistan. For instance, The Kharkhano market established in 1985 in Peshawar, which has 4,500 shops, owned by both Pakistani and Afghan traders, shows the extent of contraband between the two countries. Similarly, the filed survey in 2001[12] by the Institute for Afghan Studies shows that considerable number of goods were imported in Afghanistan and were re-exported back to Pakistan and Iran through unofficial border crossing points. (Table 2)

Total unofficial trade of Afghanistan was estimated at $1,256 million. Unofficial exports were $1,080 million in 2000, the bulk of which, $941 million, went to Pakistan and the remaining $139 million to Iran. Total unofficial annual imports of Afghanistan are estimated at $176 million, of which $94 million were imported from Iran, and $82 million from Pakistan.[13]

Table 2: Afghanistan: Field Survey Trade Estimates, 2000

	In US$ million	*in percent of total*
Total Imports	1,202	100.0
Of Which: for domestic consumption	396	33.0
For Potential re-exports	806	67.0
Total Exports	1,227	100.0
Of which: indigenous exports	130	10.6
Re-exports	1,097	89.4

Source: Field Survey.

According to government officials in the Ministry of Finance, "Afghanistan has 14 legal crossing points over its borders and 89 illegal ones" (most of them on the border with Pakistan) . One of the reasons for the illegal crossing points, between Afghanistan and its two major partners, Pakistan and Iran, is the long, uncontrolled and largely undefined borders. Moreover, same ethnic groups and tribes live across the borders in these countries. For instance, Pashtun tribes live across the border between Afghanistan and Pakistan and the Balouch live across the border between Afghanistan and Iran. They traditionally had free exchanges, which resulted in implicit free trade of goods and services between them.

Timber Contraband

Another illicit business, which has flourished following destabilization of Afghanistan is the illegal exploitation of Afghanistan's forests and trafficking of Afghan timber to Pakistan and from there to Gulf Countries.

In the mid-1990s, an estimated 2.9 percent of the land was forested, but war, illegal exploitation, and the need for firewood have removed an estimated 50 percent of that resource. In 2003 an estimated 3,150 tons of timber products were harvested.[14]

In fact the country has also been robbed of its precious forest resources by Afghan and non-Afghan timber mafia and smugglers.[15]

Fig. 7

➤ Forest cover change, Nuristan, Kunar and Nangarhar provinces, 1977 and 2002

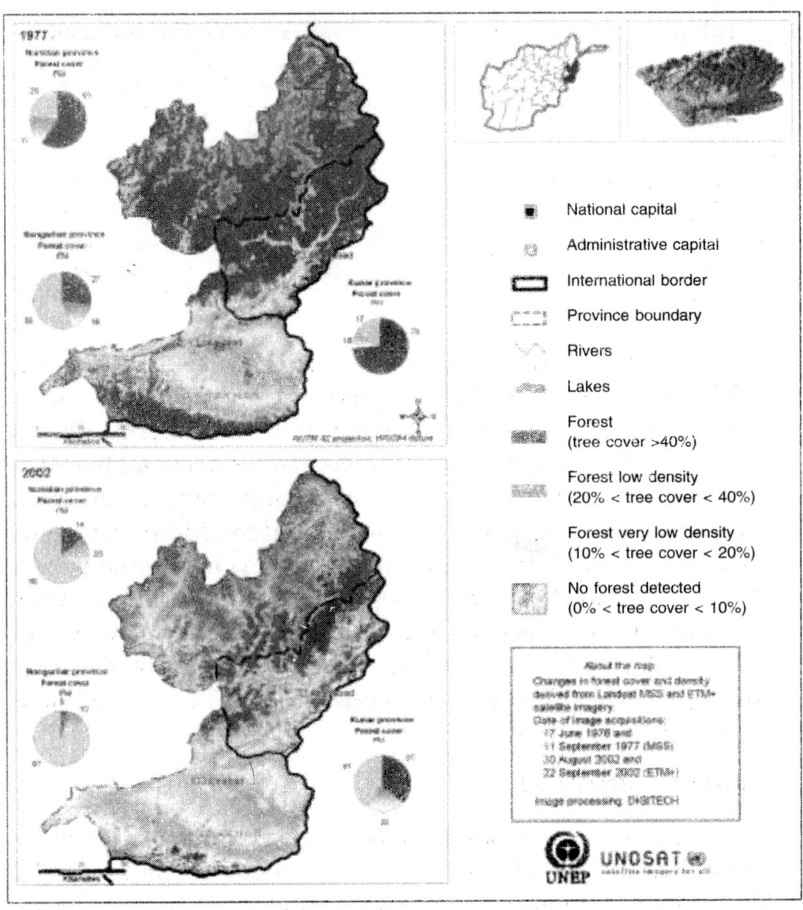

Source: UNEP Report 2002.[16]

The Fig. 7 shows the impact of contraband on local environment, which will adversely affect local economy.

During Mujahadeen and Taliban times, local government officers reported that up to 200 timber trucks could be observed per day on the main road in Kunar province. As each truck can carry a volume of timber representing five to ten trees (44 cubic metres), this represents an off take of up to 200 ha per day from the Kunar and Nuristan region (assuming a density of 20 mature trees per hectare).[17]

Elements in the Neighbouring Countries:

Despite cultivation of poppy and some of the processing of opium to Heroin in Afghanistan, Afghans involved in the business receive a small fraction of the huge profit. (Fig. 8)

Fig. 8: 2005 Afghan Poppy crop Revenues in Billion US $

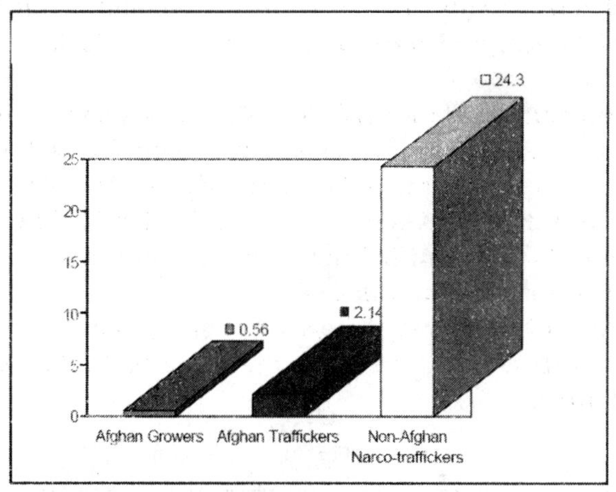

Source: USAWC.[18]

A considerable amount of profit from Afghan drug goes to the pockets of regional players. In fact Afghan farmers are the smallest recipients, and the bulk of profit in Afghanistan and in Pakistan goes to pockets of individuals and traffickers who have been involved in different types of illicit business in the region over past decades.

Past experiences elsewhere in the world has shown that profit from narcotics could serve governments covert activities. During the cold era, we have seen numerous countries paying for covert military operation by illicit and undeclared revenue. The best example was the US authorities' involvement in the Contra War.

The exit route of Afghan has been Pakistan and Iran because of the old connection known as the Golden Crescent. After the fall of the Soviets, Central Asian republics have become a secondary traffic road of opium and Heroin to Russia and Western Europe. The chart of above shows that the bulk of profit from Afghan drug goes to the pockets of non-Afghan Narco-traffickers.

Afghanistan is surrounded by undemocratic countries, some of them like Pakistan and Iran have been involved in covert military activities. For instance, Iran financially backs a number of armed movements in the Middle East and Pakistan has supported radical and terrorist movements in Kashmir and in Afghanistan.

The Iranian Revolutionary Guard and Pakistan's military are involved in lucrative businesses and no institution within these two countries could ever monitor their activities. In addition, after the collapse of the Soviet system a strong Russian Mafia emerged, which controls drug trafficking from Afghanistan to Western Europe via Central Asian Republics.

Just looking at the map below, one can assume the complicity of some of official authorities on the route of Afghan drug to Western Europe.

Fig. 9

Source: USAWC.[19]

Opium Afghanistan's Comparative Advantage

Due to major causes mentioned in part II of this paper, opium poppy has become Afghanistan's comparative advantage. In addition, the exiting contraband and drug trafficking business in the region has made Afghanistan a natural ground for drug producing. Opium cultivation requires illegal environment, which is current in Afghanistan. Production of poppy is far less expensive in Afghanistan than any other country in the region. That is why income from opium trade constitutes a large chunk of the Afghan economy. The following two graphs show interesting correlation between growth of Afghan GDP and cultivation of poppy in the last few years. (Fig. 10)

Fig. 10

Fig. 11

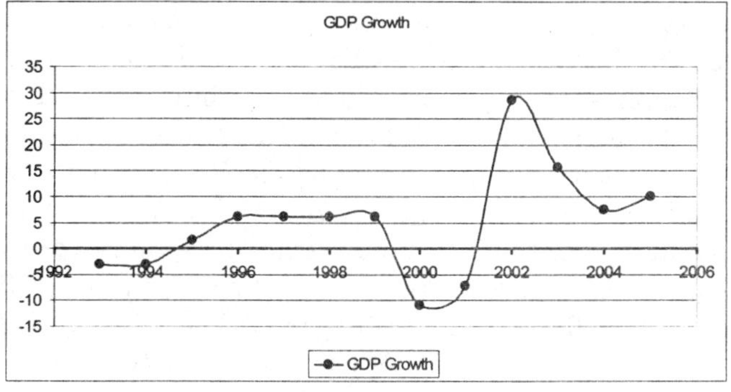

As previously stated, the Afghan economy has historically been based on agriculture and animal husbandry. Prior to the Soviet invasion in 1979, Afghanistan had a natural comparative advantage in agriculture products such as fruits, nuts, seeds, furs, skins and animal hairs. Since early 1980s, opium cultivation has become the most profitable crop for the Afghan farmers. According to the principals of free market economy, people are rational profit seeking economic agents. Hence, based on said laws widespread cultivation of poppy crops has most probably been the obvious rational choice of Afghan farmers in different parts of the country. Opium poppy is an ideal cash crop, which brings poor farmers an ideal amount of return. It is a highly efficient crop given Afghanistan's current circumstance such as drought, existence of a demand market, and long-term crop storability capacity. According to William Byrd and Christopher Ward (2004), opium poppy remains the most important development issue for Afghanistan in the years to come. *The impact of the drug industry on Afghanistan's economy, polity and society is profound, including some short-run economic benefits for the rural population and macro-economy but major adverse effects on security, political normalization, and state-building, as well as on sustainable longer-term economic development.*[20]

V. FAILURE OF NARCOTICS POLICIES IN AFGHANISTAN SINCE 2001

Brief Summary

After the fall of the Taliban regime in 2001, counter narcotics policy has become a priority for major Western countries mainly Britain. The British authorities have taken the lead in counter narcotics policy in Afghanistan and have contributed substantial amount of money in the war on drug. One of the reasons for their involvement is the fact that Britain has become one of the biggest victims of Afghan drug. "Afghanistan supplies 70% of the world's heroin and 90% of the British market, making the success of the Afghan harvest a key determinant of the street price of British heroin."[21] The British authorities have helped and financed Afghanistan to establish counter narcotics capacity in the national police force.

In 2003, Afghanistan adopted its first Afghan National Drug Strategy (ANDS), which has an ambitious goal of interdicting and eradicating opium cultivation, countering trafficking, enhancing regional and international cooperation, and providing development assistance to opium poppy growing areas. However, in 2004 there has been a consensus among stakeholders that ANDS was a failure. The common believe was the Afghan Ministry of Interior didn't have the capacity to deal with narcotics issues and was going through an important structural reform. Therefore, in 2004 the Afghan authorities promoted the Counter Narcotics Directorate, which was part of the Afghan Ministry of Interior, to a full ministerial rank.

In 2006, the Afghan government with the assistance from Britain and the US released an updated five-year strategy for tackling the illicit drug problem. In fact the core of this updated strategy does not differ substantially from its 2003 version. The emphasis is again on interdiction and eradication of opium cultivation, and drug processing and trafficking in the country.

Following, the record harvest in 2007, and the growing consensus among majority of experts about the linkage between the insurgency and narcotics in Afghanistan, the US has decided to offer a new counter narcotics strategy for Afghanistan.

2. US's New Counter Narcotics Policy in Afghanistan

In fact the treats from opium production and drug trafficking for the stability of Afghanistan are as dangerous as the insurgency by the Taliban. For instance, Antonio Maria Costa, executive director of the U.N. Office on Drugs and Crime, has been urging NATO to take a more active role in countering the spread of drug trade. "Since drugs are funding the insurgency, NATO has a self-interest in supporting Afghan forces in destroying drugs labs, markets and convoys."[22] Similarly the US administration favors military coordination between counter-narcotics and counter-insurgency forces.

One of the principal reasons that I am on this trip with General Craddock and Ambassador Nuland is to pursue a course that has been successful for us, and that is aligning the interdiction forces with those counter-insurgency forces. The alliance between these high value drug traffickers and the insurgents clearly has grown and it is through the relationships and work and partnerships that we have built on the interdiction side together with the military side that is our way forward.[23] This concern is reflected well in the new counter narcotics policy.

The new counter narcotics policy in Afghanistan, formulated by the U.S. authorities, is not much different from the previous British policy. The US's Five Pillar Plan is based on improving public information, alternative development, eradication, law enforcement, and justice reform, which seems to be an approach mainly based on the Colombian model. It doesn't take into consideration Afghanistan's deteriorating security and volatile political situation. The U.S. plan focuses on increasing development assistance, coordinating counter narcotics and counter in surgency planning and operations, and enhancing political will in the counter narcotics effort both within the Afghan government and its NATO allies.

Immediately after its release, the new strategy has been criticized by respected Afghan Scholars and experts such as Dr. Barnet Rubin, and Paul Fishstein, Director of the Afghanistan Research and Evaluation Unit. In addition, there are a number of independent think tanks such as the Senlis Council, which advocate a totally different policy for fighting narcotics in Afghanistan. But the issue of narcotics in Afghanistan has become a sensitive political issues in the majority of Western capitals and therefore inputs from individuals and independent institutions in the formulation of counter narcotics policy are not welcome by the politicians.

Reasons for failures of Counter Narcotics Policies in Afghanistan

The new US counter narcotics policy, like the previous British policy, does not take in consideration the underlying factors mentioned in part II of this paper, which have pushed Afghans to opt for opium cultivation. Western policy makers ignore most of the factors behind poppy cultivation and drug trafficking highlighted in this paper. Instead they look at narcotics from the law enforcement perspective alone. They rely on the capacities of the Afghan government, and NATO forces to deal with the issue, which have faced growing new challenges in the southern and southwestern parts of the country. In addition, since the last two years, the security and political situations have been deteriorating and the insurgents have moved their operations closer to Kabul to border provinces such as Logar and Wardak. The following factors will undermine the US's new policy similar to what happened to Britain initial counter narcotics policy in Afghanistan.

Unsecurity

Lack of security and rule of law is indeed one of the major factors behind farmers decision to grow opium. However the Afghan government and NATO forces in Afghanistan are having hard time to improve security. In fact the goal of Washington's new counter narcotics strategy, which is to fight the insurgents and the narco-traffickers simultaneously, is overly ambitious.

The number of Afghanistan's National Army around 35,000, is too small to secure Afghanistan's borders, fight the insurgents and take part in opium poppy eradication; The 70,000 Afghan National Police has been corrupt, infiltrated by the insurgents and highly influenced by the drug lords, and most of the time official from Ministry of Interior and police officers are themselves involved in drug trafficking; And NATO is short of soldiers to fight the Taliban and all recent appeals by Jaap de Hoop Sheffer, NATO's Secretary General, to increase NATO's participation in Afghanistan have not been met by the member countries.

Until now NATO forces in Afghanistan have avoided to intervene directly in the eradication and interdiction of opium cultivation and drug processing factories. According to James Appathurai, a NATO spokesperson, NATO will not intervene directly in the war on narcotics but instead would train Afghan Police and provide transportation and other logistical supports.[24] In Fact eliminating, eradicating, and interdicting drug trafficking and processing centers in Afghanistan, is a challenging task that requires at least tripling the military and police resources in the country.

Weak Central Government

The Afghan government is mired with serious problems. In the whole of southern Afghanistan, government institutions are virtually non-existent a few kilometers away from the center of provinces and districts. Provincial governors rely on powerful warlords and drug lords for their own protection, and in exchange close their eyes on their illicit activities. At highway checkpoints, the police do not stop luxury SUVs belonging to powerful lords, and courts of law most of the time rule in favor of wealthy defendants. Corruption has become an accepted norm and seeking personal wealth the ultimate goal for elite politicians.

For example justice reform will take numerous years to mature. The Afghan Minister of Counter Narcotics, Colonel General Khodaidad, has said during a TV interview that his agency disposes the list of prominent people and senior government officials who have been involved in drug trafficking. In the entire drug trafficking cases with the Afghan justice, aside small traffickers, none of big names has been mentioned. Hajji Bashir Noorzai, who represents the powerful drug mafia in Afghanistan, was arrested in New York. In fact the US authorities avoided his arrest in Afghanistan for fear of being released by corrupt Afghan justice system.

Lack of Economic Development

Poverty, unemployment, and low productivity are indeed the causes that push Afghan farmers and small traffickers to become involved in the illicit drug business because they have no other alternative. UNODC, by providing the example of wealthy farmers in the case of Helmand province, is wrong in its 2007 report on Afghanistan that there is no correlation between poverty and opium cultivation in Afghanistan. One could say that Helmand farmers are wealthier because they have been cultivating opium over the past couple of decades. In addition, if farmers and poorer provinces such as Bamyan are not cultivating opium is not because they abstain themselves willingly but because other factors such as government presence and influence of local leaders are key factors in interdicting opium cultivation.

In fact alternative crops have become the most common expression in Afghanistan. Huge amounts of money has been spent on "alternative livelihood" by international development agencies and Non-Governmental Organizations. Yet the majority of farmers are as poor as they were five years ago. An Afghan farmer with an average of 7 to 10 family members seeks to survive on less than $1,000 a year. They have a variable income based on the harvest of their crops, which could be affected by the caprices of nature. Sickness or death in the family can deplete a family's annual budget. They have to struggle with all their financial shortages without government assistance or any private lending institutions. They have heard about, but never seen, the much-talked about alternative development policies.

VI. CONCLUSION AND POLICY RECOMMENDATIONS:

More than six years after the fall of Taliban regime, narcotics remain a major obstacle for the stability of Afghanistan. Lack of progress in Afghanistan as a result of a dysfunctional government justifies infuriation of Afghans. NATO countries have been revising their military mission in Afghanistan. Actually eliminating Al-Qaeda and getting rid of the Taliban has become more challenging today than immediately after 9/11 attacks in 2001. In addition, the policy to eradicate opium poppy fields in the insurgent infested territories, which served as a political justification for Britain to send more troops in Afghanistan, is another big disappointment. Today, the overall NATO's aim is reduced to preventing Afghanistan from sliding back into chaos.

The failure of counter narcotics policy in Afghanistan reside less on its implementation but more on its formulation. Most of the time these policy are written by experts in the field who have no knowledge and understanding of Afghanistan's society, history of illicit business, and factors that have forced Afghan farmers to grow opium poppy. Afghan players such as government officials, the Afghan parliament, and the civil society have limited contribution in the formulation of policies which are funded by the major Western countries.

Narcotics in Afghanistan are not uniquely a short-term law enforcement issue. It is a well established economy that feeds and sustains millions of poor Afghan households. In addition, powerful international drug mafia and secretive government agencies in the neighboring countries extract maximum of profit from illicit drug economy in Afghanistan. However, only poor Afghan have been punished by the current failed policy.

An effective and efficient counter narcotics policy must take in consideration all of the underlying causes and issues which have been mentioned in this paper. In addition, there is no short term and permanent solution to this issue. In fact the example of Nangarhar has shown that opium cultivation could be reduced in one year but could increase in the next. As long as, an accepted mechanism is not developed, opium eradication will remain temporary effort in most parts of the country.

The issue of narcotics should be linked to long-term development project not only in Afghanistan but also to tribal zone in Pakistan, instead of short-term law enforcement policy. The following recommendations might help the Afghan government and donor countries to successfully adjust the exiting counter narcotics policy to the reality on the ground:

- Reforming of Afghanistan's legal and judiciary system,
- Reforming of Afghanistan's Ministry of Interior,
- Creating a mechanism, to seek the cooperation of key Afghan stakeholders,
- Creating a mechanism to seek regional cooperation,
- Offering a better alternative livelihood policy,
- Investing in the economic sector where it creates big number of jobs,
- Replacing drug-lords' lending system by legal credit institutions.

REFERENCES

1. The Golden Crescent is the name given to drug production in the geographical area shared by the three countries Afghanistan, Pakistan, and Iran.
2. Lemar Aftaab: Afghanmagazine.com: http://www.newsweek.com/id/118534/page/3 April 02, 2008.
3. Iqbal Khattak: Increase in Poppy Cultivation in Pakistan in 2003: http://www.mamacoca.org/FSMT_sept_2003/en/doc/

khattak_pakistan_poppy_2003_en.htm

4. Data collected from the Afghanistan Central Bank.
5. Afghanistan Opium Survey 2007, UNODC: http://www.unodc.org/pdf/research/AFG07_ExSum_web.pdf
6. *Ibid.*
7. *Ibid.*
8. SIMAA: Study of Socio-Economic Impact of Mine Action in Afghanistan: http://www.reliefweb.int/library/documents/2001/mapa-afg-30jun.pdf
9. ICARDA: http://www.icarda.cgiar.org/afghanistan/PDF/NA_Horticulture.pdf
10. MeryCorps: http://www.mercycorps.org/files/file1198714955.pdf
11. FAO: http://www.reliefweb.int/library/documents/2003/fao-afg-4dec.pdf
12. Afghanistan's International Trade with neighboring countries, Field Survey 2001: Institute of Afghan Studies: http://www.institute-for-afghan-studies.org/Afghan%20Reconstruction/Economy/intltrade.pdf
13. *Ibid.*
14. Library of congress: http://lcweb2.loc.gov/frd/cs/profiles/Afghanistan.pdf
15. UNEP Report 2002: http://postconflict.unep.ch/publications/afghanistanpcajanuary2003.pdf
16. *Ibid.*
17. *Ibid.*
18. USAWC: http://www.strategicstudiesinstitute.army.mil/pdffiles/ksil514.pdf
19. *Ibid.*
20. Byrd, William and Ward, Christopher. (2004) *Drugs and Development in Afghanistan.* World Bank Social Development Papers, 18, 2.
21. Wintour, Patrick: Guardian Unlimited: http://www.prisonplanet.com/britain_losing_new_afghan _opium_war.htm
22. Statement by Antonio Maria Costa, 16 November 2007:< http://www.reuters.com/article/featuredCrisis/idUSL1658537> March 25, 2008
23. Statement by Karen Tandy, Drug Enforcement Administrator: US Embassy in Kabul, September 25, 2007, <http://kabul.usembassy.gov/092507.html> March 25, 2008.
24. News Report by CNN: UN Urges NATO to Stop Afghan Opium Trade, November 17, 2007: http://edition.cnn.com/2007/WORLD/asiapcf/11/17/afghan.opium/index.html#cnnSTCText March 25, 2008.

CHAPTER 14

Pakistan-Afghanistan Relations

Savita Pande

INTRODUCTION

The never quiet 1500-mile-long Pakistan-Afghanistan border is in particular turmoil since 9/11. Reports from all quarters since late 2007 show spread of militancy on both sides of Pakistan-Afghanistan border, more popularly known as Durand line, a demarcation contested by Afghanistan.... It is an open truth that militants have acquired ground inside Pakistan and their writ runs beyond the Federally Administered territories (FATA) of Pakistan.... Of particular concern has been the phenomenal rise in number of suicide attacks since the overthrow of Taliban more than six years ago by western forces a la Operation Enduring Freedom. Writing in the *Survival*, Seth Jones says, "I conducted extensive interviews with United States, NATO, United Nations and Afghan officials in Afghanistan in 2004, 2005, 2006 and 2007. The conclusions are stark. There is significant evidence that the Taliban, Hezb-i-Islami Gulbuddin (HIG), al-Qaeda, and other insurgent groups use Pakistan as a sanctuary for recruitment and support. In addition, there is virtual unanimity that Pakistan's Directorate for Inter-Services Intelligence (ISI) has continued to provide assistance to Afghan insurgent groups."[1]

Historically, Pakistan Afghanistan conflict has its roots in the "great game"—the geopolitical struggle between the British Empire in the Indian subcontinent and the Russian empires holding the Central Asian lands. This was the time when Afghanistan, hitherto torn by feuds and rivalries of ethnic and tribal forms, was evolving as the modern state.

The region that is today known as Afghanistan was long torn by ethnic and tribal rivalries. It started evolving as a modern state in the early nineteenth century when the British East India Company began expanding in the northwest of British-held India. This was also the time of The British held the Indian subcontinent while the Russians held the Central Asian lands to the north. As the expansion of two empires continued, Afghanistan, the region of overlap became the bone of contention. Wars ensued, first being one, the Anglo Afghan Wars, in 1839 however, Russian expansion, it was after the war of in 1919, Afghanistan won its independence.

DURAND LINE

The Durand Line so called after the British negotiator Sir Henry Mortimer Durand, the then foreign secretary of the colonial government of India, who demarcated the frontier between him (representing British India) and Afghanistan in 1893. It was drawn after negotiations between the British government and Afghan King Abdur Rahman Khan, founder of modern Afghanistan. This line brought the tribal lands (now a part of Pakistan) under British control. Rushbrook Williams says that after 1893 this frontier was "Freely accepted by both the sides, and became one of the best defined and clearly recognized frontiers in the world."[2] Barnett R. Rubin, says the British established a three-tiered border to separate their empire from Russia through a series of treaties with Kabul and Moscow. "The *first* frontier separated the areas of the Indian subcontinent under direct British administration from those areas under Pashtun tribal control (today this line divides those areas administered by the Pakistani state from the Federally Administered Tribal Agencies). The second frontier, the Durand Line, divided the Pashtun tribal areas from the territories under the administration of the emir of Afghanistan (Pakistan and the rest of the international community consider this line to be the international border between Afghanistan and Pakistan, although Afghanistan has never accepted it). The *outer* frontier, the borders of Afghanistan with Russia, Iran, and China, demarcated the British sphere of influence; *the British enabled the emir to subdue and control Afghanistan with subsidies of money and weapons.*"[3] Literature abounds on reaffirmation of this Durand line during the British Raj say by Anglo Afghan Treaty of 1921, reaffirmed in May 1930 by none other than King Zahir Shah's father.[4]

As independence approached, Afghanistan, stating that Pakistan was a new state, not a successor to British India, argued that all past border treaties had lapsed. It also said the Afghans had signed the treaty under duress.[5] An Afghan tribal assembly or *Loya Jirga* in Kabul reaffirmed this position, that is rejecting that the Durand Line was an international border and sought self-determination of the tribal territories as Pashtunistan, on that a little later. King Zahir Shah, while inaugurating the seventh session of Afghan National Assembly on 30 June 1949, delivered an anti-Pakistan speech and the Assembly itself proceeded to pass a resolution repudiating all treaties, conventions and agreements signed between the Afghan Government and the British Government before the birth of Pakistan. The resolution also rejected the Durand Line as the international border between Pakistan and Afghanistan. In the resolution the Afghan government also referred to the alleged repression of the 'Afghan Provinces' and states from Chitral to Balochistan and promised support of the Afghan Government in their efforts to achieve freedom for the inhabitants of these areas and places.[6] Pakistani media reports cite Commonwealth Relations, Philip Noel Baker, declared in the House of the Commons in June 1949 that in international law "Pakistan was the inheritor of the rights and duties of the former government of India and of the UK government in the territories of the North West Frontier and that the Durand Line was the international frontier."[7]

Pakistan counters by arguing that since the Agreement was sought to be concluded by the then Amir Abdul Rahman, himself, with a British official of his Amir's own choice, there could have been no question of duress.[8] Border clashes ensued across the Durand Line as the two sought support from two rival Cold War powers, Pakistan from the United States and Afghanistan with the then Soviet Union. In the light of India Pakistan relations and India Soviet Union relations Pakistan, tried to project it (Afghanistan) as part of "a New Delhi-Kabul-Moscow axis that fundamentally challenged its security."[9]

These politico-legal claims and counterclaims over Durand Line or not, the free flow of Pakhtuns across the porous border between the two, has continued unabated from time immemorial assuming alarming proportions with Soviet intervention in Afghanistan in the aftermath of which, Rashid Khan et all point out in a per brought out by IPRI Islamabad, points out, "the Durand Line had practically ceased to exist with thee free movement of people, fighters, arms and ammunition across the international border between Pakistan and Afghanistan" as refugees poured in from Afghanistan to Pakistan and mujahideen infiltrated from Pakistan into Afghanistan at free will with no checks at the border. The sealing of the border remaining an impossibility, and curbing insurgency a remote possibility partly because of the difficult terrain, the rigged border areas, and partly because of the Pakhtunwali code of Milmastia (Hospitality), Nanawati (asylum) and Badal (revenge). The code reportedly has also been made use of for making profit from "fugitives from law."[10]

The ground reality notwithstanding, the sentiments can be seen effective today as Afghanistan opposes Pakistan's proposal announced by Prevez Musharraf to fence parts of the border in February 2007 to fence and mine the border between the two countries.... To quote Karzai, "He said that the fencing and mining of the 2,640-km-long 'Frontier' cannot prevent terrorism, but 'will have deadly human consequences.... Afghanistan is asking for other means.... Let us work against places where training and funding for terrorism is taking place and where supplies are given.... The fencing or mining of the border separates families, communities and people rather than ending terrorism. We also oppose mining the border from a humanitarian perspective, as mines have killed or maimed many people, children and women of this war-torn nation,"[11] interestingly the United nations is also opposed to Pakistan's plans of mining and fencing. However, subsequently the foreign spokesperson for Pakistan said, "The Army has to identify sectors and areas, it has to be selective and it is not going to be all along the border between the two countries, because we do not want to cease movement of legitimate travelers."[12]

PAKHTUNISTAN

With disputed boundary came the issue of assimilating the Pakhtuns themselves. Successive governments of Afghanistan have demanded a separate and independent state of Pakhtunistan resting its claim on the assertion that Pakhtuns constitute one nation having common ethnicity, language, geographical proximity, culture and traditions. President Daud of Afghanistan had once remarked that the "British did a wrong many years ago and we have been fighting to rectify it. Until that is done the struggle will continue."[13] The disillusionment of the Pakhtuns with their new state was seized upon by Afghanistan's progressive nationalist leader Mohammad Daud to pursue irredentist agitation in cooperation with India against Pakistan."[14]

Sardar Daud pursued the issue "more vigorously," so did the new post-Saur Revolution leaders of Afghanistan who revived the Pakhtunistan issue and declared their support for the right of self-determination of the Pakhtuns and Baloch nationalities of Pakistan.[15] The latter post-Saur leader's objectives were clear: (1) rewarding the Pakhtuns nationalists for their support to the revolution, (2) put pressure on Pakistan because it had opposed the revolution, fearing increase of Soviet influence, (3) to mobilize the Pakhtuns population living on both sides of the Durand Line "in support of the Saur Revolution, which was facing increasing resistance from the conservative Pakhtuns tribes ."[16]

Weinbaum and Harder say Pakistan retaliated against Afghanistan's "promotion of " Pashtunistan. In the fifties it dissuaded its alliance partner United States from giving military aid to Kabul, turning the latter toward Soviet Union for the same; in 1963 through trade blockade it facilitated quick exit of pro-Pakhtunistan Prime Minister Mohammad Doud; in 1975 the then Prime Minister of Pakistan Zulfiqar ali Bhutto supported an insurrect by Islamist radicals, when that failed the insurgents were given refuge who later led the mujahideen to counter Soviet occupation of Afghanistan.[17]

Pakistani Pakhtuns nationalists, are now organized along Awami National Party and the Pakhtunkhwa Milli Awami Party, view their relations with the Pakistani state and Afghanistan differently than do Pakistan's civil and military establishment and the Islamist political parties, have sought "democratization, provincial autonomy, and friendly relations with Afghanistan."[18]

Impact of all this has been traced in a USIP briefing which says that," that the foundations of Pakhtuns identity have changed with perhaps a permanent turn toward Islamism and movement away from traditional secular, tribal leadership. It would seem that new centers of power, the influence of political Islam and the rise of the *mullah*, and the commingling with so-called "foreigners" have upended the traditional tribal identification."[19] "In 2006," says Rubin, "no secessionist nationalist movement operates among the Pakhtuns in Pakistan, and Afghanistan has not revived its irredentist claims."[20] Although, the Awami National Party in its party manifesto released in 2007 December talked of provincial autonomy and rename the NWFP as "Pukhtunkhwa," apart from merger of tribal areas with the province and amendment of Frontier Crime rule.[21]

FIRST PHASE

Afghanistan was the only country that opposed Pakistan's membership to the United Nations, laid territorial claim to the two provinces of Baluchistan and NWFP, and at the same time conditioning its recognition to granting the "right of self determination" to the people of Pakistan's North Western Frontier Province.[22] This notwithstanding, recognition was granted in 1948, the relations, albeit remained acrimonious on the twin issue of Durand line and Pakhtunistan, reaching peak in 1950 when the Afghan King Zahir Shah and the Prime minister hoisted a Pakhtunistan flag, made anti-Pakistan speeches and afghan Air Force dropped Anti Pakistan leaflets later in September Afghans conducted raids in frontier areas. Pakistan till 1979, continued to buy time, making appeals for peace now and then, but firmly denying Afghan claims on Durand line and Pakhtunistan.[23] After

Daud overthrew Zahir Shah in 1973 ties improved and some bilateral visits took place.[24] As Daud started crackdown on opponents, Gulbadin Hikmatyar and Burhanuddin Rabbani, both the active resistance leaders escaped to Pakistan Zulfiqar Ali Bhutto used them to destabilise Daud's government.[25] Interestingly, Matinuddin says both Pakistan and Afghanistan lost opportunities of settling the Durand line, first in July 1977 when Bhutto had released ANP men detained for supporting the Pakhtunistan demand in return for Daud's acceptance of Durand Line, but Bhutto himself was overthrown in a coup, and then, and then during his 1978 visit, Daud had reached an agreement to the effect, but before the agreement could be finalized, Daud himself was murdered in a coup.[26] Daud, to counterbalance the growing Soviet influence sought huge financial assistance from oil-wealthy Arab states and Iran, "even tried to reconcile with Pakistan."[27]

One tends to agree with Weinbaum when he says, until his soviet intervention in December1979; Afghanistan had appeared as largely a political irritant for Pakistan, a petulant and resentful neighbour. Afghanistan irredentism represented by the call for Pashtoonistan, though potentially a challenge to Pakistan's national integrity was deemed manageable economically and militarily Afghanistan was no match for Pakistan. Pakistan's adversarial relations with India and Domestic regional instability posed more serious challenge for its national security."[28]

The Pakistan's Afghan policy hereafter was focused on three main forays:

1. The inflow of refugees that brought the two countries together in an unprecedented fashion.
2. Pakistan became a frontline state in the last great battle of the Great Battle of the Cold war. By 1980 Afghanistan transformed from a neighbourhood issue to a national security issue.
3. By 1990s Pakistan's governing elite saw it as a "national interest "in which they had substantial investment and which was their key to access to Central Asia.[29]

SOVIET INVASION

Soviet intervention in Afghanistan was a big development that gave a decisive push to Pakistan-Afghanistan relations. It "provided a golden opportunity to break this double threat of dismemberment and encirclement by fighting communism with U.S. support, while using U.S. and Saudi money to advance a fundamentalist agenda. This quest for gaining "strategic depth" against India by dominating Afghanistan was inseparable from the tactic of undercutting Pakhtuns nationalism by supporting Islamists. It remains a foundation of Pakistan's foreign policy to this day."[30] Pakistan became a conduit for Soviet arms, training and arming the mujahideen to overthrow the Soviet backed regime. Pakistan decided, "Rather than directly confronting the Soviet Union, Pakistan could funnel military assistance and give them sanctuary. The Islamabad Government had no intention of being drawn into a shooting war with the Soviets or their Afghan clients. It hoped to reap benefits from Moscow's threats without becoming an extension of War's background."[31]

Pakistan organized Jihad strategy, under the leadership of Gen. Akhtar Abdul Rehman. Consequently, by "mid-80s tens of thousands of arms and ammunition were being distributed by the Inter Services Intelligence (ISI) to the Afghan Mujahideen via their party warehouses.... Tens of thousands of Afghan guerrillas with their commanders came to Pakistan for training. From 1980 until 1987 Pakistan Army teams from the ISI went to Afghanistan to advise and assist the Mujahideen in their operations. All resistance commanders inside Afghanistan were required to join one of the seven Peshawar-based parties (Hizbs) as it was only through these parties that arms were distributed. There was no arms supply to individuals. Among the seven recognised parties, some were closer to the Pakistani establishment than others. About 70 per cent of the logistical support was given to the fundamentalist parties but no single party got more than 20 percent."[32] In 1981, a Pakistani airline was hijacked to Afghanistan, allegedly by Al-Zulfiqar, a terror organization led by sons of Z.A. Bhutto against the Pakistani military regime of Zia-ul Haq.[33] Most of the necessary funds originated from the U.S. Saudi Arabia and other Persian Gulf States.[34]

In the Soviet Occupied Afghanistan, Pakistan, while supporting the Afghan jihad against the ruling elite, discriminated between the Mujahideen groups, the conduits fighting the ruling regime. It is an open knowledge that the ISI preferred Hikmatyar to Massood the so-called Lion of Panjsher.[35] In 1981, a Pakistani airline was hijacked to Afghanistan, allegedly by Al-Zulfiqar, a terror organization led by sons of Z.A. Bhutto against the Pakistani military regime of Zia-ul Haq. The Afghan government of Babrak Karmal encouraged the hijackers. Says Feroze Hassan, that by that time "it was no longer just a Pakistan-Afghan regional affair, the region had become a battlefield of the Cold War. The conflict attracted the attentions of not only the United States, the Soviet Union, and China, but also the Saudis, who sought to inject their Wahhabi ideology. This prompted Iran to enter the rivalry by exporting its own revolutionary Islamic ideology. Both Afghanistan and Pakistan became turf for Wahabbi and Shia battle. The seeds for sectarian violence were sown as the Jihad to oust the Soviets raged on. As a result, a complex web of covert engagement enveloped the Pakistan-Afghan region."[36]

A major collateral of Soviet intervention in Afghanistan was the *flow of refugees* from Afghanistan to Pakistan over the decade. It is difficult to estimate the exact number of refugees in Pakistan since the Afghan refugees' offices lack precise data. Some say that while granting the refugees the refugee status, the government set up 306 camps in the NWFP, Baluchistan and Punjab to accommodate some 3.7 million refugees who had fled Afghanistan. These refugees, however, were never confined to the camps....[37] According to various UNHCR reports, the highest number of refugees registered in Pakistan was 2.78 million. The NWFP received the highest number of 1.30 followed by Balochistan 7,04168 and the Punjab 168,016.[38] The largest belong to lower class came from tribal and rural surroundings of all major provinces, particularly Kandahar, Ghanzi, Takhar, Hazarajat, Paktika, Badakshan, Helmand, Nimruz, Began and Nangarihar, they were uneducated and earned their livelihood through menial jobs;the middle class of Afghan refugees belonged to urban areas of Kandahar, Ghanzi, and Kabul were, ran small restaurants and transport business, own fruit and grocery stores and sold, among other things, rugs, carpets and arm, consolidated small business in Pakistan; and the higher class refugees from Kabul and are now the business of carpets, restaurants, antiques and loan giving business.[39]

As Pakistan became home to world's largest refugee population General Zia, however, made a good use of this refugee-mujahideen combine. These include, at home, it gave him an excuse to main martial law, especially to gain control on Tribal Areas, regionally tie down the Soviets to Afghanistan, and thus, globally acquire US military and economic support as well as acquire political capital among Arab States.[40] By 1990 UNHCR figures put the figure of refugees in Pakistan at 3.3 million, which did not include unregistered refugees. They were located in 344 villages—70 per cent in NWFP, 25 per vent in Balochistan, and 5 per cent in Punjab.[41] While Refugees flows in 1981 ran as high as 180,000 per month, it fell to 15,000 to 20,000 per month by 1982085, to 6,000 to 8000, by 1987....[42] The condition of these refugees was made attractive in terms of food, tents, allowance, health facilities. This notwithstanding, the refugees have had an adverse impact on Pakistan. These include: Unemployment of Pakistan's labour force as Afghan Refugees provide cheaper labour for agriculture, construction, and road building. Besides they also adversely impact revenue generation of the locals by controlling small business like transport, tea stalls, restaurant, small shop, etc. in places like Peshawar, Islamabad and Quetta; deforestation due to demand for fuel wood as well as due to over-grazing of their cattle; pressure on Utilities/Services; food consumption; Involvement in heinous crimes like drug trafficking, arms proliferation, dacoity, murder and car lifting, theft and prostitution; environmental degradation; administrative expenditure and Land Compensation; Over a period of 19 years the Pakistani government has spent US $ 1275.07 million (Pak Rs. 76504.2 million) for maintenance and Pay and Allowances and $ 1.2 million (Pak. 74.15 million) over the years to the land owner son whose lands around 2000 camps were established.[43] Lamdani, who after calculating pros and cons for Pakistan aforementioned facts would carry a tilt towards positive effect. Benefits accruing in the form of military hardware and the se of aid for Afghan refugees outweigh the negative impact in terms of quantifications."[44]

POST-SOVIET WITHDRAWAL

As Soviets withdrew, the Americans lost all interest and abandoned the region generally and Afghanistan and Pakistan specifically, resulting in a power vacuum of sorts, plunging Pakistan in a civil strife. In this post-withdrawal phase, Pakistan was in favour of establishing a broad based coalition and so the government that was formed in exile in Pakistan in 1988 could fill the vacuum. However, Pakistan having formed the government in exile initially did not recognize it. Calling it "premature" since it was initially for a period of one year. That notwithstanding, the parties squabbled among themselves on the issue of consultative Assembly (shura) and withdrew. Despite the fact that power had effectively transferred to a ten-member coalition, Pakistan brokered a Peshawar accord among 10 parties based in Pakistan which" attempted to restructure a legitimate government in three phases over a period of two years" While the first phase was successfully conducted, meeting of the *Shura-i-Hal-o-Aqd* held and power transferred smoothly from Mujadedi to Rabbani, the progress went thus far and no further, encouraging further factional feuds. In March 1993x Pakistan promoted yet another kinds of accords—the Islamabad Accords—which attempted to define the power of the prime minister and President, the ministry of Defence was replaced by Defence Council. The accords did not go much further as they were rejected by Masud. Pakistan brokered yet another accord at Jalalabad, with an aim to sort out differences on Defence council and form a cabinet, nothing made much impact.[45]

This of course was the political scene. Ground realities became militarized as from early 1990s; ethnic militias got engaged in wars amongst themselves. Drug trafficking boomed and Arab and other non-Afghan Islamist radicals strengthened their bases.... Essentially it was a battle between the Pashtuns (mostly led by Hikmatyar's Hizb-e-Islami, a key ally and then favorite of the Inter Service Intelligence—ISI) and the Panjsheris (led by Ahmed Shah Masud—the "Lion of Panjsher") that had entered a stalemate phase.

By 1990s impact of Afghan War was extremely serious in the domestic environment of Pakistan, which had serious implications for the region as well—the radicalized militarized Pakistan which suffered from the dreadful problems of small arms or as is called *Kalashnikovisation of Pakistan* linked to Narcotics trade. The arms supply came from the U.S, CIA to be precise till Karachi, "where the ISI took over."[46] The arms pipeline was a "leaky conduit," passing through several hands first in Pakistani Army, then through parties to commanders and then to the *Mujahideen*—these later sold in the arms bazaars or stockpiled for later use, estimates varying for leakage from 20 to 85 per cent.[47]

ENTER TALIBAN

Pakistan, still heavily involved in Afghanistan's internal battles, started backing the Taliban, the cleric students trained and cultivated in Pakistan Afghanistan Madrassas, an integral part of Gen Zia's radicalized Islamisation in Pakistan in his quest to seek legitimacy. These included, the Jamiat-e-Ulema-e-Islam (Fazal-Ur-Rehman Group), the famous Akora Khattak madrassa headed by Maulana Semi-ul-Haq, and Jamiatul Uloomil Islamiyah Binori Town, Karachi were reported to be making "large contributions to the Taliban force." The Taliban, some of them orphans of the Afghan Jihad, were propped up propped up initially with the support of the civil government of Benazir Bhutto, then in coalition with the Deobandi Jama'at-ulema Islam (JUI) led by Maulana Fazlur Rehman. Essentially, they were known to be brainchild of the interior Minister Naseerullah Babar, himself a Pashtun and ostensibly driven by incentive to open up a trade route to Turkmenistan via Kandahar.[48] The policy was embraced by ISI thereafter, during 1995; the ISI played increasing role in supporting the Taliban, and by 1996 had become Taliban's chief supporter.[49] It was this Taliban which by 1998, was ruling over entire Afghanistan barring some pockets in the Northeast placed where was in a anti Taliban rebels grouped as "Northern Alliance" (comprising former mujahideen and Soviet-backed militias, most of them from non-Pashtun).

As their reign in Afghanistan expanded, the Taliban promulgated extremely harsh Islamic law and were guided by Osama bin Laden, who came to Afghanistan after being expelled from Sudan in 1996.[50] For Pakistan, it served a dual purpose, while lending support to "pure Islamic state" in Afghanistan promised to "neutralize Pashtun irredentism but also helped to train and indoctrinate jihadis for the *struggle against India in Kashmir*."[51] They were being prepared for Jihad against those who, it was felt, were no longer adhering to the 'moral code of Islam'.[52] Ahmed Rashid says the "Flower power" adds yield from poppy cultivation to sources of income. He calls it Poppy production is so regularised that drug dealers operate a banking system which offer farmers credit in advance of their crop. A 20% of the income of the opium dealers and transporters, he says, goes straight to the Taliban war chest.[53] And yet the Pakistanis consistently denied supporting Taliban, at times admitting giving minimal logistical support, evidence to contrary notwithstanding.[54]

Goodsen identifies six major areas of Pakistani Support for Taliban: direct military involvement, indirect military involvement, logistical support, recruitment, financial aid, and diplomatic recognition."[55] Critical logistical support included "weapons, ammunition, fuel, communication equipment, maintenance of amour, airplanes and transport for men and material'.[56]

Ahmed Rashid Nasirullah Babar's Afghan Trade Cell in the Interior Ministry' coordinated activities of Pakistan International Airlines, Pakistan Railways, Pakistan Telecom, National Bank of Pakistan, Radio Pakistan, Water and Power Development Department.[57]

Interestingly, while security analysts agree that Pakistan's main motive is India—to keep the other border (with Afghanistan) Peaceful, as it is difficult to fight on two fronts simultaneously, they dispute the strategic depth theory. General Aslam Beg, the formulator of the concept, himself has reportedly said, "The need for strategic depth—a strategic partnership between Pakistan, Iran and Afghanistan—was misunderstood as an imperative only for geographical space ... to say that the strategic depth concept was developed to gain territorial space in case of war with India has no military logic, nor does it conform to the operational policy of Pakistan, which is to defend its borders and defeat the enemy if he attempts to violate Pakistan's territory."[58]

By the late 1990s the Pakistani establishment did face problems because of the Frankenstein it had created, apart from an extremely militarized domestic environments, in 1998, Osama Bin Laden attacks on U.S. embassies in East Africa, and the United States response (missile attacks),destruction Buddhist statues in Bamyan to cite two of the instances.

THE WAR ON TERROR

Pakistan support to Taliban for full seven years was unflinching even when the regime was "getting more and more isolated." To quote Kamal Matinuddin, "President Musharraf had been personally advocating the cause of the Taliban at every forum. He spoke to many world leaders and tried to convince them to remove the sanctions on Afghanistan, but to no avail. Pakistan's embassy remained in Kabul even when the other two embassies were withdrawn."[59] After 9/11, these equations changed.... General Musharraf decided to make a U-turn in Pakistan's policy towards Afghanistan and agreed to provide unstinted support to the United States in its Global War on Terrorism. While Matinuddin thinks India was the main reason for the change in policy (discussed below), Haqqani says Pakistan was left "with little choice but to make a harder turn toward the United States. Confronted with an ultimatum to choose between being with United States or against it, Pakistan's Generals chose to revive their alliance with the United States. At every stage since, Pakistan has proved to be a US ally of convenience, not commitment .as it has sought specific rewards for specific actions."[60]

Pakistan's gains have been enormous. Apart from working on international financial institutions to ease Pakistan's debt burden, (leading to Pakistan's growth of almost six per cent), the

US reversed it policy dating post Soviet withdrawal sanctions on a nuclear Pakistan, and in June 2006, the US promised supplies of high tech weapons including plans to sell up to 36 F-16 jets, besides making it a "major non–NATO Ally" in 2005, there have been regular visits of High level security officers to Pakistan with President Bush himself making an unprecedented overnight stop in Islamabad in 2006.[61]

Mushraff visited Kabul was in April 2002, Karzai was the guest at 2005 Pakistan day Parade, and again paid an official visit in February 2006, Last year, President Karzai attended Pakistan Day parade in Islamabad as Chief Guest. During his stay in the capital city he held talks with both President Musharraf and Prime Minister Shaukat Aziz, which led to the signing of 5 agreements between the two countries on enhancing cooperation in culture, media and counter-terrorism. During these talks, Pakistan and Afghanistan also discussed the possibility of starting Islamabad-Jalabad and Quetta-Kandhar bus service Bilateral trade, which four years ago was only a little more than US $ 25 million now touches a level of US $1.5 billion. Pakistan participated in London Conference of international donors for Afghanistan held in 2007 year and pledged US $ 50 million in addition to earlier pledges for assisting reconstruction process in Afghanistan. The 74 km Jalalabad-Torkham road to travel for buses, trucks and trailers was completed in two and a half years with Pakistan's technical and financial help, a regular bus service between Peshawar and Jalalabad has started since April 2006 with Pakistan handing over a number of buses to Afghanistan for the purpose of plying on this route.[62] Some 60,000 Pakistanis are, reportedly, currently employed in Afghanistan. Pakistan imports more than $ 700 million worth of goods, besides, security cooperation between Pakistan, Afghanistan and the United States has been institutionalized through Trilateral Commission, which meets regularly in Islamabad and Kabul to discuss issues relating to war against terror.[63]

However, Afghanistan is deeply suspicious of Pakistan. President Karzai and other ministers have publicly blamed Pakistan "terrorists from Pakistan" for much of the violence, including suicide attacks in Afghanistan, which have caused a number of casualties among the Afghan and NATO forces.[64] A sample of the actual relationship can be gauged from the August 2007 peace jirga, where Shaukat Azizaid Afghanistan could not blame others for the lack of reconciliation among its people, asserting, "first and foremost the Taliban are Afghans," and further, "Afghanistan is not yet at peace within itself. The objective of national reconciliation remains elusive.... They can't blame anyone else for failing to achieve this objective that lay at the heart of their malaise."[65]

Karzai, however, did blame Pakistan: "Why from your soil and administration is this evil coming to us?" he demanded, "Who is training them? By whose money are they being trained?" Of late Afghanistan has also blamed Pakistan intelligence agencies for a failed attempt to assassinate Afghan President Hamid Karzai during a military parade in Kabul in April this year; Pakistan rejected the allegations as "baseless and irresponsible."[66]

According to a 2006 *Special Report* of United States Institute for Peace, "The violence, which has spread to both sides of the frontier, escalated in the run-up to President Bush's mid-March 2006 visit to South Asia—especially in Waziristan, a craggy region of 5,000 square miles divided into the South and North Agencies, or tribal districts. Some 300 Islamist militants, civilians, and Pakistani soldiers died in the fighting, which forced tens of thousands of people to flee the Pakistani town of Miran Shah, administrative headquarters of the North Waziristan tribal district. In neighboring South Waziristan, skirmishes, rocketing, assassinations, and land-mine blasts continue.[67] Yet there have been repeated reports to Pakistan not "doing enough." John Negroponte, the then Intelligence Chief said in his testimony in January 2008 that charged that the Al-Qaeda leadership was running its operations from "secure hideouts" in Pakistan; and that hat it remained "a major source of Islamic extremism and the home for some top terrorist leaders."[68] Incidentally the United Nations has also asked Pakistan "to do more." Musharaff's in his replies to charges of not doing enough have been threefold," difficult terrain on the long frontier, inadequate attempts to control the insurgency on the Afghan side, and the hundreds of casualties the Pakistan army has suffered since deploying 80,000 troops in the border areas.[69]

After 9/11, Pakistan allied itself with the United States in its war on terror. This created a dilemma for Pakistan, as it now had to hunt down the Taliban and the Islamic militant organizations it reportedly helped create in the first place. It also had to send its troops into the tribal lands where the Pakistani military has never been welcome. Incidents of Pakistani soldiers surrendering without a fight to militant organizations became common during 2007. Pakistan nevertheless remains under pressure from the US "to do more."

RESURGENT TALIBAN

It is believed that after 2001 ISI's role became more indirect but the militant organisations like Jaish-i-Mohammed and Lashka-e-Taiba became more active in fund raising and training the younger generation of Taliban. They were aided by the madrassas and Pakistani policies of suppressing Afghan nationalism ISI's Islamists sympathies remained, as madrassas became sources of suicide bombers by 2005.[70]

Citing US military officials, *the tipping point* for Pakistan was in 2005 when the US policymakers publicly stated "that they were decreasing the number of American troops in Afghanistan and handing over authority to NATO" which, on the one hand, "encouraged Afghan government officials to increasingly turn to India as its long-term strategic partner" and on the other, "encouraged Pakistani government officials to counter this trend by supporting the Taliban."[71] Jones identifies three zones of presence of Taleban The northern front presence, is based in such Afghan provinces as Nuristan, Kumar, Lehmann Angara, as well as across the border in Pakistan; (2) the central front located in a swath of territory extending from Bajer to the Federally administered areas and such Afghan provinces as Knows, Patio and Patoka as a loose amalgam of foreign fighters, including Central Asians and Arabs; and (3) the southern front, which includes a large Taliban presence, is based in Baluchistan and the Federally Administered Tribal Areas, as well as such Afghan provinces as Helmand, Kandahar, Oruzgan, Zabol and Paktika, besides these there are many drug pedaling and other groups who "enjoy sanctuary in Pakistan."[72] Concurs the latest European report "The under-policed, mostly mountainous border area is a haven for the Taliban who launch operations into Afghanistan from bases inside Pakistan, including Peshawar where its top leaders are based."[73] Hassan Abbas, for instance argues in a January 2008 paper that that the Pakistani Taliban have effectively established themselves as an alternative to the traditional tribal elders and have Taliban killed approximately 200 of the tribal leaders and these indigenous Taliban groups coalesced in December 2007 under the umbrella of Tehrik-i-Taliban Pakistan (TTP) under the militant commander Baitullah Mehsud (suspect in Benazir assassination) from South Waziristan.[74] Taliban insurgency in Afghanistan had exacted its heaviest toll on Afghan civilians. There were 124 suicide bombings in Afghanistan in 2006, which killed or wounded "hundreds of Afghans."[75]

The ISI help to insurgents, at tactical and strategic level, which has undermined operations against the latter, reportedly includes: providing arms and ammunition to the Taliban, paying their medical bills, directly or indirectly (funding) training them in Quetta, Mansehra, Shamshattu, Parachinar and other areas in Pakistan, tipping off about location and movement of Afghan and coalition forces. Explaining the existence of these "training camps, staging areas, recruiting centers (madrassas), and safe havens Jalali has argued." The operations of a 70,000-strong Pakistani military force, deployed in the border region, mostly in the Waziristan tribal area, have been effective against Al-Qaeda and non-Pakistani militants, but they have not done much toward containing the Taliban. This means that more effort is needed to stop cross-border terrorist activity in Afghanistan. However, as long as the Taliban continue to use Pakistani territory for attacks on Afghanistan, the suspicion that Pakistan is playing a double game in Afghanistan will persist."[76]

However there is also a perception that Taliban cannot seriously threaten the Kabul government, they only have small scale operations, their strategy being long, term, believing that their term will come as international powers go away.[77] To defeat the Taliban will require a long-term commitment of the international community to Afghanistan's security and a Pakistani government more willing and able to deny anti-Kabul forces safe haven.

Experts say that underlying Pakistani actions in the region is concern about bolstering security against India. The USIP report notes Pakistan sought to support a "client regime in Afghanistan" that would be hostile to India, "giving the Pakistani military a secure border and strategic depth." By supporting Islamist militias among the Pashtun, Pakistan's government has tried to neutralize Baloch and Pashtun nationalism within its borders. The International Crisis group in October 2007 reported that Pakistan still supports Pashtun Islamist parties in a bid to counter Baloch and Pashtun forces. "Using Balochistan as a base of operation and sanctuary" and recruiting from its extensive madrassa network, the report says, the "Taliban and its Pakistani allies are undermining the state-building effort in Afghanistan." Pakistan's President Pervez Musharraf has repeatedly denied this.

ONE WORD ON INDIA

It is a common knowledge that Pakistani actions in the region are related to balancing its security fears vis-à-vis India. Seth Jones says, Pakistan government's strategy in Afghanistan has, for decades," been to balance India and keep a foothold in Afghanistan."[78]

Matinuddin says change in Musharaff's Taliban policy came because of India. To quote him," (Musharaf) did so because he wanted Pakistan to get back into the mainstream and frustrate Indian eagerness to get Pakistan declared a terrorist state. He was afraid that India might seek the assistance of the United States to crush the freedom movement in Kashmir. He was also concerned about the safety of the strategic assets, which could come under attack if he refused to cooperate with the United States."[79]

India's help to Afghanistan, in this phase (Since 11 September) in terms of several hundred million dollars, has been reported to be range from, helping political candidates (during the 2004 presidential and 2005 parliamentary elections), construction of the new Afghan parliament building, and road construction, including in the borders, evoking Pakistan's concerns further...[80] Pakistan has accused India, particularly since 2003 of using its consulates in Jalalabad, Kandahar and Herat to launch and promote 'terrorist activities' in Pakistan, particularly in strife torn province of Baluchistan. Federally Administered Tribal Areas (FATA).

The latest report of European Council for Foreign Relations explains Pakistan's fears "*of encirclement by India.* Delhi's assistance to Afghanistan has been considerable with Indian-donated Tata buses now an obvious part of Kabul's public transportation system. India is also making important contributions to Afghan education, including rebuilding Habibia High School in Kabul, and President Karzai—who was educated in India—has visited Delhi several times. But this support is seen in Islamabad—and perhaps even more so in the Pakistani military headquarters in Rawalphindi—*as part of a deliberate strategy to encircle Pakistan.*"[81]

SUGGESTIONS FOR FUTURE

Seeing the nature and developments in the relationship, there can hardly be a traditional conclusion to the paper. What can however be attempted is an effort to put together suggested paths to how issues can or should be handled.

Saaying that the greatest threat to the U.S. position in Afghanistan comes from Rawalpindi's continued determination to use Pashtun fundamentalists to break apart the historic Indo-Afghan alliance, which was renewed after the fall of the Taliban.Vanni Cappelli has argued that "the United States should change course and commit itself to a tripartite American-Indian-Afghan alliance aimed at containing Pakistan and the Islamic ideological and terrorist threat that it poses."[82] The pillars of this policy would be (1) cutting off all U.S. military and economic aid to Pakistan, (2) placing Pakistan on the list of state sponsors of terror, (3) brokering a resolution of the Kashmir question that grants Kashmiris a substantial autonomy shored up with economic development, (4) reconstructing Afghanistan, With special emphasis on building its military capability and securing semi permanent U.S. basing rights, and (5) providing covert economic and military Support to any efforts that India and

Afghanistan would make to counterbalance Pakistan's support for insurgent groups within their countries Pakistan.[83]

Barnett Rubin argues: "success is not possible without a coherent US strategy not only towards Pakistan and Afghanistan but also towards the Pakistan-Afghanistan relationship." He recommends recognition of an international border by the two countries and cooperative development of the tribal areas on either side. *It also suggests transforming the status of the tribal areas in Pakistan and empowering the people by allowing them to participate in elections.*[84]

The UN, Afghanistan and Pakistan should stop arguing and start cooperating to tackle the problem of terrorism together. The UN Deputy Chief said, "This war of words, this rhetorical contest between two governments, two partners, must end," Alexander said. "Pointing fingers leads nowhere. What we really need, and what Afghans most need, is a constructive engagement and joint action to tackle a very serious security challenge."[85]

Many oppose the Fencing Plan, saying that Pakistan's idea of constructing a fence along the border is "neither practical nor politically desirable" Jalali has sought, "Invigorating the Tri-Partite US-Afghan-Pakistani Commission on fighting terrorism and close operational cooperation between Afghanistan and Pakistan" for ending the insurgency.[86]

Stressing on the regular meetings of the Tripartite Commission, comprising senior officials of the three countries (Pakistan, Afghanistan and the US) Kamal Matinuddin goes further by asking Pakistan to "give up its previous policy and strictly adhere to a policy of non-interference in the internal affairs of Afghanistan." Support Karzai, "wholeheartedly coordinate with Iran and make use of the presence of the Pakistan army in the Tribal Areas for the economic development of that part of Pakistan."[87]

Others suggest multilateralism, keeping in mind Afghanistan has been admitted to several regional organizations, like the Economic Cooperation Organization (ECO), (became 10th member in 1992, the Asian Development Bank (ADB), and the Organization of the Islamic Conference; South Asian Association for Regional Cooperation (SAARC) (in November 2005, it became the eighth member). Besides, in December 2002, regional states together with Russia and the United States that had been members of the Six-Plus-Two grouping created to contain the Taliban joined with Afghanistan in the signing of a Kabul Declaration of good-neighborly relations.

Given the fluid situation within Pakistan and Afghanistan and state of institutions within, there is some sense in the multilateral solution, detailed modalities can be debated but it has to begin with non interference in internal affairs.

REFERENCES

1. Seth Jones, "Pakistan's Dangerous Game" *Survival*, Vol. 49, no. 1, Spring 2007, p. 15.
2. L.F. Rushbrook Williams, *The State of Pakistan*, (London: 1962), pp. 62-63.
3. Barnett R. Rubin, "Saving Afghanistan," *Foreign Affairs*, January-February 2007, p. 2, emphasis added.
4. See for instance Olaf Caroe, *The Pathans*, 550 B.C.-A.D. 1957 (London: Macmillan & Co Ltd, 1965), 465.
5. S.M. Burke, *Pakistan's Foreign Policy: An Historical Analysis* (London : Oxford University Press, 1973), p. 87.
6. Burke, p. 74
7. Ghayoor Ahmed "The Truth about the Durand Line," *The Dawn*, online edition, January 18, 2007, http://www.dawn.com/2007/01/18/op.htm#2
8. Olaf Caroe, *The Pathans*, 550 B.C.-A.D. 1957 (London: Macmillan & Co Ltd, 1965), p. 381.
9. *Ibid*, p. 3.
10. Dr. Noor ul Haq Dr Rashid Ahmed Khan Dr. Maqsudul Hasan Nuri, *Federally Administered Tribal Areas of Pakistan, Paper No 10, IRI, http://ipripak.org/papers/federally.shtml*
11. I Ram Mohan Rao, "Fierce Afghan opposition to Pakistan's proposal to fence and mine the Durand Line," http://www.dailyindia.com/show/102187.php/Fierce-Afghan-opposition-to-Pakistans-proposal-to-fence-and-mine-the-Durand-Line—also see "Pakistan Progress on Afghan Fence," Afgha.com, May 10, 2007, citing British Broadcasting Corporation, http://www.afgha.com/?q=node/2896
12. Shaiq Hussain, "Afghan Border Mining to be Elective," *The Nation*, January 2007, http://www.nation.com.pk/daily/jan-2007/4/index5.php

13. Khan, Azmat Hayat, The Durand Line; its geo-strategic importance (Peshawar, Area Study Centre, University of Peshawar, 2000), p. 185 cited in Dr Noor ul Haq Dr Rashid Ahmed Khan Dr Maqsudul Hasan Nuri *Federally Administered Tribal Areas of Pakistan, Paper No 10, IRI, http://ipripak.org/papers/federally.shtml*
14. Vanni Cappeli, "Containing Pakistan: Engaging the Raja-Mandala in South-Central Asia," *Orbis*, Winter 2007, p. 3.
15. On the occasion of officially celebrated Pashtunistan Day, the state owned newspaper, The Kabul Times wrote: 'The people of this country have unbreakable and age old bonds of proximity with the Pashtuns and Baloches, who thirty years after the departure of the British from the Indian sub-continent are still struggling for the right to determine their own destiny." cited in Dr Noor ul Haq Dr Rashid Ahmed Khan Dr Maqsudul Hasan Nuri *Federally Administered Tribal Areas of Pakistan, Paper No 10, IRI, http://ipripak.org/papers/federally.shtml*
16. *Ibid.*
17. Marvin G. Wein baum and Jonathan B. Harder, "Pakistan's Afghan Policies and Their Consequences," *Contemporary South Asia*, Vol. 16, No.1, p. 28.
18. Barnett R. Rubin and Abubakar Siddique, "Resolving the Pakistan-Afghanistan Stalemate," United States Institute for Peace, Special Report, October 2006.
19. C. Christine Fair, Nicholas Howenstein, and J. Alexander Their, "Troubles on the Pakistan-Afghanistan Border," USI Peace Briefing, December 2006, http://www.usip.org/pubs/usipeace_briefings/2006/1207_pakistan_afghanistan_border.html
20. *Ibid.*
21. Bureau Report, "ANP manifesto stresses autonomy," *The Dawn*, December 17, 2007, http://www.dawn.com/2007/12/17/top4.htm
22. Dennis Kux, "The United States and Pakistan, 1947-2000: Disenchanted Allies" (Washington DC, 2000), p. 19. S.M. Burke, *Pakistan's Foreign Policy: An Historical Analysis*, 1988, pp. 73-4.
23. Syed Mujtaba Rizvi, *The Frontiers of Pakistan: A Study of Problems in Pakistan's Foreign Policy*, Army Education Press, Rawalpindi, 1971, p. 144.
24. Zahir Shah visited Pakistan in 1968; his visit was reciprocated by Finance Minister, Muzafar Ali Khan Qazalbash in 1970 to explore the possibilities of increasing trade and economic callaboration Syed Mujtaba Rizvi henceforth Mujtaba, The Frontiers of Pakistan: A Study of Problems in Pakistan's Foreign Policy, Army Education Press, Rawalpindi, 1971, p. 159.

25. Kamal Matinuddin, *Power Struggle in Hindokush* (1978-91), Wajidalis Lahore, 1991, p. 23-24.
26. *Ibid.*
27. Marvin G. Weinbaum, "Afghanistan and its Neighbors; an ever Dangerous Neighborhood," Special Report 162, United States Institute for Peace, June, 2006, http://www.usip.org/pubs/specialreports/sr162.pdf, p. 4.
28. Marvin G. Weinbaum, "Pakistan and Afghanistan: The Strategic Relationship," *Asian Survey*, Vol. 31, No. 6, (June, 1991), p. 492.
29. Larry Goodsen, *Foreign Policy Gone Awry: The Kalashnikovization and Talibanization of Pakistan*, (OUP, New York), p. 153.
30. Vanni Cappeli, "Containing Pakistan: Engaging the Raja-Mandala in South-Central Asia," *Orbis*, Winter 2007, p. 63.
31. Marvin G. Weinbaum, "Pakistan and Afghanistan: The Strategic Relationship," *Asian Survey*, Vol. 31, No. 6, (June 1991), p. 492, p. 497.
32. Babar Shah "Pakistan's Afghanistan Policy: An evaluation," *Strategic Studies*, 2000, vol.2, 3, pp. 178-179.
33. The Afghan government of Babrak Karmal reportedly 'encouraged' the hijackers.
34. MohammadYousaf and Mark Atkin, *The Bear Trap, (Jang Publishers, Lahore, 1992) pp. 81-83.*
35. Imtiaz Gul, *The Unholy Nexus*, (Lahore: Vanguard, 2002), p. 272.
36. Brigadie Feroz Hassan Khan "Rough Neighbors: Afghanistan and Pakistan," *Strategic Insights*, Volume II, Issue 1 (January 2003) Center for Contemporary Conflict at the Naval Postgraduate School in Monterey, California, http://www.ccc.nps.navy.mil/si/jan03/southAsia.asp
37. Noor Muhammad Jadmani, "Afghanistan: Its Impavt on Pakistan Economy," NIPA Karachi Journal, Vol. 8, no 1, 2003, p. 82.
38. Mansoor Akbar Kundi, "A hard Nut to crack" *The Nation*, January 9, 2007, http://www.nation.com.pk/daily/jan-2007/9/forex.php
39. *Ibid.*
40. Richard Cronin, "Pakistani Capabilities to Meet the Soviet Threst from Afghanistan," in Theodore L Eliot, Jr and Robert L. Pfaltzgraff Jr Eds *The Red army on Pakistan's Border* (Washington D.C. Pergamon Brasseysa, 1986), pp. 19-43, S.M. Burke and Lawrence Ziring *Pakistan's Foreign Policy*, (OUP Karachi, 19990) seind ed, pp 443-455.cited in Goodsen p. 154.
41. UNHCR "Fact Sheet Pakistan" 2, no 2 cited in Goodsen, p. 155.
42. Goodsen, p. 157.
43. Noor Muhammad Jadmani, pp. 83-84

44. *Ibid*, p. 86.
45. Rasul Bux Rais, Asian Survey, Vol. xxiii, No. 9, September 1993, pp. 907-910.
46. Youssaf and Atkin, pp. 78-112.
47. Edward Girardet, "Corrupt Officials reap Spoils of Afghan War" Christian Science Monitor, September 7, 1988. cited in Goodsen, p. 159. He reports of having personally seen these arms in the bazaar in Tribal Agencies in Peshawar.
48. Ahmed Rashid, "Pakistan and Taliban" in William Maley, ed, *Fundamentalism Reborn? Afghanistan and the Taliban* (New York, New York University Press, 1998), pp. 72-89.
49. Ahmed Rashid, "Pakistan and Taliban" in William Maley, ed, *Fundamentalism Reborn? Afghanistan and the Taliban* (New York, New york University Press, 1998), p. 87.
50. Barnett R. Rubin, "Saving Afghanistan," *Foreign Affairs*, January-February 2007, p. 24.
51. Marvin G. Weinbaum, "Afghanistan and its Neighbors; an ever Dangerous Neighborhood" Special Report 162, United States Institute for Peace, June 2006, p. 6, 2006, http://www.usip.org/pubs/specialreports/sr162.pdf, p. 5.
52. Pakistan's Afghanistan Policy: An Evaluation, p. 193.
53. Ahmed Rashid, Taliban Exporting Extremism, *World Affairs*, November/December 1999, p. 139.
54. Anthony Davis, "How the Taliban Became a military Force," in Maley 69-71, Rashid, pp. 72-89.
55. Goodsen, p. 166.
56. *Ibid*, p. 167.
57. Ahmed Rashid, Pakistan, p. 51.
58. General Mirza Aslam Beg, "Afghanistan Turmoil and regional security Imperatives," paper read at conference in Tehran December 22, 2002. Brigadie Feroz Hassan Khan "Rough Neighbors: Afghanistan and Pakistan," *Strategic Insights*, Volume II, Issue 1 (January 2003) Center for Contemporary Conflict at the Naval Postgraduate School in Monterey, Californiahttp://www.ccc.nps.navy.mil/si/jan03/southAsia.asp
59. Lt. Gen. (Retd.) Kaml Matinuddin, "Post 9/11 Afghanistan," South Asia Journal, January-March,2004He however adds Pakistan was, however, gradually getting disenchanted with the Taliban, as they were paying no heed to the advice being given to them by Islamabad. A personal letter from Musharraf to Omar advising him to understand the seriousness of the present situation did not make a difference.

60. Hussain Haqqani, *Pakistan: Between Mosque and Military* (Vanguard Books, Lahore, 2005), p. 322.
61. Daniel Markey, "A False Choice in Pakistan," *Foreign Affairs*, July-August 2007, p. 2.
62. Rashid Ahmad Khan, "Pak-Afghan Relations," *The Nation*, August 23, 2006, http://www.nation.com.pk/daily/august-2006/23/columns1.php
63. *Ibid.*
64. Ibid Rashid Ahmad Khan, "Pak-Afghan Relations," The Nation, August 23, 2006, http://www.nation.com.pk/daily/august-2006/23/columns1.php
65. Ajai Sahni, "A Contagion of Disorders," *South Asia Intelligence Review* [SAIR, Weekly Assessments and Briefings, http://www.satp.org/satporgtp/sair/index.htm,Volume 6, No. 5, August 13, 2007.
66. Ayaz Gul, "Pakistan Denies Involvement in Karzai Attack," Voice of America, Islamabad 26 June 2008, http://www.voanews.com/english/2008-06-26-voa31.cfm
67. Barnett R. Rubin and Abubakar Siddique," Resolving the Pakistan-Afghanistan Stalemate" United States Institute for Peace, Special Report, October 2006, p. 3.
68. Tariq Fatemi, "US pressure to do more," *The Dawn* online addition, January 20, 2007, http://www.dawn.com/2007/01/20/op.htm
69. By Simon Cameron Moore, "Afghan reconstruction" Reuters Alertnet, July 27, 2006, http://www.alertnet.org/thenews/newsdesk/SP41202.htm
70. UNAMA, 'Suicide attacks in Afghanistan', Report of the UN Assistance Mission in Afghanistan (UNAMA), Kabul, 7 September 2007, pp. 11, 28 and 90.
71. Seth Jones, "Pakistan's Dangerous Game," *Survival*, Vol. 49, Spring 2007, p 18.
72. Jones, p. 21.
73. Daniel Korski, "Afghanistan: Europe's forgotten war" *Policy Paper*, European Council on Foreign Relations, January 2008, p. 25.
74. Hasan Abbas, "A Profile of Tehrik-i-Taliban Pakistan," *CTC Sentinel*, Vol. 1, no. 2, pp. 1-3.
75. Abdul Waheed Wafa, "Pakistan should crack down on Taliban, UN official says," *International Herald Tribune*, January 2007, http://www.iht.com/articles/2007/01/09/news/afghan.php
76. Ali Jalali, 'The Future of Afghanistan', *Parameters*, vol. 36, no. 1, Spring 2006, p. 5.
77. Weinbaum Special Report, p. 11. It is also "designed to register

doubt that international peacekeepers and the central government can protect the mostly Pashtun population. It is also intended to keep NGOs and international agencies from contributing to reconstruction and improvement in the lives of ordinary Afghans in these areas."

78. Seth Jones, p. 17.
79. Lt. Gen. (Retd.) Kaml Matinuddin, "Post 9/11 Afghanistan," *South Asia Journal*, January-March 2004.
80. Amin Tarzi, 'Afghanistan: Kabul's India Ties Worry Pakistan', *Radio Free Europe/Radio Liberty,* 16 April 2006, http://www.rferl.org/featuresarticle/2006/04/B5BFE0BE-ED5D-43DE-A768-99A6AB1E6C5C.html
81. Daniel Korski, "Afghanistan: Europe's Forgotten War," *Policy Paper,* European Council on Foreign Relations, London, January 2008, p. 26.
82. Vanni Cappelli, "Containing Pakistan: Engaging the Raja-Mandala in South-Central Asia," *Orbis*, Winter 2007, p. 69.
83. Vanni Cappelli, "Containing Pakistan: Engaging the Raja-Mandala in South-Central Asia" *Orbis,* Winter 2007.
84. Barnett Rubin, "Afghanistan's Uncertain Transition from Turmoil to Normalcy," CRS, No. 12, Council on Foreign Relation, March 2006.
85. Abdul Waheed Wafa, "Pakistan should crack down on Taliban, UN official says," *International Herald Tribune,* January 2007, http://www.iht.com/articles/2007/01/09/news/afghan.php
86. Jalali, p. 5.
87. Lt. Gen. (Retd.) Kaml Matinuddin, "Post 9/11 Afghanistan," *South Asia Journal*, January-March, 2004.

CHAPTER 15

The Future of Taliban

Kalim Bahadur

The exact origin of the Taliban according to many writers is shrouded in mystery.[1] This myth has been really promoted in order to cover up the role played by the Pakistan's agencies in the creation and training of the group. There is no doubt that, many Afghan students of the *madrassas* in the frontier region of Pakistan had joined the various Jihadi groups fighting during the Soviet intervention therefore, there was nothing peculiar about the so-called Taliban force which came into existence in 1994 to be given the name of Taliban. This creates the false image as if the entire force comprised of the students of the *madrassas*. It was certainly not the army of the *madrassa* students.[2] The Taliban came into existence in 1994 during the growing chaotic warfare in Afghanistan among the various Jihadi groups. The pupils of a *madrassa* in Kanadhar, led by one Umar, helped in punishing some criminals who had assaulted and killed some women. Umar, later known as Mulla Umar, was not an Islamic scholar, as he had not completed his education in any *madrassa* and was not eligible to be called a Mulla. The group came to the notice of the Pakistani agency, the ISI. This was the moment when Pakistan's relations with the Rabbani regime in Kabul had deteriorated. Even the ISI's favourite Afghan Mujahideen leader Gulbuddin Hekmatyar, had also failed to come up to the expectations of Islamabad. The

Peshawar Agreement had collapsed. The emergence of Taliban at that juncture was a godsend opportunity for Pakistan's agencies. Soon a large arms and ammunition dump in the vicinity was put at their disposal.[3]

The political system in Afghanistan over the last hundred years had evolved into a fragile structure of power headed by the monarchy. This equation was broken by first Sardar Daoud Khan in 1973 and later by the Khalq in 1978. The Soviet intervention to defend the Khalq regime proved counter productive. They could not put in place a new power structure. Pakistan's military ruler General Ziaul Haq who was facing international isolation found it expedient to put Pakistan in the frontline against the Soviet occupation. Pakistan was looking to secure a satellite regime in Afghanistan in the name of what was called the strategic depth, whatever it might have meant. The Pakistani agencies caught on to Taliban and later promoted them as the main strategic force serving the strategic interests of Islamabad.

The Taliban started their conquest of the country with the attack on Kanadhar which, it was believed, fell without much resistance but not without the support from across the border. The fall of Kanadhar, according to reports, was not entirely due to the superior strategy or bravery of the Taliban but money had played an important part in the victory. Incidentally, buying of the opposition warlords played an important role in the rapid advance of the Taliban during the next two years. Generous supplies of latest weapons and reinforcements from across the border gave the Taliban a heady start on ward to future victories. Their swift advance after Helmand and Ghazni put the conquest of the entire country within their sights. Slowly the myth of Taliban invincibility spread partly by the Pakistani media and the ISI. The induction of the former soldiers and officers of the Afghan army and also of the Pakistani advisors gave the Taliban the military edge over the Jihadi groups whose experience was limited to guerilla war against the beleaguered Soviet soldiers. The Taliban successes were not without setbacks and even routs. First attempts to take Herat, Kabul and Mazar were defeated by Ismail Khan, Masood and Malik Pahlwan. Each time reinforcements from Pakistan were rushed to help the Taliban.

Large amount of money and defection from the defenders the second time ensured almost peaceful entry of the Taliban in these cities in the second attempts.

Extremist Islam has never been popular in Afghanistan. In fact Afghans have been very tolerant in religious matters. This was because of the influence of the Sufism in the country.[4] Sufism has been a trend in mystical Islam which originated in Central Asia and Persia. There are several Sunni Sufi orders and among them Naqshbandiyah and Qadriya are the most popular in Afghanistan. The members of the former Sufi order have been close to the Afghan ruling families. Saudi Wahabism could not take roots in the country mainly because of the influence of Sufism. It was only after the Khalqi revolt in 1978 that there began the flow of Saudi arms and money which also brought in Wahabism in Afghanistan. The Afghan Ulama did not join the fundamentalist parties because they propounded an entirely different view of Islam, rejected nationalism, ethnicity and tribal loyalties. Mawdudi had opposed Pakistan movement because he believed that the concept of nation was against Islam. The Taliban never systematically put forward their view of what kind of an Islamic society they were aiming at. They like all traditional Ulama wanted a mechanical implementation of the *shariat* laws according to their interpretation of Islam mixed with tribal traditions. The arrival of Arabs in Afghanistan during the early eighties at the height of the Jihad against the Soviet army introduced a new factor in the war in Afghanistan. Till then there were very few Arabs fighting alongside the Mujahideen. One Prof Abdullah Azzam who had links with the Muslim Brotherhood and had fought with the Palestinians arrived in Islamabad in 1984 and later came to Afghanistan along with Osama Bin Laden in 1986.[5] Thereafter large number of Arabs came to Afghanistan and participated in the war. Naturally both the Saudis and the Pakistani intelligence supported this mobilization of the Arabs in the war against the Soviet army. It also had the support of the United States agencies. It was only after the Kabul fell to the Mujahideen in 1992 that the American realised the danger of the Arab movement under the leadership of Osama bin Laden and Abdullah Azzam. The United States persuaded the Pakistan and

Afghan agencies to arrest Arabs in Afghanistan and many Arabs also left because of the internecine fighting erupted among the Mujahideen groups. Osama bin laden returned later to Afghanistan to play an important role during the Taliban regime. He floated the organisation, A1-Qaeda with the avowed objective of fighting for the resurrection of Islam in the world. "Our fight will be against the enemies of Islam," he is reported to have told his followers. With this message, his organisation started networking with outfits of similar ideas all over the world. By 2000, his networking spread over 60 countries and four continents. By late 1999, the Taliban and Al-Qaeda had become synonymous.[6] Interestingly Osama was and engineer by training and not an Islamic scholar and has nowhere given his world view according to his understanding of Islam.

The Taliban were not an Islamic movement it was an armed movement which appeared in response to the chaos and lawlessness of the various Jihadi groups. It is ironic while most of the Jihadi groups belonged to Islamic fundamentalist parties and espoused the ideal of setting up an Islamic state, the Taliban did not represent any new interpretation of Islam or any of its schools of thought but belonged to the traditional Islam which aims at implementing the Islamic laws combined with the local Mullas' religious practices and Afghan Pushtun tribal traditions. Even the leader of the Jama'at-i-Islami of Pakistan Qazi Hussain Ahmed did not accept the credentials of the teachers of the Madrassas where most of the Taliban had received their education. He called the teachers of those *madrassas* as uneducated Maulvis.[7] However, the Jama'at-i-Islami, which would denounce the least deviation from their concept of Islam never, distanced itself from the blatant distortion of Islam by the Taliban. Most Islamic movements in Afghanistan including the one led by Bacha Saqa which over threw the regime of King Amanullah in 1929 were not inspired by the ideal of setting up an Islamic state as propounded by Islamic ideologues like Mawlana Mawdudi, Syed Qutb and Ayatullah Khomeini. The ideology of the fundamentalist parties appealed to the students of the modern educated schools of colleges and the modern strata of the society.[8] These ideologues interpreted Islam not as a religion but as a political theory. Islamic fundamentalism came to Afghanistan through students who went to Al Azhar. Their support base remained confined to the Pushtuns and they were at war with other ethnic communities and minority sects of the country. Most of the Taliban who came from the Madrassas established by the Jamiatul Ulama-i-Islam led by Mawlana Fazalur Rehman and Mawlana Samiul Haq were influenced by the Deobandi School however; it would be erroneous to equate the Taliban as one of the fundamentalist parties like the Muslim Brotherhood and the Jama'at-i-Islami. These parties consider Islam as a complete code of life.

The Taliban had emerged so suddenly and in such political circumstance that it was not possible for them to have well thought out ideology and probably they were not prepared for it. They were opposed to most of the Islamist parties because of religious and political reasons. They were not even intellectually capable of offering a new interpretation of Islam. Their world view and also their understanding of social and political life first came out when the Taliban captured Herat. They had earlier taken over Kanadhar but it was almost in ruins and hence their edicts on women and girls' schools went unnoticed. Herat was a well administered city with a relatively liberal society. It had many girls' schools. When Taliban took over they immediately issued orders on dress, closure of girls' schools and the behaviour of the population, particularly banned women working.[9] Even boys' schools had to be closed as many teachers in those schools were women. The Taliban rule resulted in many Persian speaking Heratis migrating to Iran. In fact the fall of Herat signaled the beginning of the end of the Rabbani regime in Kabul .

The Taliban phenomenon was a part of the Muslims' response to the modern world particularly in the post second world war, the break up of the colonial world and the emergence of many independent countries, many of them Muslim majority countries but poor and under developed. The emergence of Israel and successive defeats of the combined power of the Arab countries had created among the Muslim particularly the West Asia a religious vulnerability.

The Taliban in spite of the large material and intellectual support from the armed forces of Pakistan could not evolve into a strong military force and were time and again defeated by their opponents. By 1997 Taliban were in control of almost 90 percent of the country. This led to the recognition of the Taliban by Saudi Arabia, United Arab Republic and Pakistan after their entry into Mazar Sharif in early 1997. The Taliban had suffered a devastating rout after their first entry in Mazar Sharif in May 1997. They were able to capture the city a year later in 1998.

Women are the first victim of any so-called Islamic regime. Women were forbidden to go to work. Taliban were not the first or the last in this interpretation of their religion. The major decision of the MMA regime, which took over in the Pakistan's North Western Frontier Province in 2002, was to pass the infamous Hudood Ordinance in the province. The MMA fought hard first in the Supreme Court of Pakistan and later in the National Assembly when the government attempted to amend it. Afghanistan had been at war for almost two decades and there were thousands of women and children whose bread earners had been killed during the various wars. Banning women from any work actually led thousands of women and children to starve. Women had no option left but to take to prostitution. The Taliban regime's treatment of women aroused the human rights activists through out the world and drew wide spread protests. Usually the first step of the Taliban as of all Islamic rulers is the introduction of *amar bil maroof wa nahian al-munkar* (the department of the promotion of virtue and prevention of vice). It is implemented by kind of religious police. The Taliban carried this edict to the most ridiculous level. It compelled women to cover themselves from head to foot, forbade them to wear high heel shoes, or wear make up, making no noise with their shoes, etc. The police would be on look out for any violation of these and other rules and punishment would follow publicly and on the spot. Men were not expected to be on roads at the time any prayer and had to keep regulatory beards etc. These laws were even imposed on foreigners including Pakistani football team which wore half pants during the football match.[10] The Taliban were ever ready to cut their nose to spite the world. The destruction of the Bamiyan Buddhas was another example of this attitude of the Taliban leadership. The destruction of the priceless inheritance of the Pre-Islamic art of the country aroused world wide indignation.

Taliban were ready to go to any extent in their wilful defiance to the international opinion which was demonstrated in their refusal to handover Osama bin Laden after the 9/11 terrorists attacks on the twin towers of the world trade center in New York. The Taliban had no chance once the United States had decided to attack Afghanistan and destroy them. For several days Mulla Umar gave the impression he had some well thought out plan which he would unleash in due course of time. The Taliban were decimated by the U.S.invasion in 2001 Mulla Umar and others took to their heels. Osama bin Laden also disappeared. In fact most of the remnants of Taliban took shelter in the Pakistan Afghan frontier areas particularly in Waziristan with the knowledge and connivance of the Pakistan's agencies. None of the top leaders of the Taliban could be apprehended by the US forces.

The fact that the Taliban after suffering the devastating rout could manage to survive and resurrect themselves was mainly due to the some of the grave errors by the coalition forces. One observer of the Afghan scene has remarked that far from achieving the objectives the 2001 Afghan war, the U.S led coalition merely pushed the core leadership of Al-Qaeda and the Taliban out of Afghanistan and into Pakistan with no strategy for consolidating this apparent tactical advance.[11] They were soon allowed to regroup their forces and began to carry out attacks on the US and the Afghan government forces from the sanctuary of Pakistan territory. Ironically instead of Pakistan getting strategic depth in Afghanistan it was the Taliban who got strategic depth in Pakistan territory. Very soon after the destruction of the US attention was diverted to Iraq but apart from that the unfortunate reality was that the US had no plans for the post Taliban rehabilitation of Afghanistan. The Taliban should not have been allowed to escape into Pakistan's tribal belt. The Pushtuns of Pakistan living in the frontier region had played an important role in the rise of the Taliban and their successful campaigns in

Afghanistan. Pakistan's agencies were also deeply involved first with the Mujahideen and later with the Taliban. There was no shortage of recruits for the Taliban who came from the many *madrassas* and also from among the population along the frontier and tribesmen from Northwest Frontier Province who belonged to the same racial stock as that of the Pushtuns from Afghanistan. Pakistan under General Musharraf ever since 9/11 had been following the line of being on the one hand a very enthusiastic part of the war on terror on the other hand the military agencies doing all to help the resurgence of the Taliban. In the period soon after the Taliban escape the coalition forces neglected the south and eastern parts of the country which also included thee opium producing areas. This helped the Taliban immensely to revive their strength.

The coalition had fallen short on the post-Taliban rehabilitation and economic reconstruction of Afghanistan. The dependence of a large section of population on the drug economy is a source of great help to the Taliban. The Karzai regime has some positive achievements in building democratic institutions. But the regime still lacks legitimacy and its writ is accepted in a very limited part of the country. Karzai is seen as a ruler who had been imposed by a foreign power. The old Afghan tradition of fighting against the foreign invaders still plays an important motivational role in mobilising the Afghans for the Taliban.

The war in Afghanistan may be long drawn out. The Nato army will have to provide support for the Karzai regime for a long time to come. The rise of the fundamentalist movements in the region surrounding Afghanistan helps create an encouraging atmosphere for the Taliban. The fundamentalist movements from Algeria to Mindanao in Philippines encourage Islamic movements in the neighboring countries It does not seem possible for the Taliban to regain control of the entire country in the foreseeable future. They would remain at best one of the sizable groups vying for power in Afghanistan.

CHAPTER 16

Afghanistan: Concerns of the Periphery

P.L. Dash

INTRODUCTION

No other country of the South-Central Asian region has been so prone to political volatility as has been Afghanistan since 1979. On the Christmas eve of that year, when Soviet troops moved into Afghanistan to safeguard the national security interests of the erstwhile Soviet Union, an intense Cold War rivalry began to take shape that continued up to 15 February,1989, when nine months before the fall of the Berlin Wall, Gorbachev decided to pull out of Afghanistan. True to his avowed declaration in Vladivostok in July, 1986, Gorbachev assessed the Afghan imbroglio and quickly concluded that entrapment of the Soviet Union in a prolonged battle was of no gain to his country. Over 17 thousand Soviet soldiers, mostly youngsters, had already lost their precious lives. As death toll mounted, with each passing month, it was making the Soviet Union nervously sapless, draining its resources to the bleeding point of sanguinary entanglement from which there was apparently no escape route. In consonance with his New Thinking in foreign policy, Gorbachev understood the gravity, depth and magnitude of the Soviet involvement in Afghanistan and reached the conclusion that total withdrawal was the only wise course left to be followed in the changing context of Perestroika. He pursued that course determinedly and ensured that last Soviet soldier from the Afghan soil left before the summer of 1989. The Afghan situation was casting a pall of gloom over the entire process of secessionism wrecking the Soviet Union then.

Ever since then, Afghanistan has remained at the centre of turmoil. The Soviet collapse brought to the region cataclysmic changes in political equations. Two fundamental changes that happened in and around Afghanistan were: NATO's eastward expansion as partners of Peace and the advent of the Taliban. These were two irreconcilable forces. A truculent theocracy, whose basics were rooted in age old traditions, began to confront the efforts of a mighty, modern military block, whose unmatched potential held atop its supremacy above others. Newly independent Central Asian countries were rapidly gaining geo-strategic importance for the United States. Thus a quadrangular clash of interest was shaping up in the region involving the Taliban in Afghanistan, the US in Central Asia, the Russian Federation in its former prefectures and NATO as a military collective pursuing the unseemly role of a peace maker.

9/11 suddenly changed these equations. It drew the US attention to the Central Asian region as never before. Afghanistan became the epicentre of terror that nurtured and harboured the Al-Qaeda and the world wide terror network under the leadership of Osama Bin Laden. Determined to stamp out the remnants of Taliban from the Afghan soil, as the US proceeded to gain control over that country through a joint military efforts, the Taliban received body blows to their very existence and fled to the safe haven of mountains in Waziristan. Ever since then a new political equation has taken shape. The US and the Hamid Karzai government in Afghanistan on the one hand joined by coalition forces of NATO members and the independent Central Asian countries, enjoying Russian support on the other took position around volatile Afghanistan that has become a safe haven for many things illegal and illicit. The tug of war continues and its gloomy shadow darkens the regional picture so incredibly that Afghanistan remains a real concern for all in the region to handle.

NEIGHBOURHOOD DIMENSIONS

As political equations began to mutate to take a new shape in the post-Soviet phase, it was apparent that the Soviet Union was no longer Afghanistan's immediate neighbour. In the neighbourhood there emerged independent and sovereign states with whom Afghanistan has had no experience of pursuing sovereign diplomatic relations. And among its immediate neighbours were three Central Asian countries: Turkmenistan, Tajikistan and Uzbekistan. All three countries looked introspectively at the existing Taliban regime in Afghanistan vis-a-vis their emerging framework of relations with that country. They, however, related themselves with Afghanistan very gingerly. Tajikistan was the only country across the Pyandz river that became victim of an unprecedented civil war, where three rival factions fought with one another: native Islamists influenced by hardliner Taliban, local communists influenced by Moscow and democrats who were trimming with ideas of liberty and equality. Their fight took too bitter a turn to be too soon resolved. And the civil war continued for long five years.

Three other cross-boundary ethnic groups provided a different colour to the whole shape of things then emerging. Native Afghans on the southern side of the Pyandz fought with native Tajik on the northern shores of the river. The Afghan Uzbeks fought with the Afghan Tajik as much on the Tajik soil as on the northern Afghan territories. The Pamiris, the Garmies and the Gorno-Badakhshanis fought among themselves. The Tajik and the Uzbeks also fought thereby implying as if the area was pregnant with ethnic animus that would rip apart the neighbourhood. The spiralling effects were called in Tajikistan 'Afghan spill over' and in Afghanistan it was mutually responded as 'Tajik effects'. Such were the complementary mutuality of terminologies used to ascribe each other's sanguinary predicament. It was interesting to note that when Afghanistan was passing through the gruelling years of Taliban reign, Tajikistan was simultaneously passing through an equally tumultuous phase of civil war. Both neighbours were not in a position to help each other.

Further interesting was the neighbourhood reaction of Turkmenistan. The Turkmen president, Saparmurad Niyazov maintained cordial relations with the Taliban in Afghanistan. At the same time he distanced himself from the ongoing episodes in Tajik civil war by maintaining positive neutrality. Welcome to the Taliban and neutrality with Tajikistan was how Turkmenistan approached the emerging regional scenario to pursue its policy of 'positive neutrality'. When all other countries showered vituperation on the Taliban on their truculent approach to social issues, Niyazov's friendly treatment of the Taliban in the resorts of the Caspian coast raised eyebrows worldwide. Everybody was agog to know how one dictatorial regime was approaching another authoritarian theocracy in the neighbourhood. The salience of camaraderie was only known to Niyazov, who wanted to avoid troubles along the border from where he apprehended Islamism to spill over to Turkmen countryside. Harking back to the past approach of Niyazov, one could feel that he handled the Taliban problem deftly and adroitly upheld Turkmen sovereignty from the pernicious influence of insurgent Islam. While other Central Asian neighbours of Afghanistan were crying foul about radical Islamic spilling over to their territories, Turkmenistan was comfortable with coexistence with the Taliban and never made an issue out of it.

However, what worries one and all in the Afghan neighbourhood is the uncertain phase of development that country has been passing through. Foreign troops, first in the form of coalition forces and then since 2003 direct NATO forces are stationed in the country. A NATO commander recently admitted that "two third of the country is not under the government control."[1] The worrisome Taliban resurgence is rapidly gaining ground, thereby ruling out a military solution to the Afghan problem. Various ethnic factions are at loggerhead with one another across the country, thereby precipitating tense interethnic relations. No tangible progress on rebuilding the war ravaged country is visible on the socio-economic front and this creates disillusionment among the public to abhor as much foreign forces as the Karzai government. Millions of Afghan refugees, still living outside Afghanistan, are yet to return to their homeland. The illegal narcotic trade is droning the country as if forever. The Durrand line dividing the Afghan-Pakistan border is the safe haven for terrorists, who often sneak into urban areas as suicide bombers to embarrass the Karzai government and foil the nation building plan of European combine. Engineers and technologists, who are engaged in rebuilding Afghanistan, are routinely kidnapped by Taliban/Al-Qaeda supporters. All these are not very happy signs of a country passing through an extraordinary transition to build a civil society. It is in this context, the contiguous region and the periphery assume greater significance now than ever earlier.[2]

KANDAHAR CONCERNS

Long before the western efforts to stamp out Al-Qaeda/ Taliban began to take concrete shape, there happened an incident that the west did not care about. The hijacking of the IC814 on the very new year eve of this millennium implied the bent of mind of the Islamic terrorists to take maximum mileage out of hostage taking. The timing was Christmas break of 1999, thereby further implying that Islamic terror will remain a force to reckon with in the millennium to come. The conditions of the hostage takers that a few prisoners of some like minded terrorist outfits be freed from the Indian jail in exchange of the hostages was further testimony of their strength to bargain a hard deal. And that was what really happened. When the Indian airlines plane on a scheduled flight from Kathmandu to Delhi was detoured first to Amritsar and then to Dubai before it finally landed in Kandahar, the intentions were very clear: this time the terrorists would strike a hard deal. Round after round of negotiations failed to obtain concessions from the hostage takers. Even at the apex level, no relaxation in attitude was apparent. Meanwhile the hostage takers had already killed one passenger to send a message to others to fall in line and not create panic or commotion inside the plane.

Since the Taliban and the Pakistani authorities were acting hand in globes with each other and their mentor the US was vacationing during Christmas, no extraneous help was feasible. In fact, ignoring at that point in time the Taliban warning on terror subsequently cost the US heavily: the 9/11 was the outcome one year eight months later. The Kandahar hijacking episode not only heightened terror prospects in the region, but also it had several regional and global ramifications. Among the regional concerns were an already volatile periphery that would be further close to another type of hostage taking. Hostage taking of different kinds such as of journalist, Daniel Pearl, Japanese engineers in Kyrgyzstan and Beslan school tragedy were few of the incidences that could be traced to terror originating from Islamists. Secondly, Kandahar certainly emboldened the Taliban to look to the future of terror with optimism. As long as someone else was ready to finance or even mastermind the operations, the Taliban had least to lose. Indifference of the US to intervene in the matter facilitated the growth of Al-Qaeda within Afghanistan and this had further emboldened the Taliban to take the world for granted. And that continued until the 9/11 was successfully carried out. A timely US intervention, not with double standard but with frankness, may have influenced future trajectories of Al-Qaeda terror and averted future tragedies of 9/11, Beslan and the ilk.

However, that was not to happen. The US was not much of help to India at the moment of that crisis, when hundreds of lives were at stake. Nor was any other country in the periphery. India stood isolated in sense that the much despised Taliban-Al-Qaeda combine overtly supported by Pakistan stood on one side and India with her passengers as hostage stood at the receiving end of the other spectrum. Russia and other Central Asian countries were not much of help too. The Indian cabinet of ministers met in New Delhi to chalk out a strategy to deal with the Taliban and it assigned the job to foreign minister Jaswant Singh to sort out the problems. It was one of the most gruelling times for the minister. The Taliban bargained with the Indian government and obtained freedom for three hardcore terrorist from the Indian jails.

The swap deal of prisoners with hostages was a unique thing the Taliban regime obtained from the Indian government. More so, minister Jaswant Singh, willy-nilly had to accompany the freed terrorists in the same plane to Kandahar to oversee the safety of hostage-terrorist swap handover. Although the minister was severely criticized for accompanying the released prisoners, he apparently did not have any other option to travel, when a chartered flight was denied to him and the Aviation Research Centre of the RAW too denied him a plane to travel. Time was too pressing for Singh not to travel to Kandahar. Lest the situation would slip out of control, he chose to travel with terrorists, who were just then released. To the utter amazement of the world, in full public view televised all the world over, the three released terrorists travelled by a jeep to Pakistan. This evidently showed the evil nexus of terror links in the periphery and that too direct linkage with Pakistan.

Kandahar induced an unstoppable process of lawlessness by the Taliban in the entire region. The wayward way women were ill-treated, nurses tortured at hospitals for no reason and school education stifled was evidence of the doomsday approaching. In those few years of their reign the Taliban have meted out a crushing blow to development. The country is experiencing now acute shortage of school teachers, nurses, paramedics, computer trainers and so on. Kandahar hijacking had opened up the lead of a simmering container in Afghan society which the western world could have noticed then. Failure to notice such insinuating, societal changes landed the entire world on a place, where a bullying Taliban regime was discernible. Look at how the Taliban Leader Mullah Omar was openly criticizing the US on Pakistan television in immediate aftermath of the 9/11. Look at how daringly, the Taliban destroyed the Buddha on the Bamiyan with their despicable shootings and with utter disregard to the cross-cultural ethos of Afghanistan along the Great Silk Road. Look at how the released prisoners from the Indian jails openly drove to their safe haven in Pakistan. This drives us back to the periphery of Pakistan as a terrorist hub, that can no longer be ignored. The longer you linger with duplicitous diplomacy, the more parlous it would prove for the region.

THE STAKEHOLDERS

It would be nearly 30 years next year in December, Afghanistan has remained in turmoil; hence in the limelight of the world. Located at the receiving end are poor Afghans, who have lost on all occasions. When their sovereignty was trampled by the Soviet forces in December, 1979 under the façade of building socialism, the local stakeholders wondered why socialism. Illiterate and inexperienced in the art of modern state building and governance, people thought that socialism will provide a magic wand to prosperity. But that was not to happen. Within a few years, when people got disillusioned with social transformations, they wondered why was socialism at all needed. Their experience with the Allah in the heaven and his representative the Mullah on earth was strikingly contrasted with socialism in practice. This created a social divide with the powerful clergy placed on one side with their followers and the Afghan communists supported by the Soviets on the other spectrum of the society that set the stage for a prolonged fight between various forces as stakeholders on the Afghan soil. What widened this Afghan schism was the combined US-Pakistani role in training the mercenary Mujaheeds to oust the Soviets from Afghanistan. As long as the Soviet forces remained in that country, Pakistan was the training ground and Afghanistan was the battle front. The major stakeholders in this game were the Soviets and Afghan communists. Both of them have failed eventually and have lost miserably. When the Soviet forces left Afghanistan lock, stock and barrel, they created too big a vacuum to be filled too soon. The Americans and the Pakistanis were well aware of how they bled the Soviet and Afghan forces. They were further aware that the country was trekking a dangerous cliff through a terrible route to stability. Thus these two countries shunned Afghanistan and left the Taliban to fill the political gap that was created after Soviet withdrawal. But they had invested in Afghanistan for years with the hope to reap some dividends and that was yet to materialize. The sudden Soviet withdrawal dashed their hopes, when the Taliban openly clashed with the Americans on issues of political governance. This was indeed a 'clash of civilization': an ultramodern, western democracy advocating the art of modern state building on the ruins of dilapidated feudalism to a society that lived ages behind in pre-feudal stage and recently ravaged by years of socialist experiment. It is on this troubled water that other stakeholders such as the Taliban, the US and Pakistan were trying to fish together with Osama Bin Laden, hand in gloves with the Taliban, negotiating a social contract with illiterate masses of Afghanistan for resurgence of Islam on the ruins of failed socialism. This situation sustained until the disastrous event of 9/11.

However, 9/11 further polarized the Afghan situation with Taliban and Osama on the one hand and the US and Pakistan on the other. Both sides were asserting themselves as stakeholders until the night bombardment by allied forces began, thereby bringing into picture several more stakeholders. The Afghan situation began to transform from a purely regional crisis to an international crisis, with wider ramifications and with active, military involvement of NATO and allied forces, Taliban, Osama bin Laden and his Al-Qaeda outfits and of course the US Pakistan combine. The old stakeholder, Russia and its former prefectures in Central Asia provided logistics to the war against terror of which Afghanistan became the battle ground. A potential neighbour, Iran, was sidestepped in view of the existing US-Iran hostility that apparently did not suit US regional interest. Very conveniently, all have branded Iran as an extremist Islamic country. All have forgotten that Iran was the country that salvaged Tajikistan from the mire of misery when the later was passing through a bloody civil war in 1992-1997. And the thus far the reconciliation deal holds good among the rival factions of Tajikistan, where communists have been sharing power with the Islamists and democrats. Can the Tajik deal, negotiated by Iran's mediation, be a role model for Afghanistan? Perhaps yes, sans the US from regional geopolitical entanglement.

Now, years after the elected government of Hamid Karzai ruled the country, there is everything but governance. Karzai is unpopular among the public. Perceived as an American stooge, he enjoys power as long as he is able to strike a balance of power equation with different warlords and drug lords operating in the provinces and virtually controlling the routes of narcotic trafficking. These powerful lords dwarf Karzai in stature. Although some of them are ministers in the Karzai cabinet, they remain ministers as long as their interests are safeguarded. They bother least about the stability in the country or stability of the government. Thus while the internal political situation remains unstable, the spill over effects of this instability coupled with a mighty money flow coming from illicit drug trade that facilitates export of radical Islam to the neighbourhood is widely felt across the border. This makes Afghanistan's neighbours—Iran, Turkmenistan, Tajikistan, Uzbekistan, China, Pakistan as well other countries in the proximity such as India, Russia, and the US vulnerable to the impact of the lethal combine called Islam and drugs. Money laundering, weapons and women trafficking make the situation more perilous. Unfortunately, all stakeholders are not a party to the current reconciliation process in Afghanistan. Many of them are not even indirect participants. From the days of the Geneva accord signed on 14 April,1988[3] till the advent of Karzai government, the stakeholders have varied depending on the geopolitical changes in the region. One could sum up it precisely by saying that the Soviet forces have been replaced by the forces of allied powers; and it makes little difference to the masses in Afghanistan.

DEMOCRACY DEFICIT

To single out Afghanistan as an undemocratic country is foolhardy. All countries in the periphery of Afghanistan are more or less undemocratic. Adoption of a constitution, regular election of a president, a prime minister or a parliament and a judiciary in place do not ensure the country democracy. The western perception of democracy 'by the people, for the people and of the people', where liberty, equality and fraternity are to be constitutionally upheld by an independent judiciary is grossly misinterpreted in the region. The neighbouring countries around Afghanistan present three types of regime : Pakistan is currently transitioning from a military dictatorship to a seemingly democratic set-up. China is a communist country transitioning to the path of capitalism for over two decades now. For the past 15 plus years, Uzbekistan and Turkmenistan have been transitioning from Soviet socialism to a national model of state building under an authoritarian presidential form of government. Tajikistan established a unique form of coalition democracy in the process of its transition from socialism through a bitter civil war to modern state building. Iran passed through its bitter years of intrastate war that it fought with Iraq, when it transitioned from a kingdom to a theocracy and ever since has been groping in wilderness to assert itself as a modern state. Afghanistan's history of the past thirty years has been replete with pangs of transition from a kingdom to communism and from there to Karzaism supported by western powers. In view of this complex regional development, one of the real concerns of the periphery is deficit of democracy and its consequential impact on the neighbourhood including on Afghanistan.

The very process of evolution of democratic ethos on the ruins of antiquated kingdoms, socialism or military dictatorship has not been well rooted in these countries, primarily because the level of understanding of democracy differs from country to country and in Afghanistan it is the lowest in the region. Thus hovering over the state building process and groping between dictatorship, restoration of kingdom, theocracy and modern democracy, Afghanistan stands today where it is: in the midst of laying the foundation stone of democratic building blocks for the future. And in the process it has encountered stupendous difficulties. The difficulties are aggravated by the presence of two diametrically opposite to each other forces on the Afghan territory: the allied forces led by NATO and the USA; and the Taliban/Al-Qaeda forces led by Osama Bin Laden. The irreconcilability of these forces perpetuates the negative prospects of the ongoing war in Afghanistan and this is what creates the roadblock in state and democracy building in Afghanistan.

The Afghans are a freedom loving people. However, they do not want that freedom to be seemingly coming from the west. They prefer indigenous democracy to foreign sponsored system of governance. This is simply because the US record of democracy building is replete with sanguinary battles and resultant bloodbath. In the post-Soviet years, without the fear of a super-power confrontation, the US has gone to several countries to build democracy. They are Somalia, Haiti, Kosovo, Bosnia, Iraq and Afghanistan; and in none of these countries there is political stability or democracy. The stakeholders of democracy are the people and they have been waging a protracted fight against foreign sponsored governance system that has been imposed on them from outside. The real apprehensions of the people rest around the big issue of their country falling prey to the neo-colonial aspirations of the US and other powers. That the country has been divided by allied forces corroborates these apprehensions.

Further concerns are the deep rooted clan-tribal loyalty. This is a traditional system that has remained in the Afghan society for centuries, where the local village chieftain is the master of his territory and his devotion and loyalty are only to the provincial chieftain, who lords over everything from local taxes to narcotic trafficking. They also maintain their own security forces to safeguard their interest. These chiefs are perceived by the people as genuine protectors of the Afghans; and not the foreign forces. This clan tribal loyalty is too deep rooted to be too soon wished away. It is this traditional loyalty that is clashing with the imposition of democracy from the top. The whole debate about the Karzai government not being so successful in clamping central control over provinces rests on this fractured system of governance, where the centre supported by the west has the Karzai government in place and the provinces look differently at their virtual fiefdoms. Although Karzai has been able to ensure a compromising coalition with some of the provincial chiefs, the periphery remains automatically decontrolled from the centre simply because writ of the central government has no locus-standi among the populace.

NARCOTIC NETWORK

Over the years, and particularly ever since the Soviets withdrew their forces, Afghanistan has emerged as the largest opium producing country not only in the region but also in the world. Afghanistan has therefore been one of the biggest concerns of the world in recent years in terms of narcotic trafficking. The country occupies centre stage when it comes to poppy cultivation and opium production in the world. It is from here that 90 percent of the world opium is produced and transported to major drug centres across the world.

Drugs trade is a complex issue that begins with the farmers, who produce the raw material called opium or coca. But they are illiterate and innocent farmers unaware about the pernicious implications of their produce. They produce opium because in the Afghan terrain fertile land is unavailable and nothing else worthwhile could be grown for a livelihood. When poppy "yields eight times the income of a comparable area of wheat" the preference of the farmer naturally veers toward poppy cultivation. In Afghanistan "some 448,000 households farmed 165,000 hectares of poppy in 2006, just a third of a hectare per household, producing an income of $ 1,700 a year per family.[4] Although this was a fantastic income by Afghan standard, compared to coca cultivating Colombian household, the Afghan farmers just got one seventh of their Colombian counterpart. However, there is a vast space to be covered between where the opium is grown, heroine is refined and drugs are trafficked.

The poppies are grown in the field, but opium is cooked in farms and homes. Cooks demand a price for their art of producing the opiate from the poppy. The better the 'cook', the higher the price he demands and greater is the quality of his cooked stuff that ensures the resultant kick of the opiate. Hence the demand of a quality cook in rural areas is great. Heroin is extracted from the opiate in the laboratory. The technology and the precursor chemicals are imported from Europe or from the US. The market target is again Europe and the US. However, Russia remains the huge market for Afghan drugs and all possible efforts are made to transport drugs to the Russian Federation, which lies in the immediate neighbourhood. The immediate neighbours in Central Asian countries, particularly Tajikistan and Turkmenistan serve as a conduit passage for drugs trafficking to the Russian Federation. The biggest of all heroin seizures has taken place in Tajikistan, not necessarily because it is easy to implement the interdiction measures there, not exactly that the police is more efficient there than elsewhere, but primarily because Tajikistan remains the most potent transit zone between Russia and Afghanistan. In 2005, the breakdown of all Central Asian countries bordering with Afghan north shows that 78 percent all drug seizures happened in Tajikistan followed by 16 percent in Uzbekistan and 6 percent in Turkmenistan. That year per 100,000 citizens the quantum of heroin seizure in Uzbekistan was

2 kilogram, in Tajikistan it was 36 kilogram, 4 kilogram each in Turkmenistan and Kazakhstan and five kilogram in Kyrgyzstan.[5]

However, the worry is not limited alone to how much of the transacted drugs have been seized or how much remained unseized. The estimated unseized amount is pegged at 96.5 metric tons, while the seized drug quantity is some 8.5 metric tons. This raises the eyebrows as to how effectively to curb the menace of narcotic trade. All interdiction steps have largely been futile for a variety of reasons. First, for the past several years, particularly since the allied intervention in October 2001, Afghanistan has remained a divided country: divided not in a geographical sense, but in an innovative sense of 'divide and rule'. Daan Everts, the former civilian representative of the NATO Secretary General in Kabul, has candidly admitted to Al Zajeera in a special interview the Balkanisation of Afghanistan. He said: "you have a little 'German Afghanistan' in the north, an 'Italian Afghanistan' in the west, a 'Dutch Afghanistan' in Uruzgan and a 'Canadian Afghanistan in Kandahar' and so on. Geographically, we have been fractured, but also sectorally with equal ineffectiveness – like giving the justice sector totally to the Italians, counter narcotics to the British, the police to Germans and anti-terrorism to Americans."[6] Such division has greatly facilitated drug peddling by agents, who have used to their advantage the absolute absence of coordination among various foreign agencies.

Secondly, in this complex territorial and administrative mess-up, the transportation routes of drugs in mountainous Afghanistan takes a strange zigzag turn. From the farmers and cooks at the poppy production level in remote villages, where the government cannot dictate the poppy cultivation right up to city centres, where opium labs are located, the transaction via-media are the mule grazers. For instance, a local influential village chieftain, who is simultaneously a drug dealer, requests the mule man to carry a packet to the next point through which he passes. The packet of drug is loaded on the mule sack. The mule does not cross the check points, he meanders across the ravine and mountains across the mountainous territory separately from his owner. The sniffer dogs even cannot approach the mule for fear of a strong kick and the mule carries the stuff easily and unsuspectingly. The mule man meets the mule a mile away from the check point and they proceed ahead to their destination where the drug packet is delivered. The business is smooth, transaction carried out effectively, packet is delivered at the target on time, and life goes on without any suspicion. Within the country, this is largely the network of drug transportation. The farther march of narcotic is in different forms: opium travels through villagers and its refined product – heroin – through numerous drug dealers and point men specially engaged in the art of this trade.

Thirdly, no sophisticated weapon can detect the drugs transportation through farmers and mules at the grassroots. Modern surveillance system has to descend down to the grassroots reality to grapple with the extant problem. And the extant problems are too daunting to be tackled by foreigners. The Afghans are themselves not interested to stem the rot already set in their society by the impact of narcotic use. They consider opium cultivation a gainful profession, a lifeline of survival to which alternative means of livelihood are either absent or unavailable. No foreigner can ever imagine the pangs of abject poverty and its impact on the miserable living conditions. There is an inherent abhorrence for foreigners which the allied or NATO forces cannot discern. Afghans have been too difficult a nation in history to be tamed. And they take solace from their history to eschew everything mundane to fight for their homeland which no foreigners can take away. The real concerns of the Afghans are examples of history itself. And they will not allow their land to be occupied by foreigners forever.

Fourthly, while foreigners fathom the magnitude of narcotic problem from the vantage point of the west, the Afghans perceive it from the regional ethnic vantage. There is a clear ethnic connotation to the ongoing narcotic trade from Afghanistan. Ethnic Afghan Tajik prefers to trade with their co-ethnic brethren from Tajikistan. Similarly ethnic Afghan Uzbeks prefer to trade with Uzbeks from Uzbekistan for the simple reason that these Uzbeks or Tajik know Russian language well. And all of them prefer to trade with Russia because it is highly profitable. The Afghan narcotic network spreads from the husbandmen in rural Afghanistan to ethnic chieftains in Afghan-Tajik and Afghan-

Uzbek borderlands from where it marches to Russian Federation and Europe. All along the way there are refining laboratories with huge network of paid agents, operating clandestinely to perform the job of agent in transporting drugs from one point to another. It is these agents who supply precursor chemicals, mostly acetic anhydride, to the labs and take refined drugs in lieu for sale in the markets

The ultimate aspect of this narcotic networking is the huge profit margin that traders get. Per kilo rates vary from place to place. Farther from home, greater the profit is the principle normally followed in drugs trade. Closer to home the profit margin is less. Even sometimes, closer to home the quantum of profit greatly varies. In March 2007, in the province of Balkh on Uzbek-Afghan borders, if a kilogram of heroin was priced at $2194. A few hundred kilometers away in the Badakhshan province on Afghan-Tajik borders, cost of the same quantity was pegged at $3,500 although a good road connects the two places. The price differentials have well-knitted the network of drug trafficking. Drugs quickly move from a low priced zone to a high price zone. For instance, after narcotic enters Tajikistan, the prices shoot up in the process of transaction. In Gorno-Badakhshan province, while the price of a kilogram of heroin is just $3-4 thousand, in capital Dushanbe it costs some $ 12-17 thousand. By the time it reaches Moscow the cost spikes up to $150-200 thousand and in Europe it is escalated to $ 250-300 thousand.[7] In contrast, the profit margin for the farmer is abysmally low. A farmer gets just $90 for a kilogram of opium in Pakistan-Afghan borders, whereas the wholesale price in either country is nearly $3000. The American wholesale price for this amount of opium is some $80,000.[8] The price variation remains by far the most motivating factor for traders to trade and traffickers to trafficking drugs. While opium cultivation for the farmers remains the most alluring source of income, for middlemen and agents it serves as a surety to prosperous life. It is this allurement that engages traffickers in the shadowy business of narcotics trade replete with risks. The contagion of narcotic business affects everybody: farmers at the grassroots, middlemen and agents across the transaction routes, government at the apex level of governance, foreigners at their level of afflictions, the mafia as main controller of this profitable trade and virtually one and all. Sometimes it affects even teen age children. Therefore, there ought to be a common strategy to deal with the menace; unfortunately that is lacking.

CONCLUSIONS

An analysis of contemporary and current phase of development in Afghanistan provides us with evidence of real concerns of the periphery. What is alarming is the impact of a volatile Afghanistan on the periphery. The limitation of an article does not provide adequate space to treat drugs trade In alliance with religious extremism. That remains a potent force of destabilization. The combined effects of religious extremism and narcotic money can produce a lethal concoction that may inebriate the region for ever. The political stability and economic volatility of Afghanistan continue to overshadow regional stability in Central Asia and beyond. Years of Soviet and American engagements have proved futile to a point that military solutions ought to be ruled out as an Afghan panacea. The socio-political role of the religious clergy has not been adequately addressed. And certainly foreign forces cannot address that issue due to their limitations that Afghan society imposes on them; nor billions of dollar that have been poured into rebuilding the country can address that issue. Trekking on the dangerous cliff of narcotic trafficking and Islamic extremism, Afghanistan has few choices to ensure a stable future: it has a choice thrown at it by Hamid Karzai to work in tandem with the west and build democracy. It has also a choice to embrace the Taliban and return back to primitive practices of Shariat Islam. The third choice is a compromise between local provincial chieftains to come together to realize the essence of globalization and assess the position of Afghanistan therein; and work accordingly on a cooperative platform. None of these alternatives seems to yield fruit so far, while the future remains uncertain and in oblivion. For the time being one thing that comes as certain is the replacement of Soviet Union by allied/ NATO forces. While a peaceful solution of the Afghan conflict evades the country, the Taliban lurk in between as a viable force across Afghanistan sans Kabul to return to power.

Traditions thus clash with modernity and both vie to assert themselves on the political contours of Afghanistan.

REFERENCES

1. Govind Talwalkar, War Lords Rule Afghanistan, The Asian Age, 18 March, 2008, p. 10.
2. Ruslan Sikoev, Muslim Clergy in the Socio-political life of Afghanistan, Russia and the Muslim World, No. 3, 2007, pp. 80-87.
3. For text of the Geneva Accord please refer to S.V. Nair, Afghanistan: Perspectives for Reconciliation and Peace, Panchsheel Publishers, New Delhi, 1988. Also refer to D.R. Goyal, Geneva Agreement on Afghanistan: Framework for Peaceful Development, *Soviet Review*, No. 6, 1988, pp. 52-54.
4. The World Drug Report, 2007, The United Nations, New York, 2008, p. 183.
5. UNODC Delta Database, *Ibid*, p.185.
6. M.K. Bhadrakumar, A New Journey in Search of the Taliban, *The Hindu*, January 23, 2008, p. 14.
7. Irina Komissina, Azhar Kurtov, Narkotiki Tsentral'noi Azii: Novaya Ugroza tsivilizatsii, Russiya I Musulmanskii Mir, No. 1, 2001, p. 59.
8. P.L. Dash, Central Asia: The Heroin Highway to Hell in Eurasian Vision edited by Mahavir Singh and Victor Krassilchtchikov, Anamika Publishers, New Delhi, 2003, p. 307.

CHAPTER 17

Afghanistan: Facts and Problems

Wadir Safi

Afghanistan sat in the heart of Asia, after getting her external independence from the British in 1919; has been ruled by an absolute monarchy for decades.

The coup de' tat of Sardar Daud, cousin and brother-in-law of X king, Zahir Shah, in 1973, finished the hereditary kingdom of Mohammadzai dynasty in Afghanistan for ever.

Daud, too, by proclaiming the republican regime didn't last long and was removed from power by a bloody coup in April 1978, led by the pro-Soviet Peoples democratic party of Afghanistan.

The unwise policies of PDPA caused national uprisings all-over the country which paved way for the enemies of Communism and revival of religious Fundamentalism. Thus, the Cold War era ended with the collapse of World Socialist System including its Warsaw Pact, dismemberment of the Soviet Union and Eastern block, totally. This, changed the bipolarity of the world, created after the Second World War, to one Super-State playing in international relations forcefully.

A huge movement of Afghan population caused millions of refugees, homelessness and statelessness that still exist and as a consequence, Afghanistan turned to a ground of various interferences by neighboring and other states of the world. The peaceful land of Afghans fills into a fierce civil war and new phenomena of International Terrorism and Drugs mafia prevailed in the region.

After April 1992, Mujahedin parties couldn't establish a strong central government and were defeated by the religious students (Taleban). Since, Taleban were not aware of the governance, at all, after September 11, 2001 events, Bonn Conference established a coalition government which, by the help of international community have a constitution and apparently, elections for president and parliament have taken place.

The present situation in the country and region is not stable; ISAF couldn't do much for security; coalition and NATO forces are still engaged in war, especially, in the South, South-west, South-east and Eastern provinces bordering with Pakistan, along the Durand Line. Up to this moment, Afghan population and their war torn country is suffering most,

The future is looking dark and uncertainty prevails all over the naturally beautiful territory.

Since, Afghanistan is the home of different ethnic population, many-sided problems exists that can be tackled with only by strengthening lasting peace and security. This, needs a national and international strategy to be followed, taking into consideration internal and external (regional) conditions, economically, politically and militarily to be dealt with. First of all, with all neighboring states of Afghanistan who seek their own national interests here by all means. Then, in regional and international scale.

So, in my mined, UNO can convene an international conference of Afghanistan's neighbors plus all states having the right of Veto in security council of UNO in order to draw a plan for coordinating international efforts toward a durable peace and security for the benefit of all and humanity to fight against international terrorism and drug traffic. Such a plan must be guaranteed by big powers to be applied properly. World players must look deeply if the distribution of world resources and power, in the existing various national interests, are done justly or unjustly? Because, this makes the main source and basis of conflict on national, regional and international level.

Afghanistan, having very hard times in the whole 18th and 19th centuries, had a status of a Buffer State between Tsarist Russia and British Empire in the Indian Sub-Continent, was always in war, either outside the territory or inside wars between kings and princes, fighting for local or central power. At the same time, wars with British colonial power which continued even in the early 20th century, still in the second half of the 20th century fighting the red army, marks this country's history with atrocities as the consequences of all wars and causes lots of problems.

To specify Facts and Problems in this country, the following periods should be studied:

A. 1919 – 1964
B. 1964 – 1973
C. 1973 – 1978
D. 1978 – 1992
E. 1992 – 2001
F. 2001 – Up to now (April 2008).

A. 1919-64

In the year 1919, after February 20th, when King Habibullah Khan was assassinated, his son, Amanullah Khan, the governor of Kabul, seized power and proclaimed the war of independence, known as Third Anglo-Afghan War. Afghanistan's independence over its foreign affairs, too, was recognized in 1921by the United Kingdom and became an independent nation.

Amanullah used his influence to modernize the country, created new cosmopolitan schools for both boys and girls in the region and overturned centuries-old traditions such a strict dress codes for women. He increased trade with Europe and Asia. He also advanced a modernist constitution that incorporated equal rights and individual freedoms with the guidance of his father-in-law and foreign minister Mahmud Tarzi. Unfortunately, this rapid modernization created a backlash and reactionary uprisings later served as one of the accusations when he was overthrown.

At the time, Afghanistan's foreign policy was primarily concerned with the rivalry between the Soviet Union and the United Kingdom. Each attempted to gain the favor of Afghanistan and foil attempts by the other power to gain influence in the region.

After Amanullah traveled to Europe in late 1927, opposition to his rule increased. An uprising in Jalalabad culminated in a march to the capital, and much of the army deserted rather than resist. In early 1929, Amanullah abdicated and went into temporary exile in India. From India, the ex-king traveled to Europe and settled in Italy, and later in Switzerland. Died in 1960, Zurich.

Shortly after a rebellion by Pashtun tribesmen and forces of Habibullah Kalakani, supported by religious elements, began against the monarchy, Mohammad Nadir was exiled due to disagreements with King Amanullah. After the overthrow of Amanullah Khan's monarchy by Habibullah Kalakani, Mohammad Nadir returned to India and acquired military support from the British. He returned to Afghanistan with his British supported armies and took most of Afghanistan from Habibullah Kalakani. By October 13 of 1929. Mohammad Nadir Khan captured Kabul and subsequently sacked the city. After killing Habibullah Kalakani, he declared himself King of Afghanistan on October 16, 1929.

Mohammad Nadir Shah quickly abolished most of Amanullah Khan's reforms, but despite his efforts to rebuild an army that had just been engaged in suppressing a rebellion; the forces remained weak while the religious and tribal leaders grew strong. In 1930, there were uprisings by the Pashtun Shinwari tribes of the south and as well as by the Tajiks of Kabul province and north of Kabul. The same year, a Soviet force crossed the border in pursuit of an Uzbek leader whose forces had been harassing the soviets from his sanctuary in Afghanistan. He was driven back to the Soviet side by the Afghan army in April 1930, and by the end of 1931 most uprisings had been subdued.

Nadir Shah named a ten-member cabinet, consisting mostly of his family, and in September 1930 he called into session a loya jirgah of 286 which confirmed his accession to the throne. In 1931 the king promulgated a new constitution. Despite its appearance as a constitutional monarchy, the document officially instituted a Royal oligarchy, and popular participation was merely an illusion.

During his reign thousands of Afghan intellectuals were either imprisoned or killed. Many fled abroad, especially to the Soviet Union. The already-in-crisis press was heavily censored and power was distributed among his own relatives and family members.

On November 8, 1933 while distributing awards within the palace grounds, the King was shot dead by a teenager named Abdul Khaliq.

After the assassination of his father, Zahir Khan was proclaimed King on the same date. For the first thirty years he did not effectively rule, ceding power to his parental uncles, Sardar Mohammad Hashim Khan and Sardar ShahMahmud Khan. This period fostered a growth in Afghanistan's relations with the international community as in 1934; Afghanistan joined the League of Nations while also receiving formal recognition from the United States. Throughout the 1930s, agreements on foreign assistance and trade had been reached with many countries, most notably Germany, Italy, and Japan.

Following the end of the Second World War, Zahir Shah recognized the need for the modernization of Afghanistan and recruited a number of foreign advisers to assist with the process. During this period Afghanistan's first modern university was founded. During his reign a number of potential advances and reforms were derailed as a result of factionalism and political infighting.

Zahir Shah was able to govern on his own in 1963 and despite the factionalism and political infighting a new constitution was introduced in 1964.

B. 1964-73

The years of democracy didn't go well, because Zahir Shah's private advisors were scared him from a real transfer of power through free elections and causing problems for the regime. This resulted to interferences in the process of elections and thus destroyed the concept of free and fare elections. The other big mistake was abstention from signing the Law of political parties by Zahir Shah until the end of his reign. But, parties developed by the people themselves without even taking into consideration the absence of such a law. By this time, political and social movements developed to the extent that university students through their demonstrations were able to change the cabinets many times, including their premiers. The private newspapers, about twenty, were publishing independently that some of them even not respecting the public opinion of Afghan society and national culture. Khalq, and Parcham were pro-Soviet, socialist oriented papers that later developed to become political parties having the same titles. It was in this period that religious movements also took roots and Afghan Moslem Youth party was established unofficially. Later, in this period, the situation became so tense that, under the premiership of Mohammad Musa Shafiq, general elections for the parliament were postponed. Peoples Democratic Party of Afghanistan proclaimed by Babrak Karmal during a demonstration of students in the city publicly, undermining the non-existing of its law.

During all these turmoil, Daud Khan, a royal family member, who was deprived the right of being prime minister by constitution was active against the regime, too. He was regularly meeting with the leftist parties and planning against kingdom.

C. 1973-78

In 1973, while Mohammad Zahir shah was in Italy undergoing eye surgery and treatment, his cousin and former Prime Minister Mohammad Daud Khan staged a coup d'etat and established a republican government. As a former prime minister, Daud Khan had been fired by Zahir Shah a decade earlier. In the August following this coup, Zahir Shah abdicated rather than risk an all-out civil war. The July 1973 coup ended 226 years of royal rule controlled by the Durrani tribal confederacy. As Afghan Marxists were Daud's allies, they had expected to share power and get rid of Daud. PDPA used Daud's regime for arresting and even executing hundreds of Moslem Youths movement's members. They even killed under torture the previous prime minister, Mohammad Hashem Maiwandwal.

By 1975 Daud had moved carefully to purge the Marxists from his cabinet. In 1977 he attempted to consolidate his position by promulgating a new constitution which concentrated power in his presidency and channeled popular support through a single party system. Later Daud wanted a shift away from the Marxists in his foreign policy and moved close to Iran, Pakistan and Egypt.

Since, Marxists had penetrated in the army and the air force; they launched an assault on Daud's palace that overwhelmed his republican Guards in 1978.

D. 1978-92

The April 1978 Coup d'etat that finished with Daud and his team, proclaimed their regime the Democratic Republic of Afghanistan. Afghan Marxists named their coup a revolution (Saur Revolution). The PDPA party was not a united one and they split very soon into factions which brought for the support of their rule the Soviet army into Afghanistan in December 1979.

As the Afghan nation knew PDPA's ideology and it was not in consistence with their way of life and belief, they started resistance and national uprising took more momentum after they saw foreign troops entering their land. Especially after President Taraki's issuing different Decrees which touched every aspect of their life.

Afghan resistance received the support of Western countries that established warring parties for them in neighboring countries, mostly in Pakistan in order to prepare them for better fight against the Soviet Red Army. The resistance became so strong, particularly after receiving anti-air missiles by Mujahedin that Soviet State decided to withdraw its troops by February, 1989, after signing an agreement through the mediation of UNO in Geneva. Finally, the last pro-Soviet government was collapsed in 1992 and power was transferred in April 1992 officially to a Mujahedin government made in Pakistan, at the head, Sebghatullah Mujadidi, in the building of foreign ministry of DRA.

E. 1992-2001

Immediately after Mujahedin's taking over power, different parties' difference rose and internal wars began for expanding their grips over the lands in all Afghanistan. First, it demonstrated in the capital Kabul to the extent that in twelve districts of the capital, separate rules were operating. Soon after coming into power, different ethnic groups started to defend their interests from the point of view of language, religion, geographic location and etc. They were even baking by different foreign states according to their investments which had been made during fighting period against the foreign troops.

It is clear that all UN's efforts from 1992 to Nov. 2001, Bonn Conference, failed in the hands of the so called Islamic state of Afghanistan. During this period, unfortunately, Afghan mojahedin were not successful in having a constitution to unify the country and strengthen the National Unity. This, led to their collapse in the hand of Taliban movement, supported, logistically by Pakistan government in September 1996.

As, Taliban were not familiar with the governance according to positive laws and even Islamic Law, and from the other side were not recognized by international community and couldn't get a place in the UNs, they mostly relied on the helps of others, even individuals and fundamentalists groups which were enemies to the West, especially the USA. Finally, situation changed after September 11, 2001, attacks in USA and UNO, security council decided to get rid of the Taliban regime and thus were attacked in December 2001 and a new government was brought into power by the decisions made in Bonn Conference including all Afghan parties except Taliban.

F. December 2001 Up to now, April 2008

The new government in Afghanistan now, has a Constitution, a President through elections, a Parliament completed with a Judiciary. The whole international community is helping the economy, state-building process and establishing the Rule of Law.

ISAF, consisting of 36 countries are responsible for the security of Kabul and USA, British, Canadian and Holland forces are fighting Taliban gun-men and Al-Qaeda, at the same time, Narcotics smugglers along the Durand Line, in the South, West and East of Afghanistan.

It seems that this war is yet to be over for different Internal and External factors in and around Afghanistan. At present, Security is the main issue all over the Afghan territory, besides, economic problems are threatening the life of the majority, reconstruction is not satisfactory, unemployment is a source for the enemy of the government to hire fighters from them, dependence on foreign countries even for primary needs of life, are the main problems regime is facing. Corruption and official bribery is the characteristic of the state that decreases trust of the people on the authority of the government.

Operations of foreign troops, not taking into consideration the life of the civilian population and searches without respecting traditions and culture of locals, are the main causes of dissatisfaction of the Afghans inside their homeland.

Neighboring countries intervention, seeking their own national interests are very forceful objections towards the development inside Afghanistan and establishing lasting peace in this war-torn country and in the region.

All these, in my mined, must be paid serious attention to by the international community again and in order to remove differences of interests, the UNO must be more active than states individually and every help be done through this organization in Afghanistan. The cause of security in the region and the world over is the main goal for which Afghanistan, in this part of the world has become very important, for this very reason, a real and clear coordination is needed between all the forces involved in this part of Asia. If international community help to resolve the existing issues between different States in this region, Kashmir problem, Durand Line question, Iran's views and Afghanistan's northern neighbors, and look at them realistically; I believe, it will be possible to cut the roots of international terrorism in the countries where exists and peace will not be far to be established. Of course, constructive negotiations are the last and only way for solving all the problems in our world.

CHAPTER 18

Afghan Reconstruction Amidst Chaos

Chintamani Mahapatra

No one spoke of Afghan reconstruction until a few years ago. No country ever had a credible policy to assist Afghanistan economically during the larger part of the post-Second World era. Who would have shown much interest in a country that is land-locked, that has few natural resources, and that has been in the backwater of economic development for centuries? Superpowers are not known for attaching too much importance to economic backwaters of the globe. Afghanistan for until late 1970s attracted no attention from the United States or the former Soviet Union. But since then served as the centerpiece of the Cold War conflict until almost the fag end of the survival of the former Soviet Union.

The US certainly abandoned Afghanistan after the Soviet troop withdrawal. It spent huge resources in fighting the Soviet presence but spent little towards the economic infrastructure building or developmental activities in that country. In a little more than a decade since the desertion of Afghanistan, the US faced a direct attack on its territory from a group of terrorists who had a base in the caves of that country. The US retaliation against the 9/11 attacks of 2001 began in October of that year, but has not ended yet. It is turning into a military quagmire. Unlike in the past the foreign forces in Afghanistan are doing the fighting against the insurgents and terrorists and simultaneously trying to re-build the Afghan economy as part of the overall strategy of ending religious extremism and radicalism.

STRATEGIC CENTRALITY

It is ironical that an economic backwater of Southwest Asia is the touchstone of any long term solution to the menace of religious radicalism and militancy. Thus Afghanistan is not an insignificant actor in international politics. It is strategically central to the solution of growing international insecurity for decades. It is strategically located sharing borders with a nuclear capable Islamic country—Pakistan; the emerging global power—China, the most powerful country of the Persian Gulf—Iran; and the new Central Asian Republics of Uzbekistan, Tajikistan and Turkmenistan.

For more than three decades this geographically land-locked and economically backward country has been at war with itself and with the external forces. Three external powers have been largely responsible for the prolonged warfare in Afghanistan—the Soviet Union, the United States and Pakistan. The Soviet military intervention in this country in December 1979 turned it into one of the fiercest battle grounds of cold war that ended after about ten years with withdrawal of Soviet troops in 1989. After that it became the main theatre of international terrorism in the wake of Pakistani intervention in the then Afghan civil war that led to the emergence of one of the most fundamentalist and aggressive Islamic groups—the Taliban. The Taliban government in Kabul gave shelter to notorious Osama bin Laden-led Al-Qaeda which was responsible for the 9/11 terrorist attacks on the US. This incident turned Afghanistan into the central battle field of the US-led war on global terrorism since 2001. Afghans have since been tolerating presence of thousands of American and NATO forces that are there to eliminate terrorist networks. Ten years of Soviet intervention, twelve years of Pakistani interference and about seven years of American-led military involvement have turned Afghanistan into perhaps the most-war devastated nation in world history.

Yet Afghanistan stands out as a classic case where no external actor has been able to sustain its influence and military presence without heavy cost. Afghans successfully averted being colonized by the Europeans; prevented the Soviets from turning them into a Communist bastion; did not permit Pakistan to achieve its much desired "strategic depth" and now have fiercely been opposing the US-led Western effort to stabilize the country under occidental terms and conditions.

Thus it is the underdeveloped Afghanistan that is partly accountable for the 9/11 incident that shook the world and changed the US image of the world order for ever. The sole superpower of the post-Cold War era that claimed victory in the cold war bore the brunt of terrorist attacks and began its global war on terrorism with the bombing of Kabul. Afghanistan has so far resisted being tamed and shaped by the Western powers. On the contrary, success in Afghanistan has become very vital to NATO's long term relevance. If NATO with full American participation becomes unable to achieve its goals in Afghanistan, can it have a credible out of area operation policy? In any case, NATO has already become a two-tier alliance, one group of members supporting Afghan reconstruction as the primary goal and the US and a few others advocating security and stability as the most important goal. A divided West cannot be expected to bring Afghanistan under their influence and control.

Significantly, neither of the goals—stability and reconstruction—appears to be heading for a success any time soon. While Afghanistan continues to remain a breeding ground of international terrorists with footprints around the world, reconstruction activities in the country are facing enormous challenges and difficulties.

MOUNTING COMMOTION AND CHAOS

The fundamental question is whether reconstruction activities are feasible in the midst of a mindless insurgency. The related concern is whether insurgency of the Afghan kind can be tackled only through military means. The equally puzzling question is at what proportions and by what method the strategy of winning the hearts and minds of people and the strategy of combating terrorists/insurgents need to be simultaneously implemented.

The report card of Afghanistan reflects a trend of growing violence and persistent instability. According to one source that compared the relative figures of 2004 and 2007, security incidence in that country totaled 900 in 2004 and 8, 950 in 2007. Roadside bombs exploded 325 times in 2004 and 1469 in 2007. There were only 3 cases of suicide bombings in 2004 and the figure went up to more than 130 in 2007. Seen from another angle, the US-led coalition forces dropped 86 bombs in Afghanistan in 2004, whereas the number increased to 3572 in 2007. The task of the coalition forces was not confined to killing terrorists or fighting insurgents. It also included a war on drugs that provided the financial resources to the insurgents. One of the significant sources of turmoil in Afghanistan is poppy cultivation; and the international security forces witnessed the poppy cultivation rise rather than fall during the same period. Poppy production in 2004 which was 131K hectors rose to 193K hectors in 2007. The apparently unending tumult in the country perpetrated by drug lords and terrorist groups was mirrored in the phenomenal rise in the number of security forces deployed to tackle it. Total number of coalition forces in Afghanistan was 26,000 in 2004 and this increased to 50,000 in 2007.

According to David W. Barno,, Director of Near East South Asia Center for Strategic Studies and National Defense University of the US, "The enemy in Afghanistan—a collection of Al-Qaeda, Taliban, Hezbi Islami, and foreign fighters—is unquestionably a much stronger force than the enemy we faced in 2004."[1] The Atlantic Council recently issued a warning, "Make no mistake, NATO is not winning in Afghanistan." The Centre for the Presidency's Afghanistan Study Group made an assessment that the "mission to stabilize Afghanistan is faltering." The International Crisis Group has not been very optimistic when it says· "Afghanistan is not lost but the signs are not good." After quoting all these negative images of events in Afghanistan, Gary L. Ackerman, Chairman of House Foreign Affairs Committee, said: "The Bush Administration seems singularly incapable of pulling together all the elements of national power into a coherent strategy that will assure us victory in Afghanistan."[2]

Reconstruction activities cannot take place when rising number of Afghan fighters are ready to sacrifice their lives to defend their cause, right or wrong, and join the suicide squads. Unfortunately even the international aid agencies have not been spared. The suicide bombing rate in Afghanistan in 2007 was up by 600% from 2005 and all insurgent attacks were up by 400%. The Chairman of the Joint Chiefs of Staff, Admiral Mike Mullen, recently told the House Foreign Affairs Committee that suicide bombings were up in Afghanistan by 27% in 2007 over 2006.[3] The UN Secretary General, on the other hand, gave an equally grim picture in his report of March 2008 that 40 convoys delivering food to the Afghans under the World Food Program were looted in 2007; 130 attacks were launched against various humanitarian programmes and that 40 relief workers were killed and 89 abducted in Afghanistan in 2007.[4]

GROUNDS OF FAILURE

Why has the situation in Afghanistan been so grim and gloomy? What explains the failure of the most sophisticated military forces with most modern weapons of the most powerful military alliance of the globe—NATO—in tackling terrorists and insurgents in that country? How does one account for the difficulty of international aid agencies in providing the much needed assistance to the helpless people of the strife-torn Afghanistan? Are the Taliban and other Afghan insurgent enemy of their own people? If not, why are they targeting the aid agents as well? There is no single answer to these closely connected questions and concerns.

First of all, the US and its NATO allies have underestimated the strength of the enemy and the difficulty of fighting in the terrain of that country. The amount of resources devoted to tackle the Afghan problem is also a deplorable amount compared to what was spent in Bosnia. Afghanistan is about fifty percent larger than Iraq in landmass and its population is four million more than that of Iraq. Yet, the Western coalition forces number about 160,000 troops in Iraq and less than 60,000 (57000 to be specific) in Afghanistan.[5] According to US Congressman Gary Ackerman, "All you have to do is look at the differences in resources expended in Bosnia compared to those expended in Afghanistan. To restore order and create a nation in Bosnia the international community put in 19 soldiers for every 1,000 inhabitants. In Afghanistan that number is 1 per every 1,000 Afghans.... Per capita assistance in Bosnia is $679 but in Afghanistan it is only $57. And that's before American resources got diverted to Iraq." According to a RAND publication, the number of US troops per capita in Afghanistan has been considerably less than almost every nation-building effort since World War II. US military adopted a "light footprint" approach to prevent large scale resistance of anti-Soviet type witnessed during the 1980s. It also appeared over confident that small number of ground troops with use of air power was sufficient to ensure security.[6]

Secondly, too many cooks spoil the broth. The enthusiasm with which a large number of countries joined the US in its war against Al-Qaeda in the aftermath of the 9/11 and stayed on to make their contributions was remarkable. But lack of proper coordination led to different actors moving in diverse directions creating more confusion than contributing to solution of the problem. As Ackerman has articulated: "After the attacks of September 11, there was extraordinary goodwill and support from the international community for American efforts to rid Afghanistan of terrorists and establish a functioning democratic state... We assumed the responsibility of training the army; the British tackled the narcotics trade; the Germans agreed to train the police; the Italians offered to rebuild the judicial system. On paper this plan looked pretty good.... The trouble with this plan was that each nation headed off in its own direction, at its own pace and the results reflect that. The Afghan National Army is still incapable of operating effectively.... Opium production in Afghanistan has skyrocketed.... The Afghan National Police are uniformly considered a disaster.... And the judicial system has utterly failed to demonstrate to ordinary Afghans that criminals will be prosecuted. Secretary Rice has said that in Afghanistan there are too many cooks. She's right, but she missed the more fundamental problem: there's no recipe."[7]

Besides lack of coordination among the multiple actors, the problem has been compounded over the years because of division within the NATO members over the goals of the mission. While Washington often calls for more help from NATO, such appeals frequently fall on deaf ears. Germany, Italy, Greece, Turkey and many other NATO partners have in fact showed strong reluctance to counterinsurgency participation in violent parts of southern Afghanistan. Germany, Spain and Italy prefer to concentrate more on reconstruction and development activities rather than combat operations. Indeed, a massive number of people in these countries are against combat operations by their troops, whereas a large number of Americans support combating Afghan terrorists and Islamic extremists.[8]

Then there is dearth of strategic coherence even within the international community making efforts in Afghanistan to re-build the country, particularly among separate civilian special representatives of the United Nations, of the European Union and NATO with no clear authority of one over the other. The US and other major countries are reluctant to be coordinated by any one of them. Significantly, NATO-led ISAF has 40 contributing nations, which works with five regional commands and 26 Provincial Reconstruction Teams. Many countries have their own national requirements that restrict where ISAF Commander can deploy troops and under what circumstances.

Thirdly, one of the crucial actors in the international efforts to bring peace and stability to Afghanistan—Pakistan—had its own old and new baggage of problems that came on the way. The strategic North West Frontier Province of Pakistan bordering Afghanistan was never under the de facto control of Islamabad. This region hosted the fleeing Taliban fighters and Al-Qaeda members from Afghanistan and Islamabad was any thing but a helpless bystander. As and when President Pervez Musharraf came under Washington's pressure and militarily intervened in the region, the outcome was unsuccessful. At times, the Musharraf regime tried a carrot and stick approach, but it did not work either. To the contrary, it generated suspicion that Islamabad's military regime was mending fences with the pro-Taliban tribal leaders. The 2008 Annual Threat Assessment Report of the

Director of National Intelligence of the United States pointed out that "Using the sanctuary in border area of Pakistan, al-Qa'ida has been able to maintain a cadre of skilled lieutenants capable of directing the organization's operations around the world." It alleged that every major insurgents group the Taliban, Haqqani network, Hezb-i-Islami and al-Qa'ida, has established a command and control apparatus on the Pakistani side of the border. Al Qa'ida, in particular, "has revitalized itself and returned to the operative style it enjoyed prior to 9/11," according to Seth G. Jones. He also maintains that parts of Pakistani Government, especially current members of the ISI Directorate and Frontier Corps, continue to provide support to the Taliban and Haqqani network.[9]

Fourth problem in Afghanistan was related to the functioning of the police department. American analysts strongly believed that the Bush Administration should have taken proper care to provide timely assistance to the Afghan police, including training and equipment to look after the day to day law and order situation. But instead, it entrusted the job of training to the Germans. When Germany was proved inefficient, the State Department's Bureau of Narcotics and Law Enforcement contracted DynCorp to train the police. When the White House and the Pentagon were not satisfied by the State Department's performance, the US military took charge and led the mission to train and equip the Afghan police. Now the Inspector Generals of the State Department and the Department of Defense have expressed unhappiness over the state of Afghan police and complain that it lacks "uniforms, armored vehicles, weapons, ammunitions, police stations, police jails, national command and control and investigative training."[10]

Fifthly, the amount of international assistance has never been adequate. There has always been a great chasm between the promises made at donor meets and the actual inflow of assistance. Whatever amount of assistance has been delivered, on the other hand, has not reached the target due to corruption and lack of honest and sincere governance. Moreover, a World Bank Study has pointed out that the main beneficiary of assistance is the urban elite, whereas Afghanistan is basically a rural country. This has triggered deep-seated dissatisfaction and bitterness among the rural people.

Sixthly, there are other contradictions that have complicated the reconstruction efforts. Prominent among them is eradicating poppy cultivation. While the wider goal of ending poppy cultivation is laudable one, rehabilitation of farmers who depend on this for their livelihood has not been addressed. Aerial eradication of poppy cultivation has caused impoverishment among the farmers and generated more alienation. It has provided the golden opportunity for the Taliban to recruit new members.

Seventhly, internationally initiated Afghan reconstruction programme after the fall of Taliban was an extraordinary effort to start with. It had a minimalist and a maximalist goal. The minimalist version aimed at destroying terrorist safe heavens, re-building the Afghan State and set in motion the effort to normalize the functioning of the Afghan economy. The maximalist one was ambitious and aimed at establishing a modern Afghan society. Neither of the goals has a satisfactory progress report, mainly because the Afghans are not in the forefront of the effort and "the prominent foreign role has had increasingly negative effects."[11] The result is continuing violence, lackluster governance, human disaster and terrorist breeding. The Afghan reconstruction under the auspices of the United Nations, NGOs, international donors with the help of the US, NATO and Afghan coercive agents has eluded successful completion largely because of lack of proper understanding and appreciation of Afghan culture, values and beliefs. In other words, the concept of cultural relativism, developed by an American anthropologist, Franz Boas, perhaps has an answer to this illusive goal of Afghan Reconstruction. This concept emphasizes that customs, values, artistic expressions and beliefs need to be understood as products of a particular culture rather than theoretical preconceptions and classifications of outsiders. The imposition of cultural values or political systems from outside would not always be easy or inexpensive and it was clearly vindicated by the earlier Soviet failure and the current US inabilities. While of late there have been more serious research in the US and Europe to understand Afghan history and culture, the academic findings have not yet formed the inputs into policy making.

ANTIDOTES

Is there no end to the Afghan problem? Is it a perennial phenomenon? Will the Afghans have no peace and stability in their country? Will Afghanistan never be prosperous? These are difficult questions. Afghanistan has traditionally been more peaceful and stable when external agents do not interfere in that country. Like every other country, there are internal divisions and domestic problems in that country. But somehow the Afghans are not in the driver's seat. The decision making process in that country is dominated by foreigners. It is because Afghanistan has truly become the epicenter of terrorism and is central to combating international terrorism. How can foreign nations stay away from Afghanistan? But then external powers have also remained ineffective in tackling the problem

Many scholars, political leaders and think tank specialists have been constantly examining the Afghan problem and coming out with various remedies at different times. Such suggestions can be summarized as below:

First of all, the US and NATO members need to abandon their dominating behaviour and take into broader confidence the regional actors that have serious stakes in the Afghan stability. Only if a regional effort is made connecting Afghan and Pakistan dimension to Western strategy can one expect shift in a positive direction. The exclusion of regional actors in the vital decision making process for tackling the Afghan problem is a grave mistake of the US-led coalition of forces. Until India, Iran, Pakistan and some of the Central Asian Republics and, of course, Russia become part of a collective decision making and implementing authority, there would be no solution of the issue.

Secondly, while it is futile to expect or demand quick withdrawal of the US from the Afghan scene, the Bush Administration needs to take more active initiative to organize and coordinate the mixture of international military and civilian efforts in Afghanistan into a comprehensive strategy to prevent the actors from moving in too many different directions. Certainly the Afghan imbroglio will survive the Bush Administration. Both the presidential hopefuls in the current presidential race promised to invest considerable attention and energy on Afghanistan, but the key would be a judicious combination of civilian and military approach and neither of the approaches should dominate the other. Now that Barrack Hussein Obama had won the presidential election, it remains to be seen whether he can deliver on his promises.

Thirdly, in the face of European, Japanese and many other countries' unwillingness to direct participation in combat role in Afghanistan, the United States has to take the lead in counterinsurgency operations in the south and east of Afghanistan with adequate troops on the ground. The US cannot afford to be the hostage to the Vietnam Syndrome and its current experiences in Iraq and has to do more and rely less on outsourcing.

Fourthly, it is necessary to have unity of command among the international community or aid agencies. When practically war is going on and uncertainty prevails all over the country, piecemeal efforts by multiple agencies is bound to lack the direction and efficiency.

Fifthly, the Provincial Reconstruction Teams (PRTs) need thorough revamp. They are dominated by soldiers, with token civilian personnel from the State Dept or USAID. At the moment there is no commonality among a multiple number of PRTs and they have been operating with little transparency and unity of purpose. It needs to be changed.

Sixthly, the role of the military in reconstruction and development activities need to be curtailed. In the relatively peaceful and stable part of the country, Afghan civilian agencies with their international civilian counterparts should take the lead in reconstruction works.

Seventhly, an integrated approach to Afghan agricultural development needs should be addressed by providing seeds, fertilizer, irrigation facilities and other complimentary requirements as part of the strategy to end poppy cultivation in that country.

Last but not the least, the differences between the modernist approach to state-building and the traditional method of decision making process in Afghanistan need to be combined for a lasting solution. Afghanistan is not ripe for replicating the Western liberal democratic model. The traditional Afghan power politics likewise cannot be allowed to have a freehand. The local leaders have to be made stake holders in the new governing structure and a compromise is imperative.

Jonathan Goodhand has rightly recognized that the "state in Afghanistan was built on shaky foundations.... There have never been a territorial sovereign state in Afghanistan and there have always been multiple sovereigns including small scale local chiefs, tribal confederations, bandits or war lords.... Throughout history there has been struggle between a modernizing state and traditional borderland communities. Power has shifted back forth many times in history and the struggle is still on, despite external intervention."[12]

Afghanistan is an illustration of the negative side of globalization. It is symptomatic of what can happen elsewhere in the world. The complex web of interdependence that has emerged in the wake of rapid rise in the pace of globalization enables instability and injustice, underdevelopment and inequality in one part of the world to threaten every other part of the world. Afghanistan is not an issue that can be resolved by a superpower with a few proxies. It is not a problem that can be fixed by military muscle flexing by a superpower and its alliance partners. External intervention of any kind cannot work in this country unless a substantial number of local citizenry are convinced that the outsiders have come to fight a common enemy.

Do majority of Afghan people appear convinced that the Americans and Europeans are there in that country to bring peace and stability to their country? Do Afghan masses feel that myriad aid agencies have entered their country with a pure missionary zeal to alleviate their sufferings? If yes, resolution of the Afghan problem can be sighted in the near future. However, if majority of Afghans consider the foreign troops as invaders and the aid agencies as pawns of the invading powers, there is no end to the conflict even in the distant future.

REFERENCES

1. David W. Barno,, Director of Near East South Asia Center for Strategic Studies, NDU, statement at House Foreign Affairs Committee Testimony. The Hearing was on "Strategic Chaos and Taliban Resurgence in Afghanistan," 2 April 2008.
2. Statement of Chairman Gary L. Ackerman, House Foreign Affairs Committee Hearing on 'Strategic Chaos and Taliban Resurgence in Afghanistan," 2 April 2008.
3. Testimony by Mark L. Schneider, Senior Vice-President, International Crisis Group to the House Foreign Affairs Subcommittee on Middle East and South Asia, 2 April 2008.
4. *Ibid.*
5. Barno, n. 1.
6. Seth G. Jones, RAND Corporation, "Getting Back on Track in Afghanistan," Statement before the Committee on Foreign Affairs, Subcommittee on the Middle East and South Asia, US House of Representatives, 2 April 2008.
7. Ackerman, n. 2.
8. Jones, n. 6.
9. *Ibid.*
10. *Ibid.*
11. Astri Suhrke, "Reconstruction as Modernization: The 'Post-Conflict' Project in Afghanistan," *Third World Quarterly*, vol. 28, no. 7, 2007, p. 1291.
12. Jonathan Goodhand, "From War Economy to Peace Economy? Reconstruction and State-Building in Afghanistan," *Journal of International Affairs*, vol. 58, no. 1, Fall 2004, p. 156.

CHAPTER 19

Afghanistan in US Strategic Calculations: The Post 9/11 Regional Geo-political Dynamics

Jagmohan Meher

> *"We are not going to be a political football for neighbors in the region as we were in the 1990s. The soil of Afghanistan cannot be used by any country against a third country."*
>
> —President Hamid Karzai

The devastating terrorist attacks on the United States on September 11, 2001, and the subsequent American reaction thereof brought about a systemic transformation in the geo-political situation in South-west Asia—a region which includes both South Asia and the Persian Gulf and stretches into Central Asia. The United States reacted decisively displaying its military prowess forcing a change of government in Afghanistan; replacing the extremist Taliban regime and putting the terrorists' leadership on run. It acquired military bases in Afghanistan, Central Asian States and Pakistan, and stationed its military units in all these countries. Untying the menace of terrorism by putting a firm deterrence in the form of military presence in this volatile landmass was perhaps the aim of the United States.

The anti-Taliban war looked as a walkover for Washington, the stabilization process made the Americans confident, and the United States appeared to be comfortably placed in Afghanistan and the region. But despite these notions of "accomplishments,"

Afghanistan seems to be tilting towards another round of insurgency, instability and insecurity. The Taliban appear to be on the move once again with the same Pakistani-backing and members of the NATO Forces have already admitted that they were "not winning against the Taliban."[1] Eventually, the trouble is deeply rooted in the geopolitics of the region more than any other factor, which is not entirely under the control of Washington. It is only a matter of common knowledge that without the continued involvement of neighboring countries—both at governmental and non-governmental levels—Afghanistan's long war could not have been pursued.

1. Afghanistan's strategic location at the "faultline" of four civilizations—Islamic, Russian Orthodox, Chinese and Hindu—has been a significant factor for the region's instability.
2. Afghanistan's internal political fragility and external vulnerability continue to exist due to the country's fragmented social structure and rule of warlords and their linkage to regional actors.
3. The existence of terrorist groups in Pakistan, many of them backed by elements of the country's military and fundamentalist Islamic groups like the Jamiat-ul-Ulema-i-Islam remain as the forces of instability both in Pakistan and Afghanistan—even in the face of Pakistan's announced crackdown.
4. Central Asia's huge oil and gas deposits continue to provide incentives to the regional actors including Russia who strive for their say in the region's geopolitics. That remains as an impediment in the region's political development vis-à-vis the US military presence.
5. Afghanistan's ethnic linkages and geo-political susceptibility with neighboring countries—Pakistan, China, Tajikistan, Uzbekistan, Turkmenistan and Iran—continue to hunt the country despite American military presence, and that in turn will prolong the United States' presence.

What are then the regional geo-political dynamics of the United States' military presence in Afghanistan? How the anti-American forces are going to react to an enduring US military presence in South-west Asia? What strategic measures and policy initiative could be taken by the United States and the regional actors to bring about a lasting peace in the region? These are the questions which haunt us when we go for any serious analysis. This paper will look into the United States' geo-political ambition in the region in the pre as well as post-9/11 era and examine how the US military presence in the region affects the regional geo-politics in the long-run. The study, however, puts forward the idea that the US approach on Afghanistan has never been 'country-specific'; rather, it is driven by the regional geo-politics and strategic interests. Therefore, a regional policy framework, taking into consideration the geo-political dynamics of Afghanistan and her neighboring countries is warranted to bring about a lasting solution to the ongoing problem. Touching upon the historical facts, the study concludes that the US policy of supporting the unruly forces for its short-term gain and its hard-line stance in dealing with some nations in the region are somehow misguided and detrimental towards the Afghan peace process, as the same forces maintain their power and authority only by preventing the emergence of a functioning state.

PRE-9/11 AMERICAN PERCEPTION

With the withdrawal of Soviet troops from Afghanistan in 1989, the United States also slowly lost interests and allowed the Afghan warring factions to fight among them in a protracted civil war. The US policy during this period was one of benign neglect and apathy. Incidentally, with the rise of the Taliban, when the Americans found that a new out fit was in place and that could serve their strategic interests in the region, they extended tacit support and then gradually fostered it openly. A retrospective analysis of Washington's policy towards the pre-9/11 Afghanistan shows that the United States was ready to accept the fundamentalist regime to further its geo-political ambition in the region.[2] After the bombing of the American embassies in Dar-e-Salaam in Tanzania and Nairobi in Kenya in1998 by Al-Qaeda, however, Washington had to review its Afghanistan policy, while continuing its regional drive on a broad strategic setup.

In fact, a popular perception emerged in the whole region that the United States was allied with Pakistan and Saudi Arabia to promote the emergence of the Taliban. This US policy redefined the American perception towards the whole region. Initially, two important factors motivated the American decision. First, after the disintegration of the Soviet Empire and the independence of the Central Asian Republics, American strategic eye caught the oil and natural resources. Afghanistan's strategic location was, however, seen as a conduit for expanding American influence in the new Republics. The hand-in-glove relationships of some American officials with the Taliban leaderships were thus motivated by economic interests in Central Asia.

Secondly, the geo-strategic argument was that since the Taliban was pro-Pakistani, and at the same time anti-Russian and anti-Iranian, the United States ought to accept it. As per this argument, it was not an American affair to ascertain how the Taliban treats its own people, or to cater to "a stable Afghanistan with an aesthetically challenged government than a convulsed Afghanistan that offers a playground for Iranian and Russian devilments."[3] Nevertheless, the US hoped that after long years of turmoil, the Taliban would unite the country. A Sunni-dominated government in Kabul would serve as a bulwark against the influence of Iran in the region.[4] Containment of Iran had become an American strategy in the region, especially, after the Teheran government declared its readiness to extend port facilities to the newly independent Central Asian Republics. American interests in Afghanistan also increased when it became clear that the Rabbani government in Kabul had been drawn closer to Teheran, after the killing of Iran-backed Shia leader Abdul Ali Mazari by the Taliban in early 1995. What was more alarming for the Americans and the Pakistani intelligence agencies was the Iranian diplomatic success in bringing together of the erstwhile enemies of the Afghan war, Rabbani and Hekmatyar in an agreement in June 1996.[5]

Afghanistan, being a transport-junction and land-approach between the landlocked countries of Central Asia and the littoral states of the Indian Ocean, remains strategically important. Therefore, the competition over control of trade and pipeline routes from Central Asia to the Arabian Sea (Indian Ocean) transformed relations between Iran and Pakistan, and Teheran's initiative in this respect was openly supported by Russia and India. Taliban's ability to provide security for trade, and the projected pipelines was considered strategically advantageous to both Islamabad and Washington. Significantly, around this time, in the spring of 1996, a partnership between the American company UNOCAL and the Saudi Company DELTA had concluded plans for a multimillion-dollar ($2 billion) oil and gas pipelines from Turkmenistan to Pakistani Baluchistan via Herat and Kandahar.[6] Pakistan with the American backing (as an American company got involved) and Saudi Arabia considered the deal very lucrative since it was not just the trade route, but potential oil and gas pipelines were at stake.

In the meanwhile, American officials believed that the Taliban would serve as a bulwark against Russian and Iranian interests, and provide a US ally, Pakistan, "an overland link to the immense profits to be made from trade with the Central Asian Republics." Obviously, the new militia promised to open doors for the construction of giant oil and gas pipelines facilitating the route from Central Asia down through Afghanistan to Pakistan and world market. It was visualized that the Taliban's most important function was to provide "security for roads, and potentially, oil and gas pipelines that would link the states of Central Asia to the international market through Pakistan rather than through Iran."[7] It may be noted that the US was appeasing the Taliban at a time when the fundamentalist militia was training the Kashmiri, Uzbek, Tajik and Uighur radicals; thus spurring the growth of destabilizing fundamentalist movements throughout the region.

But the hand-in-glove relationship could not last long. The real colours of Taliban came out soon with the ever-increasing terrorist attacks by the Taliban's guest Osama bin Laden's Al-Qaeda networks in different parts of the world. After August 1998 terrorist attacks on U.S. Embassies in Nairobi (Kenya), and Dar es Salam (Tanzania), that killed more than two hundred people, the U.S. intelligence community concluded that the attacks were organized by Osama bin Laden. The Clinton administration took a serious view of this incident and wanted extradition of Bin Laden to the United States. But the Taliban categorically denied that their Saudi guest had anything to do with the US Embassy bombings, and hence the question of extradition did not arise. Then the United States ordered its Navy warships, already floating in the Indian Ocean, to launch cruise missiles against Bin Laden's terrorist training camps in Afghanistan.

The United States soon realized that the Taliban would not be able to unite and govern Afghanistan on its own and that the ongoing civil war there was likely to continue indefinitely. The Taliban proved a sad disappointment to their mentors in Washington who had hoped that the new militia would provide a new outlet to the US policy in the region.

THE POST-9/11 US INVASION

After the 9/11 terrorist attacks on the US, America's war preparation and subsequent regional policy-drives show that Washington's post-9/11 policy was not specifically Afghan-centric, but it had full-fledged regional geo-political imperatives. The huge military built-up in the region and permanent nature of military presence therein tell their own story.

MILITARY PREPARATION

America had a massive war preparation before it launched its air operation in Afghanistan. In addition to its permanent facilities in the Indian Ocean island of Diego Garcia, and floating aircraft carriers in the Arabian Sea, and Naval base off the coast in Oman, Washington used base facilities in Pakistan as well as Central Asian Republics. This was the biggest mobilization since the 1991 Gulf War. The US arsenal included B-1 and B-52 bombers, dozens of fighters and support aircraft that were ordered to the Gulf and the Indian Ocean region along with elite Special Operations troops. The aircraft carrier *USS Kitty Hawk,* which was already in the Indian Ocean was now fully loaded with helicopters and special operation forces for combat use and commando raids. American Navy planes, flying from carriers stationed in the Indian Ocean, also began patrolling specified "kill boxes" for what the Pentagon more precisely said was "engagement zones." With the unfolding of events, the United States increased the number of special operation forces and CIA teams, and engaged them in working with various opposition elements.

From Diego Garcia, B-52 and B-1 bombers, from Oman, F-15Es, and AC-130 gun-ships, and from the three aircraft carriers based in the Arabian Sea came the rest "combat punch." It was also stipulated that reconnaissance and refueling flights would originate from Diego Garcia and the Persian Gulf region, and air support and relief missions to come from Central Asia where the Tenth Mountain Division of the US Army helped protecting airfields. At the pick of the war, about 60,000 American forces were involved in this operation, out of which about half were in the Persian Gulf. In addition to this, America's friends and allies added more than 15,000 troops. Also about 15,000 Northern Alliance fighters, mostly from Tajik and Uzbek ethnic groups, and thousands of Pashtun soldiers joined in the winning side in November 2001. So compared to Afghanistan's military capability, it was a huge preparation by the United States to remove the Taliban regime from power in the shortest possible time.

In addition, the support extended (coercively acquired?) by Pakistan and Central Asian Republics made the American war efforts easier and brought about a quicker than expected military victory for Washington.

PERMANENT MILITARY PRESENCE

No Afghan or, for that matter, no American has an answer as to how long the United States will fight its war against terrorism in Afghanistan. From their nature of military presence as well as official statements it is clear that the United States has no strategy about how and when to leave Afghanistan. The United States has created and expanded the remnant military bases and replaced its Marine expeditionary forces sent into the country during the war with Army regulars settling in for a "long haul." Both Army and Air Force units have established permanent military bases.[8]

In the context of nation-building in Afghanistan, just on the eve of the second anniversary of the September 11 terrorist attacks, President Bush vowed to stay the course noting that "America has done this kind of work before" in Germany and Japan after World War II.[9] The President reminded the Americans that it took four years to hold the first elections in Germany after the war ended in 1945, and 54 years to win the wider struggle against Communism engaged there. The President displayed America's determination making it clear that the United States would not cut and run.[10] But probably, what the President failed to understand is that Afghanistan is ethnically more complex and geo-politically more explosive than Japan and Germany.

Similarly, when Donald Rumsfeld was asked by an American soldier when he expected the campaign against terrorism to end, the US Defence Secretary compared the military's role to that of police officers and firefighters who would always be needed. The Pentagon chief said, "You can't tuck in and hide and pretend that it's going to go away. It isn't. The only solution is to do what we're doing."[11] The trend, therefore, is towards a "long haul" in Afghanistan.

After three and a half years of the American military presence in the country, on 23 May 2005, President Bush and President Karzai signed a joint declaration concerning "strategic partnership" between the US and Afghanistan. The agreement stipulated that US military forces will continue to have access to Bagram Air Base and other mutually determined facilities, and that US and coalition forces "are to continue to have the freedom of action required to conduct appropriate military operations based on consultations and pre-agreed procedures." It was also declared that the US will "consult with respect to taking appropriate measures" if Afghanistan perceives that its "territorial integrity" or "independence is threatened."[12]

The Afghan opposition to the agreement was clearly visible as anti-American demonstrations erupted in several cities following its signing. This shows that Afghans, though needing the US assistance to ensure security and root out Taliban/Al-Qaeda elements, are not in favor of a permanent and prolonged American military presence.[13] Afghans have developed a sense of xenophobia about the Americans and a sense of resentment that foreigners are working in the country is intensifying.[14] Fearful about their own future, more and more people are switching gears back to neutral stance or to supporting the Taliban or their local warlords (instead of US-backed Hamid Karzai).[15]

American and western long-term commitment in Afghanistan was clearly visible during the recent NATO summit in Bucharest, Rumania. In a joint news conference with Afghan President Hamid Karzai, NATO Secretary General Jaap de Hoop Scheffer hailed the alliance for renewing its commitment to Afghanistan's security, and for recalibrating its tactical approach. This new approach is embodied in a four-page "strategic vision document," which will act as a guide for future reconstruction/ counter-insurgency operations in the country. De Hoop Scheffer asserted thus: "It will set out the path to a new phase in our Afghanistan engagement—what used to be a predominantly military effort will begin to shift towards a more balanced approach, with a stronger emphasis on civilian efforts and Afghan ownership." The strategic vision document calls for a "shared long-term commitment" for the NATO-led International Security and Assistance Force (ISAF) in Afghanistan. It also outlines support for enhanced Afghan leadership and responsibility in the reconstruction process, greater coordination of civilian and military reconstruction efforts.[16] So from all indications, it is clear that the American and the Western troops are going to be there in Afghanistan for a long time to come. Keeping all these facts into consideration, it is necessary to look at the geo-political dynamics in the region in a proper perspective.

REGIONAL GEO-POLITICAL DYNAMICS

The analysis so far points at two realities: first, the high-handed American military entrenchment, second, its permanent nature of military presence. Thus, it is crystal clear that the impact of September 11 and the American anti-Taliban war in Afghanistan that followed have changed the entire geo-political landscape in the region. It is a momentous event in the history of Afghanistan as it is the first arrival of Western Armies since Alexander the Great conquered the region in 334 B.C. In this radically altered scenario, Afghanistan's neighbors share lots of global and regional geo-political concerns because the stability of Afghanistan has a larger meaning for all of them. The US military presence in this volatile landmass was bound to have a profound effect on the strategic thinking of all the countries, as none of them have ever had discarded the region as a sphere of US influence which now appears to be an unconcealed reality. Hence, the regional geo-politics will partly be shaped by what happens in Afghanistan in the near future, including the nature and duration of the US presence. If the situation in Afghanistan deteriorates, then unalloyed security concerns will dominate. If Afghanistan stabilizes and yet the US presence lingers on and becomes permanent, the emerging geo-political trends will be in a state of flux. However, out of such a fluid situation, a few ongoing developments are worth examining as they appear to have far-reaching geo-political implications for Afghanistan as well as for the countries in the region.

Within weeks after the September 11 attacks on the US, Russian President Vladimir Putin opted for closer relationship with Washington, and launched a massive supply operation for the Northern Alliance.[17] Russia and the US acted for a time as *de facto* allies in the anti-terror campaign. Putin's decision to support Bush included acceptance of the US forces and, then their military bases in Central Asia, sharing of substantial intelligence, and offer of over-flight rights, etc. In fact, it was for the first time since the World War II, intelligence cooperation between the US and Russia was in full swing. Moscow was instrumental in securing the consent of Central Asian leaders to allow Americans to set up military bases and use them in the war against the Taliban regime. Russia also very generously extended necessary humanitarian relief during the first weeks of the war. The Russian President seems to have realized that security and stability on Russia's borders was essential in order to pursue the developmental agenda. Hence, the US invasion of Afghanistan as well as closer cooperation with Washington became acceptable to Moscow.[18]

But, this perception did not last long and the Russians began to grow apprehensive about the long-term American military presence in Afghanistan and Central Asia. The fear of possible "encirclement" by the US seems to have prevailed on the Russian psyche. The US interest in expanding the existing infrastructure in the region to meet future strategic contingencies made the Russians uneasy. Russians felt that the US was establishing itself permanently in their own sphere of influence and that could spark a series of geopolitical contests.[19]

While the US went to Central Asia only to "solve the Afghan problem," Russia has more immediate regional interests that compel Moscow to maintain a long-term presence. Russians fear that the US might seek control of Central Asia's oil and gas reserves and that Moscow could end up having NATO on its borders. America's unilateral moves based solely on its own self-interest have led to unsettling strategic dynamics,[20] according to Moscow. There are reports that Russian money and weapons are reaching to previously favored military commanders of the then Northern Alliance,[21] which annotate a different story.

Central Asian states, especially Uzbekistan, Tajikistan and Turkmenistan, which form Afghanistan's northern border, welcomed the US military and economic assistance since 2001 and in turn, ensured logistical support for the US military operations in Afghanistan. But off late, these former Soviet Republics seem to have raised their price of cooperation with the United States and look more critical and suspicious about the US strategic design.

The United States had negotiated long-term use of a major military base in Uzbekistan to expand the global reach of American forces.[22] American military planners believed that the US Special Operations Forces, intelligence and reconnaissance missions, and air logistics flights have to use the Karshi-Khanabad (K2) airfield in southeastern part of the country, which is strategically located. However, the US regional position was questioned with Uzbekistan's decision in late July 2005 to evict US military forces from this airbase. Russia rushed to fill the geopolitical vacuum by rapidly strengthening bilateral ties with Uzbekistan.[23] After strong diplomatic parleys by the United States, at the recent NATO summit in Bucharest, Uzbekistan consented to giving NATO forces an overland re-supply route to Afghanistan. NATO planners feel that an overland rail supply route would greatly ease the logistical hassles connected with reconstruction and counter-insurgency operations in Afghanistan.[24]

Tajikistan has stronger ethnic and cultural ties with Afghanistan than any of its northern neighbors. But the country has also always felt vulnerable to Muslim radicalism which emanates from Afghanistan. So the government in Dushanbe facilitated the US military operations against Al-Qaeda/Taliban in 2001. But after six years of the Afghan operation, things are now changing in a wrong direction. Illegal ethnic-Tajik militias appear to be using the threat of a resurgent Taliban as an excuse to hoard weapons and more forcefully protect their interests, such as ruling over land they have controlled since the Taliban's collapse or defending drug export routes that are a major source of income.[25] These entrenchments of the militias with cross-border support—if left unchecked—could exacerbate tensions in the country at a time when its security situation is already on a razor's edge. Under these circumstances, American support to some Tajik warlords will automatically add fuel to the fire.

Turkmenistan alone among the former Central Asian Republics had cordial relations with the Taliban. A proposed 1,000 mile gas pipeline to Pakistan through Afghanistan attracted considerable interest among American and other western investors during the Taliban rule in mid-1990s. The project, however, became a victim of international condemnation of the Taliban's linked to Al-Qaeda and global terrorism. The post-9/11 US policy towards Turkmenistan has not changed much. While the United States may be engaged in a variety of ways, Washington's focus is clearly on energy. Accordingly, the US is working to secure Ashgabat's commitment to export a sizable share of its gas via a planned trans-Caspian pipeline—a project that has Washington's strong backing. In addition, US official would like to see American and European firms gain opportunities to help Turkmen entities develop the country's reserves.[26] This American policy is not going well with the regional powers who consider it as undue US "intrusion" in their sphere of influence. Some Pentagon officials are thinking about the possibility of base facility and deployment of US forces in

Turkmenistan as well. Such a deployment could exert pressure on Iran to comply with international demands for curbing its nuclear programme.[27]

Kyrgyzstan does not share a border with Afghanistan but plays a very strategic role on America's war against terrorism. This is because of the American air base just outside its capital Bishkek. As per the US-Kyrgyz lease terms, the US facility at Manas can only be used in support of ongoing military actions in Afghanistan. But the regional powers are quite apprehensive about the US long-term motive in the region. During August 2007, Shanghai Cooperation Organization (SCO) summit, Iranian President Ahmadinajad was interested in the SCO's efforts to check US influence in Central Asia. In particular, the Iranian leader sought assurances from the summit host Kyrgyzstan, that an American air base outside of Bishkek would not be used for any potential US attack on Iran. China is believed to be more seriously interested in getting the US out of Kyrgyzstan. A Chinese security expert believes thus: "In the long run, countering the US military presence is the more important goal than countering Islamist extremist forces, so getting American forces out would be a gain."[28]

America's regional policy in the Southwest Asia has some direct bearings on the emerging geo-political trends in Afghanistan. One of the main planks of the American neoconservative agenda is the use of military force against unfriendly regimes. The recent bellicose statement on Iran, notwithstanding the chaos in Iraq, sets the tone of Washington in coming days. President Bush has said that military action against Iran is a possibility. There are also reports that the US is using Pakistani guerilla groups such as Jundullah to launch attacks on military and civilian bases in Iran.[29] It shows that the US will continue to pursue an aggressive policy towards the region. An air campaign to destroy Iran's nuclear sites or a full-fledged military invasion would probably prompt Tehran to unleash a clandestine war on the US forces in Afghanistan (and also in Iraq). This kind of situation could be far more explosive and deadly for the Americans than it already is. Iranians have been known for their opposition to the Taliban, but they can influence the forces opposed to American presence and destabilize their already insecure neighbors. In the event of an US attack on Iran, new security concerns will crop up and the ongoing geo-political situation will take a new dimension.

Another track of the US policy that will have perpetual adverse repercussions in the Afghan situation is towards Pakistan. The US has made it clear that General Pervez Musharraf would continue to play a pivotal role in the US war on terror, even if his cooperation in tracking bin Laden and his colleagues over last six years is widely acknowledged to be inadequate.[30] There is also every possibility that Pakistan would not allow capture of Laden (and others) just because Islamabad wants to further its own agenda, which is different from that of the US. A look at General Musharraf's record since he took over power in Pakistan shows that he is playing tricks.[31] It seems that General Musharraf finds it advantageous to permit Al-Qaeda and the jihadist Taliban to function in his country since without that threat looming large; Washington will have no use for him and his country. And yet, he will remain an indispensable card in the American strategic thinking.[32] Islamabad's efforts to prevent the Taliban/Al-Qaeda infiltration into Afghanistan are accurately described as "inconsistent, incomplete, and at times insincere."[33] Given this kind of a strategic situation, a low-level Pakistani support to the insurgents will continue to exist and the region across the Durand Line will remain volatile.

Before the US invasion of Afghanistan, India's concern was to check the destabilizing forces of Islamic extremism and international terrorism emanating from Pakistan and Afghanistan. So, India joined hands with Russia and the Central Asian states and continued its support to the Northern Alliance.[34] After the events of September 11, India advocated that its perception about Afghanistan's Taliban regime, Pakistan, and Al-Qaeda in promoting international terrorism had been vindicated. Therefore, Indians openly expressed their support to America's anti-terror war and opted for closer military and strategic cooperation between New Delhi and Washington. Like Pakistanis, many Indians view Afghanistan and Central Asia as an extension of its regional geopolitical competition with Islamabad where

Afghanistan had to play a vital role because of its geographical location.

But protracted American military presence in Pakistan, Afghanistan and Central Asia, will also come as an impediment on India's regional geo-political interests and diplomatic clout. The US will have a say on every Indian move in the whole South-west Asian region. Whether it is gas pipelines through Turkmenistan-Afghanistan-Pakistan-India, or oil/gas "lifeline" from Iran-Pakistan-India,[35] America will be a factor in the pipeline politics so long as they have military presence in the region. Another constraint on India's strategic interest vis-à-vis Pakistan is the entrenched and permanent nature of American military presence in Pakistan on the pretext of fighting the Taliban in Afghanistan. US presence restricts India's freedom of maneuver against Pakistan.

Almost all of Afghanistan's neighbors except Pakistan continue to endorse US-led operations that are aimed at defending Afghanistan against insurgency. But none of them seem comfortable to accept a long-term US military presence anywhere in the region. For India, China and Russia, terrorists' threats in Jammu and Kashmir, Xingjian and Central Asian regions and Chechnya respectively clearly exist. Recurrent killings and explosion of suicide bombers in the volatile Indian state reminds the policy makers in New Delhi that Pakistan has not stopped its policy of cross border terrorism. The Time to time terrorist attacks in Xingjian has taught Beijing that the menace is not out of bound for the communist country. Similarly, the Beslan school tragedy in Russia's North Ossetia Republic in 2004 and hostage taking in a Moscow theatre earlier claiming hundreds of victims in both the incidents awakened Russians to the dreadfulness of religious extremism and terrorism linked to Afghanistan.[36] There were also reports of Taliban hand in Andijon massacre of Uzbekistan in May 2005 where hundreds of innocent lives were lost.[37]

At the same time, Afghanistan's neighbors have apprehensions on what they call US grand design. They perceive that the US is now well entrenched with all its military might in the entire region and that it is not going to go back any time soon. And that the American geo-political drive is motivated by the containment of China, Iran and extracting Central Asian oil and gas to the world market, in addition to putting the NATO right their in the door-step of Russia. As per this argument, American strategists believe that it would be convenient for them to deal with an unruly China and Iran while based in Pakistan, Afghanistan, and Central Asia. Washington can have a close watch on the developments of the communist China and the unruly Iran, and the position would give access to more strategic mileage to the US foreign policy interests in the geo-politics of the region. Secondly, as stated above, through its military presence and economic and political support in the Central Asian Republics, Washington hopes to get access to the regions tremendous untapped reserves of oil.

These strategic and geo-political ambitions of the United States have led to considerable resentments among the countries surrounding the region. Russian, Chinese, and Iranian unhappiness is particularly visible in this context. In order to keep the Americans away from their "dirty games" in the region, these countries will continue to support the ethnic and tribal groups through whom they consider to promote their own geo-strategic interests. For instance, Chinese will continue to be perturbed by expanding US presence on its southwestern frontiers and support the anti-US forces; Russians to Tajiks and Uzbeks; and Iranians to their Shia minority ethnic group in the northwestern part of the country. Because these countries perceive that through its military presence in the region, the United States is unduly interfering in their "sphere of influence." In this sense, the overarching American geo-political objective in the region will be kept off balance by the regional powers, and that will continue to keep Afghanistan fragile and fragmented. In the process, America might get bogged down militarily in this landlocked country that has a long history of fighting against the foreigners.

Despite some high-handedness on terrorism and religious extremism, the regional actors complain that the US was not responding fully to the terrorist threat because it was not affecting the US interests directly. Leaders of Afghanistan's neighbors have pointed fingers at the US for its "selective approach" and "double standards." They view that while the enduring American military presence in Afghanistan and the region is not going to eliminate the specter of terrorism and Islamic fundamentalism, the menace provided a good pretext to the US entrenching itself in the region.

CONCLUSION

The January 2006 London conference, attended by more than sixty countries and international agencies produced a document called "Afghanistan Compact." The document predicated on every aspect of Afghanistan's social and economic development. On the country's security challenges, Pakistan was not even named in connection with the growing insurgency. Instead, the Compact called for "full respect of Afghanistan's sovereignty, and strengthening dialogue and cooperation between Afghanistan and its neighbors." Such a call to neighboring countries may mean different dimensions of strategic compulsions to different regional actors. The following situations could somehow mitigate the existing powers of unraveling forces in heralding a reconciliation process.

- The most desirable outcome from the current fragility would be: a hundred percent honesty and sincerity on the part of the United States in the ongoing reconstruction efforts and on disarming the warlords in a steady process without being looked like an occupying foreign power which the Afghans will not accept.
- Peace in Afghanistan also requires that the neighboring countries are convinced of American good intensions and that in turn, they abandon plans for hegemony and interference in Afghanistan's internal affairs.
- American focus on its "war against terrorism" in Afghanistan should not overshadow the threats emanating from warlords and drug traffickers which are more damaging to the population than terrorist violence.
- One way of diluting the Taliban insurgency is to show western sensitivity on their demands and rehabilitation, and a substantial dialogue as the British Defence

Secretary Des Browne suggested recently. Brown emphasized that in his opinion, some elements within the Taliban can be persuaded to change sides and that would relieve the intolerable pressure currently faced by the British Armed Forces as it struggles to fight on multiple fronts. The Defence Secretary admitted that the pressure was unsustainable, "We can't do this for ever and we aren't."[38] The British Defence Secretary's proposed negotiations with the Taliban could well be the beginning of a new Western policy of rapprochement with militant Islamic groups in Afghanistan as well as in the whole of South-west Asian region. It is a complete repudiation of the militant policy of bombs and bullets employed by the Anglo-American axis in its so-called "war on terror," but it appears foreseeable.

- If the United States wants to rebuild Afghanistan, Washington must consider that outsiders can play an important role in generating trust among former enemies and strengthening their overall commitment to the peace process. For instance, Warlordism in Afghanistan is not only an internal problem intrinsically blended through its tribal and ethnic loyalties, it is also linked to the regional actors.[39] So the US must understand that part of the solution lies in the countries of the region as well. Therefore, Washington must start with a framework for regional cooperation. And the country which is required to be brought to such a framework first is Iran, because of its strategic location and close ethnic ties with Afghanistan. That will clearly send a strong message to other regional actors about American honesty and sincerity, and bring about a drastic change in the Afghan situation. The present "containment" mindset of the neo-conservatives in Washington may not be conducive to such an idea. But if the beginning is from nowhere, Americans finally may well get there.

Bringing about such a situation in this war-ravaged country will depend on how the United States acted upon in the coming days. The present trend does not look conducive to permanent peace in the country. The American peace efforts so far appear fragile, and the country is passing through a thin edge of instability as it is still being haunted by so many divisive and centrifugal forces. Afghanistan remains critical to the future of its neighbors, as instability in this land-locked country has the potential to destabilize the whole region. A potent combination of drugs, weapons, and militants traverse Afghanistan and cross into its neighbors and beyond, and hence, the seeds of instability remain intact.

The Bonn process, reconstruction of the country and its national security are not intrinsic to Afghan situation alone. It is in fact, heavily loaded with regional geopolitics. And within this geo-political entanglement, the regional actors look at the US presence in suspicion. As stated above, many believe that the geo-political factors such as Central Asia/Caspian energy resources; China's Xinjiang, Iran, etc. are the reasons for US interest in Afghanistan. And, if that is the case, and the United States remains bogged down in a growing insurgency in the country, and if the US missiles take more innocent lives, Washington's strategy could well backfire. The (Tribal) Pashtuns have a saying, "Kill one person, make 10 enemies." This is a war in which the more people you kill, the more enemies you make, and the faster you lose.

REFERENCES

1. For a comprehensive study on the subject, see Meher, J. 2006, Understanding the Dynamics of Afghan Instability, *Contemporary Central Asia,* Vol. 10, (no. 3) pp.1-31.
2. See Meher, J. 2004: *America's Afghanistan War: The Success That Failed,* New Delhi, Kalpaz Publication, pp.199-227.
3. Garfinkle, A. 1999, Afghanistanding, *Orbis,* Vol. 43, (no. 3) p. 415.
4. Burns, J.F. and Levine, S. 1997, For Afghans, Taliban's Rise to Power Was Deliverance from Tyranny, *International Herald Tribune,* 2 January.
5. Stobdan, P. 1996-97, War in Afghanistan, *Asian Strategic Review* New Delhi, Institute for Defence Studies and Analysis, p.259.
6. Rubin, B.R. 1997, Women and pipelines: Afghanistan's proxy wars, *International Affairs,* Vol. 73, (no. 2) p. 288.

7. Rubin, B.R. 1997, U.S. Policy in Afghanistan, *Muslim Politics Report*, no. 11, p. 6.
8. In addition to their permanent military presence in Afghanistan, the United States has laid down its long-term footprint with several Army and Air Force bases in Kyrgyzstan, Uzbekistan, and Pakistan which shows that the Americans are not going to go back any time soon.
9. Waldman, A. and Filkins, D. 2003, 2 U.S. Fronts: Quick Wars, but Bloody Peace, *The New York Times*, 19 September.
10. Ibid.
11. Jehl, D. 2003, Afghan Front Heats Up, and Rumsfeld Urges Patience, *The New York Times*, 8 September.
12. Constable, P. 2005, Karzai Dismisses Taliban Threat, Minimizes Differences with US, *The Washington Post*, 25 May, p. A16. Also see, 2005, the Joint Declaration of the United States-Afghanistan Strategic Partnership, *Office of the Press Secretary*, The White House, Washington DC, 23 May.
13. Ghufran, N. 2006, Afghanistan in 2005: The Challenges of Reconstruction, *Asian Survey*, Vol. 46, (no. 1) p. 92. Regional actors such as Russia, China, and others also expressed their concern over the new US-Afghan strategic partnership.
14. See Editorial, 2006, Afghanistan: Unraveling, *The New York Times*, 1 June. The editorial writes: "Afghans have long been renowned for their hostility towards foreign troops on their territory, as the 20th century Russians and the 19th century British learned the hard way. Until now they have made a conspicuous exception for the 21st century Americans, who helped them shake off Taliban misrule and then promised their poor and war-shattered country an international rebuilding effort on the model of the post World War II Marshall Plan. More than four years later, Afghanistan's patience is running out."
15. Aizenman, N.C. 2005, Afghan Crime Wave Breeds Nostalgia for Taliban, *The Washington Post*, 18 March p. A01.
16. Wild, D.B. 2008, NATO: In Afghanistan for the Long Haul, eurasianet.org, 03 April.
17. In fact, Russians were supplying money and weapons to the Northern Alliance for a long time, but in a small scale. See Risen, J. 1998, Russians Are Back in Afghanistan, Aiding Rebels, *The New York Times*, 27 July.
18. For a comprehensive approach on the subject, see Meher, J. 2006, Afghanistan in Indo-Russian Strategic Calculations: The Post 9/11 Trends, *The ICFAI Journal of Governance and Public Policy*, Vol.1, (no. 2), pp. 48-69.

19. For a balanced view on the post 9/11 geopolitical scenario in terms of "the American Intrusion" and "Russian Responses," see Buszynski, L. 2005, Russia's New Role in Central Asia, *Asian Survey*, Vol. 45, (no. 4) pp. 546-65.
20. Berman, I. 2004-05, The New Battleground: Central Asia and the Caucasus, *The Washington Quarterly*, Vol. 28, (no. 1), pp. 59-69.
21. Weinbaum, M.G. 2006, Afghanistan and Its Neighbors: An Ever Dangerous Neighborhood, United States Institute of Peace, *Special Report No. 162*, p. 16.
22. Tyson, A.S. and Wright, R. 2005, Crackdown Muddies U.S.-Uzbek Relations:. Washington in Talks on Long-Term Use of Base, *The Washington Post*, 4 June.
23. See Shlapentokh, D. 2005, Russia's Foreign Policy and Eurasianism, *eurasianet.org*, 2 September.
24. 2008, Uzbekistan: Karimov Approves Overland Rail Re-Supply Route for Afghan Operations, *eurasianet.org*, 07 April.
25. Synovitz, R. 2007, Afghanistan: Armed Northern Militias Complicate Afghan Security, *eurasianet.org*, 11 April.
26. Weitz, R. 2007, United States makes push to improve relations with energy rich Turkmenistan, *eurasianet.org*, 20 September.
27. Cohen, A. 2005, Uzbekistan: A Policy Providing Ground for Washington, *eurasianet.org*, 31 May.
28. As quoted in Kucera, J. 2007, Shanghai Cooperation Organization Summiteers Take Shots at US Presence in Central Asia, *eurasianet.org*, 20 September.
29. See 2007, Overture from Iran, editorial, *The Times of India*, 7 April, p.16.
30. For the US position on the issue, see Rajghatta, C. 2007, US Defends Pak again," *The Times of India*, 23 May.
31. For Pakistani involvement in Afghanistan after 9/11 incident, see Meher, J. 2003, Bush on Afghanistan: Dozing at the Dossier of Musharraf, *Mainstream*, 27 December, pp. 91-94.
32. Subrahmanyam, K. 2005, Asian Drama: After Iraq, US Targets Iran with Pak Support, *The Times of India*, 20 January.
33. A scholarly depiction on the subject is available in Weinbaum, M.G. Afghanistan and Its Neighbors: An Ever Dangerous Neighborhood, p. 10.
34. The anti-Taliban alliance led by the legendary Tajik commander Ahmed Shah Masud who was killed in September 2001.
35. Former Indian Petroleum Minister Mani Shankar Ayar talked about extending such pipeline to China and eventually to Myanmar.
36. Katz, M.N. 2004, Russia and America after Beslan, *eurasianet.org*, 13 October.

37. Tarzi, A. 2005, Afghanistan: Was Taliban Involved in Uzbek Violence? *eurasianet.org,* 19 May.
38. As quoted in Lall, R.R. 2008, We should talk to Taliban, says UK minister Des Browne, *The Times of India,* 31 March, p. 15.
39. For a theoretical perspective on Warlordism and the American policy thereof, see Meher, J. 2008, Dealing with the Devils: The Other Side of Bush's Afghanistan War, *The Icfai Journal of International Relations,* Vol. 2, (no. 1) pp. 23-43.

CHAPTER 20

Resurgence of Taliban in Afghanistan: Implications for India and Pakistan

Nalini Kant Jha

As euphoria generated by wining of democratic forces in Pakistan has gradually subsided, the grim reality of resurgence of Taliban in southern and eastern Afghanistan and Federally Administered Tribal Area, (FATA) of Pakistan, which has virtually become a mini-Taliban state with Pakistan almost losing its control over it, is stirring in our face. This is not at all surprising, as the Pakistan army under the leadership of its former boss, General Pervez Musharraf, virtually handed over the area to the Taliban where they are now training and preparing for cross-border attacks. Peace deal with the Taliban has resulted in a three-fold rise in attacks on NATO troops and summery justice and other abhorrent practices are now enforced by Taliban leaders. Not surprisingly, the newly elected government in Pakistan is confronted with a similar challenge, but on a much larger scale than President Musharraf had to deal with a year ago, when in July 2007 he had to storm the Lal Masjid in the heart of Islamabad expelling the terrorists holed up there. Today it seems as if the North West Frontier Province Capital Peshawar is in imminent danger of falling in to Taliban hands.

With the Taliban resurgence on both sides of the Durand-line, and Pakistan having signed deals in north and south as well Waziristan, Pakistan's eroding sovereignty in these areas, the contours of a *de façto* independent Pashtoonistan are emerging. Is Pakistan, therefore, in the process of achieving its notion of 'strategic depth' or falling into a 'strategic ditch?'

The present article is an attempt to shed light on the implications of the resurgent Taliban for Pakistan as well as India. The paper argues that in the long-term, the Taliban are likely to create problems not only for India but for Pakistan as well. For, no Afghan government including the Pashtoon dominated Taliban regime that was recognized by Pakistan has accepted the division of the Pashtoon along Durand-line.

II

Contrary to its literal meaning, Taliban, which means students, are acting as Islamic warriors in Afghanistan and adjoining areas. These dreadful monsters were created in 1994 by Pakistan. At that time, the Pakistanis did not bother to ponder over its impact on their own society. Pakistan Inter-Services Intelligence (ISI) militaristic policies, which consisted of bleeding the Indian Army in Kashmir and turning Afghanistan into their virtual fifth province, had blinded them to its consequences. Their ill-conceived strategy has failed once again. Consequently, the Indian military has emerged stronger from the long conflict in Kashmir. In the Spring of 1992, the Communist regime fell and Ahamed Shah Masood's forces entered Kabul. Pakistani officials instructed their trusted men and surrogate Gulbudin Hekmatyar (leader of *Hezb-e-Islam*), who had just been appointed the Prime Minister of the newly established coalition government in Kabul, to burn down the city. From 1992 to 1994, the Afghan capital became a living hell.[1]

Despite intensive efforts, Hekmatyar's forces were stuck in southern and eastern parts of Kabul and were unable to make significant progress. Pakistani authorities decided to shift their support from Hekmatyar to a then unknown radical movement —the Taliban. Along with the ISI, the late Benazir Bhutto and Nasrullah Baber—then respectively the Prime Minister and Interior Minister of Pakistan—are also to blame because the movement was created under their direct watch.[2]

Few politicians in Pakistan and in the rest of the world ever questioned Pakistan's dangerous policy of deliberately nurturing a radical Islamist group. In September 1995, Colonel Imam (a senior ISI official), with impunity and consent of Western officials, who had an interest in the Turkman pipeline project, personally led Taliban forces to capture Herat, which is the largest city in western Afghanistan. In 1996 when Bin Laden's airplane landed in the Afghan city of Jalalabad, no alarm went off in the capitals of the West. When the Taliban were beating women, destroying schools, and holding public executions, Pakistani officials were trying to convince the rest of the world by saying that Afghanistan was a backward, fragmented, and ethnically divided country, which needed an iron hand to stabilize it. Today, the same ills that destroyed Afghanistan plague Pakistan.[3]

III

As stated at the outset, the newly elected government in Pakistan is facing bigger challenge from the Taliban and Al-Qaeda since political turmoil started in Pakistan at least over a year ago. All military pressure has shifted away from Tribal Area in Pakistan, where Al-Qaeda and Taliban have established their safe houses and training camps. The recent peace agreement between the newly elected civilian government of Pakistan and the Taliban has given the latter an implicit approval to intensify their attacks inside Afghanistan. Indeed, Al-Qaeda has benefited from the chaos in Pakistan and has had ample time to regroup and step-up bases for its attacks.

The growing terrorist activities of these forces and the pressure from the US obliged the civilian government in Afghanistan to use force, while keeping the door open for talks. The last few days of June 2008 saw paramilitary operations in Khyber Agency of the FATA, from where the criminal gangs with links to Taliban terrorists were training nearby Peshawar, making brazen forays in to the city in vehicles mounted with weapons, threatening music and video shop owners and kidnapping for ransom. Khyber is also a main supply root for NATO-ISAF forces in Afghanistan, and the pressure of these groups and their connections to Taliban posed a major threat to logistics convoys passing that way.[4]

Pakistan appears also to have been jolted by the failing negotiations in South Waziristan. So secretive were the negotiations, that there is no clarity even on who the parties to the talks were. Some say it was the Pakistan Army calling the shots on the government side. The government insists it was talking to Mehsud tribesmen and not the *Tehreek-i-Taliban* Commander, Beithullah Mehsud, named for Benazir Bhutto's killing Whatever it was, little remained of it after Beithullah Mehsud's men abducted and killed twenty eight tribesmen of government sponsored peace committee in the area. The killings appeared to be a direct message from the militants that peace can only be negotiated on their terms.[5]

Needless to add, the civilian government in Pakistan and the Army were under tremendous pressure to rethink their peace deals with the militants. Hence in the end of June 2008, the Pakistan government announced that it was alive to the threat to Pakistan from within its borders. Prime Minister Yusuf Raja Gilani announced that terrorism posed the gravest challenge to Pakistan's security, and declared that the Pakistani Territory would not be permitted to be used against other countries, especially Afghanistan. As stated earlier, within days of this announcement, the Frontier Corps, a paramilitary, moved into Khyber to clean-up the area. Thus far, it went according to the governments wishes. None of the three groups active in the area —The *Lushkar-i-Islam*, its rival, *Ansar-ul-Islam*, and a group called the prevention of Vice and Protection of Virtue offered any resistance, and there were little causalities.[6]

But as the paramilitaries set to work in Khyber, Beithullah Mehsud called off the South Waziristan negotiations and warned of retaliation in Punjab and Sindh. In Swat, the Taliban suspended talks with the NWFP government. And while the religious parties attacked the government for using the Pakistan forces against "brother" Muslims under US pressure, the Pakistan Muslim-League (N)—it already had a tense relationship with the PPP over the issue of judiciary—also joined in claiming not to have been consulted by the government of which it is a part, it described the paramilitary operations as a "military Invasion" against "our own people." The ruling Pakistan Muslim-League (O) also distanced itself from the operations.[7]

It appears that the above-mentioned political parties were afraid of emulating President Pervez Musharraf who was criticized for looking on passively as the Lal-Masjid terrorists entrenched themselves from January to July 2007. But when President Muusharraf finally took them on, public opinion in Pakistan rounded on him for doing so. Stories spread of "thousands of Kuran reciting little girls" killed in the operations. The operations set-off a wave of suicide attacks in the NWFP and other parts of the country, targeting soldiers and civilians alive.

Hence, the question now is: will the new government retain the stomach for taking the military operations into areas such as South Waziristan where the real Taliban challenge lies, especially in the event of a militant backlash resulting in military and civilian causalities that could turn public opinion hostile to the operations. It appears that the government in Islamabad is hesitant in confronting the Taliban head on as it is shy of calling these operations as "military operations" insisting that the paramilitaries are only restoring "law and order."

Obviously, the Pakistan Government's this hesitation to call a spade a spade has encouraged radical Islamist groups at the expense of moderate and democratic movements. For example, President Musharraf did not hesitate to jail lawyers who protested in favour of rule of law and democracy, but appeased murderous radical Islamist and Taliban leaders under the phony Pashtun code of conduct enforced in the tribal area. Until now, Pakistani authorities have been able to avoid a full confrontation with local Taliban groups for fear of alienating Pashtuns who constitute over 15 per cent of Pakistan's population, but are intentionally over-represented up to 25 per cent in Pakistan's Army.

Continuous pressure from the US notwithstanding, Pakistan's military authorities have resisted bringing their Punjabi elite units to the tribal battlegrounds against the Pashtun radical movements. Instead, they heavily relied on militia forces from the tribal zone to secure the area. Pakistani leaders rigorously want to avoid a rift and direct confrontation between Punjabis and Pashtuns.

In fact, there is a real risk that the "war on terror" in Pakistan might transform into a full war for autonomy or independence of Pashtun tribes from Islamabad. Pakistani authorities have broken the status quo in the tribal zone by promoting radical Islam and extremist religious leaders at the expense of traditional tribal leaders and institutions. Pakistan's policy in the tribal zone has been a continuation of former British colonial policy, which consisted of keeping Pashtun tribes economically dependent, politically fragmented, and intellectually backward. The government in Islamabad has continued to subsidise them and bribe their leaders, instead of creating a sustained economy and providing modern education.[8] It thus appears that the Pakistani authorities created Taliban to protect their interests in Afghanistan and in Kashmir, but are now faced with uncalculated consequences, which seriously threaten Pakistan's own existence. Hence it appears that instead of achieving its notion of strategic depth in Afghanistan, Pakistan is falling into a strategic ditch.

IV

In reality, however, the above assertion is only partially true. For, perpetuating instability and weakness in Afghanistan is an existential imperative for Pakistan – and the reason for this lies, among other elements, preponderantly in the defunct Durand Line.

Legally, the FATA and the NWFP lapsed back into Afghan territory after the termination of the treaty between Mortimer Durand (on behalf of the British Empire) and Amir Abdur Rahman Khan of Afghanistan, signed in 1893, relinquishing control of these regions to the British for hundred years. Since 1993, consequently, FATA and NWFP became *dejure* Afghan territory, though they continue to be illegally occupied by Pakistan.

That is why, the Afghan President, Hamid Karzai, has described the Durand Line as a "line of hatred separating two brothers." In June 2008, he threatened to send Afghan forces into Pakistan to "rescue the Pashtuns in Pakistan from ..cruelty and terror."[9] Successive Afghan Governments have, in fact, rejected the Durand line since 1949—but even the legal foundations of continued Pakistani occupation of FATA and NWFP have dissipated since 1993. This confronts Islamabad with the terrifying possibility of losing one of its four provinces the moment a stable and strong Kabul consolidates its capacities to press home its legal claim. Consequently, promoting instability in Afghanistan is, and will remain, a critical strategic goal for the establishment in Pakistan.

India, on the other hand, remains irrevocably committed to Afghan stability and strength, and is baking a multiplicity of development projects that impact directly on the country's reconstruction and on the welfare of its people. Moore significantly, several of these projects directly impact on the Pakistani stranglehold over Afghanistan. The Zeranj-Delaram Road project, for instance, will eventually link Afghanistan to the Iranian port of Chabahar and thereby relieve Afghanistan of its complete dependency on Pakistan for the transit of goods. At the same time, this will provide India a route to channel relief and developmental materials to Afghanistan, currently denied by Pakistan's refusal to concede trade and transit rights across Pakistani territory. Pakistan and its Taliban proxies also remain intractably opposed to road and infrastructure projects because these automatically act as force multipliers for counter insurgency formations, improving their response time and capacities.[10]

It may be mentioned here that after the fall of the Taliban in 2001 India had moved quickly to regain its strategic depth in Afghanistan. It backed President Hamid Karzai, reopened two Consulates in Herat and Mazher-e-Sharif, which had been shut since 1979, and opened two new ones in Kandahar and Jalalabad, provinces close to the border with Pakistan.

India also became one of Kabul's leading donors—it has pledged to spend $750 million on helping rebuild the countries shattered infrastructure. It committed funds for education, health, power, telecommunications, food aid and helping to strengthen governance.[11] About 400 Indians are working in Afghanistan on projects which also involve 25 private companies. The thrust areas are infrastructure development, humanitarian assistance and institutional and human resource development. The reconstruction projects are chosen by the Afghan Government. Nearly 600 Indo Tibet Border Police (ITBP) and Central Industrial Security Force (CISF) personnel are deployed for the security of these projects.[12]

India is erecting power transmission lines in the north, building more than 200 km roughly 125 miles of road, digging tube wells in six provinces, running sanitation projects in Kabul, working on lighting up 100 villages using solar energy and, significantly, building the country's new parliament building. It has given at least three Airbus planes to Afghanistan's ailing national airline. Several thousand Indians are engaged in development work. As observed by an astute observer of developments in Afghanistan, Ahmad Rashid, "India's reconstruction strategy was designed to win over every sector of Afghan society, give India a high profile with Afghans, gain the maximum advantage and, of course, undercut Pakistani influence."[13]

India's closeness in Afghanistan is also reflected in bilateral trade, which has grown rapidly, reaching $225 million in 2007-08. Besides, India has cut a number of trade deals with Afghanistan involving Iran and central Asian States. As stated earlier, since India cannot trade directly with Afghanistan using Pakistani territory, it is building the Zeranj-Delaram Road to shorten the distance to Iranian ports to facilitate its trade linkages with Kabul.

Needless to add, Pakistan has been alarmed with increasing Indian influence in Afghanistan since the ouster of Taliban. When India began reopening the Consulates, President Musharaff made his displeasure clear straightaway. "India's motivation in Afghanistan is very clear, nothing further then upsetting Pakistan. Why should they have Consulates in Jalalabad and Kandahar, what is their interests? There is no interest other than disturbing Pakistan, doing something against Pakistan."[14]

V

The conflict between the Pakistan-Taliban position, on the one hand and the Afghan- Indian perspective, on the other, is, therefore, irreducible and no 'peace process' or 'confidence building measures' are going to diminish the structural contradictions that underlie violence and terrorism in the region. The suicide car bombs attack on the Indian embassy in Kabul in July 7 that resulted in the death of four people including India's defence attaché R B Mehta and senior diplomat BV Rao as well as injury of 140 peoples is the latest manifestation of Taliban's hostility to Indian reconstruction work in Afghanistan. While no one has yet admitted being behind the attack, Afghanistan's Interior Ministry has said that the action was coordinated by an intelligence agency active in the region on obvious reference to Pakistan's ISI.[15] The intelligence agencies of India and Afghanistan too have accused the ISI of masterminding this incident.[16]

Pakistan's intelligence agency will, of course, not admit its hands in any of these events, growing violence in Afghanistan clearly points out towards the "Great Game" going on between neighbours seeking to gain influence in Afghanistan. And as the experience of past few years shows, India being one of the main donors in rebuilding Afghanistan, will have to be ready for facing these kinds of threats at least in the short run. To recapitulate some of these events, an Indian national working for a construction company was killed by unknown attacker in Kabul in 2003; a driver with India's state-run Border Roads Organization was abducted and killed by the Taliban while working on the road in November 2006; in January 2008, two Indian were killed in an attack on the key road linking Zerang and Herat with Kandhar; and in April this year, a Taliban suicide bomber killed two personnel of Border Roads Organization.

The primary target of Taliban, of course, is the Karzai government in Kabul. In January 2008, for instance, six people were killed in a Taliban attack on Serena Hotel. Two months later six people died in a car bomb attack on a military convey. In April, there was an assassination attempt on Afghan President Hamid Karzai. The authorities in Kabul accused Pakistan's ISI of involvement in this attack as well. In June they attacked a prison in Kandhar.[17]

It will, however, be churlish for New Delhi to ignore challenges posed by Taliban in collaboration with Al-Queda and

ISI to this country. While India need not unnecessarily get involved in internal war in Afghanistan, as advised by a well informed commentator,[18] threats from Taliban to this country should not be underestimated. In fact, Taliban has never been friendly to India. It indeed backed the hijacking of IC 814 to Kandahar in December 2001 in which the Indian government had to return dreaded Pakistani terrorists captured with great difficulty.[19] Understandably, Islamabad was still smarting over the loss of control of what it considered its strategic backyard and objected to India's growing influence inside Afghanistan. With the revival of the Taliban in Afghanistan, these virulent anti-India forces are active for undermining India's hold in Afghanistan.

VI

What can India do to protect its interests in Kabul? Regrettably Indian discourses have not taken up seriously about the contours of our Afghan policy. Given the "Euro Atlanticist" outlook of our think tankers, it is not surprising that the Afghan problem is of low priority. The fact that the attack on the Indian embassy in Kabul came close to heels of internal assessment sent by the Indian mission to South Block that Taliban fighters were exploiting the poor security situation in the country and there was an urgent need to beef up security for Indian installation, clearly demonstrated the casual and careless attitude of *babus* in New Delhi. The officials knew that the mission was a sitting duck but delayed installing a bomb shield around it because it is a rented building. Besides, the sophisticated security equipments for the chancery and the residence were denied on the grounds that the building is located on hired premises. What has made matters worse is that the construction work of permanent embassy building in moving in a snail's pace. Only the construction of the boundary wall could be completed in the last two years The report also says that the security personal deployed in extreme cold conditions are functioning without adequate clothing for such situations.[20]

Though more security personnel and armoured vehicles are being sent to Kabul now to step up security, it is obviously not enough. What is needed first and foremost is the strong resolve to fight terror. Unfortunately, the political instability in New Delhi is conducive for such a resolve. Not surprisingly, recently when a proposal for covert action against some Pakistani-supported militant groups was made, the top echelons in Delhi sat over it South Block must realize that only tough action and not merely lip service can ward off such threats.

REFERENCES

1. Haroun Mir, "It is Payback Time," *Times of India* (Lucknow), April 9, 2008
2. *Ibid.*
3. *Ibid.*
4. Nirupama Subramaniam, "Cracking Down the Taliban, Possibly," *The Hindu* (New Delhi), July 3, 2008.
5. *Ibid.*
6. *Ibid.*
7. *Ibid.*
8. Mir, n.1.
9 K.P.S. Gill, "ISI for Kabul's Woes," *The Pioneer* (Lucknow), July 14, 2008.
10. *Ibid.*
11. Soutik Biswas, "In the Line of Fire: India will be Targeted for its Role in Afghanistan," *Times of India*, July 11, 2008.
12. Ashok Mehta, "Pakistan's Proxy War," *The Pioneer*, July 10, 2008.
13. Biswas, n. 11.
14. Cited in ibid.
15. Editorial, "Terror in Kabul," *Times of India*, July 7, 2008; editorial, "Dastardly Act," *The Hindu*, July 9, 2008; B. Raman, ISI's Shadow in Kabul," *The Pioneer*, July 9, 2008; and Mehta, n.12; and Haroun Mir, "The Long Arm of Pakistan," *Times of India*, July 2, 2008.
16. Saurabh Shukla and Danish Karokhel's dispatch from Kabul, "Why India is the New Target," *India Today* (New Delhi), vol. 33, no. 29, July 14-21, 2008, p. 52. See also, See also, B. Raman, "Terrororising Afghanistan," *The Pioneer*, July 17, 2008
17. *The Hindu*, July 9, 2008. See also, Devyani Rao, "Peace Eludes Afghanistan," *The Pioneer*, February 12, 2008.
18. M.K. Bhadrakumar, a retired official belonging to the Indian Foreign Service, argues that Taliban's well defined agenda is to capture power in Kabul from where it was summarily evicted in the autumn of 2001. Its repeated message to the outside world is to "live us alone." Hence, India need not be involved in fratricidal war

in Afghanistan. See his, "Reading the Afghan Equations Correctly," *The Hindu*, April 19, 2008

19. Nalini Kant Jha, "Dealing with Pakistan," in his, ed., *South Asia in 21st Century: India, Her Neighbours and Great Powers* (New Delhi: South Asian Publishers, 2003), pp.97-112.
20. Shukla and Karokhel's dispatch from Kabul, n. 16.

CHAPTER 21

Resurgent Afghanistan: Implications for India

Prashant Agarwal

Geographically and culturally Afghanistan located in the northeast portion of the Iranian plateau through which India was linked with the Middle East and both these regions with China and Central Asia. Thus, throughout the history of India, Afghanistan was used as a buffer state by the rulers of India. During the 19th century, when the British Empire expanded northwest from the Indian sub-continent toward Central Asia, it first tried to conquer Afghanistan. But after the two unsuccessful attempts settled for making it buffer against the Russian empire to the North.[1] The expansion of the British and Russian empires in the 19th Century had contributed towards not only disturbing the ethnic balance of the Afghanistan but also throwing Afghanistan into turmoil for the entire century.

The fear of Russian design towards Indian frontiers through Afghanistan or Persia always effected the British-Indian defence policy and the Afghan wars of the 19th Century were a direct result of this policy. The "Russian Peril" was first mentioned by Governor General Bentinck (1828-1835 AD) and overshadowed British-Indian defence and foreign policy throughout the19th Century and lasted upto 1907, when under the pressure of the 'German danger' the Czar was induced to sign an armistice agreement, thus, giving the British a spell of relief. During the Russophobia years, the Britishers had established a three-tiered border to separate their empire from Russia through through a series of treaties with Kabul and Moscow.[2] The first frontier separated the areas of the Indian subcontinent under direct British administration from those areas under Pushtun tribal control (today this line divides those areas administered by the Pakistani state from the Federally Administered Tribal Agencies). The second frontier, the Durand Line, divided the Pashtun tribal areas from the territories under the Administration of the emir of Afghanistan (today this line demarcated as International border between Afghanistan and Pakistan, although Afghanistan has never accepted it). The outer frontier, the borders of Afghanistan with Russia, Iran and China, demarcated the British sphere of influence in this area.[3]

In the beginning of the twentieth century, the Third Anglo-Afghan War (1919) resulted in with the recognition of Afghanistan's full sovereignty. The country's first sovereign King Amanullah, tried to build a strong nationalist state. He was keen to develop Afghanistan as a modern developed country by using scarce resources very carefully, but his effort collapsed after a decade. The reason behind his debacle was the outside interference of the regional powers. The British helped another contender, Nader Shah, consolidate a weaker form of rule.[4] A weak centralized power had once again provided an opportunity to the tribal leaders to regain their territory and power. As a result, Afghanistan was once again came under the control of tribal leaders and central government's jurisdiction was only limited only around the Kabul region.[5] Afghanistan's internal unrest peaked in 1928-33, ending when Mohammed Zahir Shah began his reign as king.

Then, 1947, came the independence and partition of India, which even more dramatically altered the strategic stakes in the region. After the British left the borders of Afghanistan, in their wake the Afghan government decided to press irredentist claims to Pakistan's North West Frontier Province which led to strained relations between the two Islamic nations. Afghanistan looked towards Soviet Union for aid and trade and traditionally opposed to foreign alliances, would not enter into the US supported Baghdad Pact. By the 1950s Afghanistan was considered to be in the Soviet sphere of influence. Aid was the Soviet Union's most effective foreign policy tool in Afghanistan. Afghan troops were trained and re-equipped along Soviet lines by large numbers of Soviet military advisors; the Soviets built irrigation systems, dams, roads and airfields.[6] Unfortunately, they had not established a single production unit in Afghanistan. Backwardness of Afghanistan was prerequisite for enhancing the Soviet influence in the region. Soviets did the same thing which Americans were doing with Pakistan.

During this period, tension between Afghanistan and Pakistan was flared up. Afghanistan claimed that Pakistan was a new state, not a successor to British India, and that all past border treaties had lapsed. A loya jirga in Kabul denied that the Durand Line was an international border and called for self determination of the tribal territories as Pashtunistan. Frequent skirmishes across the Durand Line began with the covert support of both governments. At the same time, Islamabad was aligning itself with the United States in order to counter India—which in turn provided an opportunity for Afghanistan to rely more on Moscow for greater economic and military aid. This alignment of Afghanistan and India with Moscow gave an impression to Pakistan that New Delhi-Kabul-Moscow axis fundamentally challenged its security.[7] To counter this threat, Pakistan developed a capacity with US assistance for covert asymmetric warfare which it eventually used in both Afghanistan and India. Pakistan's campaign against Afghanistan gave a lot of experience to Pakistan about the unconventional form of operations now known as terrorism. This experience was later on successfully used by Pakistan against India.

In the early years of Cold War, Afghanistan pursued a policy of nonalignment. The two superpowers developed informal relationship while supporting two different institutions and parts of the country; one Afghan leader famously claimed that he light his American cigarettes with Soviet matches.[8] But honeymoon between the two super powers ultimately proved hazardous to Afghanistan's health and does not last long. The presence of both the superpowers in Afghanistan soil ultimately forced the tribal forces to organize themselves in order to save their ethnic identity and tribal power. This situation brought to power with the help of a military coup by a radical faction whose harsh policies against the tribal leaders provoked an insurgency in Afghan territory. Soviet military intervention of 1979 in Afghanistan converted this insurgency into a jihad against the invaders. The presence of Soviet forces in Afghanistan put this region on the epicenter of the Cold War politics. The United States, Pakistan, Saudi Arabia, and other US allies began spending billions of dollars to back the anticommunist Afghan mujahideen who were fighting against the Soviet forces. This support provided a strong foundation to the forces who indulged in jihad at local level and after the end of cold war converted into regional and global jihad.

In September 1980, Francis Fukuyana of Rand Corporation prepared a report on *"The Security of Pakistan."*[9] After the publication of this report, the US-Pak collusion in this region assumed a new dimension and in a way reached a new level of co-operation. This report clearly spelt out that Pakistan could pay a significant role in the area, which comes under the "Soviet Orbit." It was also visualized that Pakistan could play an important role in reestablishing US credibility and in enhancing its prestige in the gulf region after developments in Iran.[10] The report also recommended the upgrading of the 1959 Executive Agreement between USA and Pakistan into a full fledged treaty to "enable Pakistan to face both the Soviet Union and India."[11] The civil war seemed to come to an end with the 1988 Geneva accords, which provided for the withdrawal of Soviet troops. After the Soviet withdrawal from Afghanistan, military assistance to mujahideen was also stopped. But, by that time, the entire region was proliferated by small arms supplied by the United States. The Klashinokov culture was flourished in the region and the worst part of this; it was supported by the Pakistan with the help of US supplied weapons. The US ignored this situation because both US and Pakistan were keen to wipe out Soviet influence from Afghanistan entirely. The result was a continuation of conflict and eventually, state failure.

In the early 1990s, as the Soviet Union collapsed and the emergence of United States as a sole super power, the stability of the entire region was disturbed. Drug trafficking boomed and

Arab and other non-Afghan Islamist radicals strengthened their bases. Pakistan was again disturbed by the radicals and also heavily involved in Afghanistan's internal battles, backed the Taliban, a radical group of mostly Pashtun clerics.[12] With the help of Pakistan's supplied deadly small arms, the Taliban had established control over most of the Afghanistan by 1998 and pushed back the mujahideens and other ethnic groups mostly non Pashtun to a few pockets of territory in the north east. As their grip over Afghanistan was established, the Taliban leadership introduced harsh Islamic laws in order to establish greater control over Afghanistan ethnic groups and also to align various other Islamic terrorist groups of other countries. During this critical period, Osama bin Laden, who came to Afghanistan after being expelled from Sudan in 1996,[13] took over the leadership of Taliban.

The Taliban embraces intelligent and often, affluent young Muslims unaffected by the legacy of the Cold War, but polarised against the West by extreme *Salafi* ideology. More than 50 years ago the influential *Salafi* writer, Sayyid Qutb (1906-66) identified the United States as an enemy of Islam, a theme that bin Laden has monopolised. By portraying modern Western civilisation as the personification of evil and American influence as its manifestation, he has created a radical fundamentalist reaction. The belief system is so powerful that devoted followers are locked in a life or death struggle against the opponents of Islam, willing to martyr themselves for the cause.[14]

During the late 1990s, the US interest in the South Asian region was gradually decreased. This gave an opportunity to the Talibans to spread its reach throughout the Muslim world, where it had developed a large cadre of operatives and in Europe, where it can claim the support of some disenfranchised Muslim locals and members of the Arab and Asian community. It had also developed close relations with well organized mafia groups of different regions of the world, involved in drug and small arms trafficking. During this period, the Al-Qaeda had also focused its activity against Israel and other local issues. The Clinton Administration began to recognize the growing threat in Afghanistan after the Al-Qaeda bombings of two US embassies in Africa during 1998. But it never took decisive action, and when the Bush administration took office, it also gave priority to other concerns. It took 9/11 to force Bush administration to recognize that a global terrorist opposition was gaining strength—using physical capital that the United States and its allies had supplied, through Pakistan's intelligence services in pursuit of a Cold War strategic agenda. Before Bush administration overthrew the Taliban after 9/11, Afghanistan had been used as a breeding ground for the Al-Qaeda. According to some estimates, Al-Qaeda had trained up to 60,000 Afghan jihadists there.

When the US administration overthrew the Taliban in 2001, it did so with a "light footprint": using Special Forces with CIA support to coordinate Northern Alliance and other Afghan commanders on the ground under the Air force cover. After a rapid military campaign, it backed the UN effort to form a new government and managed the political transition. International Security Assistance Force (ISAF) was formed to help the new Afghan government to organize new military and police forces and also to provide security for the newly formed Afghan government. In 2003, the ASAF came under NATO command (the first ever NATO military this type of operation outside Europe) and gradually expanded its operations from just Kabul to most of Afghanistan's 34 provinces.[15] More than 40,000 US and allied forces are currently engaged in security assistance and counter terrorist operations under NATO command. The UN Assistance Mission in Afghanistan coordinates the international community's support for political and economic reconstruction.

Despite all out efforts to stabilize Afghanistan, it continues to face significant internal threats. Widespread trade in opium and heroin provides drug producers and traffickers with the resources and motivation to resist any efforts to curb the illicit narcotics trade. The money earned by this trade has been utilized by the Taliban fighters and other terrorist groups to not only organize their activities all around the world but also provide enough resources to purchase latest weaponry from the open market with the connivance of some regimes who are promoting this kind of activities in their own interests.[16] As a result, even today, Taliban fighters and terrorist groups and still active in parts of the country, and attacks on civilian reconstruction workers and forced them to leave the country. Regional warlords maintain thousands of militia fighters who could be used to challenge the authority of Afghanistan's new central government.

The US occupation of Iraq and other international involvements gave ample opportunities to the Al-Qaeda to reorganize and planned their activities in the new emerging world order. After Iraq, now Bin Laden is trying to extend his strategy by exploiting tense and hostile relationship between Iran and United States. They have also established two new centers at Iraq and Pakistan to expand its reach beyond Afghanistan. To vividly showcase its strength, Al-Qaeda records most of its operations and transmits the gruesome coverage to jihadi Web sites all over the world. US invasion of Iraq provide them an opportunity to propagate that Washington had imperialist designs and that jihad against US forces was working.[17] Decisively defeating Al-Qaeda will be more difficult now than it would have been a few years ago. But it can be still achieved if US and its allies implement a comprehensive strategy over several years, targeting on both attacking Al-Qaeda's organization and philosophy and simultaneously altering the local conditions that allow them to thrive. Otherwise, it will only be a matter of time before Al-Qaeda once again strikes against their enemies.

Afghanistan is always a key factor for India and as long as India and Pakistan remain hostile to each other, Afghanistan will remain strategically important to both the countries. The increasing Indian presence in reconstruction activity has irked Pakistan and its Afghan protégés. Pakistan has raised objections to India opening consulates in Jalalabad, Herat and Kandahar and is also opposing India's deployment of Paramilitary forces in Afghanistan especially along the areas close to its borders. Pakistan's allegations range from Indian consulates printing false Pakistani currency to RAW's alleged recruitment of Afghans to carry out acts of sabotage and terrorism on Pakistani territory. Pakistan also accuses India of setting up a network of terrorist training camps located inside Afghanistan all along the Pakistan-Afghanistan border.

Today, Pakistan is also facing challenges from super active Pushtun nationalism in Balochistan and the Federally

Administered Tribal Areas. To counter this, Pakistan is taking all out help from Al-Qaeda for not only establishing their identity as a leader of Muslim world but also promoting fundamentalist activities in India. With the help of Islamabad, Al-Qaeda has developed closer ties with Kashmiri terrorist groups such as Lashkar-e-Taiba and Jaish-e-Muhammad. Islamabad has exploited this deadly combination in their own interests and organized several terrorist activities in India. Therefore, India's engagement with Afghanistan is vital for its ongoing battle against terrorism and curtailing the influence of terror outfits in J&K-Lashkar-e-Toiba (LeT), Jaish-eMohammed (JeM), Harkat-ul-Mujahideen, which drive moral and material support from the trans-border Taliban-Al-Qaeda nexus.

Apart from the five years of Taliban rule (1996-2001), India has enjoyed good economic and cultural relations with Afghanistan. Indian movies and movie songs are reportedly a staple part of the Afghan culture, while Afghan shawls and dry fruits among other things, come into India both legally and illegally. It is a gateway to the oil and mineral rich Central Asian Republics. The much awaited gas pipe lines through Afghanistan from Central Asia and Iran will certainly boost our relations and increase interdependency. This interdependency will also strategically important for curbing terrorist activities in the region and would ultimately rattle Islamabad. After the fall of Taliban, the massive reconstruction activities for the country offer a lot of opportunities for Indian companies. Apart from presenting aircraft to kick start its Ariana airlines, India has been active in building roads, schools, hospitals, power and communication networks, besides providing training to its military, police, bureaucrats, diplomats, engineers and even businessmen and students.

It is an acknowledged fact that as long as India and Pakistan remain hostile to each other, Afghanistan will be strategically important to both. It is more important for Pakistan that it not have unfriendly powers on both its east (India) and west (Afghanistan) borders On the one hand, good relations between India and Afghanistan will ultimately squeeze Pakistan strategically. On the other hand, close relations between

Islamabad and regime at Kabul supported by US and NATO may be seen as anti-Islamic which will ultimately harm the Pakistani claim of Islamic leadership. Anti Kabul attitude of Pakistan government will adversely effect its long affiliation with Washington. Either way the costs are too high for Pakistan and helped India to effectively indorse their presence in Afghanistan.

REFERENCES

1. Prasad, Bisheshwar, Editor, Defence of India: Policy and Plans, Orient Longmans, 1963, p. 22.
2. Singh, Nagendra, The Theory of Force and Organization of Defence in Indian Constitutional History, Asia Publishing House, New Delhi, 1969, p. 11.
3. Rubin, B.R., Saving Afghanistan, Foreign Affairs, Vol. 86, No.1, Jan./Feb. 2007, p. 63.
4. *Ibid*, p. 63.
5. Isby, D.C., War in a Distant Country Afghanistan: Invasion and Resistance, Sterling Publishing Co, NY, 1989, p. 15.
6. *Ibid*, p. 15.
7. John K. Cooley, *Unholy Wars, Afghanistan, America and International Terrorism*, 2nd edn., Pluto Press London, 2002, p. 225.
8. Robin, B.R., *op. cit.*, p. 64.
9 This report records observations of Fukuyama's Trip to Pakistan in mid 1980s.
10. Chopra V. D., "Pak-Nuclear Bomb and India's Options," The Patriot (New Delhi), August 13, 1985.
11. Baral, Jaya, Krishna, and Eshwar, Anand V, "United States Arms Supply to Pakistan: A case study of America's South Asia diplomacy, "Punjab Journal of Politics, Vol. 6., No. 2, July-December, 1982, p. 38.
12. Bakshi, G.D., Afghaistan: The First Faultline War, Lancer Publishers, New Delhi, 1999, p. 126.
13. Rubin, B.R., *op. cit.* f.n.-3, p. 65.
14. Huntington , S.P., Al-Qaeda: A Blueprint for International Terrorism in the Twenty-first Century?, *Defence Studies*, Vol. 4, No. 3, 2004, p. 231.
15. Rubin, B.R., *op.cit.* f.n.-3 p. 65.
16. Riedel, Bruce, Al-Qaeda Strikes Back, Foreign Affairs, Vol. 86, No.3, May/June 2007, p. 25.
17. *Ibid*, p. 29.

PART III

AID EFFECTIVENESS AND INTERNATIONAL INITIATIVES

CHAPTER 22

Geopolitical Lessons of Afghanistan for the International Community

Farkhod Tolipov

New geopolitical stalemate characterizes the overall military and political situation in Afghanistan nowadays. The strategic equation in this country has been solved until now on the principle of 'no war, no peace'. The overall efforts of the international community on the reconstruction of Afghanistan produced more questions than solved.

Operation "Enduring Freedom" (OEF) is quite unique in terms of peace enforcement and peacekeeping activities. Since 2003 NATO has been commanding the operation in Afghanistan, the country which is far away from the zone of responsibility of the Alliance. The Shanghai Cooperation Organization (SCO) and the Collective Security Treaty Organization (CSTO) also pretend to play more visible role in Afghanistan. In such a very complicated situation Central Asian countries find themselves entangled. The geopolitical perplexity put Central Asians at least within the symbolical triangle: US-RF-PRC. These three great powers seem to pursue three different agendas in the region. The divergence of strategies cannot but distort the very counter-terrorist agenda in Afghanistan.

Is it really an international community that has been solving the Afghan question? Is the so-called anti-terrorist coalition a genuine coalition? Who is doing what in this country? Do all the international actors pursue the same agenda there? What lessons can we draw from war on terror in the territory of Afghanistan? Why do not the closest neighboring countries participate in the military operation? What is the degree of southern threats to the regional security of Central Asia? Is it possible to work out a new "Road Map" for the stabilization and reconstruction of Afghanistan? These and some other related issues are elaborated in this article.

NEW GEOPOLITICAL STALEMATE

One of the main lessons of Afghanistan is the "discovery" that terrorism and counter-terrorism have a geopolitical dimension. The permanent geopolitical struggle in the zone of IRAFPAK (Iran, Afghanistan, Pakistan) which always had the form of the "zero sum game" have once led the situation in this region to the geopolitical stalemate.[1]

That stalemate of which Afghanistan became a main victim was one of the sources of the global threat of terrorism that emanated from this country at the end of the 20th century. The very start of the counter-terrorist operation in that country revealed the triplex of world community's delusions about the means and ways of the Afghan conflict resolution:

(1) It was widely perceived that the conflict concerned was a solely internal affair of Afghanistan. However, the conflict proved to be not an internal affair, and external interference proved to be extremely needed, inevitable and the only possible option among the means of the conflict resolution.

(2) It was widely believed that the Afghan conflict didn't have a military solution. However, the solution of the conflict proved to be primarily military.

(3) It was widely recognized that the Islamic Movement of "Taliban," or part of it, could be admitted to the future coalition government of Afghanistan. Moreover, the "Taliban" itself already stood in one step to the international recognition as a country's legal and real government. However, only after 11 September 2001 the

> "Taliban" was blamed and condemned for what had always been obvious—international terrorism.

So, international community was misled by: (1) wrong assessment of sources and driving forces of the Afghan conflict; (2) the quite obsolete conceptions of international interference in a conflict and means of peace-enforcement, and (3) the inadequate vision of the new form of social and political arrangement in Afghanistan.

Moreover, the international community encountered a kind of a dilemma: "universal counter-terrorism versus national counter-terrorism" or "geopolitics versus counter-terrorism." Such a dilemma can have immense implications for Central and South Asia. Juxtaposition of two realities—international and uniting by character struggle against terrorism, on the one hand, and the conflict-prone and dividing by character geopolitical rivalry in Central-South Asian macro-region, on the other hand,—is currently taking place with respect to the operation in Afghanistan.

As a matter of fact, one has to take into serious consideration that neither terrorism nor the conditions for terrorism are eradicated in Afghanistan. This will be done with the completion of two interrelated tasks: gaining a full success in the military phase of the counter-terrorist operation and creation of a full fledged state and nation. Who controls the territory—the state or other forces—is in fact the first simple and obvious, in a conceptual sense, question which is, at the same time, too complicated in a sense of implementation with respect to Afghanistan. In other words, it is a question of the nation- and state-building. (Let's remember that in the last days of their ruling the "Taliban" resorted to the nationalist rhetoric and called Afghans to unite in fighting "American invaders" (having forgotten even about their own foreign mercenary fighters).)

Now, demilitarization, decriminalization, and rebuilding of the state should be the three priorities if the world community is to eliminate any possible future challenges to international security emanating from Afghanistan. "The events of September 11, 2001, taught us that weak states, like Afghanistan, can pose as great a danger to our national interests as strong states. Poverty does not make poor people into terrorists and murderers. Yet poverty, weak institutions, and corruption can make weak states vulnerable to terrorist networks and drug cartels within their borders."[2]

Meanwhile, just because Afghanistan lost its statehood and terrorist network grew up in its territory on the background of and due to massive, intensive and destructive external influence, the very process of nation- and state-building cannot but be developed via the massive, intensive and constructive external presence. Dr. E. Krakowski's arguments deserve to be mentioned: "The key to the Afghan problem is to be found not within Afghanistan but in the countries surrounding it...While it is true that the Afghans are fiercely independent and have stood up to mighty conquerors, it is also true that it is the neighboring states that have fanned and maintained ongoing warfare for now more than twenty years. It is also this external intervention and the chaos it has engendered that has allowed the country's gradual hijacking by an international terrorist network."[3] This is another lesson one can draw from the geopolitical stalemate in Afghanistan.

Using the expression of one analyst, one can assert that as the US-led war against international terrorism completed six years on October 6, 2007, with no end yet in sight, it is uncomfortably apparent that Operation Enduring Freedom has turned into Operation Enduring Taliban in Afghanistan.[4] This is the essence of the new geopolitical stalemate in this country and South Asian region in general.

WHO IS DOING WHAT?

The OEF is believed to be a military undertaking of the so called international anti-terrorist coalition. But the formation of this coalition was a spontaneous, even "emotional" process. This is reflected nowadays in how different international actors act in Afghanistan.

UN

The United Nations Organization finds itself in a quite awkward situation. Despite the adoption of the anti-Taliban Resolutions and legitimization of the military action in Afghanistan in 2001, the organization seems to remain, so to speak, an old UN not a new one. The old, classical UN has been the organization of the cold war that very often fell victim of different geopolitical struggles of world powers. The new one should correspond to post-cold war realities and be free from geopolitical divisions. As long as the Afghan process has a deeply rooted geopolitical nature, the UN will always face prevalence of great power interests at the expense of great power concert.

NATO

The NATO is, perhaps, the only organization that has the real and strongest capacity to play the role of a sponsor of the overall peace process in Afghanistan. It commands the very OEF and assists the reconstruction tasks in the provinces of the country.

NATO's mission serves, among other things, as a means of deterring of Islamic extremism from South. The neglecting of this task can lead the international community to pre-9/11 situation and even to some new versions of 9/11 in the future. At least, the understanding of the likelihood of such a worst scenario must convince us not only to acknowledge the NATO presence in Afghanistan, but also to think of what else the international community, the UN, can do in terms of either military and non-military actions in Afghanistan, as well as to contemplate on regional countries' format of participation in the conflict resolution and reconstruction.

The agreement was reached at the summit on the transit of cargo from Europe through the territories of CIS countries toward Afghanistan. If such a project is to be realized it will symbolize three simultaneous achievements by the NATO: (1) some new form of engagement of the CIS countries, especially Russia, in Afghanistan reconstruction; (2) new positive signals to Afghans about the international community's taking care of their country; (3) further legitimization of the NATO's out-of-area operation.

The Bucharest summit of the NATO 1-4 April 2008 indicated that the Alliance's presence in Afghanistan will last at least until 2012. The period which is left till that "deadline" is more or less enough for making the overall efforts on the Afghan state-building and security more visible and more satisfactory. It is clear that by that deadline in almost all neighboring countries the current leaders will be gone and a new generation of leaders will come. That's why the NATO's, so to speak, "2012 strategy" looks well worked out.

SCO

The SCO has not yet completed its institutional and conceptual formation. Therefore, it is premature for it to climb to 'high policy' level, that is regional security missions. Nevertheless, the SCO member-states declared on its last summits their intention to deal with the regional security matters. Particularly, the counter-narcotic activity of the SCO is envisaged. In any case, the organization cannot but bring with it a new geopolitical dimension to the Afghan process.

CSTO

Afghanistan can become a polygon for bridging partnership between the CSTO and the NATO. On 18 June 2004 session of this quasi-alliance in Astana (capital of Kazakhstan) "The Main Directions of dialogue and interactions with the NATO" were adopted. The Secretary General of the CSTO Nikolay Bordyuja delivered the NATO Secretary General a suggestion on establishing contacts between two organizations concerning the threats from Afghanistan.

The NATO operation in Afghanistan is a temporary mission and sooner or later the troops of the Alliance will withdraw, Russian expert argues. At the same time, the CSTO's presence in Central Asia is permanent. That's why it is in the interests of the Afghan government to establish positive contacts with this organization which aspires to become effective and operational in the region that is adjacent to Afghanistan.

The perspectives of cooperation between the CSTO and Afghanistan will depend on three factors: 1) readiness of Afghanistan to cooperate with the CSTO in fighting drug traffic, terrorism, extremism and other common threats; 2) cooperation between CSTO and NATO, between Russia and the US; 3) readiness of CSTO member states themselves to provide real assistance to Afghanistan comparable to economic assistance of Western states.

The question "Who is doing what in Afghanistan?" is pertinent not only to international organizations but primarily to major state actors who, besides following common multilateral goals, pursue their own interests, the latter having geopolitical nature. Let's consider some of them.

Russia, for example, is now comfortable with the current status-quo in Afghanistan because, as Russian analysts argue, NATO does the job there which Russia itself is incapable to do and which, at the same time, meets Russia's security interests. At the same time, from geopolitical point of view, Russia would accept, as well, a prolonged instability in the country, as long as such a status-quo serves its traditional geopolitical interests.

But in the longer perspectives, traditional geopolitics cannot cope with non-traditional threats. Therefore, the Russian expert Dmirtri Trenin is right when he argues, that "the Russians have no reason to feel any *schandenfreude* as a result of the difficulties faced by the NATO and the United States in Afghanistan. If the international efforts fail to stabilize that country, Moscow will be faced with a resurgent Taliban threatening Russia's soft Central Asian underbelly. There is therefore a clear need for closer consultations between Russia and the West on how to turn the tide against Islamist radicals. Helping the moderates to hold on to Kabul and the Afghan provinces is a far better alternative than having to start reconstituting the Northern Alliance in Taloqan."[5]

The United States, has the 9/11 events on the background which justify its military presence in Afghanistan. At the same time, Washington seems to have started its "Greater Central Asia" (Central Asia plus Afghanistan) strategy (see below).

Pakistan is, perhaps, the only country whose international behavior and geopolitical doctrine will have a decisive impact on the Afghan fate in the long term perspective. Ahmed Rashid pointed out that Pakistan is now fighting proxy wars on two fronts, in Kashmir and Afghanistan and even though the repercussions from these wars—Islamic fundamentalism, drugs, weapons and social breakdown—are now aggressively spilling into the country, there is no reappraisal or policy review. Pakistan is now ripe for a Taliban-style Islamic revolution, which would almost certainly jeopardize stability in the Middle East, South and Central Asia.[6]

Iran's role in Afghanistan is also a part of geopolitical game. Currently, Iran seems to feel itself just like Russia—comfortable and anxious, comfortable with the emerged status-quo and anxious about the stabilization of Afghanistan in favor of the United States.

Taliban itself, surprisingly, can be considered in the list of actors (the one acting against the coalition). As was said above Operation Enduring Freedom has turned into Operation Enduring Taliban in Afghanistan. Terrorism is growing and becoming more mature. Taliban effectively exploits the unique nature of Afghanistan and Afghans: absence of control of the territory, ethnic and religious fragmentation, backwardness, tribal relationships, opium economy, specific neighborhood of the country, severe climate and topography, fierce aforeignism.

Trying to resolve ethnic problems and keep states together needs persistent and consistent diplomacy rather than virtual bribes to keep various warlords quiet.[7]

CONCEPTION OF 'GREATER CENTRAL ASIA'

Why do not the closest neighboring countries participate in the military operation? What is the degree of southern threats to the regional security of Central Asia? These two questions are important for understanding Afghanistan's fate in the broader context which encompasses Central and South Asia. The perception of threats to their national security from South determined, to a great extent, the regional behavior of Central Asian countries throughout the whole period of independence. Right after 9/11 all Central Asian countries entered the international anti-terrorist coalition and provided their territories for the deployment of coalition contingents.

However, such a position of some of these countries did not persist until now. Uzbekistan, for example, demanded the United States military contingent, which was deployed in Khanabad town in the wake of 9/11, to withdraw from the country in 2005. Kyrgyzstan, in turn, despite the pressure from Russia and China "tolerates" the US military presence on its territory (airport Manas) because this helps to fill up the Kyrgyzstan's budget.

One of the most prominent American expert of Central Asia Prof. Frederick Starr advanced an idea of "Greater Central Asia" (GCA) by which he meant 5 Central Asian countries plus Afghanistan which constitute a single region. Starr points out that the very fact of reconstruction of Afghanistan will symbolize a significant victory over terrorism, but the failure can cause the breakdown of already existing achievements. The GCA is deemed to serve as a regional forum for cooperation in and development of this region through planning, coordination and realization of a number of programs which will be worked out in the United States.[8]

The emergence of such a zone of cooperation that contains extremist forces and perform an attractive model for other developing Muslim societies, Starr believes, might yield serious benefits to both the region and the United States. Indeed, it is likely that Washington equipped its Central-South Asian strategy with this conception of GCA. One of the tokens of such a policy seems to be the appointment of one official in the State Department as responsible for Central and South Asian affairs.

Nevertheless, it has to be said that "Greater Central Asia" nowadays looks just like a Bigger Central Asia, not Greater Central Asia. To my mind, two problems cause some skepticism about the GCA project, for the time being: (1) simple addition of Afghanistan in the notion Central Asia only for geographical reasons will distort the real political composition; (2) Central Asia itself has not yet become an integrated region, despite the proclamation of integrative perspectives in 1991, because so many interstate problems and mistrust prevailed among five Central Asian countries throughout all the period of independence.

Afghanistan today cannot be regarded as part of Central Asia even for the sake of big regional project; it can only join Central Asia—the region *now demonstrating* its strategic attractiveness, and Central Asia, in turn, can accept Afghanistan in a GCA format only if and when that country *will demonstrate* its strategic attractiveness.

One of the reasons for strategic unattractiveness of Afghanistan is its turning into a narco-state. It is well known that one of the main sources of financing of terrorism is narco-business. A big portion of the Afghan opiates are being transferred through the territory of Central Asia. The experts notice that about 70% of drug traffic that passes the territory of Kyrgyzstan has been controlled by the Islamic Movement of Uzbekistan (IMU).[9] This channel was used by the IMU for the illicit trade of weapons, as well as gold and precious stones which are mined in Afghanistan. Extract

Taliban, as it is also known, got up to 20% ($40-50 mln.) of benefits from drug business. Afghanistan became the major producer of drugs in the world. In 1981 Afghanistan had produced 31% of world drugs, in 1990—41%, by 2002—70%. Today from 70 to 90% of heroin in Europe is produced from the Afghan opium. Production and trade of narcotics constitute more than 50% of Afghanistan's GDP. Most agricultural lands in this country are used for the production of opiates.

As a result, the scale of drug traffic through the territory of Central Asia is growing. The common share of Uzbekistan, Tajikistan and Turkmenistan as transit countries for Afghan drugs increased from 0.1% in 1994 to 13% in 2000 and 23% in 2001. The increase of drug trade is observed in Kazakhstan and Kyrgyzstan as well, which do not have common borders with Afghanistan.

Interesting to note that Uzbekistan's President Islam Karimov who participated in the NATO Bucharest summit stated that Uzbekistan is ready to sign an agreement with the Alliance on providing of the corridor for transit of non-military cargo through the border crossing point Termez-Khayraton, which is practically the only existing railway connection to Afghanistan.

Uzbek President also suggested to revitalize the diplomatic process on achievement of peace and stability in Afghanistan, which functioned through 1997-2001 under the name "6+2" under the UN aegis. The "6+2" format was composed by Uzbekistan, Tajikistan, Turkmenistan, Pakistan, Iran, Afghanistan plus the US and RF. He suggested, taking into account the current realities in the region, to transform the "6+2" format into the "6+3" implying the participation of the NATO.

CONCLUSION

What was and is the main purpose of the Operation Enduring Freedom? The answer is "Fighting terrorism." This purpose has not been reached throughout almost seven years since October 2001.

Meanwhile, a paradoxical situation arose in the Afghan context: the interests of main geopolitical rivals—contradictory to each other on the global level—objectively fully coincide in Afghanistan: they all need stability and peace in this country. Thus, the international community needs to work out a new Grand strategy for the overall Afghanistan's becoming what is now called a Newly Independent State. This Grand Strategy should offer a kind of a Road Map.

In October last year a sensational statement was made by the President Hamid Karzai, according to which some posts in the government might me given to the leader of Taliban Mulla Omar and the Chairman of the Islamic party of Afghanistan Ghulbiddin Khekmatyar. It is symptomatic and not accidental that those offers were rejected by both leaders, to the embarrassment of Karzai. Any attempts on negotiations with the Taliban are doomed to the deadlock. The current Afghan political system or that to emerge under the international aegis—on the one hand, and the Taliban-style state—on the other, cannot be considered compatible or reconcilable. That's why such attempts reminds us those delusions of the international community which are mentioned above, and can hardly be parts of the new Grand Strategy.

Meanwhile, on the April 2008 NATO Bucharest summit an alliance's new strategy on Afghanistan was adopted. That strategy contains 4 main direction of action: (1) strengthening of laws in Afghanistan; (2) strengthening of the central government;

(3) reconstruction of the social sphere; 4) acceleration of the solution of the Afghanistan-Pakistan border area issue.[10]

It seems to me that some other points might also be emphasized in the strategy, namely: (1) demilitarization; (2) decriminalization; and (3) economic revitalization of the country.

The adoption of a "Pact on Peace" in the zone of IRAFPAK (in South Asia in general) might be important.

The International Convention on "Struggle against terrorism" will be important as well.

In the end, I would like to remind three important conclusions made by Ahmed Rashid in his book. These three theses still remain actual and should be taken seriously by the international community until it is too late.

First. If the Taliban were to conquer the entire country, the Central Asian states would have to accept the Taliban reality, but they would be unlikely to trust their energy exports to go through Taliban controlled Afghanistan and Pakistan.[11]

Second. For Muslims everywhere Saudi support for the Taliban is deeply embarrassing, because the Taliban's interpretation of Islam is so negative and destructive. Increasingly, Western popular perception equates Islam with the Taliban and Bin Laden-style terrorism. Many Western commentators do not particularize the Taliban, but condemn Islam wholesale for being intolerant and anti-modern.[12]

Third, any serous peace process would need much greater commitment to peace-making in Afghanistan from the international community than it has shown so far.[13]

REFERENCES

1. F. Tolipov. Geopolitical Stalemate in Afghanistan, in *Central Asia and Caucasus*, No. 6, 2000.
2. The National Security Strategy of the USA, http://usinfo.state.gov/topical/pol/terror/secstrat.htm, September 2002.
3. Statement by Dr. Elie D. Krakowski, Senior Fellow, Central Asia/Caucasus Institute, the School of Advanced International Studies, the John Hopkins University and Senior Fellow, American Foreign Policy Council at a Hearing on "The Future of Afghanistan" before

the House Committee on International Relations, November 7, 2001.

4. Raman, B. Operation Enduring Taliban, in *International Terrorism Monitor*. Paper No. 135.
5. Trenin, D. NATO and Russia: Sobering thoughts and practical suggestions, in *NATO Review*, July, 2007.
6. Rashid, A. Taliban. Militant Islam, Oil & Fundamentalism in Central Asia. (Yale University Press, Nota Bene, 2000), p. 210.
7. *Ibid*, p. 209.
8. Starr, F. A Partnership for Central Asia, in *Foreign Affairs*, July/ August, 2005.
9. *Svante E. Cornell, Regine A. Spector*. Central Asia: More than Islamic Extremists. - The Washington Quarterly, Winter 2002.
10. http://www.afghanistan.ru/doc/11714.html
11. Rashid, A. Taliban. Militant Islam, Oil & Fundamentalism in Central Asia. (Yale University Press, Nota Bene, 2000), p. 211.
12. *Ibid*.
13. *Ibid*, p. 215.

CHAPTER 23

India's Role in Reconstruction Process and Political Transformation in Afghanistan

Anil Bhat

INTRODUCTION

India's ties with Afghanistan are ancient and civilisational. Cultural linkages across South Asia make it imperative for India to seek special and bilaterally-beneficial relationship with Afghanistan. But there are important strategic aspects to this relationship as well. Depending upon which side of the border one stands, Afghanistan appears both a geopolitical nightmare and a land of tremendous opportunities. Unfortunately, as history testifies, that country has remained a geopolitical nightmare for centuries. Strategically sandwiched during the Great Game, it has never managed to emerge out of the plague of external interference. Great power interventions in Afghanistan have been primarily responsible for its collapsed institution and incessant disruptions. But the role of regional actors, especially since the British left the subcontinent, is equally responsible for the present situation Afghanistan finds itself in. Specifically, Pakistan's nefarious strategic interests in Afghanistan have not augured well for the latter and have resulted into a spiral of degenerative processes. The current phase of Afghanistan's reconstruction efforts is also being affected by a similar trend.

This paper attempts to contextualise India's role in

Afghanistan's reconstruction and political transformation and the constraints these efforts are faced with. The first section is largely informative and briefly lays down the extent and diversity of India's contribution to Afghanistan's reconstruction. The second section underlines Pakistan's response to India's assistance programme, which has been to sabotage and derail reconstruction efforts. The concluding section argues that India's efforts have been constrained by Pakistan's posture to its activities in Afghanistan and that India could do more, and better than most, if only Pakistan is willing to cooperate.

I

During the three decades of King Zahir Shah's rule—probably the only period of stability Afghanistan experienced in the 20th century—and the period before the advent of the Taliban, India had a major presence there, providing assistance in the fields of education, medical, engineering and defence. In the aftermath of the September 11, 2001 terrorist attacks, US-led forces launched their assault against Taliban and Al-Qaeda in Afghanistan in early October that year. The Northern Alliance, which was officially recognised by India, also played a major role in the initial defeat of the extremist regime. Once the US coalition forces moved into Afghanistan, India was the first country to set up its diplomatic mission under the aegis of former Ambassador, Mr S K Lambah. Without any delay, Indian and Afghan officials got down to identifying the various fields and categories of cooperation and assistance and within record time India began implementing the programme. This involved activities in both countries; Indian representatives being positioned in Afghanistan and teams of Afghan officials from their different departments, who began coming to India for training. India also took lead in the battered country's reconstruction and pledged efforts in truly diverse fields. It pledged reconstruction related assistance to Afghanistan in the Tokyo Conference. Mr Lambah attended this Conference as well as the one at Bonn in December 2001, which laid the foundation for the reconstruction process. Later, India also took a leading role in two regional economic conferences on Afghanistan held in Kabul and New Delhi in 2005 and 2006 respectively. Besides, Afghanistan's inclusion in formal South Asian regional process through SAARC has also received encouragement and support from India.

A brief glance at the diversity and range of India's efforts in Afghanistan:

FINANCIAL ASSISTANCE

- India announced a financial assistance of US$ 100 million for Afghanistan. Of this assistance, US$ 31.5 m was operationalised during 2002-03 and US$ 30 m has been operationalised during 2003-04 (details below).
- The Government of India further announced US$ 70 m (over and above US$ 100 m) for upgradation/ re-construction of road from Zaranj to Delaram in Afghanistan.
- India is contributing US $ 200,000 per annum to the World Bank managed Afghan Reconstruction Trust Fund.
- India announced food assistance of 1m tons of wheat to Afghanistan. A part of this assistance (85517 tons of wheat) was converted into high protein biscuits (9526 tons) and sent to Afghanistan for its school feeding programme from November 2002 to June 2003. The deliveries of the second tranche of high protein biscuits (7496 tons) against 76 521 tons of wheat will commence in December 2003. As a result of the assistance, 972,000 Afghan children are receiving a package of 100 gms of biscuits every day.
- India decided to gift 300 vehicles to the Afghan National Army, which have been delivered.
- In addition, the Indian Government is also providing scholarships to Afghan students for higher education and training Afghan nationals in various fields in India under its regular schemes/programmes.

AID TO AFGHAN BUDGET

US $ 10 m were transferred to the account of the Afghan Government in July 2002 as cash subsidy to the Afghan budget US$ 200,000 have been paid to Afghan Reconstruction Trust Fund in year 2002 and 2003.

HUMANITARIAN ASSISTANCE

Winter clothing was sent to provide immediate humanitarian relief in Nov.-Dec. 2001. Another consignment of around 25 tons of winter clothing was sent in February 2003. A consignment of 20,000 blankets was sent to Herat on 4th and 6th February 2002. Earthquake relief consisting of 200 tents, 10000 blankets, and nearly 10 tons of medicines was delivered to Afghanistan in April 2002.

HEALTH

The reconstruction of Indira Gandhi Institute of Child Health in Kabul commenced in September 2003. A team of 13 Indian doctors and paramedics are working at Kabul since November 2001. The team is attending hundreds of patients daily and disbursing medicines at the polyclinic (OPD) of the Indira Gandhi Institute of Child Health (IGICH). The Indian Medical team is also running an Operation Theatre at the Koh-e-Markaz Hospital in Kabul. A 6-member team of Indian doctors and paramedics is running an Operation Theatre at the Civil Hospital in Mazar-e-Sharif since April 2002. A 4-member team of Indian doctors and paramedics has started its work in Herat on April 12, 2003. A 4-member team of Indian doctors and paramedics is working in Shebargan since end-May, 2003. A 4-member team of Indian doctors and paramedics started its work in Kandahar in September 2003. More than 175 tons of medicines, medical instruments and equipment have been sent to Afghanistan since November 2001. An artificial limb/ Jaipur foot fitment camp was set up for Afghan amputees at Kabul military hospital in January 2002. Nearly 1000 artificial limbs were fitted during the camp. Another artificial limb fitment camp was set up from October 21-December 4, 2002 at Mazar-e-Sharif and Meymaneh fitting around 600 artificial limbs. During the camp, training was also provided to eight local artisans on the artificial limb maintenance. On conclusion of the camp, the fitment centre alongwith tools, machinery and raw materials was handed over to the Afghan authorities and named as Indo-Afghan Rehabilitation Centre in Mazar-e-Sharif. A large number of rehabilitation aids like wheel chairs, crutches, hearing aids, audiometers were also gifted. Two batches of six Afghan doctors and paramedics each from Indira Gandhi Institute of Child Health attended training in areas of their specialisation at All India Institute of Medical Sciences from August 19-November 18, 2002, and May 29-August 27, 2003 respectively. Extension was provided to one of the trainees of the first batch for advanced training for three months.

AVIATION CIVIL (AIRCRAFTS, SPARES AND SERVICES)

The Indian Government has gifted three airbus aircrafts, along with essential spares including two engines, and services including crew support to the Ariana Afghan Airlines. The first two aircrafts were handed over in September and December 2002 and the third aircraft in March 2003. 51 Ariana Afghan Airlines officials have been trained by Air India. Flight Engineers Ground Basic Classroom Training was provided to 8 officials of Ariana Afghan Airlines at Indian Airlines Training Centre, Hyderabad for a period of six weeks in September-October, 2003.

TRANSPORT

Government has gifted 274 buses to the Afghan Government for its public transport system. Of these, most of the buses are operating in Kabul city, 25 in Kandahar and 25 in Herat. Small numbers of buses are also operating in other cities.

FOOD AID

9526 tons of fortified biscuits have been supplied for School Feeding Programme in Afghanistan from November 2002 to June 2003. The deliveries of the second tranche of high protein biscuits (7496 tons) to Afghanistan will commence in December 2003. As a result of this assistance, 972,000 Afghan children are receiving a package of 100 gms of biscuits every day.

EDUCATION

The reconstruction of Habibia School has commenced in September 2003. Two English language Instructors are teaching English at the Institute of Diplomacy since Feb 2002 to the officials of the Ministry of Foreign Affairs and other Government

Departments of Afghanistan. Two additional English language teachers are teaching English at the Ministries of Information and Culture and Labour and Social Welfare since March 10, 2003. 8646 educational kits were gifted to the students of Habibia School in Kabul in Aug-Sept 2002. The Government has gifted 20,000 desk-cum-benches for schools in Afghanistan. In-service training was provided to seven Afghan teachers from the Ministry of Education of Afghanistan by Delhi Public School Society from September 4-October 15, 2003. Fifty slots have been allocated to Afghanistan for training at various institutes in India under Indian Technical and Economic Cooperation Programme. 43 Afghan nationals have attended the training under the Programme during 2002-03 in the fields of Rural Industry Promotion (3), Training Methods and Skills for Managers (4), Small Business Planning and Promotion (7), Urban Development Management (4), Audit of Receipts (3), Legislative Drafting (5), Development Journalism (1), Audit of Public Enterprises, (1), Participatory Planning and Management of Watershed Projects (5), Micro Planning for Poverty Reduction and Sustainable Development (3), Sustainable Development in Agriculture and Rural Development (2), Educational Planning and Administration (4) and Urban Infrastructure Planning and Management (1). 10 slots were allocated to Afghanistan under General Cultural Scholarship Scheme of Indian Council of Cultural Relations for higher studies in India in 2002-03, of which three have been utilised by Afghanistan (one each at School of Architecture and Planning, Delhi, Delhi University and Osmania University, Hyderabad). 4 slots have been allocated to Afghanistan under the scheme for 2003-04. 10 slots have been allocated to Afghanistan under the Cultural Exchange Programme Scholarship Scheme for 2003-04.

DIPLOMACY

Three batches of 20 Afghan Diplomats each have been trained at the Foreign Service Institute in February-May 2002, August-November 2002 and July-September 2003. 15 officials from Presidential Secretariat of Afghanistan were trained at Foreign Service Institute from October 2002-March 2003. Two

Afghan diplomats attended a two-week module on Professional Course for Foreign Diplomats in January 2003.

CULTURE, HERITAGE, MEDIA, SPORT

The Broadcast Engineering Consultants India Limited has commenced the following works in September 2003. Setting up of a modern offset Printing Machine along with DTP Facility Setting up of a new 100 kw SW transmitter Setting up of TV Satellite Uplinking/Downlinking facility. A consignment of musical instruments was sent for the Afghan Radio and Television to Kabul on 10th February 2002. Another consignment of musical instruments was gifted to Kabul University in April 2003. The Government has also gifted musical instruments to the Ceremonial Band of the Presidential Guard of Afghanistan in June 2003. US $ 20,000 were granted for the repair of Hazrat Ali Shrine in Mazar-e-Sharif in September 2002. Two batches of 15 Afghan journalists each and third batch of 19 Afghan journalists have been trained at Indian Institute of Mass Communication from August-October, 2002, January-March, 2003 and June-August, 2003 respectively. Two choreographers were sent from ICCR for a period of two weeks in April, 2003 for assisting Afghan authorities in producing programme for national day celebrations on April 28, 2003. Indian Council of Cultural Relations has allocated two slots to Afghanistan for learning music in India during 2002-03, of which one has been utilised by Afghanistan.

SECURITY AND RULE OF LAW

Afghan National Army The vehicles given to the Army have been put to good use not only for the Army but also for public service. But defence is one sector now in which there is no cooperation as compared to earlier for obvious reasons, i.e. that it is the US which is in charge of the situation there and as such, there is no scope of any further cooperation at this stage. Resumption of the previous kind of defence cooperation can only be possible after the exit of the US from Afghanistan. There, however, seem to be no prospects of such a move by the US anywhere in the near future.

Police Training was imparted to 250 Afghan police officers

and cadets in twelve different courses in India from July-September 2002.

Eighteen Afghan judges and lawyers were trained at the Indian Law Institute, New Delhi from February-May, 2003.

CONSTITUTIONAL LOYA JIRGA

Sixty five electronic voting machines have been made available to United Nations Assistance Mission for Afghanistan for voting during the Constitutional Loya Jirga in December 2003 alongwith deputation of four experts for operation and technical support.

AGRICULTURE

Nearly 67 tons of vegetable seeds have been supplied to the Ministry of Agriculture of Afghanistan in three Phases in Aug.-Sept. 2002, February 2003 and August 2003. 15 officials from the Ministry of Agriculture have attended a training course in the field of Cooperative Farming and Marketing at RICM, Banglore from December 2-March 3. 16 officials from the Ministry of Agriculture have attended a training course on Operation and Maintenance of Agricultural machinery and equipment at CFMTTI, Budni, Bhopal from January-May, 2003. A sericulture expert was deputed to Afghanistan for a period of one week (July 14-20, 2003) to suggest possible areas of co-operation and assistance to Afghanistan in the field of sericulture.

INFORMATION TECHNOLOGY

An IT specialist has been deputed to Afghan Government since June 20, 2003 for a period of one year. A LAN network with Internet access via VSAT was established alongwith supply of necessary equipment in the office of the Foreign Minister of Afghanistan. The LAN has been extended to additional twenty nodes alongwith supply of necessary equipment. A computer-training centre was set up in Kabul from July 02-Jan. 03 for providing computer training to Afghan officials. The centre was handed over to the Afghan Ministry of Foreign Affairs in January 2003. Two Computer Training Centres have been set up in Kandahar and Herat in August 2003. Another two Computer

Training Centres have been set up at Pul-e-Khumri and Jalalabad in November, 2003.

BANKING

Three experts from RBI were deputed to assist the Da Afghanistan Bank in July 2002. Six experts from various banks in India have been deputed to the Da Afghanistan Bank in July-August 2003 for a period of one year.

COMMERCE

A Preferential Trade Agreement was signed between India and Afghanistan on March 6, 2003 and has come into effect since May 2003. The Agreement provides duty-free access to the import of fig-dried, pistachio (open and closed shell), mulberries dried, pine nuts roasted, melon fresh, asafeotida, lapis lazuli, ruby, and emeralds from Afghanistan. A 50% concession has been extended on duty on green, black and red raisins, apricots dried, walnuts, plums dried, almonds, raisins golden, cherries sour dried, fresh grapes, apples, apricots, pomegranates, anise seeds, caraway seeds, linseeds, sesame seeds, liquorice roots, apricot nuts bitter, and alpha alpha seeds. The construction of a cold storage of 5000-ton capacity in Kandahar has commenced. A training programme and workshop on marketing and enterprise development for twenty women entrepreneurs from Afghanistan organised by Consortium of Women Entrepreneurs of India commenced on November 17, 2003

URBAN DEVELOPMENT

Civil engineering lab equipment and measuring instruments were gifted to the Ministry of Urban Development and Housing of Afghanistan in May 2003. The Government has decided to gift 76 utility vehicles/ equipments (water tankers, rear drop tippers, dump trucks, bulldozers, motor graders and garbage tippers) to the Kabul Municipality from Eicher International Ltd, Tata International Ltd., and BEML. 35 of these vehicles from Eicher International Limited have been already handed over to the Kabul Municipality and another 35 vehicles from Tata International Ltd. will be delivered in end-November.

INFRASTRUCTURE DEVELOPMENT

Road Construction Feasibility study and detailed project assessment for upgradation of road stretch from Delaram to Zaranj in Afghanistan have been carried out by a team of experts. Water Resources WAPCOS has carried out detailed Project assessment for rehabilitation of six Mini/Micro hydro projects, Khanabad Irrigation Project, Quargha reservoir and Amir Ghazi Dam in Afghanistan. WAPCOS carried out the field survey and water analysis to identify location of 50 deep wells in Herat province of Afghanistan. Following the survey, the work of drilling of 24 deep wells in Herat province commenced in September 2003. WAPCOS has carried out the feasibility study and detailed project assessment (March-August 2003) of completion of Salma Dam Project in Herat Province.

INDUSTRY

A team from Ministry of Small Scale Industries and NSIC had visited Afghanistan and carried out feasibility study for rehabilitation of Industrial Park in Kabul. Twenty officials from the Ministry of Light Industries and Foodstuff of Afghanistan have commenced training in the field of light industry at National Institute of Small Industries Extension Training (NISIET), Hyderabad from October 13, 2003 for a period of eight weeks.

TRAINING

Diplomacy: Three batches of 20 Afghan Diplomats each have been trained at the Foreign Service Institute in February-May 2002, August-November 2002 and July-September 2003. 15 officials from Presidential Secretariat of Afghanistan were trained at Foreign Service Institute from October 2002-March 2003. Two Afghan diplomats attended a two-week module on Professional Course for Foreign Diplomats in January 2003.

Medical: Two batches of six Afghan doctors and paramedics each from Indira Gandhi Institute of Child Health attended training in areas of their specialisation at All India Institute of Medical Sciences from August 19-November 18, 2002, and May 29-August 27, 2003 respectively. Extension was provided to one of the trainees of the first batch for advanced training for three months.

Journalism: Two batches of 15 Afghan journalists each and third batch of 19 Afghan journalists have been trained at Indian Institute of Mass Communications from August-October, 2002, January-March, 2003 and June-August, 2003 respectively.

Police: Training was imparted to 250 Afghan police officers and cadets in twelve different courses in India from July-September 2002.

Judiciary: Eighteen Afghan judges and lawyers were trained at the Indian Law Institute, New Delhi from February-May, 2003.

Agriculture: 15 officials from the Ministry of Agriculture have attended a training course in the field of Cooperative Farming and Marketing at RICM, Banglore from December 02-March 03. 16 officials from the Ministry of Agriculture have attended a training course on Operation and Maintenance of Agricultural machinery and equipment at CFMTTI, Budni, Bhopal from January-May, 2003.

Civil Aviation: Ariana Afghan Airlines officials have been trained by Air India. In-service training was provided to seven Afghan teachers from the Ministry of Education of Afghanistan by Delhi Public School Society from September 4-October 15, 2003. Flight Engineers Ground Basic Classroom Training was provided to 8 officials of Ariana Afghan Airlines at Indian Airlines Training Centre, Hyderabad for a period of six weeks in September-October, 2003. Industry: Twenty officials from the Ministry of Light Industries and Foodstuff of Afghanistan have commenced training in the field of light industry at National Institute of Small Industries Extension Training (NISIET), Hyderabad from October 13, 2003 for a period of eight weeks. A training programme and workshop on marketing and enterprise development for twenty women entrepreneurs from Afghanistan organised by Consortium of Women Entrepreneurs of India commenced on November 17, 2003.

English Language: Two English language Instructors have been teaching English at the Institute of Diplomacy since Feb 2002 to the officials of the Ministry of Foreign Affairs and other Government Departments of Afghanistan. Two additional English language teachers have been deputed to Kabul since March 10, 2003 to teach English at the Ministries of Information and Culture and Labour and Social Welfare.

Computers: A computer-training centre was set up in Kabul from July 02-Jan 03 for providing computer training to Afghan officials. The centre was handed over to the Afghan Ministry of Foreign Affairs in January 2003. Two Computer Training Centres have been set up in Kandahar and Herat in August 2003. Another two Computer Training Centres have been set up at Pul-e-Khumri and Jalalabad in November, 2003.

Miscellaneous: Fifty slots have been allocated to Afghanistan for training at various institutes in India under Indian Technical and Economic Cooperation Programme. 43 Afghan nationals have attended the training under the Programme during 2002-03 in the fields of Rural Industry Promotion (3), Training Methods and Skills for Managers (4), Small Business Planning and Promotion (7), Urban Development Management (4), Audit of Receipts (3), Legislative Drafting (5), Development Journalism (1), Audit of Public Enterprises, (1), Participatory Planning and Management of Watershed Projects (5), Micro Planning for Poverty Reduction and Sustainable Development (3), Sustainable Development in Agriculture and Rural Development (2), Educational Planning and Administration (4) and Urban Infrastructure Planning and Management (1). 10 slots were allocated to Afghanistan under General Cultural Scholarship Scheme of Indian Council of Cultural Relations for higher studies in India in 2002-03, of which three have been utilised by Afghanistan (one each at School of Architecture and Planning, Delhi, Delhi University and Osmania University, Hyderabad). 4 slots have been allocated to Afghanistan under the scheme for 2003-04. 10 slots have been allocated to Afghanistan under the Cultural Exchange Programme Scholarship Scheme for 2003-04. Indian Council of Cultural Relations has allocated two slots to Afghanistan for learning music in India during 2002-03, of which one has been utilised by Afghanistan. (These details are till as of 2 December, 2003).[1]

II

As should be obvious from this, India's role in Afghanistan's reconstruction and political transformation has been intense and engaging. India opened consulates in Herat and Mazhar-e-Sharif in August 2002 and in Kandahar and Jalalabad in December 2002 to co-ordinate its efforts. The Embassy was closed on 26 September 1996 after the Taliban took over Kabul. Though it does not share borders with the country, India considers Afghanistan to be part of its extended strategic neighbourhood. However, renewed Indo-Afghan ties have not gone down well with Pakistan. Pakistan is wary of the Indian diplomatic presence. It strongly believes that an Indian presence abets and promotes activity inimical to Pakistan's interests. President Musharraf contended that India's decision to open these consulates had "nothing to do with the promotion of economic ties," but intended to "harm Pakistan." The Afghan Foreign Minister, Abdullah Abdullah, clarified that the activities of the Indian consulates were "in the limits of their duty as consulates in accordance with international norms and principles."[2] President Karzai assured President Musharraf that Afghan soil would not be allowed to be used against Pakistan. In spite of these assurances, Pakistan, despite its peace process with India since November 2003, still nourishes suspicions of 'evil intent' on India's part. It accused India, specifically the Research and Analysis Wing (R&AW), of disseminating false currency and running training camps for Afghans to carry out destructive activities, especially in the tribal areas bordering Pakistan. India rubbished these allegations and maintains that, as two sovereign countries, India and Afghanistan have full right to determine the nature and content of their bilateral relationship.

Afghanistan, in terms of its stability or otherwise, has historically had a marked impact on South Asia. Its geo-strategic location by virtue of its contiguity to the vital regions of the Persian Gulf, Central Asia and South Asia sucked in the intrusive influence of external powers like the US, Russia and China. South Asia is deeply impacted by Afghanistan as a result of the long Pak-Afghan border, the Durand Line, which is disputed by Afghans of all political hues. Pakistan in its games of the "pretender power" in South Asia has used Afghanistan, along with Kashmir, as a pawn in the South Asian power games. The exit of the Taliban from Afghanistan imposed heavy losses on Pakistan in virtually every conceivable field. Afghanistan, along with Kashmir was the strategic centre-piece of Pakistan's foreign, military and state-sponsored terrorism policies for over a decade. Strategically, Pakistan today loses the strategic depth that it tried to build up so zealously during the last decade. Its Western frontiers can no longer be perceived as secure. Pakistan's Islamic credentials have taken a beating, both domestically and externally. It is being perceived as an Islamic nation which did not have a second's compunction in ditching the Islamic Emirate of Afghanistan and its own creation, the Taliban. Possession of an 'Islamic Bomb' alone cannot guarantee Pakistan's aspirations for the leadership of the Islamic World. In South Asia also, Pakistan's image gets affected considerably. South Asian states which would cozy-up with Pakistan to discomfit India would now have to think twice of Pakistan's reliability to stand by them.[3] The strategic losses of Pakistan resulting from the Afghanistan events impact heavily on Pakistan's pretensions to emerge as the 'second pole' in South Asia politics.

In the face of Pakistan's uneasiness with Indian efforts in Afghanistan, it was logical that India would have to pay the price. It paid. And the most terrible of them have been loss of Indian lives. On April 28, 2006, Kasula Suryanarayana, an Indian telecommunications engineer working for a Bahrain based firm in the Zabul Province, was reportedly abducted by the Taliban. His abductors demanded the withdrawal of all Indians working in Afghanistan in lieu of his release. Even before the Indian government's special team reached Kabul to negotiate his release, Suryanarayana's beheaded body, with apparent torture marks, was recovered on April 30 at Hassan Kariez district of Zabul, clearly indicating that his abductors had no intent to negotiate. The message they wanted to convey was one of terror and intimidation.[4] This was not the first instance. Earlier, in November 2005, Maniappan Kutty, a driver working with the Border Roads Organisation's project of building the Zaranj-Delaram highway, was abducted and killed by the Taliban. On November 8, 2003, an Indian telecommunications engineer working for the Afghan Wireless Company was shot dead. In 2003, two Indian engineers—P. Murali and G. Vardharai—working on a road project in Zabul province were abducted. Their release three weeks later came about after intense negotiations by Afghan tribal leaders with the Taliban militia, which was demanding the release of 50 imprisoned militants in return for the Indian engineers.

Afghanistan's Defence Minister Abdul Rahim Wardak's visit to India in April 2008 was a significant step in an effort to strengthen defence ties. Afghanistan considering to send its armed forces officers for specialised training in Indian counter insurgency warfare institutions amounts to getting around the problem of a major Indian Army presence there. Wardak's visit, heading a seven member high-level Afghan delegation, was a first ever to India by an Afghan Defence Minister in almost two decades. He sought India's help in revitalising Afghanistan's Soviet era MIG fighters and 8-10 MI 35 helicopter gunships through spares, training of technicians and pilots and medical equipment. Wardak, a serving Four Star General in the Afghan Army, and his delegation, comprising top Afghan army and Air Force officials, visited Indian Army's 15 Corp Headquarters in Srinagar, counter-insurgency school in the state and Army High Altitude Warfare School located at Gulmarg to get a first hand briefing Indian Army's experience in conducting counter-terrorism operations. Sure enough, within days of this visit a suicide bomber killed three Indian road engineers and an Afghan in southwestern Afghanistan in the second deadly attack on road builders in a week. A Taliban spokesman claimed responsibility, the Pakistan-based Afghan Islamic Press news agency reported.[5]

Now, such incidents raise concerns about the safety of Indians working on reconstruction projects in the conflict-ravaged country.[6] But more importantly, it is important to link such incidents with the intentions and unintended consequences of Pakistan's Afghanistan policy. The Islamisation of Pakistan under the Zia regime had a decisive impact on that country's tribal regions, where the writ of the Pakistan state was always weak. This prompted Pakistan's search for "strategic depth." The Taliban were propped up by Pakistan in early 1990s to attain this strategic depth, quell sub-nationalist aspirations plaguing the country, negate resurgence of the Durand Line dispute, and bleed India in Kashmir from bases in Afghanistan. This architecture came to collapse in the aftermath of 9/11. But so inextricably linked are Pakistan's interests in Afghanistan's instability and its policies towards India that Pakistan has been opposed to Indian efforts. A strong, democratic Afghanistan with thriving bilateral relations with India would mean that the demon of the Durand Line and other issues will be raised again and Pakistan will stand to lose a lot in case such a situation arises. Aside the fact that these issues are gaining prominence once again, Pakistan continues to abet and aid Taliban and Al-Qaeda remnants and other hardliners against Indian interests in Afghanistan.[7] And it is these elements that have been responsible for the spate of abduction and killings of Indian workers.

Pakistan also remains vary of Indian efforts for two additional reasons. Afghanistan's well-being allows India to capitalise on its Central Asian strategy, especially the proposed gas pipeline from Turkmenistan. Additionally, the reconstruction process in Afghanistan remains an inalienable part of the global "war on terror." The US government aims to install democracy and robust institutions in intervened states. Democracy promotion is an area where the interests of the US and India coincide. This would help further to strengthen Indo-US relations. Pakistan is likely to squirm in a situation like this given its excessive dependence on the US for economic and military requirements. These are factors that need to be accounted for when we attempt to understand Pakistan's discomfort with India's role in Afghanistan.

III

This paper has laid down the diverse and lasting nature of India's contributions to Afghanistan's reconstruction and political transformation. It has also argued that Pakistan's response to India's role in Afghanistan has been hostile and also suggested the reasons why that is the case. This section very briefly suggests the importance of India to Afghanistan's present and future and in what ways could India do more than most countries who have pledged their support to Afghanistan.

India is the largest regional donor to Afghanistan having invested nearly US $ 800 million. India remains central to processes of regionalism in South Asia given its overwhelming superiority compared to the rest of the states. It is stable and democratic. Its economy is robust and growing by leaps and bounds. Democracy is generally good news for peace and institution sustenance. Though real and genuine democracy in Afghanistan may take a long time to come, it is important to notice the difference culture makes in political transformation. Attempts by the US to install puppet regimes with very limited influence will be treated with hostility of some degree or other. On the other hand, if India plays a greater role in these efforts, it is likely to be received well. India and Afghanistan's cultural linkages will be of tremendous help here. Besides, ever since Independence, India has been a vocal supporter of Afghanistan, and, contrary to the trend, not used that country for its vested interests. Being the largest economy in the region, the scale of assistance India could offer to Afghanistan remains singular. It has credible infrastructure support base, both civilian and military, which could be galvanised to greater effects for Afghanistan's betterment. Indeed, it would not be far-fetched to suggest that only India could provide a sustainable and lasting support towards Afghanistan's path to recovery which, at the moment, seems to be heading nowhere.

CONCLUSION

The next few months following the recent installation of a civilian government in Pakistan, preceded and followed by bloody jihadi attacks, are expected to be trying ones indeed. Whether the Pakistan Army, now commanded by a former head if the ISI, who is reported to have been close to the now retired General Parvez Musharraf, relaxes or releases its stranglehold over civil affairs and foreign policy of Pakistan, remains to be seen. Considering the history of Pakistan Army and the ISI and old links that both have had with jihadi groups and the Taliban, such a process cannot come about easily or soon. While there is a fair public sentiment of better tie with India and leaders both PPP and PML-N have made statements sounding encouraging to

India on one hand, on the other, Prime Minister Yousuf Raza Gillani has stated that "sacrifices of Kashmiris will not be forgotten." As such, there is no guarantee of India—Pakistan relations improving to the extent that Pakistan begins allowing India road transit to Afghanistan and is able to rein in the Taliban or prevent it from attacking Indians engaged in reconstruction and assistance projects there. Over a thousand Indians are engaged in reconstruction and developmental works in Afghanistan for last six years as part of New Delhi's commitment to help in rehabilitation of the war-torn country. Of them, about 300 personnel of BRO are engaged in construction of Delaram-Zaranj highway to provide shorter connectivity between Kabul and Iran. In the wake of fresh terror attack on a convoy of BRO workers in Afghanistan—the security of Indians engaged in reconstruction work in the trouble-torn country is being beefed up after a fresh assessment of the threat to them.[8] Fresh speculations, just as they first arose in 2006, that India might be asked to dispatch troops to Afghanistan to buttress the ISAF presence there has apparently rung alarm bells in the Pakistani establishment, which asked the US to ensure that Indian security presence in Afghanistan remained restrained.[9] This came after US President George Bush publicly asked India to increase its presence in Afghanistan. India, though committed to its presence in the Afghan reconstruction drive, has stayed out of the security operations there except to provide greater protection to its own people, which it has done by sending Indo Tibetan Border Police. If the US had taken up the Indian offer to send troops to Afghanistan, in the past five years, with their experience, they could have effectively trained Afghan security forces to higher standards than those at present.

Since the manuscript went to press, the terrorist bombing of Indian Embassy in Kabul on 7 July 2008,along in Afghanistan has led the US to adopt more a aggressive posture towards Pakistan. All of this bears out this paper's primary contention and the recommendations it has offered.

CHAPTER 24

US Role in Afghanistan's Reconstruction and Political Transformation

Saleem Kidwai

INTRODUCTION

No other country in Asia has suffered so much of physical and material destruction in recent years as Afghanistan. It is the only country which faced the attack and occupation of world's two super powers, the Soviet Union and the United States in the quarter of a century. The civil war shattered the entire economic structure and nothing was left intact From 1992 to 1996, Kabul and other cities saw worst form of destruction. The present day Afghanistan is nothing but a legacy of blood and fire caused by the Mujahideen in fighting and battles between the Taliban and the Northern Alliance forces. It continues to be ripe with instability and there is very little sign of reconstruction. The daunting task of rebuilding Afghanistan involves not only building the security structure but also rebuilding country's educational, judicial and administrative system. Essential services like electricity, water and adequate economic opportunities are also conspicuous by their absence. Kabul needs massive international assistance. Reconstruction of country's shattering infrastructure and transition away from a war economy based on narcotics, weapons and smuggling are crucial pillars for success in Afghanistan. Hence the rationality of the task of democratization and rebuilding of Afghanistan so as to ensure peace and stability in this country is not only the responsibility of government and people of that country but the international community including the lone super power, the US.

What are the important issues of rebuilding and reconstruction of Afghanistan? What has been the role of the US in assisting the task of reconstruction in Afghanistan? What are the impediments in this regard? What is the impact of 9/11 on Afghanistan? Was the attack on Afghanistan a short term response to the perceived and alleged terrorism network masterminded by Osama bin Laden, a guest of Mulla Omar? What were the linkages between the Afghan crisis and the issue of terrorism? What are the long term goals of the US in Afghanistan? Has the US achieved its objectives in Afghanistan? What are the stakes of the US in Afghanistan? What is the nature of American involvement in Afghanistan? Why did the US intervene in Afghanistan? The paper seeks to find answers to these and similar questions.

WHY AMERICAN INVOLVEMENT?

The American involvement in Afghanistan began in October 2001 after dozen years of only marginal interest in the country's civil war and stymied development. For a variety of reasons, Washington regarded Afghanistan a sanctuary of various terrorist organizations after the Soviet military withdrawal from that country. The war against international terrorism started from Afghanistan. While none of the hijackers involved in 9/11 incident belonged to Afghanistan, but those who masterminded that event had operated from that country. Al-Qaeda bases in Afghanistan provided training, forces, networking to various terrorist groups. President Bush in a speech on 20th September 2001, to a joint session of the Congress, announced the start of a 'war on terrorism', and demanded that the Taliban leadership in Afghanistan turn over all the Al-Qaeda leaders base there, close every terrorist training camp in the country, hand over all terrorists to appropriate authorities, and give the US full access to terrorist training camps."[1] The US backed by UN Security Council invaded Afghanistan to remove Taliban from power and succeeded The American-led strikes were in retaliation to what according to the Bush administration described the Al-Qaeda-led attacks on its soil on 9/11.The people of Afghanistan who had suffered endlessly because of more than two decades of violence and war faced another catastrophe when US military machine began to target their country resulting into more pain and agony. The US declared that it was on a warpath. With the support of Northern Alliance, the US forces were able to capture one Afghan town after another including capital Kabul. Thus, the process of dismantling the Taliban regime and liquidation of the Al-Qaeda network in Afghanistan which was unleashed by the Bush administration in the aftermath of 9/11 reached to its logical conclusion. It resulted into the induction of a new setup in Afghanistan heavily dominated by the US supported regime.

US ASSISTANCE IN RECONSTRUCTION

The US initially conceived Afghanistan essentially a military operation. Little thought was given in the Pentagon-directed mission to the country's future beyond conceding to others the responsibility for pressing Afghan political leaders to agree on an interim government and raising international and donor interest. Nation building as such was not on the agenda of Washington. The American financial commitment would be modest because other nations and international creditor agencies were expected to assist with the bill for humanitarian and reconstruction activities. Thus, the US joined in convening an international donors conference at Tokyo in January 2002 at which Washington promised only 296 million dollars as reconstruction aid for 2000-3 on top of the 320 million dollars already pledged to Afghanistan for humanitarian assistance. Without a broadly conceived development agenda, Washington was mostly satisfied to see humanitarian aid consume much of the foreign assistance. The all critical rebuilding of Afghanistan's water and power systems was not addressed. No progress was registered on reconstruction of major roads, most of all Ring Road connecting Kabul with Heart, for which funding by the US and Japan had been kept aside. The US excused the delays in initiating reconstruction with the argument that most large-scale projects would have to wait for an improved security environment. The US officials failed in initial period to appreciate the interconnection between security and reconstruction, and how progress in one was contingent on the other

SHORT-TERM OBJECTIVES AND LONG-TERM GOALS

Later on the US realized that its military objectives could not be achieved without considerable involvement in Afghanistan's economic restructuring and political stabilization The geo-political and geo-strategic location of Afghanistan is such that the complexion of its state matters a lot to the neighbouring countries. A violent, militant and instable Afghan state is a source of instability and disorder in the three Asias: Central, South and West. For America, the past experience of abandoning Afghanistan had proved to be counterproductive because the country became a breeding ground for various militant groups having an anti-US agenda... Therefore after 9/11, Washington embarked on a long term policy for Afghanistan with a major purpose of transforming that country from a tribal, anarchic and violent to stable and democratic state according to its own standards. Unlike in the 1980's when Washington pursued a policy of disengagement from Afghanistan after the withdrawal of Soviet troops from that country in 2001, it made it clear that this time it meant business and had come to stay.

A decision to redirect and restructure American policy, intended to accelerate most programmes, was agreed in Washington in June 2003.[2] Over a period of months, the US led Operation Enduring Freedom (OER) forces were increased to 18000 troops. Training for the Afghan National Army (ANA) was given new urgency. To accelerate its development Washington appropriated in supplemental legislation 28 million dollars for the year 2004, incliding new funds for the military infrastructure and soldiers salaries and training.[3] During 2004, the US also provided equipments and trucks and laid plans to supplement the ANA arms and defense services. American military advisers involved themselves more directly in training Afghan units. The US also agreed to underwrite an army academy. The creation of national police academy also took on greater priority. The US State Department through a private contractor assumed most of the training in nine regional centers around the country. The Kabul government backed financially by the US and Japan finally made strides during 2004 in a planned programme of disarmament.[4] To complement other policy adjustments, the US in mid 2003 adopted personnel and structural changes in managing the reconstruction effort. Zalmy Khalilzad who had been a Special Presidential envoy to Afghanistan, was sent to Kabul as ambassador. He came with his own team of advisers forming a separate Afghan Reconstruction Group (ARG) that took over most of the planning and monitoring activities from the US embassy. The new management approach was meant to overcome bureaucratic turf war in Washington, miscommunications between Washington and Kabul and at times contrasting military and civilian priorities in Afghanistan.[5] The ambassador khalilzad 's personal style appeared to be too high profile for a light foot print policy of the United States.[5]

Poppy production which spread in every one of Afghanistan's provinces caused grave concern in the US.[6] American domestic pressures mounted for greater efforts to reverse the trend. The US administration insisted on a stepped up eradication programme in the belief that terrorist groups are profiting handsomely from the production along with dedicated traffickers. Drugs are also regarded a serious drag on reconstruction plans. Consequently President Karzai signed on to a more dedicated eradication programme that saw implementation in 2004.These actions coincided with demands by the US Congress for a more robust effort that contained an explicit threat to tie Afghan aid to progress in drug eradication. Between 2003 and 2004, spending by the US Congress for assistance for Afghanistan went from 740 million dollars to 1.9 billion dollars, most of the latter in a supplemental appropriation legislation passed in 2004, for 2005 provided 980 million dollars in reconstruction and humanitarian aid, but could rise in another supplemental bill in 2005.A gain Washington took a lead in attracting reviewed pledges from the international community. With donors at the Tokyo Conference, having failed to deliver fully on their pledges a second conference was convened in Berlin in March-April 2004 where 8.2 billion dollars in bilateral aid was committed for the year 2004-2006.For the full period, the US pledged 2.9 billion dollars in non-military assistance. Separately Washington also backed loan pledges from the World Bank. The US Congress in December 2007 passed the 31 billion dollars in funding for Afghanistan. The package is known as the Consolidated Appropriation Act, 2008.The funding of the effort in Afghanistan also indicates the US anxiety to continue with the operations that many of its lawmakers now admit, were distracted by the operations in Iraq. The cost of the US government to fund the war in Afghanistan has cost the US government 88.2 billion dollars from 2001until 2006, whereas the pledged funds for reconstruction were11.4 billion dollars for the same period

The US involvement in Afghanistan profited from the fact that from the outset the international community understood the purpose of the mission that unlike Iraq, where the international community is not that supportive to the US military operations and occupation, in Afghanistan the situation is relatively different. Major NATO members and other countries including some from the Muslim world are a part of the international force in Afghanistan. The main task of that force is to ensure security and combat terrorist activities carried out by Taliban remnants and al-Qaeda. Washington considered Afghanistan a sanctuary of various terrorist organizations. Significantly Afghanistan unlike Iraq, is not a source of major resistance against the US led presense. Few Afghans view these forces as occupiers. The largely welcoming environment in sharp contrast to Iraq derives from the exhaustion of a quarter century of conflict and war and the widely shared conviction that resource—poor Afghanistan cannot succeed on its own. However Afghans understand the difference between those who sought to rule over them and those who had come to aid them But history proves the fact that attacking and invading Afghanistan is not difficult but getting out of Afghanistan is an uphill task, So far, Washington has used the terrorist events of 9/11 and the threat of terrorism to justify its military presence in Afghanistan but it is not certain for how long America can sustain its military engagements in that country. No external power has managed to establish its long term writ on Afghanistan. British and Soviet Union examples must be taken into account in this regard. For how long America with the support of its allies can sustain operations in Afghanistan remains a fundamental question as far as the future of that country is concerned. It would be better if the US concentrates on humanitarian assistance and the process of reconstruction and rebuilding instead of identifying itself as suppressing the local resistance. Another area of concern is the heavy US investment on the physical and political survival of one man. In order to keep Hamid Karzai protected, the US contracts the job of guarding the President to a private American firm President Karzai is often thought to be too close to the Americans. The biggest challenge is the transformation of Afghanistan state from a tribal and authoritarian to a modern and democratic one The main issue at hand confronted by the US supported Kabul regime is the legacy of centuries of feudal and tribal setup which is considered as a main impediment as far as the process of rebuilding Afghanistan and democratization of that country is concerned. Throughout history in the ancient land of Afghanistan, the tribes have enjoyed an almost independent status. Most conquerors passing through left them alone. However after the Emergency Loya Jirga in 2001 and the introduction of western democracy, these ancient old Afghan traditions had been replaced overnight and the door opened to the world of globalization alien to the tribal society. The question is :are the common people in Afghanistan familiar with democracy and the political process which the Bush administration wants to introduce ?What about sardars and tribal leaders of that country who are intolerant and parochial in their approach vis-a-vis critical issues as before? Can democracy be introduced in Afghanistan because of American and NATO's military presence and some financial aid for rebuilding and reconstructing that turbulent and war ridden country? If democracy is an implication of 9/11 in Afghanistan, then by now something positive should have occurred in terms of cutting war lords down to their size, establishing the rule of law and ensuring some semblance of political tolerance. Afghanistan has been for the US a test case for whether a moderate Islamic democracy can be rooted in countries with little or no experience at open societies and politics.

CONCLUSION

The need and urgency of rebuilding Afghanistan existed immediately after the withdrawal of Soviet forces from that country but the world looked at the other way and failed to unleash the process of reconstruction and rebuilding of that war torn state. As Afghanistan was ignored by Washington, the outcome was the worst form of destruction and bloodshed among the Mujahideen groups and the ultimate seizure of power by the Taliban. The US role in Afghanistan may be characterized as a qualified success.[8] The post Taliban situation in Afghanistan is certainly better than both the Taliban era and the fifteen years preceding it, from the Soviet invasion and the decade of Mujahideen resistance to the 4 years of Rabbani government. However several errors occurred in setting Afghanistan on a course towards recovery and stability, As a result Afghanistan is still in a grip of instability and violence. Resurgence of Taliban, factional fighting and lawlessness, easing of opium production and culture of warlordism still exist on the Afghan political scene. There has been a lack of infrastructure projects carried out by the donors which has hampered economic integration, resources and job benefits of a total of 13.4 billion dollars pledged at the Tokyo and Berlin Conferences for the period 2002-2007 against a needs assessment of 27billion dollars demanded by the Afghan government for the same period of time, only 39 billion dollars have actually been disbursed of which only 0, 9 billion worth of projects have actually been completed, The costs and complexity of the tasks were underestimated. The US reconstruction policy lacked coordination and appeared ineffective. Overall the American commitment in Afghanistan can be characterized as light footprint. Despite a desire to bolster the central government, Washington was reconciled to have NGOs as the main conduits for aid. As German Foreign Minister J Fischer has rightly put it in a globally circulated article 'Things are not going well in Afghanistan." Sometime at the turn of 2001-2, the Bush administration concluded that the stabilization and reconstruction of Afghanistan was no longer its top priority and decided to bet instead on military led regime change in Iraq." Afghanistan can thus be seen as the first victim of the Administration 's misguided strategy"[9] he rising violence and insecurity has impeded the development al activity and has led to disillusionment among the people. Clearly the US policy in Afghanistan is floundering. One finds a huge gap in US policy between the stated goals and the rhetoric of establishing democracy and stabilizing the country. The Bush administration has maintained a light foot print and demonstrated great reluctance in the nation building exercise. Rebuilding and construction of Afghanistan is not just limited to economy and military but it is a gigantic task including the important organs of the Afghan state. Essentially, the task for the US is to buy for Afghanistan to emerge as a normal developing country, allowing institutions to take roots, governance to improve and a normal political process to get underway.

To sum up, despite international assistance and proclamations of improvement, Afghanistan remains one of the poorest countries in the world. The country ranks at the bottom of all major development indicators. The Bonn agreement's stated purpose was to end the tragic conflict in Afghanistan and promote national reconstruction, lasting peace, stability and respect for human rights in the country. However the coalition forces have not succeeded in bringing back durable peace and stability to the war-ravaged land. The most significant recent development has been the upsurge in violence in the south, south-east and east of Afghanistan. Security has once again become the paramount concern. According to Karl Inderfurth, former US Assistant Secretary of Stat e for South Asian Affairs, "Almost six years after US-led military forces removed the Taliban and its Qaeda support network from power, major challenges are seriously undermining popular support in the government of Afghan President Hamid Karzai, A resurgent Taliban and a growing sense of insecurity throughout the country rampant corruption, ineffective law enforcement and a weak judicial system a failure to provide social services, lagging reconstruction, a booming drug trade and too many warlords."[10] The international community headed by the US has made immense efforts to bring back peace and stability. But a lack of cultural understanding on the part of both the Afghan and international community due to entirely different cultural roots, education, religious and social views has generated obstacles to stabilization. Ancient tribal traditions, warlords, geographic location, climate, drought and religion also play an important role to the hurdles faced in Afghanistan. The world community has disregarded the magnitude of the crises and has failed to act in a manner appropriate to Afghanistan's conditions. The lack of coordinated, targeted and adequately funded action has exacerbated the humanitarian crisis. A change of approach is the need of hour. If Washington pursues realistic aims, and does so with perseverance, its main goal—a central government that can drive back the Taliban, hold the country together, and with the help of international community, ensure Afghanistan's development-is achievable

REFERENCES

1. Global security.comText: The Bush announces Start of a War on Terror, <http;//www.global security.org/military/library/news/2001/09/mil-010920-usia.htm>
2. See discussion in S Fredrick Starr, "US Afghanistan Policy: Its Working," Central Asia—Caucasus Institute, John Hopkins University, October 2004, pp. 4-7.
3. *Ibid*, p. 28.
4. Kenneth Katzman, Afghanistan: Post-War Governance, Security and US Policy," Congressional Research Service Report for Congress, Washington DC, Dec., 16, 2004, pp. 26-27
5. Khalilzad served as ambassador until March 2005.
6. Marvin G. Weibaum, Rebuilding Afghanistan :The Impediments, Lessons and Prospects' in Francis Fukunasma (Ed.), Nation Building: Beyond Afghanistan and Iraq (Baltimore at Washington DC, John Hopkins University Press).
7. According to the latest UN World drug Report 2007, opium production increased by 595 to 165,000 hectares in 2006 which is the largest ever found in Afghanistan.
8. Marvin Weibaum, 'The US Involvement in Afghanistan since 9/11: Staqrtegic Objectives, Security and Reconstruction' in Moonis Ahmar (Ed.), The Challenge of Rebuilding in Afghanistan, University of Karachi, 2005, p. 165.
9. Fischer Joschka, "Afghanistanand the Future of NATO," Turkishweekly, 3 January 208.URL;http;ww.turkishweekly.net/news.php?id=5127
10. *International Herald Tribune*, 29 May 2007.

CHAPTER 25

Mainstreaming the Gender in Democratization of Afghanistan: The Role of United Nations

Yeshi Choedon

One of the main threats to international peace and security in the post-Cold War era is the internal conflicts emanating from the 'weak' or the 'failed' states. These conflicts not only have spill over effect on the neighbouring states but also the territories of such states tend to become the safe haven for terrorist network. The United Nations has been intervening in these conflicts either on the humanitarian ground to prevent genocide and ethnic cleansing or on the grounds of maintaining international peace and security. Invariably, the United Nations gets involve not only in peacekeeping and peace making activities but also take on the task of peace building to prevent such states from recurring relapse into conflict situation.

Peace Building involves extensive task of recovery, reconstruction, rebuilding infrastructure and institutions, which have been destroyed or weakened during the internal conflict. It also involves in establishing some new social, economic, political institutions, which would make the state durable and stable. The similar effort has been also known by the term "nation building." The central thrust of these activities is to install a stable and effective government that would able to manage its internal and external relations and obligations. The United Nations also emphasized the importance of bringing gender perspectives to the center of all UN conflict prevention and resolution, peace-building, peacekeeping, rehabilitation and reconstruction efforts.

In the case of Afghanistan situation, after the Taliban regime was over thrown, the international community favour to establish an Interim Government run by the locals themselves. The relief, recovery, reconstruction and rebuilding of state has been attempted through such government with the assistance of international community. Theoretically, this practice seems to be sound as ownership of the administrative lies with the local people themselves, without much of outside intrusion. The international community extended assistance to build local capacities to establish a stable, durable and legitimate government. The high priority has been accorded to democratization of Afghan polity, as it is believed that democracy would bring about greater acceptance and legitimacy of the government among the people, compare to other forms of government. In the in the democratization process, the conscientious attempts have been made to mainstream the gender to give voice to Afghan women, who were the worst victims of Taliban regime. The United Nations has been guided in this endeavour by the Security Council resolution 1325 adopted in October 2000. In fact, Afghanistan is one of the first countries where the United Nations conscientiously tried to operationalize the concern of gender mainstreaming in the peace operation.

This paper begins by briefly tracing the major attempts made in Afghan history to improve the status of women. Particularly, the paper discusses how the Soviet's move to bring about progressive social change, including the status of women, further fueled the fundamentalist movement and in turn served as the ground for Mujaheddin to expel the Soviets to regain control over both women and Afghanistan. The paper highlights the unprecedented violence and oppression against the women during the Taliban's rule in order to contextualize the present attempt to empower the Afghan women.

The main focus of the paper is to examine various strategies and techniques adopted by the United Nations to articulate and sensitize the gender issue in Afghan polity. It highlights the various mechanisms that the United Nations assisted to put in places to facilitate Afghan women's participation and increase their capacities. It concludes with analyze of major constraints and challenges confronted the United Nations in its attempt to mainstream the gender in democratization process in Afghanistan.

BACKGROUND

The current effort to empowering Afghan women is the third phase of series of major attempts made in the recent history of Afghanistan. The first major reforms were introduced during the reign of King Amanullah who passed a family law in 1921 banning child marriage, freeing widows from the domination of their husbands' families, requiring judicial permission before a man could take multiple wives and removing some family law questions from the jurisdiction of the mullahs. However, the overthrow of King Amanullah in November 1928 resulted in the total abolition of all progressive legislation and measures affecting women.

The second major attempt was made during the Soviet occupation of Afghanistan from 1978-1988. Along with its aggressive programme for social change, the Soviet attempted to introduce reform to improve the status of women in Afghan society. Women were encouraged to enroll in universities and to take jobs in government as well as business and the service sector. By the early 1980s, under the communist backed governments, women held 70 percent of teachers' jobs as well as 50 percent of government jobs and 40 percent of medical posts in Afghanistan. (Khattak, Saba Gul: 2002, 19) These reforms and achievements further fueled the fundamentalist movement and in turn served as the ground for Mujaheddin to expel the Soviets and regain control over both women and Afghanistan. (Goodson, Larry: 2001)

During the Taliban's rule in Afghanistan since the mid-1990s, violence and oppression against the women increased. They introduced harsh policy of gender discrimination that had progressively instituted a system of sexual apartheid. In the first few weeks of its rule, the Taliban enacted measures limiting women's freedom of movement and right to work, girls' access to schools. Throughout its rule, the Afghan women faced multiple restrictions ranging from denial of access to equal rights, mobility and education to marriage and divorce. In fact, women's space under the Taliban was virtually annihilated as they were banned from public life. (Verdirame, Guglielmo: 2001, 374)

The latest phase is the offshoot of the "war against terrorism" as it is also projected as war to liberation the Afghan women. In fact, the gender issue attaining the focal point in the latest war in Afghanistan did not come as a complete surprise. Whatever may the reasons for such projection, the United Nations has been making conscious attempts to make difference to Afghan women after the collapse of the Taliban regime. This attempt is particularly visible in its effort to inject gender issue in the democratization process, which has been the high priority in the international agenda, expecting to bring not only the legitimacy but as a mean for moderation of ethnic and other differences in Afghanistan. Its effort in gender mainstreaming has been guided by the UN Security Council resolution 1325, which acknowledged "the important role of women in the prevention and resolution of conflicts and in peace-building" and stressed "the importance of their equal participation and full involvement in all efforts for the maintenance and promotion of peace and security." (UN Security Council Resolution, 2000)

The role of the United Nations in gender mainstreaming in the democratization process can be categorized into two broad themes of articulation and sensitization of the issue in the Afghan society and other major stakeholders; and assisting to put in place various mechanisms to facilitate women's participation and build their capacities to participate effectively in the political process.

ARTICULATION AND SENSITIZATION

The Afghan government, the United Nations and other organizations have employed a variety of techniques and strategies to articulate and sensitize the need of women's participation in the democratization process of Afghanistan. The discussions were held, talks were arranged, workshops and conferences were organized, reports were prepared, resolutions were passed in various forums and tours abroad were arranged for the Afghan women to enable them to share their experiences and aspirations with worldwide. For instance, 'Afghan women's Summit for Democracy' was organised by coalition of women's organizations in collaboration with the Gender Advisor to the Secretary-General of the United Nations and UNIFEM, on December 4 and 5, 2001 in Brussels. It provided a unique forum for forty Afghan women leaders from all parts of the world to discuss their involvement in decision-making over the future of their country. The summit adopted the Brussels Proclamation which expressed not only the long held aspirations of Afghan women but also included a list of concrete demands for immediate implementation relating to the reconstruction of Afghanistan. Women leaders from around the world joined the Afghan women in Brussels in solidarity, and activists from 16 countries met in a parallel session during the Summit to formulate support strategies for the women of Afghanistan and adopted a Declaration of Solidarity. (Afghan women's Summit for Democracy :2001)

Following the Summit, a political and media tour for six delegates were organized to deliver their message to officials of the European Union, the United States and the United Nations, including the UN Security Council and UN Secretary-General, Kofi Annan. The delegates got an opportunity to interact with the members of the UN Security Council under Arria Formula on 19 December 2001 and could place their view before them. A women NGO known as 'Equality Now' issued Women's Action Update entitled 'Afghanistan; Terrorism, the Taliban and the Role of Women in Peace and Security' in 2001, which called for appropriate intervention from the United Nations, in accordance with international law, to address the crisis and calling for the implementation of UN Security Council Resolution 1325. (Equality Now: 2001)

UN Special Adviser on Gender Issues, Angela King said in 2001 that the women in Afghanistan should be made "full partners" while deciding the future of the war-torn country. She urged members of the international community to insist on women's participation in Afghanistan's future development. (UN Official Seeks: 2001) In January 2002, the Committee on the

Elimination of Discrimination Against Women expressed its solidarity with Afghan women and underlined that the participation of Afghan women as full and equal partners with men was essential for the reconstruction and development of their country. The Committee also called upon all parties concerned to respect internationally recognized principles, norms and standards of human rights, particularly the human rights of women as an inalienable, integral and indivisible part of universal human rights. (Press release: 2002)

In March 2002 the Commission on the Status of Women considered the Secretary General's report on Afghan women and passed a strong-worded resolution calling on the Afghan Interim Authority and its successors to respect fully the human rights and fundamental freedoms of women and girls; to repeal all legislative and other measures that discriminate against women and girls. (Statement of Angela E.V. King: 2002)

A three day Afghan Women Consultation was organized by UNIFEM in collaboration with the Afghan Ministry of Women's Affairs (MOWA) and the UN agencies on March 5-7, 2002 in Kabul. It brought together 60 Afghan women from several provinces with policy-makers, representatives of key ministries, UN agencies and donors. It provided a unique opportunity for Afghan women to articulate their priorities, concerns, perspectives. ("Afghan Women's Consultation Concludes ...": 2002)

For the first time in 2002, the observance of international Women day at the United Nations was focused on the situation of women in a specific country, namely Afghanistan. The theme of the day, which included a high-level panel, was "Afghan Women Today: Realities and Opportunities."

The UN expert on violence against women issued a statement at the end of her visit to Afghanistan in 2003 urging both the Afghan authorities and the international community to recognize that sacrificing respect for human rights, in particular women's rights, to the claims of stability not only falls short of the United Nations' founding principles, but is also politically shortsighted. She emphasized the need to "end the state of violence and impunity, of which the pervasive, intense violence experienced by Afghan women at all levels is a central but neglected element. The present time constitutes a unique window of opportunity that should not be missed." (Expert on violence Against Women Ends Visit to Afghanistan: 2005)

In a report of 2004 to the Commission on the Status of Women on the situation of Afghan women and girls, United Nations Secretary-General Kofi Annan specifically underscored the need for the Afghan Transitional Administration—as well as the future government—to enact new non-discriminatory laws and repeal any measures that discriminate against women and girls. He also stated that Afghan electoral processes should be monitored closely "to make certain that women are able to register, participate fully and support special measures that would guarantee that they are represented in local, provincial and national government positions." (Afghan Transitional Government should improve women's rights: 2004)

Within the framework of the celebration of women's day in March 2004, it is reported that the Ministry of women's Affairs, with the support from the UNIFEM and the Japan International Cooperation Agency, organized a series of workshops in Kabul to discuss the role that women would play in upcoming elections and the implementation of the constitution. It is also reported, "Events emphasizing the rights and duties of women in the registration and election processes were held in the provinces in March." (UN document: 2004, 13)

The above incidences are not meant to be extensive accounts but illustrative of efforts made by the UN system and others to articulate and sensitize the need for women's active involvement in the democratic process to rebuild a stable and legitimate government.

MECHANISM FOR PROMOTION OF WOMEN'S PARTICIPATION

Keeping in mind the historical legacy, conscientious attempts are made to facilitate women's participation in the political process in Afghanistan. Towards that goal various mechanisms are put in placed to promote women's participation and to ensure their foothold in the political process.

Constitution Provisions

One of the prominent mechanisms to entrench women's rights is the constitution of a country. The Bonn Agreement, which resulted from the conference attended by representatives of major groups within and outside Afghanistan, specified that the interim government produce a draft Constitution within 18 months of its establishment. In his decree of 5 October 2002, President Karzai formed the Drafting Commission consisted of nine legal scholars, including two women, to draft Afghanistan's new constitution. The preliminary draft produced by the Commission was then taken over by a new commission established by a presidential decree in April 2002, known as Constitutional Review Commission. The new Commission was composed of 35 members of varying background of religious figures to legal scholars and judges and seven of them were women. It was mandated to work closely with the Ministry of Women's Affairs, which together with UNIEFM, was collecting inputs, holding seminars and other public education programs about the constitutional rights of women. (Rights and Democracy Mission Report: 2003; Oates, and Helal: 2004). The Constitutional Loya Jirga was convened on December 2003 to debate and approve the draft presented by the Constitutional Review Commission. Among the 502 delegates to Constitutional Loya Jirga, 103 were women. To sensitize the importance of their role, "UNAMA convened a series of meetings on women's role in the constitutional and legal reform process. (UN Document: 2003, 14)

The women delegates, who were working to entrench women's rights, negotiated in a climate of fear and intimidation created by conservative factions and warlords. They suffered the humiliating, threatening and unfair treatment. When the event began, Sibghatullah Mojaddedi, a prominent religious leader and the chair of the proceedings, proclaimed to the assembled women delegates, "Even god has not given you equal rights because under his decision two women are counted as equal to one man." (Sultan, Masuda and others: 2005, 25) Men sought to silence women by refusing to allow them time to speak and even turning off their microphones. As a result of verbal threats and physically aggressive behaviour, the women's effective participation was greatly undermined.

The Afghan women wish to have many of the rights denied during the Taliban regime been incorporated in the new constitution. 'The Gender and Law Working Group' was established in December 2002 with the support of UNAMA and UNIFEM. Its goal was to provide a forum for government, NGO actors to ensure that the gender issues were addressed in Afghan's constitutional, legal and electoral reform processes. It proposed number of modifications to the draft constitution prepared by the Drafting Committee with the intention of strengthening and securing women's human rights. (Gender and Law Working Group)

However at the end, only major provision in the constitution is the Article 22 which provides: "Any kind of discrimination and privilege between the citizens of Afghanistan are prohibited. The citizens of Afghanistan—whether man or woman—have equal rights and duties before the law." This codification of equal rights for women in the new Afghan constitution provides a legal basis for women to pursue a fuller role in society. However, it also contained Article 3, which provides that "no law can be contrary to the beliefs and provisions of the sacred religion of Islam." These provisions steam from two different sources. One of the sources is Sharia law which is traditional Islamic law and which emphasizes the obligations of the believer as a member of the religious community. The other is based on international human rights law which emphasizes the rights of the individual, and the state's obligation to protect those rights. The constitution drafters attempted to reconcile Islamic and international law by creating a hybrid constitution. (Sultan, Masuda and others: 2005, 27) Lawyers and human rights experts fear that effective exercise of the equality provision of the constitution may suffer in the hand of interpreting the laws in a conservative way. So the test of constitution as a mechanism for democratization and empowerment of Afghan women lies in its enforcement.

Apart from this provision, there are provisions in the new constitution for women representation in the upper and lower houses of the National Assembly guarantee their voice in national decision-making.

Quotas

Although the United Nations does not have an institutional policy in support of quota system, it has used it successfully in Afghanistan to gain foothold for Afghan women in the governing structures. According to participants in the Bonn talks, Lakhdar Brahimi, UN Secretary General Kofi Annan's envoy, encouraged each political faction to bring at least one female delegate. In February 2002, Kofi Annan called for "temporary special measures, including targets and quotas, targeted at Afghan women." (Sultan, Masuda and others: 2005, 28) The mechanism has been widely used in every stage of the political process drawn up by the Bonn Agreement, and the level of women's participation has steadily increased. During the Bonn negotiation in 2001, only about 10 percent of the participants were women, compared to 12 percent at the Emergency Loya Jirga, 20 percent in the Constitutional drafting and Constitutional Review commissions, and 20 percent at the Constitutional Loya Jirga. (Sultan, Masuda and others: 2005, 27) As required by article 83 of the new constitution adopted in 2003, women gained 27 percent (68 out of the 249) seats in the Wolesi Jirga and around 23 percent in Meshrano Jirga, including the presidential appointees. Women also secured 29 percent (121 out of total of the 420) seats in the provincial Councils. Five provincial seats reserved for women remain vacant owing to the lack of women candidates in three provinces, while women won two provincial council seats in Kabul, in addition to those seats reserved for women.

These women appointed or elected to political positions may become mouthpieces for warlords, their husbands or other family members or political parties at the initial stage. In the long run they have the potential of campaign the cause of women and may acquire a share of influence on decision-making processed at various levels of government. Whatever may be the ultimate outcome, the quota system in the case of Afghanistan provided a critical entry point for women in the political process and formal governing structures that would not have existed otherwise. Thus, it proved to be effective mechanism to facilitate participation of women in the democratic processes in Afghanistan.

Building of Capacities

Many a time the United Nations system is engaged with this Ministry of Women's Affair (MOWA), which is the institutional expression of gender concern in the Afghan government, to build the capacities of Afghan women. For Example, the United Nations Development Programme (UNDP) is supporting MOWA with technical advisors in its efforts to mainstream gender awareness throughout the national and provincial governments. One of the primary ways MOWA is reaching out to women is through a network of 'Women's Resource Centers' established in various provinces. Women's Resource Centers' one of the most important aims is to provide political participation training for women to build up their capacities.

UNDP/UNAMA convened a conference for women delegates to the Constitutional Loya Jirga. (CLJ) with the purpose of empowering the women delegates and to assist them devising a clear and unified agenda for gender issues to be considered in the CLJ. Also at the request of the UNAMA, UNIFEM seconded three of its staff members to the Constitutional Commission to support women members. (UNIFEM at glance) Another example of enhancing Women's capacities was the UNAMA's "induction" course for all the women delegates to the emergency Loya Jirga. The UN Secretary General reported "In collaboration with the Ministry of Women's Affairs, UNAMA had conducted an induction course for the women delegates to the Loya Jirga and provided advice and assistance to them throughout the assembly." (UN Document: 2002, 7) An other example is that a Gender Section was created within the "Joint Electoral Management Body" consisted of international electoral experts whose task was to oversee the organization of the election. This section carried out activities such as public outreach, training and capacity Building programmes. During the electoral process, the Gender Section was mandated to provide support for women candidates, voters and organizations in preparation for the election. (UN Document: 2005, 4)

Another way of ensuring women's participation was through facilitation of registration and voting by women. According the Bonn Agreement, the task of registration of voters was entrusted to United Nations. The UN set up 4,000 separate male and female registration site to encourage women to come out for registration. Of a total population of 27 million, the United Nations reported that 10.3million Afghan had registered to vote. Over 41 percent of those who registered were women. 43 percent of the women registered to vote actually cast ballot for parliamentary election. (UN Document: 2005, 5)

Another example of building capacity and facilitating the women participation is through the Advisory Group on Gender chair By Afghan's Minister of Women's Affairs. It consists of representatives from international and national NGOs, professional women's associations, the donor communities and the United Nations. It provides policy, strategy and programming advice to the government. In March 2004, the Advisory Group on Gender established a subgroup, called the Election Task Force, chaired by UNAMA and it was mandated to monitor the participation of women in the election process. The Election Task Force contributed to the increase in female registered voters. It handled the obstacles faced by the women candidates in campaigning for office as well as the issue of their personal security. (UN Document: 2005, 5) Further, to increase women's participation in the elections and ensure their security, separate polling stations were set up for women. Out of a total 26, 243 polling stations throughout Afghanistan, 11, 387 were established for women for parliamentary election of 2005.

Radio has been also used to build awareness and capacities among Afghan women. Radio has emerged as a critical tool for informing and educating women about the political process as it could reach far and wide corners of Afghanistan and it could be understood by the illiterate masses as well. The UN Educational, Scientific, and Cultural Organization (UNESCO) funded the country's first women-operated-managed independent FM station, beginning in March 2003. (Sultan, Masuda and others: 2005, 31)

In recent years, UNAMA has been able to complete its programmed expansion with eight fully integrated regional offices and nine provincial offices. Its field presence provides provincial government and NGOs stakeholders with crucial capacity-building and coordinated support, as well as allows political outreach to disaffect groups. (UN Document: 2007a, 16)

Thus, above mechanisms have been put in places with aid and assistance of the UN system to build the capacities and facilitate effective participation of Afghan women in the democratization process.

CHALLENGES AND POTENTIALS

Despite the above mentioned efforts to build capacities and put in place various mechanisms to facilitate women's participation, formidable challenges are being faced by the Afghan women. First and foremost among them is the security concern. It is more than six years since the overthrow of the Taliban regime and the process of implementing Bonn Agreement been accomplished by 2005 but peace and stability is yet to prevail in Afghanistan. This is due to mixing up of priorities and conflicting pressures exerted on the project of rebuilding a government with Afghan ownership.

In the case of Afghanistan, conscious attempts were made at the initial stage itself to set up a government ran by the Afghans themselves. To gain external and internal legitimacy and for the effectiveness of government, democratization was high on the international agenda and the roadmap towards that direction was laid in the Bonn Agreement under the leadership of the United Nations.

On the other hand, the United States and its allies are more concerned about removing the perceived threats to Afghanistan's new sovereignty. (Starr, S. Fredrick: 2006) Their main concern is rooting out al-Qaeda and destroying the remnants of Taliban forces even with collaboration with local warlords. In return for their assistance, the United States got warlords incorporated in Loya Jirga and got some important posts for them in transitional authority, which undermined the UN efforts to establish a legitimate authority. These diversions from democratic process caused by extraneous factors made it difficult for Afghanistan's new government to take the country towards the path of stability and peace. (Ponzio, Richard J.: 2007)

The major fall out of the mixed priorities has been the non-implementation of Disarmament, Demobilization and Reintegration programme (DDR), which is normally carried out by the United Nations after the crisis was brought under control. Nigel Fisher, the Deputy Special Representative of the Secretary General in Afghanistan, stated that DDR had been postponed in the case of Afghanistan in order to wait for reform of the Afghan Ministry of Defense, which has been dominated by warlords and gunmen who assisted the United States in defeating the Taliban and Al-Qaeda (Rights and Democracy Mission Report: 2003) This is construed as no option for women but to wait for these changes before they could effectively participate in all spheres of societal activities.

It was not only the remnant of Taliban and Al-Qaeda elements which posed the security threat to the Afghan women. The Afghan police and armed forces also indulged in violation of women's rights and posing threat to their security. They enjoy impunity because of their powerful connection with former warlords and gunmen who hold high positions in the government. For instance Human Rights Watch Report of July 2003 stated, "Human rights abuses in Afghanistan are being committed by gunmen and warlords who were propelled into power by the United States and its coalition partners after the Taliban fell in 2001. ...These men and others have essentially hijacked the country outside of Kabul." The report warned that violence, political intimidation, and attacks on women and girls were discouraging political participation and endangering gains made on women's rights. (Afghanistan: Warlords Implicated in New Abuses: 2003)

In his press briefing on July 10, 2003, Niel Fisher, clearly identified security as a major concern and acknowledged the warring between commanders as well as the daily intimation of ordinary Afghans by their own security forces. (Oates, Lauryn and

Isabelle Solon Helal : 2004, 11) Amnesty International was informed by women and girls in the interviews that they felt their situation had remained largely unchanged. (Amnesty International Report: 2005, 11)

The UN authorized security force, International Security Assistance Force (ISAF), was mandated to provide security only in and around Kabul. The Afghan women have repeatedly demanded an expansion of the ISAF mandate to provincial level with clear cut mandate of soldering and securing of their neighbourhoods so that women could begin functioning under at least a relative sense of normalcy. (Rights and Democracy Mission Report: 2003, 14) The mandate of ISAF has been extended in 2003 by the UN Security Council and provides for the "progressive expansion of the ISAF to other urban areas and other areas beyond Kabul" (The United Nations Security Council Resolution: 2004) However, despite the establishment of Provincial Reconstruction Teams (PRTs) in all major provinces, ISAF continue to lack mandate to protect civilians. On the other hand, humanitarian organizations complain that PRTs have created confusion between military and humanitarian operations. They urged the military to focus on activities within the range of military expertise and leave other tasks to humanitarian NGOs. (Rights and Democracy Mission Report: 2003, 13)

ISAF attempts to assist the Afghan Government in extending and exercising its authority across the country should be supplemented by establishing effective Afghan police, military forces, judiciary system and rule of law in order to generate a sense of security among the Afghan women.

The second major challenge is the urban-rural divide among the Afghan women. Like many developing countries, there existed huge gap between rural and urban areas of Afghanistan. Although incremental changes and awareness of woman empowerment has been percolated in the major cities, the approximately 85 percent of Afghan women, who live in rural areas, have no understanding of the measures and mechanisms put in places to enable them to exercise their role in the new political process. This disconnect between urban and rural is partly due to inability of the national government to extend its authority in the far flank areas and delays in the provision of aid. Thus traditional customs and conservative male values continued to constrain women in the rural areas. Further, many provincial governments, local leaders, and warlords offer no support for women's empowerment.

In fact, the UN voter registration teams had restricted access to potential voters in these areas. Although they had female staff members, due to the lack of security of staff and attacks by anti-government groups made the registration of women voters in remote and rural areas difficult. There were reports of threats by the Taliban and warlords to deter women from registering; and targeted killings of Afghans holding voter registration cards. That is the reason why certain provinces in the south (Uruzgan, Zabul) had very low rates of female registrations: Uruzgan—9%, Zabul—10%. Even those who were registered were prevented from voting as family members refused to let them go to the polling stations. (Amnesty: 2004) Another reason for low turn out of woman's voters was because the United Nations could not recruit sufficient number of women polling officers to manage these polling stations. These are some of the challenges and lacuna which prevented rural women from effective participation in the democratic process of the Afghan polity.

The third major challenge is conservative elements' stronghold in the Parliament and how they prevent the women MPs from exercise their rights. Many of the warlords and religious fundamentalists got elected in the September 2005 Wolsi Jirga election because of the single nontransferable voting (SNTV) system adopted without giving sufficient thought. Under this system, Afghan voters had cast ballots for individual candidates rather than political parties. This system retarded the development of a stable party system and caused, instead, political fragmentation, thereby making national legislation the business not of ideologically coherent political parties but of regional warlords and religious fundamentalists. (Reynolds, Andrew: 2006, 113)

As the liberal-democratic and progressive parties encountered immense hurdles in getting their message across and their candidates elected, most hopes for moderation and nonviolent reform are pinned on the 68 women MPs, most of who are nonaligned and independent of traditional power structures. (Reynolds, Andrew:2006, 116) But the conservative elements in the Parliament view the women's rights as part of a western agenda. Every possible road block to the realization of women's rights has been put in place and the participation of women in decision-making processes has been stalled. Despite these obstacles, individual women have been vocal in challenging the power of the warlords and other conservative elements. For instance, at the Constitutional Loya Jirga, Malalai Joya, a woman delegate, stood up and denounced the attendance of warlords at the event. She called them "criminal who have brought ...disasters for the Afghan people," and said that they should stand before an international tribunal. (Sultan, Masuda and others: 2005, 33) She received protection from the United Nations after she received death threats. In 2007, after her successful international tour and interview with a local TV station in Kabul, the Parliament suspended Joya for three years on May 21, 2007 and ordered the High Court to file a case against her. They also directed the Interior Ministry to restrict her movements within the country. (Afghan Democracy is a Sham: 2007)

Another women member of the Parliament, Saima Khugyani, expressed her optimism for the Afghan parliament as for the first time "Communists, high officials of the Mujahideen and Warlords are all talking to each other instead of fighting each other." Nevertheless, she also expressed her concern that women MPs are being marginalized and not taken seriously. (Saima Khugyani, Afghanistan) The Un Secretary General pointed out that, "Progress towards the realization of gender equality continued to be held back by discrimination, insecurity and the persistence of customary practices" (UN Document: 2007b, 14)

CONCLUSION

The United Nations' endeavour of peacebuilding in the post-Taliban phase started with laudable objective of putting in place a stable and legitimate government ran by the Afghan themselves. Quite appropriately, democratization of Afghan polity has been accorded the central focus not only for establishing a legitimate government acceptable to all sections of the society but also as a means for moderation of ethnic and other differences in Afghanistan. As Afghan women were the worst victims of the Taliban regime, empowering the Afghan women, especially in the political process received much attention of the United Nations, particularly in the light of UN Security Council resolution 1325 of December 2000.

Various components of the UN system as well as personnel have been involved in articulation and sensitization of the need to mainstream the gender in democratization process of Afghan polity. It has been playing pioneering role in aiding and assisting the Afghan government to set up various mechanisms ensure women's participation and to build capacities and facilitate effective participation of the women in political process.

Despite all these strategies and measures, the Afghan women still face formidable challenges in terms of security, rural-urban divide and conservative dominance in the Afghan Parliament. All these challenges inhabit them from effective exercise of the foothold they have gained in its polity. These challenges and lacunas need to be addressed on priority basis as the women MPs in the Parliament, being liberal and progressive in out look and not attached to traditional groupings, have the potential of serving as counter to extremism and religious fundamentalism. There is no doubt that onus of addressing these challenges lies with the government of Afghanistan but as the international community controls most of military and financial resources, they can use the leverage to make the government earnestly tackle the hurdles that stand on the way of effective participation of the Afghan women in the political process. Further, sustained support of the United Nations is needed to enable the Afghan women to embrace the opportunity and build network with other women's movements with extensive experience in advocacy and leadership.

REFERENCES

"Afghan Democracy is a Sham ...controlled by Warlords and Drug Kings" (2007) (http://americannepali.blogspot.com/2007/05/afghan-democracy-is-shamcontrolled-by.html accessed on 28-3-2008).

"Afghan Transitional Government should improve women's rights, " (2004). http://www.un.org/apps/news/storyAr.asp?NewsID=9575&Cr=afghanistan&Cr1= accessed on 12-3-2008

"Afghan Women's Consultation Concludes..." (2002) http://www.unifem.org/news_events/story_detail.php?StoryID=82 accessed on 24-3-2008.

Afghan Women's Summit for Democracy (2001), http://www.equalitynow.org/english/campaigns/afghanistan/brussels_en.html accessed on 12-3-2008

"Afghanistan: Warlords Implicated in New Abuses" (2003), (http://hrw.org/english/docs/2003/07/29/afghan6271.htm accessed on 9-3-2008)

Amnesty International Report (2004), "Afghanistan: Women failed by progress in Afghanistan," http://asiapacific.amnesty.org/library/Index/ENGASA110152004?open&of=ENG-AFG accessed on 9-3-2008

Amnesty International Report (2005) "Women still under attack—systematic failure to protect" http://www.amnesty.org/en/library/info/ASA11/007/2005 accessed on 23-3-2008

Equality Now (2001) Afghanistan: Terrorism, The Taliban and The Role of Women in Peace and Security, http://www.equalitynow.org/english/actions/action_2101_en.html accessed on 11-4-2008.

"Expert on violence Against Women Ends Visit to Afghanistan, " (2005) (http://www.unhchr.ch/huricane/huricane.nsf/view01/615D4B5628D7E547C125704200343ECB?opendocument accessed on 12-3-2008)

Gender and Law Working Group, Kabul, "Recommendations on the Draft Constitution for Strengthening Women's Political Participation and Securing Women's Human Rights" http://www.wraf.ca/documents/glwg%20recomendation%20to%20the%20cons%20comm.pdf, accessed 4 May 2008.

Goodson, Larry (2001), *Afghanistan's Endless War: State Failure, Regional Politics, and the Rise of the Taliban,* Seattle: University of Washington D.C.

Khattak, Saba Gul (2002), "Afghan Women: Bombed to be Liberated?," *Middle East Report,* No. 222, Spring.

Oates, Lauryn and Isabelle Solon Helal (2004), *At the Cross-roads of Conflict and Democracy: Women and Afghanistan's Constitutional Loya Jirga,* Rights and Democracy, Montreal.

Ponzio, Richard J. (2007), 'Transforming Political Authority: UN Democratic Peacebuilding in Afghanistan," *Global governance,* no.13.

Press Release (2002), Solidarity and Support for Afghan women

Expressed in Statement by Committee on Elimination of Discrimination Against Women, 30 January, accessed on 12-3-2008.

Reynolds, Andrew (2006) "The Curious Case of Afghanistan" *Journal of Democracy* Volume 17, Number 2, April.

Rights and Democracy Mission Report (2003), "Seizing an Opportunity: Afghan women and the Constitution-Making Process," http://www.un.org/apps/news/storyAr.asp?NewsID=9575&Cr=afghanistan&Cr1 accessed in 23-3-2008.

Saima Khugyani, Afghanistan, http://www.wdn.org/SuccessStories/Detail.aspx?ID=5 accessed on 23-3-2008

Starr, S. Fredrick (2006), "Sovereignty and Legitimacy in Afghan Nation-Building," Francis Fukuyama, *Nation Building: Beyond Afghanistan and Iraq*, Baltimore: The Johns Hopkins University Press.

Statement of Ms. Angela E.V. King, Special Adviser on gender Issues and Advancement of Women (2002), http://www.un.org/womenwatch/daw/Afghan-april02/AK-speakingnotes-Afghan.htm accessed on 31-3-2008

Sultan, Masuda and others (2005), From Rhetoric to Reality: Afghan Women on the Agenda for Peace, http://www.huntalternatives.org/download/18_from_rhetoric_to_reality_afghan_women_on_the_agenda_for_peace.pdf

United Nations Assistance Mission in Afghanistan (UNAMA), http://www.unama-afg.org/about/_gender/Gender.htm accessed on 8-3-2008

United Nations Document (2002), A/56/1000-S/2002/737, 11 July.

United Nations Document (2003), A/57/850-S/2003/754, 23 July.

United Nations Document (2004), A/58/742/-S/2004/230, 19 March.

United Nations Document (2005) E/CN.6/2006/5, 30 December.

United Nations Document (2007a) A/61/799-//s/2007/152, 15 March.

United Nations Document (2007b), A/62/345-S/2007/555, 21 September.

United Nations Security Council Resolution (2000) S/RES/1325, 31, October.

United Nations Security Council Resolution (2004) S/RES/1563, 17 September.

"UN Official Seeks More Role for Afghan Women" (2001) http://www.rediff.com/us/2001/nov/21ny1.htm accessed on 12-3-2008

UNIFEM at a Glance, http://www.unifem.org/about/fact_sheets.php?StoryID=290 accessed on 31-3-2008

Verdirame, Guglielmo (2001), "Testing the Effectiveness of International Norms: UN Humanitarian Assistance and Sexual Apartheid in Afghanistan," *Human Rights Quarterly*, no. 23.

Index